expanding the
circle

SUNY series in Queer Politics and Cultures

———————

Cynthia Burack and Jyl J. Josephson, editors

expanding the
circle

Creating an Inclusive Environment in Higher Education for LGBTQ Students and Studies

Edited by

John C. Hawley

Published by State University of New York Press, Albany

For information, contact State University of New York Press, Albany, NY
www.sunypress.edu

Production, Eileen Nizer
Marketing, Fran Keneston

Library of Congress Cataloging-in-Publication Data

Expanding the circle : creating an inclusive environment in higher education for
    LGBTQ students and studies / edited by John C. Hawley.
        pages cm. — (SUNY series in queer politics and cultures)
    Includes bibliographical references and index.
    ISBN 978-1-4384-5461-0 (hc : alk. paper)—978-1-4384-5462-7 (pb : alk. paper)
    ISBN 978-1-4384-5463-4 (ebook)
    1. Sexual minority college students—United States.   2. Homosexuality and edu-
cation—United States.   3. Education, Higher—Social aspects—United States.
4. Gays in higher education—United States.   5. Gay college students—United
States.   6. Lesbian college students—United States.   7. Bisexual college students—
United States.   8. Transgender people—Education (Higher).   I. Hawley, John C.
(John Charles), 1947–
    LC2574.6.E96 2014
    378.0086'64—dc23   2014007251

10 9 8 7 6 5 4 3 2 1

This book is dedicated to the
American Civil Liberties Union (ACLU),
to the Association of Gay and Lesbian Psychiatrists (AGLP),
to the Gay, Lesbian, and Straight Education Network (GLSEN),
to the Human Rights Campaign (HRC), to the Parents, Families,
and Friends of Lesbians and Gays (PFLAG), and to the
many other organizations and individuals who have worked
over the years to change the environment for LGBTQ individuals
in their homes, on their campuses, and in American society.

Contents

Part II. Case Studies

Part III. Changing Student Perceptions

List of Illustrations

Tables

Figures

Acknowledgments

I would like to thank Joseph Subbiondo, president of the California Institute of Integral Studies, for his unstinting support of this book, and the National Advisory Committee of the Expanding the Circle project (http://expandingthecircle.com/purpose/), of which I am a member, organized over several years by Dustin N. Smith and Karim Baer: Genny Beemyn, director, the Stonewall Center, University of Massachusetts, Amherst; Billy Curtis, executive director of Multicultural, Sexuality and Gender Centers, University of California, Berkeley; Gilbert Herdt, founder and professor, Sexuality Studies Department, San Francisco State University; Luke Jensen, director, Office of LGBT Equity, University of Maryland, College Park; Sharon Marcus, Orlando Harriman Professor of English and Comparative Literature, Columbia University; Pauline Park, chair, New York Association for Gender Rights Advocacy (NYAGRA); Susan Rankin, research associate, Center for the Study of Higher Education, and associate professor of education, College Student Affairs Program, the Pennsylvania State University; Shiva Subbaraman, director of LGBTQ Resource Center, Georgetown University; Steven Tierney, Member of San Francisco Health Commission; chair, Counseling Psychology Department and Community Mental Health Program, CIIS; Colette Seguin Beighley, director of the Grand Valley State University LGBT Resource Center; and Nancy Jean Tubbs, director of LGBT Center, University of California, Riverside.

Our chapter by Elizabeth Cramer and Charles Ford is an expanded version of a piece that was featured in *Academe*, a journal of the American Association of University Professors, in September–October of 2011. We gratefully acknowledge their permission to republish the essay.

We gratefully acknowledge a generous grant from Amy Shachter, senior associate provost for Research and Faculty Affairs, at Santa Clara University, that supported the production of this book.

Introduction

Building on a Changing Paradigm

John C. Hawley

A child can learn social values by being terrorized by them.

—Brian Devor

The time is now.

—Shane L. Windmeyer

The first quotation is from Brian Devor, a female-to-male (FTM) transsexual who offers a stark reminder that the normal process of identity formation experienced by everyone of college age can be far more traumatizing for some, depending in part on the situation in which those individuals literally find themselves. The second quotation is far more hopeful, taken from Shane L. Windmeyer's 2006 book, *The Advocate College Guide for LGBT Students*. Windmeyer dedicates the book to the first generation of "out" students and quotes the ending of a poem by Elizabeth Marie Couch about heading off to college:

> You've done your time in purgatory,
> So let those old dogs lie.
> Make light your feet and close your eyes . . .
> It's time for you to fly. (5)

All of us working in secondary and higher education would hope that the latter sentiments are more frequently experienced by our students than those so memorably described by Brian. But, for all the hopeful changes in social attitudes in the United States in the last decade, we know that Brian's experience is still shared by far too many students. This book hopes to assess the situation and to offer examples of steps that are being taken by our colleagues in academia to "expand the circle" of acceptance that encourages a pedagogy that liberates our students from the terrors that still lurk beyond the college walls, and sometimes within them.

The surprisingly complex situation facing lesbian, gay, bisexual, trans, and queer (LGBTQ) students on the contemporary high school and college campus becomes painfully clear in Matthew Blanchard's account of his own experience. "My choice to remain in Virginia to attend university," he writes in 2012, "was a decision I regretted for a very long time. During my freshman and sophomore years of college, I remained stubbornly closeted, despite the constant haranguing and harassment, not by homophobic straight students, but by the queer kids on campus" (116). A queer classmate whom Blanchard describes with some bitterness as "out, proud and loud" discovered his "loosely veiled cyberspace identity" and revealed Blanchard's queerness to any and all, resulting in constant ridicule from more public gays. "Bred to condemn and constantly contradict all accusations against my good Catholic, conformist upbringing," writes Blanchard,

> I adamantly maintained that I was not in any way a 'faggot.' Homosexuality was a sin! I begged the culprits guilty of gay-on-gay cyber-bullying and rumor-mongering to let me be free to live my life at its own normal pace. I did not want them to force me out of the closet sooner than I felt comfortable enough to break down its doors. I especially did not want people telling me who and what I was before I had decided for myself. (116)

This student offers an example of a less-reported form of campus bullying and one that would have been inconceivable not many years ago. Times have, indeed, changed. But he also underscores the enduring truth that self-discovery and self-revelation cannot be forced without damage. In Blanchard's case, the path chosen in response to this outing was an increasingly secretive and dangerous sexual life off-campus "in the unabashed bacchanalia of sex parties where drugs were lavished upon [him] and condoms were rarely in sight" (117). When he tests positive for the HIV virus he conscientiously informs each of his former sex partners, and word gets out—to devastating effect:

> The ostracization I had first experienced as a 'holier than thou' homo-hater was carved into the cement stone of the cinderblock walls of my dormitory hallways, tacked to my door in scribbled sketches of guns, nooses, and scathing epithets; sliced and slashed into all four of my car tires, and tagged in soap on my car wind-

shield: A.I.D.S. WHORE! A.I.D.S. VERMIN! QUEER SLUT! YOU KILLED MY BOYFRIEND!! Needless to say, the hatred aimed at me by the kids on campus at the time of my diagnosis translated into my own vehement contempt and hatred of the greater LGBTQ culture and community. My unmitigated misery as victim to this venomous hatred in turn intensified my suppressed queer kid self-loathing. (117)[1]

Somewhere in this history the educational system failed not only the student attacked by others often very much like himself, but failed also the persecutors. This collection of essays seeks to provide openings to discussions that may help administrators, counselors, teachers, and perhaps students to expand the circle of inclusion and to support the journey of self-acceptance that is so crucial a part of the educational experience.

If there have been undeniable improvements for LGBTQ students (Kaminer 2012; Swarns 2012), recent publications underscore that they continue to face challenges not shared by the majority of their classmates (Harris 1997; Owens 1998; Howard and Stevens 2000; Sears 2005; Singh and Jackson 2012). They typically endure microassaults, which Kevin Nadal and Marie-Anne Issa define as "name-calling, avoidant behavior, or discriminatory actions," as well as microinsults ("often unconscious . . . verbal or non-verbal communications that convey rudeness and insensitivity and demean a person's heritage or identity," and microinvalidations ("often unconscious . . . communications that exclude, negate, or nullify the realities of individuals of oppressed groups" (235). One does not need to ponder the situation long to recognize, as these researchers do, the "various ways that systems, institutions, and environments are microaggressive in nature" (235), nor does it come as a surprise that "heterosexism and genderism toward LGBT individuals has also become less direct and more subtle" (236). Minority stressors are created by the "use of heterosexist terminology; endorsement of heteronormative culture/behaviors; assumption of universal LGBT experience [stereotypes]; exoticization; discomfort/disapproval of LGBT experience; denial of the reality of heterosexism; assumption of sexual pathology/abnormality; threatening behaviors" (243). "Experiencing heterosexism during one's youth can . . . negatively impact one's ability to gain a positive self-efficacy or navigate successfully in her or his academic and professional life. . . . Thus, microaggressions affect school achievement for LGB youth in ways that heterosexual youth are not affected. . . . it is clear that both intentional and unintentional forms of discrimination are negatively impacting LGB youth" (253). "On institutional levels, the absence of LGB-affirming spaces, role models, programs, policies, and organizations can be construed as a microaggression in itself" (255). The statistic that jumps out in any of these studies is the following: "Gay and lesbian individuals [are] 2.5 times more likely to have a mental health problem in their lifetimes compared to their heterosexual counterparts" (237). Schools can mitigate this, or ignore it. In their 2011 study Genny Beemyn and Sue Rankin record that

> Among the 1,669 self-identified LGBT students, faculty, and administrators surveyed nationwide, 36 percent of the undergraduates and 29 percent of all respondents had experienced harassment over the past year. Ninety-two percent (68) of the transgender respondents reported that they were the targets of harassment because of their gender identity. . . . [O]ne in five respondents feared for their personal safety on campus because of their sexual and/or gender identities and . . . half concealed their sexual and/ or gender identities to avoid intimidation. (85)

The implications for college personnel come quickly to the fore in the Beemyn/ Rankin study, since "41 percent [of students interviewed] believed that their institutions were not adequately addressing issues related to sexual and gender identity and 43 percent felt that their college or university curricula did not adequately represent the contributions of LGBT people" (85).

Colleges and universities have always been interested in attracting the best students to their campuses, and that is becoming increasingly evident in the proliferation of new sports centers, upscale residences, and so on. Many will have noticed the newest marketing assessment for a niche market, *The Advocate College Guide for LGBT Students*, which ranks the top twenty campuses as follows: American, Duke, Indiana, NYU, Oberlin, Ohio State, Penn State, Princeton, Stanford, Tufts, UC Berkeley, UCLA, UC Santa Cruz, U Mass Amherst, Michigan, Minnesota (Twin Cities), Oregon, Penn, Puget Sound, and USC.[2] The ranking was drawn from a 2005 national call for nominations from LGBT students currently at the schools: 680 schools were nominated, and each nominated school had at least five LGBT students and one faculty or staff member interviewed online (a total of 4,650 online interviews with students, and 560 with faculty and staff). Shane Windmeyer, the guide's editor, judged this a significant response rate since, at the time of the survey, and according to the Human Rights Campaign and the Transgender Law and Policy Institute, there were "only 561 known campuses in the United States that [had] sexual orientation as part of their campus nondiscrimination policies and just over 60 campuses that [had] the same inclusion policy for gender identity or expression" (12). Windmeyer also considered types of institutions, campus size, and regional locales in order to present a broader spectrum of options for students around the country. The questions dealt with issues of support and institutional commitment, campus policies, academic life, housing, student life, campus safety, and counseling and health, including the following:

- Are there active LGBT student organizations on campus?

- Are there out LGBT students, and out faculty and staff?

- Does the institution set a standard for its entire student body by publicizing LGBT-inclusive policies (including "same-sex partner benefits" and "trans-inclusive health benefits"?

- Are there visible signs of gay pride on campus, like Safe Space signs, rainbow flags, and so on?

- Are there audible allies for the LGBT community in the administration who bring up issues of importance to this community in public speeches, and so forth?

- Is there LGBT-inclusive housing as an option, and are there gender-neutral bathrooms?

- Is there a dedicated center or office for the LGBT community on campus?

- Are there opportunities to study LGBT issues in the classroom, with perhaps an LGBT/Queer studies major or minor available?

- Is there a generally liberal attitude on campus and a lively LGBT social scene? (13–14)

These questions align well with the recommendations Beemyn and Rankin draw from their own study. Changes initiated on various campuses that proved constructive included

> forming committees charged with the task of improving the quality of life for LGBT students and employees; creating LGBT resource centers and "safe space" programs; offering at least one course on LGBT topics; developing a formal academic program in LGBT studies; providing domestic partner health benefits; establishing LGBT-themed residential programs; including the experiences of LGBT people in student and staff orientations; and instituting nondiscrimination policies that incorporate sexual orientation and gender identity. (Beemyn & Rankin, 85)

In 1997 when J. T. Sears and W. L. Williams conducted a study similar to the 2012 research from Beemyn and Rankin, they found that at that time relatively few institutions had yet implemented the sorts of changes Sears and Williams were recommending. "Currently," they wrote,

> 595 colleges and universities offer protection against discrimination on the basis of sexual identity . . . with 392 of these schools enjoining discrimination also on the basis of gender identity . . . More than 400 institutions provide health care benefits to the same-sex partners of employees . . . These numbers may seem large, but the LGBT-inclusive campuses account for only a small percentage of accredited colleges and universities in the United States [there are around 6,900]. . . . physical and verbal harassment has been reported on every campus where research has been conducted. (86)

Given the opportunity, students themselves offer creative interventions to counter prejudice and assaults from institutions and from other students. Gary W. Harper, Asya Brodsky, and Douglas Bruce, for example, note that "it is important to also highlight the strength and resiliency demonstrated by LGB adolescents" (23). Youths in their study identified positive aspects of being gay/bisexual, notably in the greater flexibility they experienced in three categories: their choices in sexual partners, their inclination to "explore more physical places and spaces, specifically ones that are gay friendly" (30), and the ability to experiment with gender roles. They also recognized a different sort of connectedness, both with females and with the gay community. In the face of oppression, the subjects of this study found strategies of resilience in four areas: in self-acceptance and through messages of acceptance from others; in increased self-care (emotional self-care through "increased vigilance around homophobic individuals" [33]), and physical self-care in increased concern for sexual health and physical appearance; in the rejection of stereotypes through an assertion of individual choices; and activism resulting from "an individual desire to be knowledgeable about issues that have affected the LGBT community in order to guide their future aspirations" (34). Similarly, in another study Arnold Grossman, Anthony D'Augelli, and John Frank concluded that "a central process in building resilience is the development of coping skills, processes, and styles [from which] four potential aspects of psychological resilience among transgender youth were selected: a sense of personal mastery, self-esteem, perceived social support, and emotion-oriented coping" (105). The take-away for counselors on college and high school campuses is clear: "By focusing on positive conceptualizations of being gay/bisexual, interventions may help improve gay/bisexual youth's self-esteem and decrease the likelihood that they will participate in high-risk behaviors" (Harper, Brodsky, & Bruce, 36). One thinks back to Brian's experience, with which we began, and Matthew Blanchard's, and imagines what their lives might have been had someone on staff intervened at the right time. In fact, Blanchard recognized the resilience within himself and, by extension, within other gay and lesbian students. He moves to San Francisco, joins BAY Positives (Bay Area Young Positives), and finds them very helpful, but complains that "I wanted the agency to shift away from viewing queer youth as passive clients to a focus on empowering queer youth to become participatory members." Eventually, the organization responds to this criticism, and becomes "a participatory organization focused on the education, advocacy and empowerment of its 'members' as youth leaders in HIV/AIDS prevention" (Blanchard 118).[3]

Susan Driver writes that queer youth "become innovative participants in do-it-yourself media projects, popular cultural narratives, local drag performances, anti-oppression activisms, online communities, and music subcultures," and thereby "push us to become nuanced in the ways we read, watch, and listen to young people telling their own stories and envisioning their futures" (1). Students are also leading the way in discerning the practical implications of moving from *gay* and *lesbian* to *queer*. Those of an older generation generally have more trouble with the latter term, finding it too fuzzy, too inclusive, perhaps too needlessly contrary—yet students often find it just right for their self-understanding. Youth "use 'queer' as an adjective to suggest a rich and layered sense of self, evoking a transitional process, refusing to define themselves once and for all" (11–12). Jane Bryan Meek agrees, noting that

> Debates over the term queer often embody the most contentious issues within social movements organized around sexual orientation and gender—issues over the notion of an essential or fixed identity and "the policing of that identity's boundaries and the concomitant exclusion of the gay community's "others," be they female, nonwhite, working class, or transgendered," as queer theorist Thomas Piontek (2006, p. 3) articulates. My discussions with these students [at a large public Midwestern university] revealed that they are highly aware of this exclusion of "others," labeled by one student "misfits," within the so-called gay community. As articulated by my study's participants, such "misfits" often employ queer to represent their distinct positions as the marginalized within a minority. (188)

Thus, the question of class and ethnic distinction comes to the fore. Echoing Eric Rofes, Meek writes "LGBTQ students might not appeal as much to queer youth of color who might identify more strongly with their racial, ethnic, or religious identities and thus feel more legitimized in groups with such a focus" (189).

As sexual orientation becomes less an issue for students in adolescence, and less essentialized for some, "the ability of queer to simultaneously unite diverse populations as well as trouble the notion of rigid, binary-based identities makes it appealing to some LGBTQ people and dangerous to others, and thus queerness can expose ideological differences and power dynamics within LGBTQ and allied populations" (190). One imagines an "Occupy Gay" movement somewhere as inevitable, since "At least for this particular group, filling the void left by a commodified gay culture has led to the creation of a dynamic queer subculture grounded in activism, education, and creative expression" (193). Some students "are beginning to understand at an early age the problems of policing identities and are responding by actively queering identity-based community and culture" (196).

Transgender individuals are taking the lead here, as they did in the Stonewall Rebellion in 1969. Studies suggest that the parameters of the topic of nonconforming gendered lives is in creative flux and is now a more pressing topic on college campuses. In their recent comprehensive survey of individuals who identify as transgender Beemyn and Rankin find that most of the younger people they interviewed "began to identify as transgender while still teenagers," whereas "few of the older participants indicated that they had acknowledged being transgender during adolescence" (160). These investigators conclude that these results "reflect a shift in transgender identity formation and not merely survey bias" (160)—but "transgender people are still completely ignored and invisible in most institutional structures" (159). Citing the 2011 report from the Transgender Law and Policy Institute, Beemyn and Rankin draw some stark conclusions: ". . . college curricula and co-curricular activities rarely encompass experiences beyond male and female; and most faculty, staff, and student leaders lack training on gender diversity" (160). Campuses are scrambling to catch up, as more transgender students become visible:

> A rapidly increasing number of colleges and universities are adding 'gender identity and/or expression' to their nondiscrimination policies; creating gender-inclusive bathrooms, locker rooms, and housing options; providing a means for transgender students who have not legally changed their names or had gender confirmation surgeries to use a preferred name and to change the gender on public records and documents; and covering hormones and surgeries for transitioning students as part of student health insurance.

> However, more than 90 percent of two- and four-year institu-
> tions in the United States have not taken any of these steps and
> remain completely inaccessible and inhospitable to transgender
> students. (163)

In short, their investigation confirmed what will be obvious to any of us,
though seldom noticed: "genderism permeated every aspect of campus life,"
including "LGBT and other student organizations and communities" (163–
164). Not surprisingly, therefore, transgender students continue to experience
more discrimination and marginalization on college campuses than do gay
and lesbian students (164). Various authors have detailed steps that can be
taken to improve the lives of transgender students (Beemyn 2005; Beemyn,
Curtis et al. 2005; Beemyn, Domingue et al. 2005; Bilodeau 2009), including multigendered fraternities, expansion of the gender category on application forms, and, of course, grievance procedures for cases of harassment and
discrimination.

Questions of gender are, perhaps, the last hurdle that must be passed in
our society, and are as contested among gay and lesbian individuals as among
heterosexuals. Grossman, D'Augelli, and Frank argue that "whereas society
legitimates two genders, gender identities tend to vary along a continuum
from hyper-masculine to hyper-feminine; therefore, there are many gender
identities, e.g., transmen (FTM), transwomen (MTF), trannybois, tranndykes,
genderqueer, and two spirit" (105). In their study of transgender youth, these
researchers indicate that

> youth reported feeling different at an average age of 7.5 . . . [and
> were] told to stop acting outside of their gender role expecta-
> tions by their parents at the mean ages of 9 [FTM] and 10
> [MTF]. . . . The FTM and MTF youth in the study also self-
> identified as transgender at mean ages of 15 and 14, respectively;
> and they disclosed that identity to someone else at mean ages of
> 17 and 14, respectively. (112)

These researchers recommend, therefore, that "interventions to enhance psychological resilience should begin when the youth are older children or young
adolescents" (112); and, since these individuals often met with negative or
very negative responses from their parents, these researchers underscore "the
important need for psycho-education programs and other interventions with
parents of transgender youth" (112). In the absence of such programs before
transgender individuals reach our campuses, analogous programs are all the
more essential.

The collection of essays that follows investigates a broad range of issues that will no doubt suggest new lines of research for our readers. The intersectionality of diversity issues, a broader focus on other racial identities (including the complexities of multiracial identity), and greater discussion of dis/ability issues and sexual identity formation/expression—these are several such topics that we hope to see examined more fully in future studies, beyond our own.

Recommendations and Sources

In an academic environment that reflects the growing complexity of American society, Shane Windmeyer's *Advocate Guide* makes several recommendations that serve as a good prelude for those that will follow in our collection. One of the Windmeyer essays that follows his assessment of individual schools, written by Saralyn Chesnut and Angela C. Nichols, suggests academic strategies for a more inclusive LGBT classroom; for individual faculty members, they suggest using inclusive language and examples, addressing derogatory comments, establishing ground rules for dialogue, incorporating specific content into the curriculum, and learning more and involving oneself; for faculty groups and administrators, they suggest developing brown-bag lunch discussions, encouraging and recognizing outstanding work, planning annual events for academic learning, creating an ongoing development seminar for faculty, and building and institutionalizing course offerings (Windmeyer 360–362). In another of Windmeyer's essays, to improve campus housing for LGBT students Kaaren M. Williamsen-Garvey and Steve Wisener recommend being "intentional" in the recruiting, hiring, and training of housing staff "to ensure that staff at all levels are willing and able to deal with issues of sexual orientation and gender identity/expression"; writing housing policies that "include clear language that communicates to LGBT students that their needs can and will be addressed" by one's staff; offering a variety of housing options for LGBT students, such as single-room availability, an LGBT floor or house, gender-neutral options, and "private or coed bathroom availability for safety and privacy"; displaying visible symbols of support; publicizing community standards that include "an appreciation of diversity and freedom from harassment"; showing up at LGBT events; documenting and responding to "graffiti, hate speech, or other instances of discrimination," and providing and publicizing the procedures for reporting incidents; serving as a campus role model on these issues (Windmeyer 363–365). Ric Chollar offers advice about the physical and emotional health concerns of LGBT students, including their need for access, comfort, and trust in providers during the processes of: coming out;

healing from oppression; coping with stress, anxiety, and depression; surviving suicidal thoughts, plans, or attempts; coping with sexual health concerns and HIV/AIDS; reducing smoking, which is relatively high among LGBT youth ("over 43 percent of young gay men and lesbians [aged 18–24] smoke, compared with approximately 17 percent of the general population of 18–24 year-olds" [369]); dealing with abusive drinking and other drug use; overcoming overly demanding concerns about body image (e.g., "gay and bisexual men are expected, by both mainstream and gay cultures, to be fit, muscular, well-dressed, and into trends and fashion" [370] (Windmeyer 366–371). Eric W. Trekell offers ways for campus safety to support LGBT students, including the creation of an LGBT liaison officer, the active recruitment of LGBT officers, visibility at LGBT events, the appointment of an LGBT person to the campus safety advisory board, the inclusion of LGBT issues as a component of the training procedures for campus safety staff, the broadcasting of methods for LGBT students to report harassment, and attention to the special concerns of transgender individual so that campus security does not become part of the problem when confusion or confrontations occur (Windmeyer 372–374). Brett Genny Beemyn offers recommendations to improve trans inclusiveness on campuses, including the addition of "gender identity or expression" to the campus nondiscrimination policy, seeing to it that residence life staff help create transgender-inclusive housing options "including gender-neutral rooms or floors" (Windmeyer 375), converting restrooms to gender-neutral, seeing to it that "transgender students can be part of gender-specific student groups" so that students are able to "participate in campus activities in keeping with how they identify and express their gender identities" (376), making it easy for trans students to change their name and/or gender on all campus records and documents, and other similar policies (Windmeyer 375–377). W. Houston Dougharty notes the several ways that college admissions offices can reach out to and recruit LGBT youths through the school's publications, staff attitudes, college fairs, and so on (Windmeyer 379–381).

Elsewhere, Heather McEntarfer writes of three religiously affiliated institutions of higher education and details "the methods and approaches used when advocates of gay-straight alliances . . . encountered resistance from administrators" (McEntarfer 309). Another helpful resource is the collection of essays edited by Erica Meiners and Therese Quinn, in which Carolyn Ford, Becky Atkinson, Eric Rofes, Jane Gallop, and Coya Paz Brownrigg discuss the importance of teaching as a whole self, as someone whose sexuality is not erased when entering the classroom (Meiners 84–123). In the same collection, Tim Barnett's resource guide for educators includes helpful websites categorized by intended audience, films grouped by appropriate age cohort, a discussion of Sins Invalid ("a performance project that incubates and celebrates artists with disabilities" (Meiners 410), and print texts divided by likely age of readership.

Among the most helpful journals in this burgeoning field are the following: *Canadian Online Journal of Queer Studies in Education*; *International Journal of Transgenderism*; *Journal of Bisexuality*; *Journal of LGBT Youth* (formerly *Journal of Gay & Lesbian Issues in Education*); *Journal of Gay & Lesbian Mental Health* (formerly *Journal of Gay & Lesbian Psychotherapy*); *Journal of Gay & Lesbian Social Services*; *Journal of GLBT Family Studies*; *Journal of Homosexuality*; *Journal of Lesbian Studies*; *Journal of LGBT Health Research*; *Journal of LGBT Issues in Counseling*; *International Journal of Sexual Health* (formerly *Journal of Psychology & Human Sexuality*); and *TSQ: Transgender Studies Quarterly* http://www.kickstarter.com/projects/tsq/tsq-transgender-studies-quarterly

Moving the Conversation Forward

Our book is structured to reflect institutional concerns and personal choices. Part I surveys the current situation of intentional or unconscious structures in our academic units, including the administration and the academic study of LGBTQ issues. Part II flows naturally from the first, offering case studies of how individual institutions have confronted some of the problems that have been discussed in this introduction. Part III moves to the enduring problems of interpersonal relations on secondary and higher-educational campuses, moving from bullying to greater freedom in self-expression. The book concludes with an examination of the intersection of LGBTQ issues with those of the changing dynamic of the ethnic mix in the United States, especially as these questions engage the full spectrum of psychosexual and spiritual exploration.

Notes

1. An interesting sign of the times is the establishment of Spectrum clubs for gay and lesbian students at the United States Naval Academy in Annapolis, Maryland, the Air Force Academy in Colorado Springs, and the United States Military Academy in West Point, NY; as well as the Air Force Academy in Colorado Springs. Rachel Swarns writes, though, that "At the Naval Academy, where a tight-knit group of gay and lesbian friends had socialized underground, the repeal exposed an awkward divide between those who were ready to come out and those who were not. As closeted midshipmen, they all hated the law that barred gays from openly expressing their sexuality at military academies, but some still resist the new pressure to go public" (Swarns).

2. Others in the top one hundred: Antioch, Bowling Green, Bryn Mawr, Cal State Poly (Pomona), Carleton, Carnegie Mellon, Case Western, Central Michigan, Central Washington, Colby, Colgate, Colorado State, Columbia College (Chicago), Cornell, Dartmouth, DePaul, DePauw, Eastern Michigan, Emory, George Mason, Grinnell, Haverford, Iowa State, Ithaca, Kalamazoo, Knox, Lawrence, Macalester, Marlboro, MIT, Metropolitan State College (Denver), Michigan State, Middlebury, Minnesota State (Mankato), New College of Florida, Northern Illinois, Northwestern, Ohio, Oregon State, Rochester Institute of Technology, Rutgers, Sarah Lawrence, Skidmore, SUNY Purchase, Suffolk College, Syracuse, Temple, Arizona, UC Davis, UC Riverside, UC San Diego, Colorado (Boulder), Colorado (Denver and Health Sciences Center), Connecticut, Florida, Illinois (Chicago), Illinois (Urbana-Champaign), Kansas, Louisville, Maine, Maryland, Minnesota (Duluth), UMKC, North Carolina (Chapel Hill), North Texas, Rhode Island, Southern Maine, Texas (Austin), Utah, Vermont, University of Washington, Wisconsin (La Crosse), Wisconsin (Madison), Wisconsin (Milwaukee), Vassar, Washington State, Wellesley, Whitman, Williams, and Yale.

3. But his earlier experiences take a toll on Blanchard, who writes:

> We were all to-die-for adorable at twenty-something; each of us boys (and grrrls!) had climbed mountains in our Sisyphean struggle out of "Southern cruelty" and queer kid condemnations, and into the loving arms of San Francisco's skid row SROs. We naively assumed that 'It Gets Better,' but it never did. Some of us celebrated drag princess pastiche or twink boy sex-tape stardom; some of us wanted to save the world through political action, civil rights coalitions or artistic agitprop performance cooperatives. We had all escaped the torment and turmoil of 'home,' searching for freedom and romance among the infamous hills, valleys and serpentine streets of San Francisco. Little did we know that we would instead be welcomed into the arms of a chaotically corrupt, crystal-lined, tina-torn, AIDS-quilted gay mecca. (119)

Works Cited

Barnett, Tim. "Resource Guide for Educators." In Erica R. Meiners and Therese Quinn, eds. *Sexualities in Education: A Reader*. New York: Peter Lang, 2012, 401–415.

Beemyn, Genny. "Making Campuses More Inclusive of Transgender Students." *Journal of Gay and Lesbian Issues in Education* 3.1 (2005): 77–89.

Beemyn, Genny, B. Curtis, M. Davis, and N. J. Tubbs. "Transgender Issues on College Campuses." In Ronny Sanlo, ed. *Gender Identity and Sexual Orientation: Research, Policy, and Personal Perspectives*. San Francisco: Jossey-Bass, 2005, 41–49.

Beemyn, Genny, A. Domingue, J. Pettitt, and T. Smith. "Suggested Steps to Make Campuses More Trans-Inclusive." *Journal of Gay and Lesbian Issues in Education* 3.1 (2005), 89–104.

Beemyn, Genny and Sue Rankin. *The Lives of Transgender People*. New York: Columbia University Press, 2011.

Blanchard, Matthew D. "It Gets Better?" In Mattilda Bernstein Sycamore, ed. 115–122. *Why Are Faggots So Afraid of Faggots? Flaming Challenges to Masculinity, Objectification, and the Desire to Conform*. Oakland, CA: AK Press, 2012, 115–122.

Devor, Holly. *FTM: Female-to-Male Transsexuals in Society*. Bloomington: Indiana University Press, 1997.

Driver, Susan. "Introducing Queer Youth Cultures." In *Queer Youth Cultures*, ed. Susan Driver. Albany: State University of New York Press, 2008.

Grossman, Arnold H., Anthony R. D'augelli, and John A. Frank. "Aspects of Psychological Resilience among Transgender Youth." *Journal of LGBT Youth* 8.2 (2011): 103–115.

Harper, Gary W., Asya Brodsky, and Douglas Bruce. "What's Good About Being Gay?: Perspectives from Youth." *Journal of LGBT Youth* 9.1 (2012): 22–41.

Harris, Mary B. *School Experiences of Gay and Lesbian Youth: The Invisible Minority*. New York and London: Haworth Press, 1997 (copublished simultaneously as *Journal of Gay & Lesbian Social Services* 7.4 [1997]).

Howard, Kim and Annie Stevens, eds. *Out & About Campus: Personal Accounts by Lesbian, Gay, Bisexual, & Transgendered College Students*. Los Angeles and New York: Alyson Books, 2000.

Kaminer, Ariel. "Since Suicide, More Resources for Transgender and Gay Students." *New York Times* September 21, 2012 (accessed September 22, 2012), http://www. nytimes.com/2012/09/22/nyregion/after-clementis-suicide-rutgers-embraces-its-gay-and-transgender-students.html?hp& pagewanted=print.

McEntarfer, Heather Killelea. " 'Not Going Away': Approaches Used by Students, Faculty, and Staff Members to Create Gay-Straight Alliances at Three Religiously Affiliated Universities." *Journal of LGBT Youth* 8.4 (2011): 309–331.

Meek, Jane Bryan. " 'Being Queer Is the Luckiest Thing': Investigating a New Generation's Use of Queer within Lesbian, Gay, Bisexual, Transgender, and Queer (LGBTQ) Student Groups." In Erica R. Meiners and Therese Quinn, eds. *Sexualities in Education: A Reader*. New York: Peter Lang, 2012, 187–198.

Meiners, Erica R. and Therese Quinn, eds. *Sexualities in Education: A Reader*. New York: Peter Lang, 2012.

Nadal, Kevin L., Marie-Anne Issa, Jayleen Leon, Vanessa Meterko, Michelle Wideman, and Yinglee Wong. "Sexual Orientation Microaggressions: 'Death by a Thousand Cuts' for Lesbian, Gay, and Bisexual Youth." *Journal of LGBT Youth* 8.3 (2011): 234–259.

Owens, Robert E. *Queer Kids: The Challenges and Promise for Lesbian, Gay, and Bisexual Youth*. New York: Haworth Press, 1998.

Piontek, Thomas. *Queering Gay and Lesbian Studies*. Urbana and Chicago: University of Illinois Press, 2006.

Rofes, Eric. *A Radical Rethinking of Sexuality and Schooling: Status Quo or Status Queer?* Lanham, MD: Rowman and Littlefield, 2005.

Sears, James T., ed. *Gay, Lesbian, and Transgender Issues in Education: Programs, Policies, and Practices.* New York: Harrington Park Press, 2005.

Sears, J. T. and W. L. Williams, eds. *Overcoming Heterosexism and Homophobia: Strategies That Work.* New York: Columbia University Press, 1997.

Singh, Anneliese A. and Ken Jackson. "Queer and Transgender Youth: Education and Liberation in Our Schools." In Erica R. Meiners and Therese Quinn, eds. *Sexualities in Education: A Reader.* New York: Peter Lang, 2012, 175–186.

Swarns, Rachel L. "Out of the Closet and into a Uniform." *New York Times* November 17, 2012 (accessed September 22, 2012), http://www.nytimes.com/2012/11/18/fashion/military-academies-adjusting-to-repeal-of-dont-ask-dont-tell.html?hp.

Sycamore, Mattilda Bernstein, ed. *Why Are Faggots So Afraid of Faggots?: Flaming Challenges to Masculinity, Objectification, and the Desire to Conform.* Oakland, CA: AK Press, 2012.

Transgender Law and Policy Institute. (2011a). *Colleges and Universities* (accessed April 24, 2011), http://www.transgenderlaw.org/colleges/index.htm

Transgender Law and Policy Institute. (2011b). *Colleges and Universities with Nondiscrimination Policies that Include Gender Identity/Expression,* (accessed April 24, 2011), http://www.transgenderlaw.org/college/index.htm#policies

Windmeyer, Shane L. *The Advocate College Guide for LGBT Students.* New York: Alyson Books, 2006.

Part I

Changing Institutional Structures

Chapter 1

A Website Evaluation of the Top Twenty-Five Public Universities in the United States to Assess Their Support of Lesbian, Gay, Bisexual, and Transgender People

Bharat Mehra, Donna Braquet, and Calle M. Fielden

Introduction

Evaluation and assessment of information resources and services are key areas of research, study, and practice in the enactment of the information creation-organization-dissemination processes that form the core of the library and information science (LIS) professions in all its varied manifestations (Diamond and Sanders 2006; Munde and Marks 2009; Wallace and Van Fleet 2001). They have also provided practical relevance as a management tool for leaders in diverse LIS environments (e.g., public, academic, school, and medical libraries) to identify and execute change in tangible directions and operationalize improvements in the planning, design, delivery, performance, and implementation of different kinds of information services (Matthews 2007; Matthews 2003; Weingand 2001). This chapter focuses on application of evaluation and assessment in the analysis of the websites of the top twenty-five universities in the United States to identify and measure their support (or lack of thereof) of lesbian, gay, bisexual, and transgender (LGBT) people.

The development of this research is based on an intersection of three knowledge areas, as a result of which it makes a unique contribution to this collection of work, namely: information resource evaluation and assessment (Johnson et al. 2002), LGBT information representation (Jackson 1995; White 1999), and website design and development (Lawrence and Tavako 2006;

19

Plumley 2010) in academic institutions of higher learning in the United States. Evaluation and assessment of one kind of information resource (namely, academic university websites) forms the goal of this research, representation of LGBT information provides the context of study and becomes the subject of scrutiny under examination, and the specific objects being studied are the websites of the selected universities.

LGBT people have long been marginalized in American society (as well as in other parts of the world) often persecuted and treated with hate as criminals or worse (Brown and Alderson 2010; Mogul, Ritchie, and Whitlock 2011). Social, cultural, political, religious, legal, familial, and other support systems are limited and lacking for LGBT people in the manner that most heterosexuals consider their birthright and take for granted (Isay 2009; Parker & Aggleton 2007). Further, an irresponsible media is always at hand in the United States to prostitute itself in exchange for increased ratings and often more than willing to straddle its legs up in the air for the manipulative games of the politicians who have used the "gay card" during election times to distract the public, in order to avoid dealing with real issues facing the nation (Cahill 1999; Smith 2008). The audacity of the conservative religious right in trampling the democratic values of liberty, equality, and justice at every step has also known no bounds in recent years, as they continue to brainwash the ignorant public and target LGBT people as the problem (Aarons 1995), manipulating the First Amendment and the right to freedom of speech argument to new diminished levels in spreading the message of hate and demonizing an already marginalized minority (Lakoff 2002; O'Connor & Cutler 2008). For example, the opinion of authors Alan Sears and Craig Osten (Sears & Osten 2003) is that the "homosexual agenda" is to trump the rights of all other groups, especially those of people of faith, except that they fail to recognize the documented fact that it is LGBT people who have been ostracized, ridiculed, and even killed (e.g., Matthew Shepard's brutal murder and the numerous hate-crimes since) (Cortese 2005), their rights of life, liberty, dignity, and equality denied (Cobb 2006; Shepard 2010), and not the other way around (compared to people of faith).

Even within the information world, there is much literature that would simply just want LGBT people to disappear (Mehra & Braquet 2007, "Process") and/or information about them is often either completely lacking or presented in an isolated, incomplete, and fragmented manner owing to conscious or unconscious ignorance, deliberate malice, homophobia, and pervading heterosexism, among other reasons (Mehra & Braquet 2006). Moreover, in the LIS professions, LGBT people have long been considered invisible, conspicuous by their absence (Mehra & Srinivasan 2007), and are only recently beginning to get recognized as a significant underserved population, worthy of study, focus of library services in different environments, and important enough to be touched on in mainstream LIS education knowledge domains and practices (Mehra & Braquet 2011).

Academic institutions of higher learning, especially in the United States, have garnered tremendous prestige and an enviable reputation of providing cutting-edge education in the pursuit of academic excellence (Volkwein & Sweiter, 2006.). The 2010 "Webometrics Ranking of World Universities" identified 103 universities in the United States in the Top 200, based on web presence, visibility, and web access (Aguillo, Bar-Ilan et al. 2010), while the Shanghai Jiao Tong University's "Academic Ranking of World Universities" recognized more than 30 of the highest-ranked 45 institutions are in the United States, measured by awards and research output ("Academic Ranking" 2011). In light of such a positive image of academic institutions of higher learning in the United States worldwide, how are the top-ranking universities in this group representing relevant LGBT information and presenting LGBT services that exist in their academic environments? This research addresses the question to identify how such an influential assembly of members considers one of society's most disenfranchised populations to make them included and welcome in their institutions and what strategies they are employing to create safe and supportive environments for LGBT people. The purpose of focusing on the top-ranked universities in this research is to provide benchmarks and best practices that may lead to development of positive trends in practice since other lesser-ranked universities and colleges regard the top-ranked as aspirational institutions and role models, more often than not emulating and replicating their efforts and strategies (O'Shea, et al. 2007). In evaluation and assessment research and practice the role and use of such benchmarks has recently found much tangible application in service design, development, and delivery (Madhaven, Tunstel, &Messina 2009.; Dunn, McCarthy et al. 2010), and it will be worthwhile to establish such benchmarks (if they can be formulated) for representing LGBT information on web resources developed by academic institutions of higher learning in the United States. Public institutions were intentionally selected as the focus sample for this research. The underlying reason is that public academic institutions are supported by federal and state monies and tax payer's contributions, and since LGBT people pay taxes as much as anyone else living in the state or country; hence, it would be valuable to explore the extent of their needs, expectations, and representation on the websites of their public institutions of higher learning.

Traditionally, evaluation of information services has involved documentation of routine input-output like measures that present more of a perspective from the internal environment and system-centric view (Dugan, Hernon, & Nitecki 2009.), while more recently, outcome-based evaluation takes an external viewpoint presenting a customer or people-centric point of view (Smallwood & Forman 2011). The website provides an interface between the internal world of the institution and the external life of the community within which the institution is embedded. It becomes the translucent electronic facade—opaque in its limited coverage of the actual realities of experience that physicality embodies, yet, visible for the world to gaze and navigate to gain insights and understanding of the physical experience of a place, even at a distance—that has tremendous potential for shaping public perception, image building, and serving a constructive marketing agenda (Potts 2007).

Moreover, a study of web resources is key since during the past two decades the world has witnessed tremendous growth of the Internet and an almost ubiquitous adoption of the World Wide Web that has had an undeniable and everlasting impact on the way people from around the world search, find, and use information (Chowdhury & Chowdhury 2001; Muller 2003). Examining what strategies the top twenty-five public universities in the United States are using to represent LGBT information on their websites is important because such representations influence what people geographically dispersed may experience (and make assumptions), at a distance, of these institutions in terms of their campus climate and environment, based on what is (or not) represented (Weller 2010). This web representation or lack of representation of all forms of diversity (including LGBT people) shapes users' mind-set at an individual level and helps them determine whether or not the different academic institutions are attractive places for them to join (Visser 2005). Having effective LGBT representation on the university's website may thereby help attract the best students, faculty, staff, administrators, funders, and business corporations, among others, who are interested in endowing financial investments in progressive and safe areas for all people to live in. Future research will identify if any correlations exist between high-economic investments by financial investors in specific institutions and high (or positive) use of web representations for diverse groups (including LGBT people) by those institutions.

Research Methods

The methods used in this research have evolved (and been informed) as a part of a process that involved the participation of the authors and others in qualitative studies and action research conducted on behalf of LGBT people at the University of Tennessee since 2005. This chapter extends, modifies, redefines, and expands select variables from a study titled "A Website Analysis of the University of Tennessee's Peer Institutions to Assess Their Support of Lesbian, Gay, Bisexual, and Transgender People" that the authors had led as part of the Research Committee of the UT's Commission for LGBT People during January through June 2007 (Mehra et al. 2007). Twelve peer institutions recognized by UT's Office of Institutional Research and Assessment were included in the initial study that assessed their web representation of LGBT issues based on select variables from the list of "gay friendly" criteria identified in The Advocate College Guide for LGBT Students (Windmeyer 2006). The initial assessment of UT's support of LGBT people (based on the select variables) showed that the UT was ranked in the bottom two universities as compared to its peer institutions at the time. It led to identifying and mapping information-related LGBT-relevant criteria with LGBT representations, social justice activism, and interventions that promoted communitywide socially progressive changes on behalf of LGBT people (Mehra & Braquet 2007, "Library"). Information-related work activities were subsequently analyzed in the identified interventions. Efforts were proposed to integrate these in the delivery of an LIS curriculum to educate and train future librarians and information professionals to "become socially progressive curators of world knowledge," "transform them to become true leaders involved in the organization/management of information" who realized the worth of questioning heterosexist assumptions in LIS work and took appropriate actions to "rectify biases in a systematic and holistic manner that may bring about community-wide cultural, political, legal, and economic changes for LGBT people" (Mehra 2011).

Having identified ways for LIS education to extend itself in its integration of LGBT content, this research broadens the scope of study in its website assessment of top-ranked public institutions of higher learning in the United States. Table 1.1 lists the top twenty-five public universities in the United States that were selected for this research. These universities were selected from the list provided by the 2011 U.S. News & World Report ("Top" n.d.) that identifies its reason for ranking colleges and universities to help students make "one of the most important decisions" of their life, since investment in a college education is on the rise and profoundly affects students' career opportunities, financial well-being, and quality of life ("Why U.S." 2010).

The "gay friendly" criteria developed over past research conducted by the authors were reevaluated and reconsidered over a period of time via sustained discussions and debate between the three authors based on their relevance and applicability in the new context of this website study. Factors such as applicability of the criteria during changing times in the contemporary context, reflecting current trends and practices in academic environments,

Table 1.1. List of Top Twenty-Five Public Universities Identified by 2011
U.S. News & World Report

Rank	University Name	Location	Homepage URL
1	University of California–Berkeley	Berkeley, CA	www.berkeley.edu/
2	University of California–Los Angeles	Los Angeles, CA	www.ucla.edu/
2	University of Virginia	Charlottesville, VA	www.virginia.edu/
4	University of Michigan–Ann Arbor	Ann Arbor, MI	www.umich.edu/
5	University of North Carolina–Chapel Hill	Chapel Hill, NC	www.unc.edu/
6	College of William and Mary	Williamsburg, VA	www.wm.edu/
7	Georgia Institute of Technology	Atlanta, GA	www.gatech.edu/
7	University of California–San Diego	La Jolla, CA	www.ucsd.edu/
9	University of California–Davis	Davis, CA	www.ucdavis.edu/
9	University of California–Santa Barbara	Santa Barbara, CA	www.ucsb.edu/
11	University of California–Irvine	Irvine, CA	www.uci.edu/
11	University of Washington	Seattle, WA	www.washington.edu/
13	University of Texas–Austin	Austin, TX	www.utexas.edu/
13	University of Wisconsin–Madison	Madison, WI	www.wisc.edu/
15	Pennsylvania State University–University Park	University Park, PA	www.psu.edu/
15	University of Illinois–Urbana–Champaign	Champaign, IL	www.uiuc.edu/
17	University of Florida	Gainesville, FL	www.ufl.edu/
18	Ohio State University–Columbus	Columbus, OH	www.osu.edu/
18	Purdue University–West Lafayette	West Lafayette, IN	www.purdue.edu/
18	University of Georgia	Athens, GA	www.uga.edu/
18	University of Maryland–College Park	College Park, MD	www.umd.edu/
22	Texas A&M University–College Station	College Station, TX	www.tamu.edu/
23	Clemson University	Clemson, SC	www.clemson.edu/
23	Rutgers, the State University of New Jersey–New Brunswick	Piscataway, NJ	www.rutgers.edu/
23	University of Minnesota–Twin Cities	Minneapolis, MN	www1.umn.edu/
23	University of Pittsburgh	Pittsburgh, PA	www.pitt.edu/

and use of extended information and communication technologies, to name a few, were considered in the process. The criteria were also examined and modified keeping in mind new research and reports that have been developed during this time (Rankin et al. 2010). The reevaluated criteria were also tested in a pilot group of five randomly selected universities from the list by three different coders to identify which criteria were still relevant and/or needed to be redefined; the pilot study also contributed toward a refinement of some of the criteria meanings and definitions so that the three coders were on common ground while applying the framework to the entire website sample of all the universities selected for this research. This redefinition of meanings of the selected criteria for evaluating the websites helped develop consistency between the different coders while analyzing the individual institutions. The finalized criteria were categorized under three subheadings based on their function as related to: administration and policy, research and teaching, and services offered. Table 1.2 summarizes the twenty-two finalized criteria that were used and a brief definition/explanation of the criteria.

Data collection involved compiling and developing institutional profiles during summer 2011 for all the twenty-five universities selected for this research based on application of the modified and finalized evaluation criteria to assess their support of LGBT people. Typical examples of LGBT representation for each criterion in every institution were also included on the institutional profile sheet. The process involved using grounded theory principles in allowing the content found on the university websites to help identify which criteria it reflected; selective coding practices were applied as developed in the context of the website content to categorize the information and provide data for analysis (Glaser & Strauss 1967; Strauss & Corbin 2007). This generated a grade sheet of sorts that compared the different universities along the select evaluation criteria to assess their support of LGBT people. The grade sheet only identified whether each evaluation criterion was either reflected or not on the websites of the different universities. Owing to limitations of space, a detailed analysis of the range of content found under each criterion is beyond the scope of this chapter and will be documented in future publications. The three coders individually developed select institutional profiles and overextended discussion and dialogue came to a common agreement where there were differences among the coders in documenting the applicability of the different evaluation criteria for each institution's website. Appendix presents the institutional profile sheet developed for the University of California–Los Angeles to assess its support of LGBT people (dated October 2010). The outcome of the processes in data analysis was the development of such institutional profile sheets for each university selected in this research.

Table 1.2. Website Evaluation Criteria Used in this Research

Sr. No.	Evaluation Criteria and Definition
	I. ADMINISTRATION + POLICY
1.	Formal LGBT representation via committees, taskforce, commissions, etc.: Formal LGBT representation in the select university's administrative structure.
2.	Nondiscrimination statement inclusive of sexual orientation: Terms associated with "sexual orientation," specifically in the Equal Employment Opportunity/Affirmative Action (EEO/AA) Statement.
3.	Nondiscrimination statement inclusive of gender identity (expression): Terms associated with gender identity specifically in the Equal Employment Opportunity/Affirmative Action (EEO/AA) Statement.
4.	Extends domestic partner benefits to same-sex couples: Benefits for domestic partners of LGBT faculty, staff, and students.
5.	Procedure for reporting LGBT bias, harassment, and hate crimes: Procedures and policies to address LGBT discrimination and prejudice.
6.	Offers LGBT housing options: Adequate choices, options, and representation for LGBT people in housing.
	II. RESEARCH + TEACHING
7.	Information resources: bibliography, directory of local resources, etc. This includes LGBT listservs, mailing lists, and chat rooms hosted by the university.
8.	LGBT studies (courses and curriculum: Specialized courses on LGBT issues (not content that is part of other non-LGBT-themed courses; "seminars" have been removed from this variable owing to ambiguity about what constitutes a "seminar."
9.	LGBT educational events: Educational events on LGBT topics and concerns.
	III. SERVICES OFFERED
10.	LGBT and ally student organization(s): Links from the university's main resource pages to the websites of active and current LGBT organizations.
11.	LGBT resource center (office): A physical space demarcated for use as an LGBT resource center
12.	LGBT faculty and staff group(s): Visible groups for LGBT faculty and staff.
13.	Safe zone (safe space): Designated safe space programs, especially for LGBT people who had a trained support system to facilitate their operation and implementation.

III. SERVICES OFFERED *(continued)*

14.	LGBT social activities: "Fun" activities and events for LGBT people.
15.	Offers LGBT-inclusive health services (testing): Visible health services to meet the needs of LGBT people.
16.	Offers LGBT-inclusive mental health services and counseling (support groups): Adequate counseling services to meet the needs of LGBT clientele.
17.	Offers LGBT student scholarships: Specific LGBT scholarships that are provided by the university in question (not a link to information about national scholarships).
18.	Offers services for trans concerns: Representation of trans concerns.
19.	LGBT alumni group(s): Visible groups for LGBT alumni.
20.	LGBT mentoring: Mentoring efforts for LGBT students so that they can grow, develop, and succeed in their chosen paths.
21.	Intersections: Intersections of sexual orientation/sexuality with other categories of social marginalization such as race/ethnicity, income, national origins, religion, etc.
22.	LGBT recruitment: University efforts to actively pursue recruitment of LGBT students

Findings

Table 1.3 presents a comparison of the top-ranked universities along the select evaluation criteria to assess their support of LGBT people. A check mark (ü) against the evaluation criteria for the universities under study indicates that some representation of the criteria was available on the university's website. For example, eighteen universities had some information available on their websites regarding formal LGBT representation via committees, taskforce, commissions, and so on. This section briefly summarizes the kinds of examples and representations of each evaluation criteria that were found on the select university's websites. The analysis presented here is not all-encompassing or complete in any manner whatsoever; the purpose is to present an introduction of the representations to the readers to give an idea of the range of expression and further detailed discussion of each evaluation criteria and their representations will be presented in future publications. Though a discussion of the evaluation criteria that were included in the top-five and the least-five most popular among the top twenty-five universities will be presented in the next section to highlight those that can form part of "best practices" and future applications, respectively.

Table 1.3. Comparison of the Top-Ranked Universities Along the Select Evaluation Criteria to Assess Their Support of LGBT People

*University Identification → Assessment Criteria ↓	A	B	C	D	E	F	G	H	I	J	K	L	M	N	O	P	Q	R	S	T	U	V	W	X	Y	Z	Total
I. ADMINISTRATION + POLICY																											
1. Formal administrative representation	✓	✓						✓	✓	✓	✓	✓	✓	✓	✓	✓	✓	✓	✓	✓				✓	✓	✓	18
2. Sexual orientation in EEO/AA statement	✓	✓	✓	✓	✓	✓	✓	✓	✓	✓	✓	✓	✓	✓	✓	✓	✓	✓	✓	✓	✓		✓	✓	✓	✓	25
3. Gender identity in EEO/AA statement	✓	✓		✓				✓	✓	✓	✓	✓	✓	✓	✓	✓	✓	✓	✓					✓	✓	✓	18
4. Domestic partner benefits	✓	✓		✓	✓			✓	✓	✓	✓	✓	✓	✓	✓	✓	✓	✓	✓	✓	✓						18
5. Procedure for reporting bias	✓	✓		✓	✓			✓		✓	✓		✓	✓	✓	✓	✓	✓	✓	✓	✓	✓	✓	✓			19
6. Housing	✓	✓		✓		✓		✓	✓	✓	✓		✓	✓				✓		✓	✓				✓		12
II. RESEARCH + TEACHING																											
7. Information resources	✓	✓	✓	✓	✓	✓	✓	✓	✓	✓	✓		✓	✓	✓	✓			✓	✓	✓	✓			✓		19
8. Courses and curriculum	✓	✓	✓	✓		✓	✓	✓	✓	✓	✓	✓	✓	✓	✓	✓	✓	✓	✓	✓	✓		✓	✓	✓	✓	20
9. Educational events	✓	✓	✓	✓	✓		✓	✓	✓	✓	✓	✓	✓	✓	✓	✓	✓	✓		✓	✓	✓	✓	✓	✓		22
III. SERVICES OFFERED																											
10. Student groups	✓	✓	✓	✓	✓	✓	✓	✓	✓	✓	✓	✓	✓	✓	✓	✓	✓	✓	✓	✓	✓	✓	✓	✓	✓	✓	26
11. Resource center	✓	✓	✓	✓	✓	✓	✓	✓	✓	✓	✓	✓	✓	✓	✓	✓	✓	✓	✓	✓	✓	✓	✓	✓	✓		24
12. Faculty/staff group	✓	✓	✓	✓		✓	✓	✓	✓	✓	✓	✓	✓			✓		✓		✓		✓	✓				16
13. Safe Zone		✓	✓	✓		✓	✓	✓	✓	✓	✓	✓	✓	✓	✓	✓	✓	✓	✓	✓	✓	✓	✓	✓	✓		22
14. Social activities	✓	✓	✓	✓	✓	✓	✓	✓	✓	✓	✓	✓	✓	✓	✓	✓	✓	✓	✓	✓	✓	✓	✓	✓	✓	✓	26

	A	B	C	D	E	F	G	H	I	J	K	L	M	N	O	P	Q	R	S	T	U	V	W	X	Y	Z	Total
15. Health services	✓	✓	✓			✓	✓	✓		✓	✓	✓	✓	✓		✓	✓	✓	✓	✓	✓		✓				16
16. Mental health services	✓	✓	✓	✓		✓	✓	✓	✓	✓	✓	✓	✓	✓	✓	✓	✓	✓	✓	✓			✓		✓		19
17. Scholarships	✓	✓	✓	✓		✓		✓	✓	✓	✓		✓		✓		✓			✓			✓	✓	✓		15
18. Trans concerns	✓	✓	✓		✓	✓	✓	✓	✓	✓	✓	✓		✓			✓			✓				✓	✓		16
19. Alumni groups	✓	✓	✓	✓	✓	✓	✓	✓	✓	✓	✓	✓	✓		✓			✓				✓	✓	✓	✓		18
20. Mentoring	✓		✓	✓	✓	✓	✓	✓	✓						✓										✓		13
21. Intersections	✓	✓	✓	✓	✓			✓	✓						✓				✓	✓				✓			14
22. Recruitment	✓						✓								✓					✓	✓	✓		✓			7
Total	**18**	**19**	**14**	**19**	**15**	**12**	**8**	**21**	**19**	**21**	**20**	**14**	**17**	**20**	**17**	**14**	**15**	**16**	**9**	**15**	**17**	**11**	**10**	**16**	**19**	**7**	

*LEGEND: A. University of California–Berkeley; B. University of California–Los Angeles; C. University of Virginia; D. University of Michigan–Ann Arbor; E. University of North Carolina–Chapel Hill; F. College of William and Mary; G. Georgia Institute of Technology; H. University of California–San Diego; I. University of California–Davis; J. University of California–Santa Barbara; K. University of California–Irvine; L. University of Washington; M. University of Texas–Austin; N. University of Wisconsin–Madison; O. Pennsylvania State University–University Park; P. University of Illinois–Urbana-Champaign; Q. University of Florida; R. Ohio State University–Columbus; S. Purdue University–West Lafayette; T. University of Georgia; U. University of Maryland–College Park; V. Texas A&M–College Station; W. Clemson University; X. Rutgers, the State University of New Jersey–New Brunswick; Y. University of Minnesota–Twin Cities; Z. University of Pittsburgh.

Formal LGBT representation in the selected university's administrative structure was provided by units and examples that had a range of names and functional roles. For example, the mission of the Chancellor's Advisory Committee on the LGBT Community at the University of California–Berkeley is broad and encompassing to "promote a tolerant and inclusive campus environment," and the committee "regularly identifies, analyzes, and advises the Chancellor and senior administration on needs and concerns" of the LGBT community via: advising on campus climate, changing needs, and emerging populations and trends; supporting scholarly research and teaching in LGBT studies; reviewing campus and system policies, procedures, and practices, as well as reports, plans, and program proposals; helping create an affirming and welcoming environment; commenting on LGBT affecting conditions and incidents; and, serving as liaison with related committees and constituencies ("Chancellor's" n.d.). Whereas, the responsibilities of the LGBT Concerns Committee at the University of Florida is more focused on: serving as a "vehicle for a systematic and periodic assessment of the quality of life" of LGBT individuals and making "recommendations regarding the need for educational programming, establishment of specific services and programs, and other similar matters"; examining and recommending "revisions in university policies and procedures having potentially negative consequences" for LGBT individuals; and, acting as a forum "to which various individuals and groups can express concerns related to issues of homophobia and transphobia" ("Lesbian, Gay, Bisexual, Transgender Concerns" n.d.). Each kind of formal administrative unit and the nature and type of role it plays in the different institutions seem to have emerged to meet very specific needs influenced by the particular social, cultural, and political climate. Future research will examine the history of some of these administrative units and document the reasons that they emerged via collecting feedback during qualitative interviews with some key staff and personnel available in these institutions. This will help better understand the context and realities of LGBT experiences longitudinally at these institutions and trace the trajectory of administrative response over a period of time.

With regard to the inclusion of sexual orientation and/or gender identity in their EEO/AA statement, some institutions like the University of Minnesota–Twin Cities not only had different terms for each of these constructs, in addition, their nondiscrimination policy included terms drawing distinction between "gender," "gender identity," and "gender expression" (Boyd & O'Day n.d.). Use of such refined vocabulary and unique identifiers demarcating the different meanings within the larger concept in the policy reflects a deeper understanding, progressive administrative climate, and positive approach in its acknowledgment of the variations.

Different public universities provided different services in extending domestic partner benefits to LGBT faculty, staff, and students in their institutions based on the state laws where they are geographically located. For example, the University of California–Davis provides financial aid to individuals if they or their parents are in a Registered Domestic Partnership following the California Domestic Partner Rights and Responsibilities Act of 2003 ("Parents" n.d.). Purdue University–West Lafayette identifies details of the benefits it extends to same-sex domestic partners of its employees and their eligible children to include: medical insurance (including vision plan); fee remissions; dependent life insurance; Accidental Death and Dismemberment (AD&D); access to programs, services, and facilities of the university; use of flexible spending account and addressing specific tax issues; and employee leaves and time off to acknowledge domestic partners (e.g., bereavement leave, family illness leave, leave similar to the federally mandated Family and Medical Leave Act) ("Same-Sex Domestic" n.d.).

Different institutions had different procedures for reporting LGBT bias, harassment, and hate crimes. Some, like the University of California–Irvine provided online access to Intolerance Report Form ("Welcome to the University of California's" n.d.) that allowed for reporting many various issues (e.g., expressions of bias; hate speech; hate crime; graffiti/vandalism; intimidation, bullying or physical violence; bias incidents; hostile climate; and other campus climate issues), most of which specifically included LGBT-representative vocabulary in their definitions. Others, like the Ohio State University–Columbus provided access to a more broad-based information service, the Bias Assessment and Response Team that not only had a procedure in place for reporting a bias incident (defined to include "sexual-orientation group"), additionally, their website included a list of relevant student life bias response resources (e.g., university housing, student judicial affairs, student advocacy, etc.), policies and reports, diversity tool-kit project, and methods to get involved, among others, that did not necessarily refer to LGBT people or issues ("Bias Assessment" n.d.).

Offering of LGBT housing option was the last administration and policy-related assessment criteria used in this research. The University of Michigan–Ann Arbor has identified LGBT housing policies and options especially for same-sex couples and transgender-identified students ("Frequently" n.d.), while Rutgers, the State University of New Jersey–New Brunswick offers Special Interest Housing sections to include those on sex, sexuality, and gender, where section members live together either on the same floor or in the same traditional-style residence hall ("Special" n.d.).

Several universities provided various kinds of LGBT information resources to support their research and teaching missions as well as to further

LGBT knowledge and awareness of local community places, events, and activities. Further, a range of electronic social networking applications (e.g., listservs, mailing lists, chat rooms, etc.) were also identified. The University of Illinois–Urbana-Champaign provided access to their LGBT library collections and community and campus LGBT resources, in addition to their Facebook and Twitter accounts ("Resources" n.d.). The Texas A&M University–College Station focused on local categories of information resources such as LGBT associations, offices, counseling, community groups, religious organizations, advocacy and action, health services, median and events, and clubs ("GLBT Resources" n.d.).

The representation of LGBT content as an educational area of study was administratively acknowledged in different ways shaped possibly by the value and importance that the institution associated with the body of knowledge. The University of California–Santa Barbara provided information regarding LGBTQ Studies Minor in its Department of Feminist Studies ("Lesbian, Gay, Bisexual, Transgender and Queer" n.d.), whereas the University of Georgia listed a variety of courses offered across departments that examined LGBT issues ("LGBT Classes" n.d.).

Various institutions offered different LGBT educational events on campus that were represented on their websites. The University of California–Los Angeles shared information about the UCLA Queer Studies Conference in 2010 ("UCLA Queer" n.d.), whereas the University of Maryland–College Park offered a "Speaker's Bureau" whose mission has been to educate the "campus about sexual orientation, and gender identity and expression through panel discussions in classes, residence halls, and other university settings." LGBT and allied community members receive purposeful training on relevant issues and participate in discussions to disseminate accurate information, "answer questions that students, staff and faculty may have about the realities of LGBT lives," and "introduce the heterosexual, gender normative majority to visible members and allies of this mostly invisible minority" ("Speakers" n.d.).

There were varied LGBT services offered by the universities under study. Presence of LGBT and ally student organizations were high on the list and included groups focused for targeted student audiences such as the Rainbow Alliance for undergraduate students ("Welcome!" n.d.) and the GLBTQ Grad Student Support Group ("Group Counseling" n.d.) both at the University of Pittsburgh. Other institutions such as the Clemson University provided a setting for students (undergraduate and graduate), faculty, staff, and community members from different groupings to interact with each other like its Gay Straight Alliance ("Welcome to the Clemson" n.d.).

The physical presence of an LGBT resource center on campus was believed to be an important tangible marker to represent institutional show of support of LGBT people. For example, the Pennsylvania State University provided the LGBTA Resource Center ("LGBTA" n.d.), the University of Wisconsin–Madison offered the LGBT Campus Center ("About the LGBT" n.d.), and the University of Texas–Austin demarcated the Gender and Sexuality Center ("Welcome to the Gender" n.d.) for the purpose of meeting the needs of LGBT and other people through education, communications, outreach, and advocacy.

Few institutions provided groups for LGBT faculty and staff. The University of North Carolina–Chapel Hill supported the Queer Faculty and Staff Network ("Faculty" n.d.), while the UVa Pride, a LGBT Faculty, Staff, and Graduate Student Association at the University of Virginia, identified its objectives to include ("About UVA" n.d.): (1) educate the community about the needs of LGBT people; (2) develop LGBT curriculum and courses; (3) provide a safe LGBT social space; (4) provide accurate LGBT information and exchange of ideas; (5) support LGBT services and advocacy; and (6) pursue political change to further tolerance, fairness, and equality of LGBT people.

Several universities recognized the importance in identifying and designating LGBT safe spaces as a real and symbolic marker to represent their support of LGBT people. The Safe Zone Ally Program at the College of William and Mary ("Safe Zone" n.d.), modeled after the Virginia Association of College and University Housing Officer's (VACUHO) "Safe Zone Virginia" project, began in 1998 as an effort to enhance the campus climates across the state for LGBT people, and offers multiple sensitivity workshops each semester to reduce homophobia and heterosexism and make the community a safer and freer environment for all members, regardless of sexual orientation or gender identity.

LGBT social activities included "fun" activities and events for LGBT people and others. For example, the Spectrum Center at the University of Michigan–Ann Arbor provides students with the opportunity to participate in social events and activities that include: Gayz Craze–Welcome Week Activity during the week before classes begin in the fall semester; the Spectrum Center Open House in early September; Speakers Bureau panels that are orchestrated throughout the year and have involved 5,500 students per year during past years; Ally Program offered monthly for LGBT trainings; celebrating Bisexuality Day in September; National Coming Out Week during the second week of October; Transgender Day of Remembrance in November; Flaming Menorah Party; Queer Soiree celebrated around Valentine's Day; the annual Lavender Graduation in April; Spring Pride in March; and Flames on Ice involving LGBT and ally students ice-skating for the night; among others ("Frequently" n.d.).

Various institutions offered a myriad range of LGBT-inclusive health services (e.g., disease testing), in addition to mental health services (e.g., counseling, support groups). The University of California–San Diego provided specific health information for transgender people ("Transgender Health" n.d.) as well as broader Counseling and Psychological Services that were inclusive of LGBT people ("Meet the CAPS" n.d.). Similarly, the University of California–Davis compiled a list of relevant information resources specially for transgender people ("Transgender Resources" n.d.) (http://lgbtcenter.ucdavis.edu/resources/transgender-resources), in addition to focusing on trans activism and advocacy during its Trans Action Week ("Trans Action" n.d.).

Not many universities offered scholarships specifically to LGBT students. The University of Wisconsin–Madison was an exception in that it provided more than $100,000 in scholarships to incoming and continuing undergraduate and graduate students via its GLBT Alumni Council ("Gay, Lesbian, Bisexual, Transgender Alumni" n.d.). In recent years, there has been a trend in increased visibility of LGBT alumni groups who are recognizing the need to provide such scholarships and financial resources especially to address LGBT concerns at their alma mater. For example, the Pennsylvania State University–University Park had various services and resources for its LGBT alumni that included a listserv, advisory board, electronic newsletter, various special events, professional and social support network, in addition to opportunities to donate in support of LGBT causes ("Penn State LGBTQA" n.d.). Some universities pursued active recruitment of LGBT students. For example, the University of California–Los Angeles used the article titled "UCLA rates at the top for being LGBT-friendly" written by Alison Hewitt and published in the *UCLA Today* on August 10, 2010, as a recruitment tool to attract other LGBT students to the university (Hewitt 2010). Moreover, the practice of LGBT mentoring programs to involve students, faculty, and staff at some universities reflected an understanding that not only was LGBT recruitment important, but LGBT mentoring was key in order to retain and support LGBT students once they were admitted into the academy so that they could grow, develop, and succeed in their chosen career paths. For example, the goal of the GLBTA Mentor Program at the University of Minnesota–Twin Cities is to pair "mentors and mentees to provide an opportunity for GLBTA students to access support and resources and to attain personal growth; to give an opportunity for mentors to give back to their community; to provide support and growth opportunities mentors and mentees may not find otherwise; to build community among participating mentors; and to encourage community involvement" ("GLBTA Mentor" n.d.). Information regarding intersections of sexual orientation/sexuality with other categories of social marginalization in the United States such as race/ethnicity, income, national origins, religion, and so on was made available by some universities under study. For example, the University of Michigan–Ann Arbor listed an LGBT Caucus of the Students of Color of Rackham (SCOR) for students, faculty, and staff experiencing as a result of intersecting variables of sexual orientation/sexuality and race/ethnicity/national origins ("LGBTQ Student" n.d.).

Discussion

Figure 1.1 shows a distribution of the top twenty-five public universities selected under study in descending order based on a comparison of the select evaluation criteria to assess their support of LGBT people.

No public university represented all the twenty-two evaluation criteria used in this research to assess their support of LGBT people on their websites. Twelve of the twenty-six public universities (46.15%) selected under study occupied the top five positions with the highest representation of the evaluation criteria (17–21) on their websites. What does this reveal? First, there seems to be a high level of agreement among at least nearly half of the top twenty-five public universities in the United States about what information is important to represent on their websites as a marker of their support of LGBT people. Second, the fact that so many of the top twenty-five universities are "on the same page" regarding the representation of their support of LGBT people on their website, indicates the relevance and validity of the selected evaluation criteria. The information-related efforts of these public universities in representation of their support of LGBT people on their websites, provides other universities and colleges a benchmark to follow and adopt as "best practices." The fact that all the six public universities in the state of California (with branches in Santa Barbara, San Diego, Irvine, Davis, Los Angeles, and Berkeley) that were identified by the 2011 U.S. News & World Report in the top twenty-five are included in the twelve universities occupying the top five positions with the highest representation of the evaluation criteria on their websites reflects a high level of consistency across the public universities in the state in their show of support of LGBT people. Moreover, the fact that universities from other regions such as the Midwest (University of Wisconsin–Madison, University of Michigan–Ann Arbor, University of Minnesota–Twin Cities), the Southwest (University of Texas–Austin), and the Northeast (University of Maryland–College Park, Pennsylvania State University–University Park) are represented in the twelve universities occupying the top five positions with the highest representation of the evaluation criteria on their websites shows that progressive efforts are being made in other parts of the country as well. These universities that are identified in the top exemplary efforts to show support of LGBT people on their websites can serve as a role

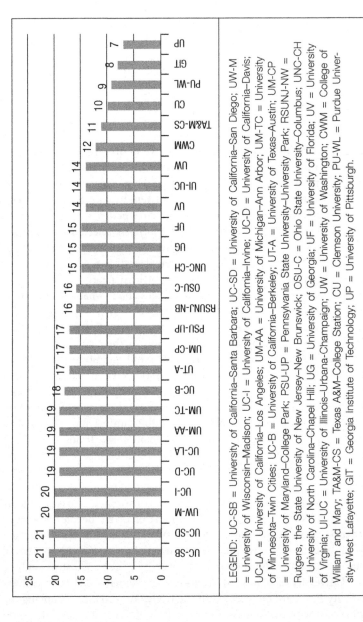

Figure 1.1. Distribution of the top twenty-five public universities in descending order, based on a comparison of the select evaluation criteria to assess their support of LGBT people.

LEGEND: UC-SB = University of California–Santa Barbara; UC-SD = University of California–San Diego; UW-M = University of Wisconsin–Madison; UC-I = University of California–Irvine; UC-D = University of California–Davis; UC-LA = University of California–Los Angeles; UM-AA = University of Michigan–Ann Arbor; UM-TC = University of Minnesota–Twin Cities; UC-B = University of California–Berkeley; UT-A = University of Texas–Austin; UM-CP = University of Maryland–College Park; PSU-UP = Pennsylvania State University–University Park; RSUNJ-NW = Rutgers, the State University of New Jersey–New Brunswick; OSU-C = Ohio State University–Columbus; UNC-CH = University of North Carolina–Chapel Hill; UG = University of Georgia; UF = University of Florida; UV = University of Virginia; UI-UC = University of Illinois–Urbana–Champaign; UW = University of Washington; CWM = College of William and Mary; TA&M-CS = Texas A&M–College Station; CU = Clemson University; PU-WL = Purdue University–West Lafayette; GIT = Georgia Institute of Technology; UP = University of Pittsburgh.

model for other universities and colleges looking to extend their support towards this marginalized population.

A cause for concern is that the Northwest and the South were conspicuous by a lack of representation of universities and colleges from these regions in the top five positions with the highest representation of the evaluation criteria on their websites. Future research needs to explore the possible reasons underlying this trend. Hence, a related point is the need to be careful in making assumptions while presenting claims of progressive efforts of LGBT support across the United States that are based solely on trends visible in the major metropolitan areas, densely populated urban settlements (e.g., New York, San Francisco, Chicago, etc.), and regions known for their liberal and supportive climates. As the data in this research reveals, there may be miles to go in terms of getting the rest of the country on board regarding adequate representation, fairness, equity, and justice on behalf of LGBT people in regions perceived as less progressive.

Figure 1.2 shows the evaluation criteria with the top five occurrences (20–26) on the websites of the top twenty-five public universities in the United States.

The fact that the two evaluation crietria (namely, LGBT student groups and LGBT social activities, both related to services offered) were represented

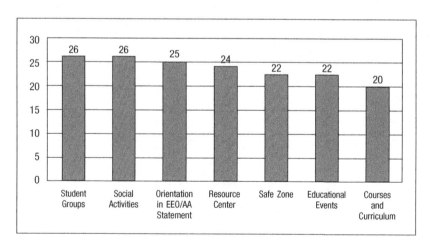

Figure 1.2. Evaluation criteria with the top five occurrence on the websites of the top twenty-five public universities.

on the websites of all the twenty-six universities selected for this study indicates how basic and important such information and services are believed to be included on the websites of the top public universities in the country. The other five of the seven evaluation criteria that were identified with the top five occurrences are considered equally important in forming part of a "bare minimum" set of best practices that other universities and colleges must adopt and integrate information about on their websites. These included: inclusion of terms associated with sexual orientation in the EEO/AA statement (administration and policy); LGBT resource center (service offered); designated safe zone spaces (service offered); LGBT educational events (research and teaching); and LGBT courses and curriclum (research and teaching). It is worthwhile to note that these best practices include four evaluation criteria representing services offered, two evaluation criteria regarding research and teaching, and one evaluation criteria representing administration and policy. The small range reflected in the twenty to twenty-six public universities (77%–100% of the total) for the seven evaluation criteria with the top five occurrences reveals a mutual agreement between these universities in their significance associated with these evaluation criteria as web markers of LGBT support.

Figure 1.3 shows the evaluation criteria with the five least occurrences (7–15) on the websites of the top twenty-five public universities in the United States. The five evaluation crietria with the fewest occurrences on the websites of the top twenty-five public universities in the United States

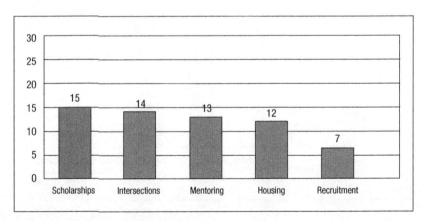

Figure 1.3. Evaluation criteria with the five least occurrence on the websites of the top twenty-five public universities.

were represented by a number of public universities in the range of seven to fifteen (27%–57.7% of the total) and this provides a few insights that deserve closer examination. First, the value of these five evaluation criteria as web markers of support of LGBT people cannot be understated owing to the fact that at least 27 percent of the top twenty-five public universities represented them on their websites. What this shows is the cutting-edge nature of these evaluation criteria as web markers of support of LGBT people that currently very few public universities are representing on their websites. Universities and colleges aspiring to become role models in their web and campus support of LGBT people should promote these efforts (in addition to representing the other evaluation criteria identified in this chapter) that will identify them as leaders in the twenty-first century. Second, the five evaluation criteria with the fewest occurrences on the websites of the top twenty-five public universities in the United States included: offering LGBT student scholarships (service offered); intersections of sexual orientation/sexuality with other categories of social marginalization (service offered); mentoring efforts for LGBT students (service offered); adequate choices, options, and representation for LGBT people in housing (administration and policy); and university efforts to actively pursue recruitment of LGBT students (service offered). It is worthwhile to note that one evaluation crieteria was related to administration and policy while the remaining four evaluation criteria focused on services offered. The inclusion of these evaluation criteria with the least occurrence on the websites of the top twenty-five public universities in the United States highlights their potential importance in future directions of growth. It suggests the need for extended efforts to recruit, retain, and ensure success of LGBT students while making certain that they have a positive experience during their academic and educational process, and that sexual orientation/sexuality issues are not allowed to derail them from their career growth and professional development. The importance of providing a supportive social and cultural environment on-campus and online for LGBT populations seems a must in this regard.

Conclusion

This web-based evaluation research painted an initial picture assessing the top twenty-five public universities in their support (and representation of that support) of LGBT people. "Best practices" and future directions were also identified based on the data collected. An underlying assumption made in this research is that what was made visible on the website is what was indicative of institutional support of LGBT people. If the university had various services and administrative policies in support of LGBT people but they were not represented on the university websites, then they were not counted in this research. People searching the university website for indicators of campus climate may initially have only the information found on the university website to go by to identify what is available (or not available) in their support of LGBT people. It calls attention to the urgent need for complete, accurate, and updated information that is made available on university websites. The often used excuse of lack of resources to support staff with technological skills and/or time to keep up with current changes on the website seem completely out-of-sync in the twenty-first century, when people around the world use the Internet as the first window to gain information and initially experience the physicality of place.

Having said that, future efforts as a follow-up to this website evaluation research will include a detailed assessment of the top twenty-five public universities and others in terms of their support of LGBT people based on: (1) deeper understanding and comprehensive representation of the evaluation criteria in terms of the range of expression and examples for each criterion; and (2) use of mixed quantitative and qualitative methods to gather data beyond information content available on the web. This is related to the fact that just because the information was made available on the university website does not mean that the particular policy or service is effective and having an impact in making the experiences of LGBT people better in a particular academic environment.

Findings in this research are based solely on information found on the websites of the top twenty-five public universities in the United States. Follow-up research will involve establishing contacts with students, faculty, and staff at these universities to verify the accuracy, currency, and coverage extent of information presented on the websites of the select institutions. Moreover, applying the website evaluation framework and criteria developed in this research to other universities and agencies will identify how the rest of the country is faring in terms of representing their support of LGBT people on their websites. Suggestions for interventions and concrete strategies in support of LGBT people at these institutions will also be made to ensure that they do not stray far behind the top identified in their domains of work.

Appendix

Institutional Profile Sheet Developed for the University of California–Los Angeles to Assess Its Support for LGBT People (Dated October 2010).[1]

I. ADMINSTRATION AND POLICY

1. *Formal representation via committees, taskforce, commissions, etcetera.:*

   Chancellor's Advisory Committee on Gay and Lesbian Community.

   http://gsa.asucla.ucla.edu/organization/chancellorial-advisory-committees/gay-lesbian-community

2. *Nondiscrimination statement inclusive of sexual orientation:*

   Personnel Policies—"It is the policy of the University not to engage in discrimination against or harassment of any person employed by or seeking employment with the University of California on the basis of race, color, national origin, religion, sex, *gender identity*, pregnancy,[1] physical or mental disability, medical condition (cancer-related or genetic characteristics), genetic information (including family medical history), ancestry, marital status, age, *sexual orientation*, citizenship, or service in the uniformed services (as defined by the Uniformed Services Employment and Reemployment Rights Act of 1994).[2] This policy is intended to be consistent with the provisions of applicable State and Federal laws and University policies [emphasis added]."

   http://atyourservice.ucop.edu/employees/policies_employee_labor_relations/personnel_policies/spp12.html

3. *Nondiscrimination statement inclusive of gender identity (expression):*

   Personnel policies—(see above).

   http://atyourservice.ucop.edu/employees/policies_employee_labor_relations/personnel_policies/spp12.html.

4. *Extends domestic partner benefits to same-sex couples:*

   All eligible family members—same-sex domestic partner.

   http://atyourservice.ucop.edu/retirees/health_welfare/enrollment_eligibility/eligibility_chart.html

5. *Procedure for reporting LGBT bias, harassment and hate crimes:*

   Report anti-LGBT incidences.

   http://www.lgbt.ucla.edu/form_reportantilgbt1.html

6. *Offers LGBT housing options (themes):*
   None.

II. RESEARCH AND TEACHING

7. *LGBT online information resources (bibliography, directory of local resources, etc.):*
   Williams Institute Reading Room—A guide to resources in the Williams Institute Reading Room, part of the Williams Institute on Sexual Orientation Law and Public Policy at the UCLA School of Law.

   http://libguides.law.ucla.edu/williamsreadingroom

8. *LGBT studies (courses and curriculum):*
   LGBTStudiesUCLA.

   http://www.humnet.ucla.edu/humnet/lgbts/index.html

9. *LGBT educational events:*
   UCLA Queer Studies Conference 2010.

   http://www.humnet.ucla.edu/humnet/lgbts/events/current.html

III. SERVICES OFFERED

10. *LGBT and ally student organization(s):*
    LGBT student organizations.

    http://www.lgbt.ucla.edu/UCLALGBTStudentOrganization.htm

11. *LGBT resource center (office):*
    UCLA LGBT Campus Resource Center.

    http://www.lgbt.ucla.edu/

12. *LGBT faculty and staff group(s):*
    The UCLA LGBT Faculty-Staff Network.

    http://www.lgbt.ucla.edu/facultyandstaff1.html

13. *Safe zone (safe space):*
    None active.

14. *LGBT social activities:*
    LGBT Faculty-Staff Network—Sponsors National Coming Out Week reception, Annual Spring Anniversary Reception, Lavender Graduation, Brown Bag lunch events, other events.

    http://www.lgbt.ucla.edu/facultyandstaff1.html

15. *Offers LGBT-inclusive health services (testing):*

    Get Yourself Tested @ Ashe Student Health & Wellness Center.

    http://www.studenthealth.ucla.edu/health_gyt.html

16. *Offers LGBT-inclusive mental health services and counseling (support groups):*

    Counseling and Psychological Services—Gay/Bi Men's Support Group.

    http://www.lgbt.ucla.edu/services1.html#studentcounseling

17. *Offers LGBT student scholarships:*

    Lambda Alumni—LGBT Scholarships.

    http://www.lgbt.ucla.edu/scholarshipresources.html

18. *Offers services for trans concerns:*

    Transgender Resources.

    http://www.lgbt.ucla.edu/transresources.html

19. *LGBT alumni group(s):*

    Lambda Alumni.

    http://www.lgbt.ucla.edu/alumni1.html

20. *LGBT mentoring:*

    LGBT Graduate Student Peer Mentor Program.

    http://www.lgbt.ucla.edu/mentor.htm

21. *Intersections: race and sexuality, etcetera:*

    BlaQue is a student organization for same-gender loving, LGBT, queer peoples of African/African American descent.

    http://www.studentgroups.ucla.edu/qa/blaque.html

22. *LGBT recruitment:*

    Undergraduate Admissions—Student Life, Gay and Lesbian Resources.

    http://www.admissions.ucla.edu/about/studentlife.htm

    "UCLA Rates at the Top for Being LGBT-Friendly." The *Campus Pride* index of colleges and universities provides students with a way to find out which schools are the most welcoming to LGBT students: UCLA is in the top twenty. UCLA has a five-star rating.

    http://today.ucla.edu/portal/ut/ucla-rates-at-the-top-for-lgbt-166129.aspx

Note

1. The websites in the Appendix were accessed on June 25, 2011. The authors have made small changes to the content for editing, spelling, grammar, and so on.

Works Cited

Aarons, L. *Prayers for Bobby: A Mother's Coming to Terms with the Suicide of Her Gay Son*. New York: HarperCollins Publishers, 1995.

"About the LGBT Campus Center." LGBT Campus Center, University of Wisconsin–Madison (accessed June 25, 2011), http://lgbt.wisc.edu/about.

"About UVA Pride." Lesbian, Gay, Bisexual, Transgender Faculty, Staff & Graduate Student Association, University of Virginia (accessed June 25, 2011), http://indorgs.virginia.edu/uvapride/about/index.php.

"Academic Ranking of World Universities—2010," Shanghai Ranking Consultancy, Shanghai, China, 2011 (accessed August 30, 2011), http://www.arwu.org/ARWU2010.jsp.

Aguillo, I., J. Bar-Ilan, M. Levene, and J. L. Ortega Priego. "Comparing University Rankings." *Scientometrics* 85.1 (2010): 243–256.

"Bias Assessment and Team Response." Office of Student Life, Ohio State University–Columbus (accessed June 25, 2011), http://studentlife.osu.edu/bias/.

Boyd, K., and M. O'Day. "Affirmative Action Plan for the University of Minnesota." Office of Equal Opportunity and Affirmative Action, University of Minnesota–Twin Cities (accessed June 25, 2011), http://www.eoaffact.umn.edu/resources/AAP2010/AAP10Text.pdf.

Brown, T., and K. Anderson. "Sexual Identity and Heterosexual Male Students' Usage of Homosexual Insults: An Exploratory Study." *The Canadian Journal of Human Sexuality* 19.1–2 (2010): 27–42.

Cahill, S. *Courting the Vote: The 2000 Presidential Candidates' Positions on Gay, Lesbian, Bisexual and Transgender Issues*. Washington, DC: The Policy Institute of the National Gay and Lesbian Task Force, 1999.

"Chancellor's Advisory Committee on the Lesbian, Gay, Bisexual, Transgender (LGBT) Community at CAL." Gender Equity Resource Center, University of California–Berkeley (accessed June 26, 2014), http://geneq.berkeley.edu/cac.

Chowdhury, G., and S. Chowdhury. *Information Sources and Searching on the World Wide Web*. London: Library Association, 2001.

Cobb, M. L. *God Hates Fags: The Rhetorics of Religious Violence*. New York: NYU Press, 2006.

Cortese, A. *Opposing Hate Speech*. Westport, CT: Praeger Publishers, 2005.

Diamond, T., and M. Sanders. *Reference Assessment and Evaluation*. Florence, KY: Routledge, 2006.

Dugan, R., P. Hernon, and D. Nitecki. *Viewing Library Metrics from Different Perspectives: Inputs, Outputs, and Outcomes*. Santa Barbara: ABC-CLIO, LLC., 2009.

Dunn, D., M. McCarthy, S. Baker, J. Halonen, and P. Maki. *Using Quality Benchmarks for Assessing and Developing Undergraduate Programs*. Hoboken, NJ: Jossey-Bass, 2010.

"Faculty and Staff Organizations." LGBTQ Center, University of North Carolina–Chapel Hill (accessed June 25, 2011), http://lgbtq.unc.edu/index.php/resources/facultystaff-organization.html.

"Frequently Asked Questions." Spectrum Center, University of Michigan–Ann Arbor (accessed June 25, 2011), http://spectrumcenter.umich.edu/prospective/studentfaq.

"Gay, Lesbian, Bisexual, Transgender Alumni Council." Wisconsin Alumni Association, University of Wisconsin–Madison (accessed June 25, 2011), http://www.uwa-lumni.com/glbtac.

Glaser, B., and A. L. Strauss. *The Discovery of Grounded Theory: Strategies for Qualitative Research*. NJ: Aldine Transaction, Piscataway, 1967.

"GLBT Resources for the Brazos Valley and Beyond." GLBT Professional Network, Texas A&M University–College Station (accessed June 25, 2011), http://glbtpn.tamu.edu/resources.html.

"GLBTA Mentor Program." GLBTA Programs Office, University of Minnesota–Twin Cities (accessed June 25, 2011), http://glbta.umn.edu/programming/mentorprogram.

"Group Counseling." University Counseling Center, University of Pittsburgh (accessed June 25, 2011), http://www.counseling.pitt.edu/services/groups.html#women.

Hewitt, A. "UCLA Rates at the Top for Being LGBT-Friendly." University of California–Los Angeles, Last modified August 10, 2010 (accessed June 25, 2011), http://today.ucla.edu/portal/ut/ucla-rates-at-the-top-for-lgbt-166129.aspx.

Isay, R. *Being Homosexual: Gay Men and Their Development*. New York: Vintage Books, 2009.

Jackson, E. *Strategies of Deviance: Studies in Gay Male Representation*. Bloomington, IN: Indiana University Press, 1995.

Johnson, D. Lamont, C. Maddux, L. Liu, and N. Henderson. *Evaluation and Assessment in Educational Information Technology*. Boca Raton, FL: CRC Press, 2002.

Lakoff, G. *How Liberals and Conservatives Think*. Chicago: University of Chicago Press, 2002.

Lawrence, D., and S. Tavako. *Balanced Website Design: Optimising Aesthetics, Usability and Purpose*. New York: Springer Verlag, 2006.

"Lesbian, Gay, Bisexual, Transgender and Queer (LGBTQ) Studies." Department of Feminist Studies, University of California–Santa Barbara (accessed June 25, 2011), http://www.femst.ucsb.edu/lgbtq.html.

"Lesbian, Gay, Bisexual, Transgender Concerns Committee." Presidential Committees, University of Florida (accessed June 25, 2011), http://fora.aa.ufl.edu/University/PresidentialCommittees/Lesbian-Gay-Bisexual-Transgender-Concerns-Committee.

"LGBT Classes." Lesbian, Gay, Bisexual, Transgender Resource Center, University of Georgia (accessed June 25, 2011), http://www.uga.edu/lgbtcenter/students/classes.html.

"LGBTA Student Resource Center." Student Affairs, Pennsylvania State University (accessed June 25, 2011), http://www.sa.psu.edu/lgbt/.

"LGBTQ Student Organizations." Spectrum Center, University of Michigan–Ann Arbor (accessed June 25, 2011), http://spectrumcenter.umich.edu/getinvolved/lgbtqorgs.

Madhaven, R., E. Tunstel, and E. Messina. *Performance Evaluation and Benchmarking of Intelligent Systems.* New York: Springer, 2009.

Matthews, J. R. *Measuring for Results: The Dimensions of Public Library Effectiveness.* Westport, CT: Libraries Unlimited, 2003.

Matthews, J. R. *The Evaluation and Measurement of Library Services.* Westport, CT: Libraries Unlimited, 2007.

"Meet the CAPS Staff." Counseling and Psychological Services, University of California–San Diego (accessed June 25, 2011), http://caps.ucsd.edu/staff_web/staff_home.html.

Mehra, B. "Integrating LGBTIQ Representations Across the Library and Information Science Curriculum: A Strategic Framework for Student-Centered Interventions." In *Serving LGBTIQ Library and Archives Users: Essays on Outreach, Service, Collections and Access,* ed. Ellen Greenblatt. Jefferson, NC: MacFarland & Company, 2011, 298–309.

Mehra, B., and D. Braquet. "A 'Queer' Manifesto of Interventions for Libraries to 'Come Out' of the Closet! A Study of 'Queer' Youth Experiences during the Coming Out Process." *Library and Information Science Research Electronic Journal* 16.1 (2006): 1–29 (accessed August 30, 2011), http://libres.curtin.edu.au/libres16n1/.

Mehra, B., and D. Braquet. "Library and Information Science Professionals as Community Action Researchers in an Academic Setting: Top Ten Directions to Further Institutional Change for People of Diverse Sexual Orientations and Gender Identities." *Library Trends* 56.2 (2007): 542–565.

Mehra, B., and D. Braquet. "Process of Information Seeking During 'Queer' Youth Coming-Out Experiences." In *Youth Information Seeking Behaviors: Contexts, Theories, Models and Issues,* ed. M. K. Chelton and C. Cool. Toronto: Scarecrow Press, 2007, 93–131.

Mehra, B., and D. Braquet. "Progressive LGBTQ Reference: Coming Out in the 21st Century." Special Issue: Learning Landscapes and the New Reality, *Reference Services Review* 39.3 (2011): 401–422.

Mehra, B., and R. Srinivasan. "The Library-Community Convergence Framework for Community Action: Libraries as Catalysts of Social Change." *Libri: International Journal of Libraries and Information* Services 57.3 (2007): 129–139.

Mehra, B., D. Braquet, E. White, R. Weaver, and C. Hodge. *A Website Analysis of the University of Tennessee's Peer Institutions to Assess Their Support of Lesbian, Gay, Bisexual, and Transgender People* (report submitted by the Research Committee, Commission for LGBT People, University of Tennessee) (accessed August 30, 2011), https://web.utk.edu/~bmehra/final.pdf.

Mogul, J., A. Ritchie, and K.Whitlock. *Queer (In)Justice: The Criminalization of LGBT People in the United States.* Boston: Beacon Press, 2011.

Muller, J. *A Librarian's Guide to the Internet: A Guide to Searching and Evaluating Information.* Oxford: Chandos, 2003.

Munde, G., and K. Marks. *Surviving the Future: Academic Libraries, Quality and Assessment.* London: Chandos Publishing, 2009.

O'Connor, R., and A. Cutler. *Shock Jocks: Hate Speech and Talk Radio: America's Ten Worst Hate Talkers and the Progressive Alternatives.* San Francisco, CA: AlterNet Books, 2008.

O'Shea, R., T. Allen, K. Morse, C. O'Gorman, and F. Roche. "Delineating the Anatomy of an Entrepreneurial University: The Massachusetts Institute of Technology Experience." *R&D Management* 37.1 (2007).

"Parents of Dependent Students." UC Davis Financial Aid, University of California–Davis (accessed June 25, 2011), http://financialaid.ucdavis.edu/undergraduate/parents/definition.html.

Parker, R., and P. Aggleton. *Culture, Society and Sexuality: A Reader.* Florence, KY: Routledge, 2007.

"Penn State LGBTQA Alumni." LGBTA Resource Center, Pennsylvania State University–University Park (accessed June 25, 2011), http://www.sa.psu.edu/lgbt/Alumni.shtml.

Plumley, G. *Website Design and Development: 100 Questions to Ask Before Building a Website.* Hoboken, NJ: John Wiley & Sons, 2010.

Potts, K. *Web Design and Marketing Solutions for Business Websites.* New York: Springer Verlag, 2007.

Rankin, S., G. Weber, W. Blumenfeld, and S. Frazer. *2010 State of Higher Education for LGBT People.* North Carolina: Campus Pride, 2010 (accessed June 25, 2011), http://www.campuspride.org/Campus%20Pride%202010%20LGBT%20Report%20Summary.pdf.

"Resources." Student Affairs, University of Illinois–Urbana-Champaign (accessed June 25, 2011), http://studentaffairs.illinois.edu/diversity/lgbt/resources.html.

"Safe Zone Ally Program at William and Mary." College of William and Mary (accessed June 25, 2011), http://wmpeople.wm.edu/site/page/safezone01.

"Same-Sex Domestic Partner Benefits." Vice President for Human Resources, Purdue University–West Lafayette (accessed June 25, 2011), http://www.purdue.edu/hr/Benefits/domestic_partner.html.

Sears, A., and C. Osten. *The Homosexual Agenda: Exposing the Principal Threat to Religious Freedom Today.* Nashville, TN: Broadman & Holman Publishers, 2003.

Shepard, J. *The Meaning of Matthew: My Son's Murder in Laramie, and a World Transformed.* New York: Penguin Press, 2010.

Smallwood, D., and S. Forman. *Everyday Program Evaluation for Schools: Implementation and Outcomes.* Florence, KY: Routledge, 2011.

Smith, C. H. "It's an Election Year: Playing the Fear Card for the Religious Right . . . Again," *Firedoglake* (blog), May 5, 2008 (accessed June 25, 2011), http://firedoglake.com/2008/05/05/its-an-election-year-playing-the-fear-card-for-the-religious-rightagain/.

"Speakers Bureau." Office of LGBT Equity, University of Maryland–College Park (accessed June 25, 2011), http://www.umd.edu/lgbt/speakers.html.

"Special Interest Housing." Housing and Residential Life, Rutgers, the State University of New Jersey–New Brunswick (accessed June 25, 2011), http://ruoncampus.rutgers.edu/living-at-rutgers/special-living-options/special-interest-housing#Sex_Gender.

Strauss, A. L., and J. Corbin. *Basics of Qualitative Research Techniques and Procedures for Developing Grounded Theory,* vol. 2. Thousand Oaks, CA: Sage Publications, 2007.

"Top Public Schools." *U.S. News and World Report* (accessed June 25, 2011), http://colleges.usnews.rankingsandreviews.com/best-colleges/rankings/national-universities/top-public.

"Trans Action Week." Lesbian, Gay, Bisexual, Transgender Resource Center, University of California–Davis (accessed June 25, 2011), http://lgbtcenter.ucdavis.edu/events/trans-action-week.

"Transgender Health Information." LGBT Resource Center, University of California–San Diego (accessed June 25, 2011), http://lgbt.ucsd.edu/Transgender_Health_Information.asp.

"Transgender Resources." Lesbian, Gay, Bisexual, Transgender Resource Center, University of California–Davis (accessed June 25, 2011), http://lgbtcenter.ucdavis.edu/resources/transgender-resources.

"UCLA Queer Studies Conference." LGBT Studies, University of California–Los Angeles (accessed June 25, 2011), http://www.humnet.ucla.edu/humnet/lgbts/events/current.html.

Visser, U. *Intelligent Information Integration for the Semantic Web.* New York: Springer, 2005.

Volkwein, J. F., and K. Sweitzer. "Institutional Prestige and Reputation Among Research Universities and Liberal Arts Colleges." *Research in Higher Education* 47.1 (2006): 129–148.

Wallace, D., and C. V. Fleet. *Library Evaluation: A Casebook and Can-Do Guide.* Englewood, CO: Libraries Unlimited, 2001.

Weingand, D. E. *Administration of the Small Public Library.* Chicago, IL: American Library Association, 2001.

"Welcome to the Clemson Gay Straight Alliance." Gay Straight Alliance, Clemson University (accessed June 25, 2011), http://clemson.orgsync.com/org/clemsongsa.

"Welcome to the Gender and Sexuality Center: Serving Women and LGBTAQ Communities." Gender and Sexuality Center, University of Texas–Austin (accessed June 25, 2011), http://www.utexas.edu/diversity/ddce/gsc/index.php.

"Welcome to the University of California's Systemwide Intolerance Report Form." Campus Climate, University of California–Irvine (accessed June 25, 2011), https://ucsystems.ethicspointvp.com/custom/ucs_ccc/.

"Welcome!" Rainbow Alliance, University of Pittsburgh (accessed June 25, 2011), http://www.pitt.edu/~sorc/rainbow.

Weller, K. *Knowledge Representation in the Social Semantic Web.* New York: Walter de Gruyter GmbH & Co., 2010.

White, P. *Uninvited: Classical Hollywood Cinema and Lesbian Representability.* Bloomington, IN: Indiana University Press, 1999.

"Why *U.S. News* Ranks Colleges and Universities." *U.S. News and World Report,* Education. Last modified August 17, 2010 (accessed June 25, 2011), http://www.usnews.com/education/articles/2010/08/17/why-us-news-ranks-colleges-and-universities.

Windmeyer, S. L. *The Advocate College Guide for LGBT Students.* New York: Alyson Publications, 2006.

Chapter 2

Conducted in a Whisper

Some Observations About the Current State of LGBT Studies, and Ten Ways We Can Shout Down the Silence

Joshua G. Adair

Prologue

In spring 2009 I taught a group of twenty-five bright, engaged, and coura-geous, students for my course in Lesbian, Gay, Bisexual, Transgender Studies at Northern Illinois University. The course introduces students to the history, culture, and contemporary social issues of lesbian, gay, bisexual, and trans-gender (LGBT) people. As a blended course, it affords the opportunity for undergraduates and graduates to mingle, and to benefit from the instruction of not one, but two, professors. Most class periods, however, I would teach the undergraduate students separately for at least part of the class period and during that time I worked closely with an intelligent, sophisticated young man named Jason. Jason, preparing to graduate at the semester's end, revealed his homosexuality in an essay responding to a newspaper article lambasting gay men and effeminacy. He bemoaned the assumption of gay men's inherent effeminacy and noted his ongoing feelings of alienation because he looked and behaved, for all practical purposes, in a stereotypically masculine man-ner. He felt ostracized for failing to embody stereotypical gayness. I admired his dissection of the nuances of gay culture coupled with his passion and eloquence about his own feelings of simultaneous dual-disenfranchisement from mainstream and queer culture.

Shortly thereafter, I inquired about Jason's postgraduation plans. He expressed uncertainty; he was considering graduate school, but had not applied. He also mentioned that he might look for a job in the business world—his degree would be in general studies—but he felt ambivalent about that option too. His lack of focus about his rapidly approaching future puzzled me, because he struck me as neither apathetic nor unmotivated. When I casually asked two of Jason's friends in the class about their career goals (juniors, both) they evinced a similar uncertainty. I could not understand how three such excellent students could maintain such indifference about their futures.

A couple weeks later, one of Jason's friends stopped by my office to discuss her research paper. During our conversation I expressed my surprise that she was not formally enrolled for the LGBT Studies Certificate of Undergraduate Study and encouraged her to do so since she had completed all the required courses. Her response, "I can't sign up because it would appear on my transcripts and then my parents would stop paying for my education," troubled me deeply. A few days later Jason submitted another response paper, this time discussing his own struggle over whether or not he ought to complete the necessary paperwork for the Undergraduate Certificate in LGBT Studies. He too had completed all the necessary coursework, but feared that allowing this accomplishment to be reflected on his official transcript might equate to career suicide. How, I wondered, was this possible? Had I not regularly recruited students for the program by citing the invaluable benefit of having demonstrable training in diversity? Is the widespread assumption still that only LGBT people study LGBT topics? Straight males and females take my classes and demonstrate as much interest in, and dedication to, learning about LGBT people and issues. That moment with Jason, more than any other as an educator, destabilized my perception of the world and reminded me of the danger one still assumes when studying gender identity and sexual orientation. Are these areas of inquiry, after all, only safe within the academy? Are those of us committed to the mission of achieving social parity simply expanding the square footage of the closet for our students? In the pages that follow, I hope to illustrate, anecdotally, my perception of the current climate of gender and sexuality studies in the United States. My discussion will be limited to my experiences as a graduate assistant and an instructor for the Lesbian, Gay, Bisexual, Transgender Studies Program at Northern Illinois University (NIU) and my most recent experiences as an assistant professor at Murray State University. Occasionally, I will also fold in anecdotes and strategies shared with me by friends and colleagues at other universities.

Parity starts at home (away from home).
Murray State University's residential college system offers its students access to a heightened sense of community among their peers as well as faculty and staff. This system, which differs considerably from traditional dorm life, helps create a home-away-from-home for many students. Faculty members are strongly encouraged to participate in the program by offering alternative learning experiences—I taught a cooking class to students one semester—that show students that faculty members are real people with real interests. As a gay man, I offer (hopefully) a positive image and help expand their minds a bit. Residential colleges offer a number of events every semester that encourage students to learn more about diversity. Residential assistants and directors that foster an open, welcoming environment for students help send the message that understanding more about sexual orientation and gender identity is integral in our world. Because students spend far more time in their residential colleges (or dorms) than the classroom, university faculty and staff must seize opportunities to educate outside the classroom and to help nurture an environment inhospitable to bigotry or ignorance.

Discipline Matters

At the end of the semester I described above, I completed my doctoral work, earning a PhD in English with a concentration in Gay and Lesbian literature as well as LGBT studies. Fortunately, I secured a tenure-track position at Murray State University in western Kentucky. I spoke proudly as I received the Eychaner Award, NIU's highest LGBT honor, telling the audience at the ceremony that I believed the world had changed tremendously when an openly gay man whose research and publications focus primarily on queer men can be hired by a university in rural Kentucky. While several of my mentors and esteemed professors at NIU had expressed concern that I might not easily secure a position after completing my degree, I felt intense gratitude that I had escaped the grueling job search that so many in my field endure. I also felt validated in the knowledge that I had been invited by NIU to speak at its weeklong Multicultural Curriculum Transformation Institute aimed at infusing the classroom with greater awareness of diversity. The institute, offered annually for a select group of faculty, encourages the revision of course syllabi across disciplines to develop greater awareness of issues of race, ability, gender, and sexual orientation. Proud to have graduated from an institution that I viewed as seriously committed to equality for all people, I eagerly prepared my presentation about strategies for addressing sexual orientation and gender identity in the classroom.

> **Subtlety is the order of the day.**
> Form a habit of speaking in respectful language that avoids sexism and heterosexism. Use *partner* or *significant other* rather than making assumptions. Require your students to do the same in their writing and when they speak. It's simple, but it makes a large impact.

My enthusiasm dimmed considerably, however, after I completed my presentation. During the talk, the professor's smiling faces and their rapt note-taking charmed me. Clearly, in my mind, these individuals sought to effect change in their own minds and the minds of their students. Once the question-and-answer portion of my presentation began, however, the tenor of the questions and their underlying tone of fear and concern shocked me. I wish to be clear here: I considered, and still do, the faculty assembled before me to be caring, concerned, and almost (with a few notable exceptions) unanimously unaware of either the necessity of addressing LGBT issues in the classroom, regardless of discipline, or the LGBT-related educational opportunities (in the classroom and beyond) available to all NIU students. Many were unaware of the existence of the LGBT Studies Program (despite our widespread publicity) and fearful of encouraging students to participate in any program that might appear on their official transcripts and then be interpreted as questionable or threatening to potential employers.

One participant, a career center counselor, described to the group (of about 30 people) her encounters with a few students who had completed the undergraduate certificate. As the official university representative responsible for helping students hone their résumés and compile job applications, her role is pivotal in students' job searches. Her advice, she shamefacedly admitted, was for students to omit that particular qualification on all application materials. "I know it sends a poor message," she observed, "but my goal is to help students find jobs." Her message resounds: securing employment demands a retreat into the closet. What message do we send students by opening a new world before them, one where gender and sexuality figure importantly not as handicaps but as valuable segments of identity, and then push them back into the "real" world with a diploma and the directive to keep quiet? Such a response enforces the ghettoizing of gender and sexuality studies as solely the province of LGBT people, and conveys the message that such studies are shameful and unrelated to the so-called real world.

> ***Your office door tells a lot about you.***
> Does your campus have a "safe zone" or ally program? If so, find out how to get involved: not only can these programs offer participants educational opportunities, they typically provide stickers or emblems for your office door that signal to students that they're welcome there regardless of their gender identity or sexual orientation. If your campus doesn't have a program, simply google "safe zone," locate an image of the symbol and print out your own. Start a trend.

Another attendee, a faculty member from the School of Business, echoed this sentiment. She noted that because homogeneity continues to characterize business studies—whiteness, maleness, straightness hold primacy—she could not, in good conscience, encourage students to participate in LGBT studies or even women's studies. To do so, she reasoned, alienates students from the professors in their major and severely restricts their employment opportunities after graduation. This professor evinced palpable sadness at relating such hard realities; clearly advising students accordingly offended her own sense of fairness. She did not wish to convey or imply personal disapproval or homophobia to her students: in fact, she feared inflicting psychological harm. However, true to her discipline, she recognizes the realities of business and directs her students accordingly. Ultimately, apparently, we must be employable professionals before we are healthy, productive human beings.

I offer both of these short episodes not as criticism, but as examples of the difficult place both students and professors find themselves when it comes to gender and sexuality studies. While I believe that each faculty member in that room would acknowledge the moral reprehensibility of implying any disapproval of LGBT people or gender and sexuality studies, convention continues to constrain their fields and disciplines. Departmental and university hierarchies communicate these values clearly. While those individuals at the workshop coming from the arts and humanities generally saw no issue with encouraging students to learn more about gender and sexuality, the faculty from the sciences, business, and education all conveyed varying degrees of reticence about encouraging students to pursue certificates in LGBT studies.

Incorporate LGBT content into any syllabi, regardless of discipline. For students who have had little or no exposure to LGBT individuals or issues, the biggest mistake an educator can make is to heighten awareness through singling out the topic. No matter what the discipline, any educator can introduce LGBT seamlessly and without fanfare so that students encountering these topics begin to see them as mainstream as anything else that might be covered in the course. For instance, educators teaching in mathematics might incorporate a same-sex couple into the language of a word problem or they might nonchalantly mention a famous mathematician's same-sex sexuality. Educators in business colleges might employ a similar strategy: one can easily imagine discussing current tax codes and their impacts on same-sex couples. The possibilities are limitless and there isn't a discipline that can't acknowledge this topic.

Intuitively, of course, the segregation of disciplines possesses a certain logic. Those fields characterized as somehow feminine (an absurdity in itself)—English, counseling, visual, and performing arts—tend to be staffed more heavily by women. Such departments, as well, tend to encourage liberal thought and generally display greater flexibility in terms of areas of study. During my time as a doctoral candidate in NIU's Department of English, I was surrounded by individuals looking at vampire literature, soft-core pornography novels, and the evil eye in Italian American literature, so no one looked askance when I decided that gay men's novels of wartime would be the subject of my dissertation. I am fortunate that my interests and the liberal nature of my discipline affords me the opportunity to research what I deem important. On the other hand, those disciplines deemed traditionally or stereotypically masculine still actively practice intolerance, refusing to acknowledge the potential benefit of gender and sexuality studies in all fields of academic inquiry. One out gay male faculty member in another university's school of business reacted with utter disbelief when I told him that I was publishing about gay men. He indicated that in his field such a choice would likely prevent gaining tenure: he did not begin to research and publish about gay men until his career was well established. To put it bluntly, in many fields we must still "play the game" until tenure bars the likelihood of dismissal. Then, and only then, can we rebel. Passing, it seems, still lives and breathes in many corridors of the academy.

Money Matters

This passive bullying of students by an institution of higher education disconcertingly reduces to little more than the issue of financial power. Those disciplines least willing to engage in teaching or encourage the study of LGBT topics also tend to garner the largest budgets. Students of business and the hard sciences tend to draw in staggering amounts of tuition and external grants. A direct correlation exists between revenue potential and homophobia: professors steer students away from gender studies because pursuing such inquiry might upset the balance of the department or negatively impact post-graduation employment statistics. Those programs more willing to engage LGBT-related topics in the classroom and departmental research, perennially struggle with ever-diminishing budgets and resources. For instance, NIU's School of Liberal Arts and Sciences serves the majority of students in the university, however, its budget pales in comparison with the other colleges.

Take a holistic approach. Reward volunteerism, build it into your course, or both. This idea builds on the extra credit option by asking students to engage a group they're not familiar with. For example, I tell students each semester that I will award extra credit points if they provide evidence of participating in a volunteer capacity and then writing a short paper about the experience. On the campus at MSU, I regularly line up volunteer positions for students in our Women's Center or our Multicultural Center. In recent years, some of my students even organized a book drive for LGBT-themed materials for our library. Some of the students had never considered getting involved in a project of that nature, but I think that experience really made an impact.

This situation gathers irony exponentially when one considers that NIU actively recruits LGBT Students. Since 2006, NIU has proudly touted its status as one of the top one hundred universities in the United States for LGBT students. After receiving high marks in Shane L. Windmeyer's *The Advocate College Guide for LGBT Students* (scoring 16 out of 20 on issues of LGBT-friendliness), NIU has actively cited this achievement as a selling point for students. From my experience as a gay student, I can honestly say in its defense that NIU strives to create a safe, friendly environment for LGBT students, although I would credit this achievement to the dedication of a relatively small group of concerned faculty and staff members rather than to institutional imperatives. Ranking both social and academic opportunities, the College Guide for LGBT Students recounts the struggle by NIU's LGBT students to be afforded equal rights as a matter of record: one gets the sense that there are no longer hurdles to overcome in order to make being LGBT, studying LGBT issues, or both safe. A brief perusal of the websites for either the LGBT Resource Center or the LGBT studies program uncovers the Advocate ranking prominently displayed alongside the icon of the guide's cover. From this, one might infer a simple motivation: students who believe NIU will be hospitable and welcoming to all varieties of diversity are more likely to matriculate. In short, NIU serves to gain tuition dollars from marketing itself as a place where LGBT people can learn and grow.

Learn about financial aid on your campus. During my time at NIU and MSU I have known a number of students who have been disowned by their parents for being LGBT. Not only does this situation take a serious emotional toll, it also seriously impairs a student's ability to finish her or his education. Students in this situation can work with their financial aid officers to become emancipated, or declared independent. The process can be tedious and time consuming, but I have been consistently impressed at how helpful our financial aid staff has been in these situations. Their help really makes the difference between students earning a degree and dropping out.

In fact, NIU boasts the distinction of being one of just a handful of universities across the nation that offers certificates of undergraduate and graduate study in LGBT studies. However, the financial realities of these programs remain quite grim and the mere existence of the program can be credited to a small cadre of remarkable faculty members who have operated the program over the last decade without extra compensation for their efforts and with little or no funding. Although the university uses these programs to draw in students (and their dollars), it refuses to commit any permanent support to the program. This is all the more troubling given the fact that the certificates of undergraduate and graduate study benefit nearly one hundred students on campus in five colleges in pursuit of various degrees and certifications.

Student interest in the LGBT Certificates has steadily grown over the last few years. In fact, in my role as the first graduate assistant for the LGBT Studies Program, I witnessed the number of the students enrolled in the program double. This was due, in large part, to my efforts and the efforts of the co-coordinators for the program in conjunction with like-minded faculty members who advertised the program in their courses. Interdisciplinary in nature, the undergraduate and graduate certificates can be earned by taking classes in counseling, health and human sciences, visual and performing arts, law, history, English, and women's studies, to name a few. In other words, students across the university benefit from the program and yet finding funding for the program has proven nearly impossible.

During my first year working for the program my graduate assistant stipend was covered in part by the College of Health and Human Sciences and the other portions were provided by Liberal Arts and Sciences (LA&S) and the Department of English. This funding, however, was short term. The program co-coordinators constantly sought new sources of funding, realizing all the while that despite the revenue the program was earning that no college or dean was willing to create a dedicated budget for the program. Because it is technically housed in the College of Liberal Arts and Sciences, other colleges were reticent to dedicate funds to the cause. Conversely, because students from many other colleges were benefiting from the program, the administrators in LA&S felt there ought to be funding contributions from those colleges. Because of bureaucratic red-tape and buck-passing, all sources of funding essentially refused to make any permanent commitments to the program. Whether this administrative inertia was the result of institution-alized homophobia, disinterest, or simple neglect, I cannot say. I suspect, however, that adequately funding the LGBT Studies Program was not seen as a priority, particularly when we managed to be successful with so little. This devaluation of the merits of the program, in my estimation, reveals latent or passive homophobia. The program served as a necessary evil: we brought in tuition dollars so we would be allowed to continue our work, but without much additional help.

While our course offerings remained stable, my second year as the program's graduate assistant was marked by diminished fiscal support. The fight to gain the cost-of-living increase for my stipend was lengthy and contentious. While this concern may seem minor, such raises are afforded campuswide and the possibility of future recruitment for my position was certainly impacted by others' awareness of these difficulties. More importantly, however, our five hundred dollar operating funds were not renewed, and we were forced to operate without any funds, begging and borrowing office supplies and ceasing to print brochures about the program. This development in itself was quite detrimental because our brochures serve as the primary form of publicity for the program and are integral in the recruitment of students.

As a result, I spearheaded a silent auction initiative that required me to work many extra hours (unpaid) in order to maintain the day-to-day operations of the program while hosting a monthlong online auction of autographed editions of books donated by NIU faculty to raise funds for the program. This initiative was ultimately successful, raising $477 for the program, which allowed us to purchase printer ink and paper and to print program brochures. Shortly thereafter the College of Liberal Arts and Sciences conceded and gave us another $500 for the last academic year. Once again, these funds were not permanent, and we dedicated our energy to planning how to stretch the funds for the purchase of supplies for the current and the coming academic years. An unfortunate side-effect of these circumstances was that I dedicated much less time to program development, because our primary concern remained keeping the proverbial wolf from the door.

It also bears mentioning that during these two years, along with the help of the program's co-coordinators, I secured three academic speakers for the benefit of LGBT studies students as well as the rest of the campus community. During my first year, we invited Dylan Scholinski, a transgender artist and author, and Richard Meyer, an art historian, to speak. Scholinski's presentation drew a record-breaking 324 students. Our venue was so full that it was impossible to fit everyone in. Meyer's presentation also drew an impressive 189 people. Typically, similar events are considered successful if more than 30 members of the campus community participate. Students, faculty, staff, and community members clearly communicated their feelings: we want to learn about these issues, they matter. During my second year, the venerable Toni A. H. McNaron, author of *Poisoned Ivy: Lesbian and Gay Academics Confronting Homophobia* (1997), addressed the campus community. Her event was also well-attended. After her primary campus presentation, we asked that she conduct a seminar about the subject of *Poisoned Ivy* and sent invitations to all high-level administrators at NIU. After all, we continue to confront homophobia, and who better to benefit from McNaron's wisdom than those individuals responsible for policy making at our institution? Our administrators responded definitively: all but two failed to appear. Those two administrators spent the presentation looking peeved, checking their watches, and departing early. One of McNaron's major talking points was the silent but pointed perpetration of homophobia via a refusal of funding. For the students in the room, particularly those at the graduate level, our administrators' early departure communicated clearly their lack of interest or true commitment to LGBT issues and rights. The lesson we learned: silence and disinterest can be just as harmful and damning as other strains of homophobic behavior.

The current status of the LGBT Studies Program at NIU is even more grim. After conducting extensive interviews and hiring my replacement, the position was reduced to half-time. The program was theoretically moved under the auspices of a new dean who appointed a new program coordinator after the previous coordinator (and founder) stepped up to take an interim director's position with women's studies. Since then, the graduate assistant works only ten hours per week, and the recruitment efforts for the program have dwindled. Student interest, however, remains strong. Unfortunately, because of the downturn in the economy, administrators exhibit even greater reticence about committing any funding to the program, although they continue to offer lip service to the wonderful contributions the program makes to the campus community. The LGBT Studies Program, it seems, proves quite helpful when the powers-that-be find it necessary to trot it out as an illustration of the university's commitment to diversity. However, it appears that they would prefer that program development continues to transpire through the volunteerism of faculty members and graduate students rather than allocating funds fairly for a growing program that students both value and benefit from.

Saving the Best for Last

While the majority of this essay might leave you feeling a sense of hopelessness or despair about the amount of work those of us dedicated to raising awareness and appreciation for all varieties of sexual orientation and gender identity still face, I hope that you will take more away from this vignette than just that.

> *Have a sense of humor.* Too much seriousness can create a stifling environment. These are serious, life-and-death consequences topics and it's important to recognize that. However, we don't want students to feel suffocated by the gravity of the situation. A smile or a cackle can have great impact and still impart seriousness.

To be certain, the challenges we face are manifold and quite possibly more insidious (because they are transacted so stealthily) than those we faced even ten years ago. The reasons behind and the justifications motivating the current brand of institutional homophobia may be easily dismissed as the result of budgetary constraints or a desire to do what is best for the students. The reality, tinged with some sadness, of this situation is that homophobia is alive and well and currently taking place by turning a blind eye, by negligently refusing to commit to permanent institutional change. Furthermore, as evidenced by my experience with the faculty at the Multicultural Curriculum Transformation Institute, the academy (NIU in this case), does not work to make faculty members aware of the services and educational opportunities available to students in regard to LGBT history, culture, and political awareness. As a result, students continue to be silenced by well-meaning individuals who want their students to find employment on leaving the university. However well-intentioned, it disconcerts me to believe that one of the last messages students receive before leaving the university is that it might have been acceptable to be LGBT on campus, even to learn about LGBT issues, but that on departing they need to pull the closet door shut after themselves. Without question, the world remains imperfect and the dangers informing those choices are quite real; professors and career counselors wish to shield these young people. However, in order for any real change to occur we must begin to explore ways that students can report their academic careers accurately, that they can learn to accept the possibility of danger in pursuit of creating further change. Without this change, aren't we all trapped in some configuration of the closet?

Use extra credit as a learning tool. Encourage students to attend gender- and sexuality-related events on campus and then write a response paper making connections between course content and the event. Every university campus I've ever visited offers events—often through the Women's Center or the LGBT Resource Center—aimed at dispelling myths and spreading awareness of issues related to gender and sexuality. Many other organizations offer related events, too, so take advantage and encourage your students to further expand their awareness. Even the most resistant students typically crave extra credit!

The upside of all this is that the world does seem to be changing, if ever so slowly. I now live in a small, conservative town in Kentucky. I teach students daily and talk to them about all manner of issues related to race, gender, class, and sexuality. I am unbelievably fortunate, I know—countless others have not been nearly as lucky. Change occurs incrementally, and I credit my current position to what I learned at NIU, both in the classroom and beyond. I am lucky in that I never tried to hide who I am, and I have rarely been severely punished for that choice. My fondest desire is to afford that opportunity to all students who enter my classroom.

Jason ultimately decided to officially register for the Certificate of Undergraduate Study in lesbian, gay, bisexual, transgender studies; his friend, for fear of her parents, did not. I felt immense pride (commingled with a little fear) for him when he related the news. I could not help but notice the smile on his face, his pride at standing up for his beliefs. However, I understood how that career counselor must feel: Did I do the right thing? Have I condemned this person to potential violence and/or discrimination because I encouraged him to live honestly? For me, enduring that fear is worth it because the damage of living in a world where you hide all the time is far worse. I cannot condemn those individuals who advise otherwise, but I do implore those administrators in the academy and beyond, who have more power than I do, to consider the potential benefits this change could catalyze.

Apart from the ceaseless frustrations of limited or nonexistent budgets, administrative negligence, and the hypocrisy of an institution that profits from students they do not fully support, there is reason to hope. For me, the hours that I spent in the classroom each week with a room full of undergraduate students present to learn about LGBT studies were some of the most fulfilling I have ever spent. If you surveyed the classroom, they looked typical: black, white, Latino/a, Chinese, male, female, wealthy, poor, straight, lesbian, gay, bisexual, and transgender. They represented a wide swath of socio-politico-economic class and they were bright, funny, and attractive. They seemed to both acknowledge and disregard difference at once. To our current college generation, it seems, we are similar in our difference. Furthermore, they wanted to learn, and they openly communicated their disbelief at our human obsession with sexual orientation and the expression of gender identity. It was, and is, encouraging to know that college-age students are starting to take for granted that binaries cannot possibly describe us and that in order to see the world in dichotomies, we must apply literal or metaphorical blinders.

From the vantage of the classroom, closeted as it is from the machinations of the administration, the world is changing. Twelve years ago, as an undergraduate, I never imagined a classroom where I would have admitted my own sexuality to my classmates. Imagine my surprise and most sincere pleasure when Jonna, a transgender student, approached me at mid-class break and told me that she knew we would be reading Julia Serrano's *Whipping Girl* the next week and wondered whether I might like to have a question-and-answer period about her experiences. I agreed that if she was comfortable, then I thought it would be a great experience for everyone. I announced it to the class after break, and I noticed the clear concern on their faces. Over the next week, I fielded a number of calls, e-mails, and office visits about Jonna's upcoming talk. Not one of those contacts was negative, though. These students expressed genuine concern for their classmate and worried that they might offend her with their questions. They respected her and did not wish her to be treated like a scientific specimen. I reassured them and encouraged them to ask whatever questions interested them and prepared myself for our next class.

Don't attack students if they make missteps.
We all unintentionally say callous or hurtful things. If we, as educators, treat such missteps as massive gaffes, however, we run the risk of that student closing her or his mind to new ideas about it forever. Maintain your calm; respond in a measured fashion. If possible, let peer pressure correct the situation. Students who perceive the approbation of their classmates are more likely to fall in line. Continually stress the importance of mutual respect; it really works.

While the initial few minutes of Jonna's talk and her question-and-answer session were awkward and polite to the point of absurdity, something magical began to happen. Jonna told the class that with Wal-Mart's new 4 dollar prescription plan she is able to get the medications that she takes to transition, for only 8 dollars a month. The class started to laugh at the irony of Wal-Mart helping people transition, and the tension subsided. Students asked questions, volunteered personal information, discussed delicate topics, and I think, learned a great deal. For the first time in my teaching career, I did not have to direct the conversation. The students were both frank and tactful, without my policing. Afterward, I received numerous e-mails from

Jonna's classmates citing the experience as amazing. That hour completely altered their understanding of what it means to be transgender. When Jonna later withdrew from the course for medical reasons, her classmates expressed sincere concern and routinely inquired about her well-being. For me, that experience proves that bottom-up change is transpiring. Considering our program's treatment by university administration, though, I wonder, are our classrooms' lively, near-magical closets where the business of teaching about sexual orientation and gender identity must still be conducted in a whisper?

> *Recognize your own limitations.* Seek out education, recruit experts, and admit what you don't know. If you feel completely out of your depth in presenting information about gender and sexuality or building it into your course, take advantage of that opportunity and seek out current books and journal articles. Nearly every campus has some kind of resource available to educators looking to expand their horizons. In addition, most campuses have experts (faculty or staff) who would be more than willing to visit your classroom and give a short informative presentation. Sometimes just inviting a guest speaker to talk for three to five minutes about campus or community services to LGBT people can make a tremendous difference in the life of a student who feels alienated for being different. Simple strategies like this signal awareness and an earnest desire to make all people feel welcome. Your campus resource centers, LGBT-related or not, are amazing places with myriad services and I try to make all my students aware of all their options.

Works Cited

McNaron, Toni A. H. *Poisoned Ivy: Gay and Lesbian Academics Confronting Homophobia.* Philadelphia: Temple University Press, 1996.

Windmeyer, Shane L. *The Advocate College Guide for LGBT Students.* Los Angeles: Alyson Books, 2006.

Chapter 3

Queering the Academy

A Case Approach to LGBTQ Studies

Molly Merryman and K. G. Valente

There is much to celebrate and commemorate since American institutions of higher education first began establishing programs committed to lesbian, gay, bisexual, transgender, and queer (LGBTQ) studies in the 1990s.[1] To suggest such is not to deny that the progress toward implementing programs has been slow and, at times, marked by controversy. Among highly publicized disputes is Yale University's rejection of Larry Kramer's endowment to establish a gay studies program in 1997 (Dolan 1998, 42; Jaschik 2009, "Kramer"). More common challenges involve attacks against state colleges and universities when they launch LGBTQ studies programs, with recent developments at the University of Louisiana at Lafayette serving as a sharp reminder (Jaschik "Defending").[2] Even so—and more than twenty years on—the hard work of developing and sustaining programs shows little sign of abating. The continuing emergence of academic programs provides an opportunity to reflect on the academic spaces that have been—and have yet to be—claimed. The project of transforming curricula so as to create spaces for LGBTQ studies is daunting in its scope, yet it is one amenable to a rich array of institutional models. Consequently, the varied and particular histories associated with laying claim to such spaces are worthy of consideration. They can provide roadmaps as much as they can signpost aspects of the academic landscape that we might contemplate as our horizons continue to expand.

Data, such as that compiled by John Younger, suggests there are approximately sixty colleges and universities in the United States and Canada that maintain LGBTQ studies. In a few cases, these are identified as sexuality studies. Most of the programs offer curricula leading to a minor. Undergraduates can, however, pursue majors in ten of these institutions, while a fewer number provide certificates or concentrations. The true extent of opportunities for sustained explorations in LGBTQ studies is likely underrepresented, since institutions can pursue other academic structures in making them available to their students.[3] Still, a generous estimate of one hundred institutions with coordinated curricular commitments would represent less than 3 percent of American colleges and universities. The National Gay and Lesbian Task Force encouraged the creation of LGBTQ studies programs in a 1995 campus organizing manual and a 2003 report on campus climate published by its policy institute (Shepard, Yeskel, & Outcalt ch. 15; Rankin 7, 43–44). Serving as a reminder of the work that remains to be done, Warren Blumenfeld calls for continued development in a 2012 issue of Diversity & Democracy published by the American Association of Colleges and Universities (21).

As evidenced by this collection of essays, annual *Expanding the Circle* conferences organized by the California Institute for Integral Studies since 2010 have provided an important forum for discussions dedicated to improving the campus climate for LGBTQ students, both outside and inside the classroom. While we have a profound respect for past programs, we felt that the time was right to build on formal presentations and informal conversations that focused on the curriculum. Imagining and inspiring particular interventions undoubtedly constitute significant aspects of the work to be done; institutionalizing these within courses of study typically engages additional levels of complexity and ingenuity. Our workshop at the 2012 institute, "Roadmaps for Establishing and Assessing LGBTQ Studies," was designed as an opportunity for sharing experiences and discussing considerations relevant to program development.

An overarching theme of the session stressed the importance of creating LGBTQ studies programs that fit the faculty, students, missions and possibilities at individual institutions. Case studies based on our own experiences establishing programs at a small liberal arts college and a large state university became the preferred means for identifying developmental points of reference that could be profitably examined in the context of this theme. Additionally, Ardel Thomas and Gregory Miraglia accepted invitations to join the session in order to present developments on their community college campuses: City College of San Francisco and Napa Valley College, respectively. These effectively linked the history of establishing the first gay and lesbian studies department in the U.S. at City College in 1990 with a spirit of professional collaboration that attended the creation of a new program at Napa Valley College in 2012. Although the session benefited greatly from contributions made and queries raised by those in attendance, this essay provides the case studies representing Colgate University, Kent State University, and Napa Valley College.[4] In these, those seeking to establish programs will find common and practical concerns that have been negotiated in ways that underscore the resilience with which we continue to transform the academic landscape.

At the same time, the case studies contained herein give rise to reflections that relate to both the past and the future of LGBTQ studies. Looking for material to build on, we were particularly struck by the lack of information available on starting LGBTQ studies programs. While works dedicated to supporting students and establishing resource centers have been published,[5] there is very little literature documenting the emergence of our academic programs. It is interesting to consider the extent to which a discipline so indebted to the reclamation of hidden histories may need encouragement when it comes to documenting its own development within the academy. Looking to the future, we might reasonably ask if the time has come to think seriously about structures that could help us to collectively address professional challenges and expectations. Our programs are emerging and evolving in justifiably distinctive ways, a reality that in part responds to tensions between seeking to inhabit and aspiring to subvert academic structures. Still, the climate of academic assessment will likely require both internal and external program reviews.[6] The development of LGBTQ studies is a legacy we should celebrate, but the organic aspects of its past may well present challenges in the future, particularly when faced with such exercises. Institutional comparisons and curricular practices will need to be considered in ways that ensure sensitivity to local environments. Documenting our efforts can serve to stimulate potentially fruitful explorations regarding the emergence of our programs within the academy as well as future professional aspirations.

Colgate University

Colgate University, a liberal arts institution located in rural upstate New York that enrolls approximately 2,800 undergraduates, incorporated LGBTQ studies within its curriculum in 2009. The minor-granting program is located within University Studies, one of four divisions that provide a foundation for academic administration. This division supports the university's signature Liberal Arts Core Curriculum, a five-course requirement that all students must complete, as well as a rich collection of interdisciplinary programs. Faculty members contributing to LGBTQ studies hold appointments in other disciplinary departments such as economics, English, and political science, a situation that is typical of many of interdisciplinary programs within the university curriculum. Unlike others, however, LGBTQ studies is currently affiliated with women's studies, although it maintains a separate director, budget, and advisory committee. That is, it is recognized as an independent interdisciplinary program situated within another.

To earn a minor in LGBTQ studies students must complete five courses, including one of three gateway offerings. Capstone expectations are, by design, flexible, with the expectation that students will supplement work in their major using analytic skills developed through the minor course of study. Currently, only three courses are specifically identified and offered exclusively through LGBTQ studies. Nevertheless, each of these has been approved to fulfill various academic requirements that all students must satisfy.

Program Origins

The impetus and initial momentum for creating an academic program emerged from the LGBTQ Supporter's Network.[7] Established in 2002, this organization represented a loose affiliation of approximately 250 students, staff, and faculty from across the university who were dedicated to improving the campus climate. Though not sanctioned in any official way, the Supporter's Network enjoyed open lines of communication with various high-level administrators, including the president of the university, the provost and dean of the faculty, and the dean of the college. A position established the same year within the dean of the college staff, which now carries the title of assistant dean and director of LGBTQ Initiatives, represented a conduit for student life concerns raised by the Supporters Network. Indeed, the institutionalization of this position beyond an initial one-year commitment, one made possible by an anonymous and specifically directed donation of 20 thousand dollars, became a focal point for much of the organization's advocacy.

The lengthy process of establishing LGBTQ Studies began in earnest in 2004, with a five-year plan developed by the Supporter's Network. This document highlighted three "needs" that the organization was committed to seeing the university meet. Two of these focused attention primarily on student life through a sustained commitment to the staff position dedicated to LGBTQ Initiatives as well as the provision of resource center. The third articulated the creation of an academic, minor-granting program that could unify and coordinate intellectual discourses. As noted at that time, several faculty members were already engaging pedagogies and scholarship associated with LGBTQ studies in courses then regularly offered within the curriculum. Establishing an interdisciplinary program, in the minds of many within the Supporters Network, would provide a structure for formally recognizing and expanding on extant curricular commitments.

Program Development and Related Concerns

Between 2004 and 2006, a curricular working group of the Supporters Network surveyed the faculty, reviewed enrollment patterns, coordinated reading groups, and organized workshops dedicated to course development.[8] These efforts helped to identify approximately fifteen faculty members in various departments who regularly offered courses that featured within the first draft of a formal proposal and were willing to pursue affiliation with LGBTQ studies. Among these offerings, three new courses were designed and approved to serve as "gateways" for the envisioned minor.[9] Community and curriculum building tasks undertaken in this period signaled the feasibility of mounting and sustaining a minor program, the expediency of which was enhanced by the fact that approving such programs in New York does not require review beyond the university's governance structures.

Other conversations affected the proposal in significant ways. Among these, discussions with the president and key administrators highlighted two questions that, in broad terms, related to support from alumni and women's studies. In the former case, the question turned on the extent to which developing an academic program in LGBTQ studies would benefit from the support of LGBTQ and ally alumni. Respectful of a tradition of dedication and involvement on the part of many Colgate graduates, members of the working group remained committed to initiating positive change from within the institution—change that might eventually encourage greater engagement with LGBTQ alumni—by moving forward with a proposal that primarily reflected ambitions promoted by the Supporters Network.[10]

The intersection of academic ambitions with curricular realities underpinned the question related to women's studies: specifically, should LGBTQ studies become a minor option available within women's studies? This question has been—and will undoubtedly continue to be—engaged elsewhere, as is evidenced by the emergence of both gender and sexuality studies. The response that emerged at Colgate from discussions with the Women's Studies Advisory Committee directed the working group to propose LGBTQ studies as an independent program. Though complicated and unspoken concerns may also bear on this decision, two interrelated positions maintained by the advisory committee are most salient. The first held that LGBTQ studies represents a distinctive field of inquiry, though one that owes much to women's studies. The second acknowledged the unprecedented consideration of situating one interdisciplinary program within another at Colgate. The significance of this point underscores, as much as it is underscored by, the university's long-standing commitment to interdisciplinary studies.

Though not directly undertaken by the Supporters Network, a Sexual Climate Survey administered in 2005 is worthy of consideration in the context of establishing LGBTQ studies. An enterprising student envisioned the survey—the first such for Colgate—as an independent study project while serving as a summer intern for the university's president. Eventually, the climate survey project became an independent study course enrolling seven students. On top of their individual teaching loads, five faculty advisers worked alongside the students and brought expertise from sociology, psychology, religion, and mathematics. The adoption of "snowball" methodologies in administering the survey instrument developed as part of the course helped to ensure that LGBTQ-identified students were represented in the nonrandomized sample; their responses made up approximately 5 percent of the 1,062 recorded. Analysis of the data provided a snapshot of student attitudes regarding sexuality in several different categories, including self-identification, social life, safety and comfort, and attitudes. Two results in particular highlighted relevant considerations for establishing LGBTQ studies when viewed in relation to the campus climate. Student responses tended to accept that sexuality has a place in the classroom. However, LGBTQ students significantly differed from their heterosexual peers insofar as they felt that their sexuality was neither represented nor respected in the classroom (Jellison & Valente).[11]

Program Approval and Curricular Integration

Institutional review of the proposal submitted in 2006 lasted two years and engendered two revisions. The first of these called for the most substantive editing inasmuch as the reviewing body recommended that the proposal maintain a strictly academic focus. This meant that portions of the original proposal referencing advocacy, agency, or empowerment were removed. Instead of speaking to improving the campus climate or enhancing examinations of diversity, the final version of the proposal discussed LGBTQ studies exclusively in terms of its analytic frameworks and scholarly contributions. Without specific knowledge of the deliberations it is impossible to know the reviewing body's reasons for requesting such changes. It should be noted, however, that the university approved a permanent, full-time position dedicated to LGBTQ Initiatives at about the same time as the LGBTQ studies proposal underwent the revision described above. Perhaps the reviewing body believed that campus climate concerns related to LGBTQ students would be best addressed through the institutionalization of the student life position that the Supporters Network explicitly championed in 2004. At the same time, members of the curricular working group believed that changes to the proposal per se would not significantly affect the academic program's anticipated articulation with broader issues through LGBTQ Initiatives.

Administrative approval of LGBTQ studies in 2008 ushered in a new round of activities. Members of the curricular working group adopted roles on the first Advisory Committee and took on a different set of administrative tasks. Perhaps the most important of these involved formalizing guidelines and procedures for vetting courses that would be offered as part of LGBTQ studies by affiliated faculty. The guidelines that eventually emerged reflected both the curricular standards maintained by other interdisciplinary programs as well as a pragmatic recognition that curricular transformations require time. Specifically, any faculty member offering a course that dedicates a significant portion of its syllabus to student engagements with sexuality as an analytic lens can seek affiliation with LGBTQ studies. At the same time, faculty offering courses with less than significant levels of engagement can contribute to the program provided the course syllabus clearly articulates this possibility and informs students about tailoring appropriate material and coursework as necessary. The program curriculum currently identifies two lists of elective offerings based on the distinction outlined.

Preparing for the program also involved revisiting its relationship to Women's studies. While the proposal reflected the outcomes of earlier conversations by describing an independent program, administrative approval of LGBTQ studies came with the proviso that it would be affiliated with women's studies for an initial period of time. Even so, the administration agreed that LGBTQ studies would have its own director and budget.[12] The rationale for this unexpected—and unprecedented—curricular arrangement ostensibly related to concerns over the potentially controversial reception of LGBTQ studies. In particular, the administration suggested that women's studies, having flourished at an institution that until 1970 admitted only men, could provide a degree of insularity. However well intentioned it was, this aspect of approving LGBTQ studies required renewed conversations with women's studies. A spirit of cooperation infused discussions between the programs. Nevertheless, reservations were addressed in a memorandum of agreement that mandated no diminution of women's studies resources—whether administrative, budgetary, or spatial—as well as a review of the affiliated arrangement that is scheduled to take place in 2013.

Beyond its relationship to women's studies, defining the program was a significant consideration throughout the early history of LGBTQ studies at Colgate. Contestations regarding the possibilities and limitations associated with LGBT and Queer studies programs—both intellectually and structurally—continue to attend their emergence within the academy, with scholars such as Jen Bacon, Trea Stewart, and Susan Talburt providing important reflections on various aspects of this discourse. For better or worse, faculty at Colgate typically mitigated confrontations and pursued appropriate compromises by situating intellectual disagreements in the context a larger goal: establishing the program. The choice of *LGBTQ* over *sexuality* as the program identifier reflects, in large part, the legacy of the now dissipated Supporters Network. The inclusion of *queer* makes a space for many colleagues who justifiably see the interrogation of categories as a critical extension of establishing (nonnormative) sexuality as an analytic category. Mindful of Talburt's reservations regarding "institutional liminality" (98–99), concerns over sustaining an LGBTQ studies curriculum through the incorporation of disciplinary courses are mitigated by the strong and long-standing commitment to interdisciplinarity at Colgate. The program owes much of its robustness to this institutional commitment, while it maintains a curricular nimbleness well suited to the university.

Kent State University

Kent State University's LGBT(Q) studies program[13] started in 2001—and was the first in the state of Ohio. Kent State is a Carnegie II, doctoral granting, eight-campus university system with 22,000 undergraduate students and 5,500 graduate students located in northeast Ohio.

The LGBT(Q) studies program is an undergraduate minor, with an introductory course that fulfills the university's domestic diversity requirement (and thus fills multiple sections online and at several different campuses). While the program is administratively located within the College of Arts and Sciences, its thirty-three affiliated faculty represent sixteen departments and programs within three (out of 11) colleges and schools. Over the past decade the expansion of faculty and student interest in LGBT(Q) studies has necessitated the need to completely update its curriculum, which has in the past been only modified slightly. This academic year (2012–2013) a complete overhaul of curriculum and structure is being conducted.

The development and approval process for the program was straightforward and fast—the process from proposal to approval took only a year. But there existed a rich legacy of student organization, faculty involvement and university activism that set the stage for an easy adaptation. Therefore it is important that the curricular developments of 2000–2001 be put into the context of prior events.

Program Origins

The roots of the program go back thirty years, to the fall of 1971, when professor Dolores Noll[14] signed up to teach a gay liberation class in the Experimental College, an addition to the university's Honors College formed as one response to the May 4, 1970 shootings of university students by the National Guard following students protesting the expansion of the war in Vietnam to Cambodia. That same semester, she became adviser of the Kent Gay Liberation Front, which was one of the first LGBTQ student organizations in history, and which has continuously been one of the most influential and well-attended organizations at Kent. The following year she taught a course called Gay Womanhood; then, in 1974 started teaching a university course called Sexual Minorities, which she taught until she retired in 1981.

No LGBTQ courses were taught until 1994, when The Sociology of Gays and Lesbians was offered. The KSU College Republicans campaigned within the university and statewide to have the course banned. The situation attracted national attention and was cited in books and articles about the 1990s university-based culture wars in which Kent State University was recognized for maintaining academic freedom in the face of internal and external pressures. This course is still offered regularly and is one of the classes students can take to fulfill the LGBT(Q) studies minor.

The next significant movement occurred in the late 1990s, when faculty and staff began an organized fight to obtain domestic partner benefits. In their meetings, they discussed other aspects of LGBTQ university life, and realized that several had an interest in starting an academic program.[15]

Program Development

The thoughts for establishing a program turned into a real effort in 2000, when the dean of Arts and Sciences appointed a faculty member to a special administrative appointment to assess interdisciplinary programs within the college. This opened up an opportunity for those faculty activists interesting in LGBTQ studies to formally propose the establishment of an interdisciplinary minor modeled on the same structure as women's studies. They established the program name,[16] developed an introductory and individual investigation course, and contacted other departments about including their classes into the program. The dean immediately supported the effort and recommended that interested faculty team-teach an introduction to LGBT studies course in order to demonstrate interest. The class filled to its capacity enrollment of thirty, and this information was presented along with the proposal to the university and the state Board of Regents for approval. This process was administered by the office of the dean of Arts and Sciences, in a further demonstration of the institutional support received by the LGBT studies program. The process started in 2000, and by fall of 2001, the LGBT studies program was approved.

Other LGBTQ Developments

Program faculty have worked closely with undergraduate students, notably the students of Pride! Kent, and in the 2000s, LGBTQ and ally students achieved a number of successes, including a range of positive actions, events and activities, and significant visibility. Among the highlights: the KSU chapter of Delta Lambda Phi, the national gay male fraternity was officially recognized by the university in 2000, and in 2003 journalism and mass communication students started Fusion, an LGBTQ magazine that has received national and regional accolades.

Expansion of student support within LGBT(Q) studies also occurred in this decade. In 2003, the program received an endowed gift to establish the Curry-Myers Scholarship for students enrolled in the minor. In 2010, two more scholarships were established, the Akron PFLAG endowed scholarship for LGBTQ students enrolled in the minor, and the donation-based LGBTQ Student Emergency Fund to support students who have been cut off from parental support because of their sexual orientation/gender identity. In conjunction with these gifts, the LGBT(Q) studies program has been working closely with university staff and administrators regarding alumni relations and sponsored gifts—and not just to support the LGBT(Q) studies program. The most significant example of this is a willed endowment valued currently at 2 million dollars along with a 25 thousand dollar cash donation that was made to support LGBTQ students at Kent State University and given because the Akron, Ohio donor recognized that ours was the only university in the area with academic and other LGBTQ student-based programs.

During this time, we also developed a northeast Ohio LGBT Collection in our library archives. As we've been receiving community support for the program, some of that support was in the form of donations of LGBTQ books, magazines, and newsletters. In determining which of these items had archival value, we decided it would be helpful to the program and the regional LGBTQ population that we establish a special collection so that important materials can be preserved and studied.

The academic program was also leveraged to open an LGBTQ Student Center—something students have been requesting since the 1970s. The minor program coordinators agreed to open and provide volunteer staff support when office space was found in the Student Center. The LGBTQ Student Center opened with a reception attended by hundreds, including the university's president and new vice president for Diversity, Equity, and Inclusion, and local and state politicians. (A highlight of this event was when the university presented its first Diversity Trailblazer Award to KSU LGBTQ pioneer Dolores Noll.)

Program Expansion and Change

When the program started in 2001, it was structured in a flexible fashion to accommodate the limited number of LGBTQ-expert faculty and existing courses with relevant content. Because so few courses had a majority of content related to sexual orientation/gender identity, a "Block B" of courses having content of theoretical or methodological interest was incorporated to fill out the minor. But in the decade since the program started, more courses have been developed at the university with relevant content; further, more LGBTQ-identified faculty have come to KSU, particularly since the inclusion of domestic partner benefits. This, combined with the solid number of minors, the increased enrollments in the introductory course (both because it fulfills the university's domestic diversity requirement and because it is a recommended course in a number of majors), and the expanding visibility of and interest in the program, has made it possible to begin work to significantly change its structure and curriculum.

While a working committee has been established and efforts have begun to change the curriculum, at the time this chapter is going to press these changes have not made it through the cycle of approval, so a definitive assessment cannot at this point be made. One of the proposed classes (LGBTQ Methodologies) has been offered and has resulted in students within the minor engaging in qualitative research, both in the course and through subsequent independent study work. But the intentions of this plan can be described. As has already been mentioned, one change is in name—to add Queer to the program title, thus having it formally become LGBTQ/Lesbian, Gay, Bisexual, Transgendered, and Queer Studies. The second significant change is to increase the numbers of courses directly offered by the program from two to six, thus bringing the control and revenue of the program to us. It has been a challenge for students to complete the minor in its current format because often departments do not offer LGBTQ-topic courses in an annual rotation. We also want to make the entire program available online (both to accommodate our regional campus students and to open up courses to students from other institutions), and we cannot control the online offerings of courses we don't "own." The new minor structure will still include those departmental courses with significant LGBTQ content, but because students will just be choosing one or two from this list (depending on whether they choose individual investigation work), they will have more opportunities in a given year to schedule those classes. The new courses being proposed for addition are Transgendered Studies, Queer Theory, LGBTQ Methodologies, and Internship in LGBTQ Studies. These courses will be developed as undergraduate/graduate classes, and after we revise the undergraduate curriculum and implement these changes, we plan on developing a graduate certificate in LGBTQ studies.

A significant development that brings together the proposed LGBTQ Methodologies course, the archival collection, graduate student outreach and increased grant-work is the "Ohio LGBTQ Neighborhoods Project." Funded with start-up money from the College of Arts and Sciences' Collaborative Research Program, this project will seek external funding in order to engage undergraduate scholars in collecting oral histories from LGBTQ neighborhood residents in the seven largest cities in Ohio. The college money supports a pilot study in Akron, Ohio during Spring semester 2013, and supported the hiring of the LGBT(Q) studies program's first graduate assistant. The four LGBT(Q) studies affiliates working on this project will engage undergraduate student researchers to help collect data and videotaped interviews within the structure of the new LGBTQ Methodologies course. Ultimately the project will result in the most comprehensive analysis of LGBTQ neighborhoods to date, with the end goal being the expansion of the LGBT archive collection, sustained community outreach, print publications, and a broadcast documentary.

These changes and developments will hopefully lead to funded positions within the LGBT(Q) studies program. While volunteer faculty have allowed the program to exist, that model has stalled the implementation of needed curricular change and course expansion; therefore by "owning" the program classes, LGBT(Q) faculty can have financial resources to compensate faculty, expand faculty pools and hire graduate assistants and undergraduate student staff.

The Kent State University LGBT(Q) studies program arose from forty years of queer activism, brave pioneers and vibrant students. It started simply because faculty and students united in quests for social justice and equality had a vision for an academic presence and structure to understand queer lives. Its initial structure was based on what could make it possible (while academically solid) within this institution, but as it and its faculty have expanded and growth, it has exceeded its planners' vision and is now being solidified and improved.

Napa Valley College

The faculty and Board of Trustees of California's Napa Valley College approved LGBT studies in 2012. Those involved with developing the certificate-granting program at the two-year college effectively responded to state legislation enacted to enhance inclusivity in education. They also established notable collaborative arrangements with, among others, the City College of San Francisco. In this, one of the oldest programs in the United States, whose history is thoroughly recounted by Jack Collins in "Matters of Fact: Establishing a Gay and Lesbian Studies Department," directly contributed in significant ways to the realization of one of its newest progeny.

Program Origins

The LGBT Studies program emerged at Napa Valley College within a relatively short period of time. Conversations with particular faculty members dating to 2010 explored two institutional possibilities. The first focused on the development of a Safe Space Program for the campus, while the second considered the creation of an LGBT Studies Certificate Program. The college recognized that both initiatives have been proven to be positive efforts to improve the overall support for LGBT students.

Highly publicized suicides among LGBTQ youth in the United States prompted a concentrated period of campuswide introspection and intervention in 2011. In particular, the college's Academic Senate expressed concerns and raised questions about the extent to which the institution served its LGBTQ students. A climate survey administered in 2010 might have provided useful information; however, respondents were not asked to identify their sexual orientation. Further, the college received a low score (one out of five stars) based on information it provided for the Campus Pride Climate Index.[17] At the same time, the college's involvement, on both local and regional levels, with Stop the Hate! programming prompted its Inclusivity Committee to ask what more could be done to improve its level of support for LGBTQ students. For their part, students recommended the development of the college's Safe Space Program. On another front the library acquired a collection of books to support various aspects of LGBTQ programming. Responding to a faculty inquiry, a local PFLAG chapter contributed 1 thousand dollars for new purchases and donated additional material to the collection from its own library.

The academic program at Napa Valley College took shape in the context of renewed concerns related to its LGBTQ students. Enactment of California Senate Bill 48, known as the Fair and Inclusive Education Act, provided additional stimulus. The act, which came into effect in 2012, requires "instruction in social sciences to include a study of the role and contributions of lesbian, gay, bisexual, and transgender Americans, persons with disabilities, and members of other cultural groups, to the development of California and the United States" ("SB 48"). In this context, Gregory Miraglia, dean of Career Technical Education, raised the possibility of establishing an LGBT studies certificate program to support, in part, the training needs of local K–12 teachers. The plan moved forward with the enthusiastic support of the Family Studies Program and the vice president of Instruction.

Program Development

The curriculum approved in 2012 incorporates an introductory course in LGBT studies, electives already on offer at the college, and contributions established through collaborative partnerships. The introductory course was specifically developed for the program and designated to meet the college's general education requirement for social sciences and multicultural/gender studies. Alongside these efforts Miraglia, as the first program coordinator, worked closely with Ardel Thomas, chair of the LGBT studies department at the City College of San Francisco. A formal agreement between the two colleges allows students at Napa Valley to complete elective courses offered at City College as part of program. Additionally, transfer agreements with City College, San Diego State University, and Sonoma State University allow students to earn either associates or bachelors' degrees based on work undertaken at Napa Valley College.

Conclusion

The queering of academic programs over the past twenty-five years has been an organic and largely individualistic enterprise. Transformations are the result of efforts undertaken by dedicated individual faculty and students at a variety of colleges and universities, rather than the products of administrative dictates or outcomes of trends from national and international scholarly/ professional organizations. Most programs were started without structural funding, utilizing courses and faculty from extant departments. Because of this, each institution's curriculum varies—reflecting the faculty, courses and centers of support that exist in those particular places.

The paucity of research and published materials on establishing LGBTQ studies programs resulted in our decision to utilize in case study format the experiences from three different educational institutions (a private liberal arts college, large research university, and a community college) that started academic programs at different times. Despite the differences in institutions and time, we see similar trends: programs started by faculty rather than administrators, the seizing of opportunities as they arise, involvement by students/ consideration of student needs, and voluntary/unfunded efforts.

As our collective stories and the recent events at the University of Louisiana at Lafayette demonstrate, the development of LGBTQ studies programs is political and contentious, something that is not surprising given that most states and our federal government provide LGBTQ people no protection from discrimination. Therefore, we maintain that at this point in history there is no right way to establish LGBTQ studies—instead we believe that each educational institution must respond to its own climate, faculty, students and support structures, and that those working toward implementation must be aware of the strategic and political challenges within their own microcosms. In the same way that nationally the struggle for LGBTQ rights is contentious and support for LGBTQ students is too often ambivalent, so too we must accept that the development of LGBTQ studies programs cannot be pursued exclusively along strictly intellectual and scholarly lines. Like it or not, our work is often a form of activism occurring in highly political individual institutions, environments made more rancorous by competitions for reduced resources.

Recent conversations at "Expanding the Circle" conferences have opened up the possibilities for more engaged work toward critically assessing the growth and impact of our programs (such as the need for expanding coursework on transgender studies, queering the curriculum and measuring program success), and have clearly demonstrated the need for a central space or structure in which we can organize, meet and discuss this interdisciplinary field. Further, as these conferences have effectively proved, exploring possibilities and developing structures will continue to benefit from collaborative engagements among academic faculty, staff, and administrators, as well as the students they teach and support.

We believe that if programs in LGBTQ studies are to survive and flourish, we need to have experts and practitioners who can encourage further growth in our field and establish best practices for our curricula. However, to the extent that we value both our "do-it-yourself" ingenuity and queer margin existences, we also acknowledge a certain ambivalence, if not mistrust, for centralized authority. We recognize that because our country still doesn't fully accept LGBTQ people as equal and valued members of society, there is considerable risk in centralizing our interdisciplinary identities, particularly at a time when interdisciplinary programs are being shut down at so many institutions. So, while we see the limits inherent in LGBTQ studies implementation stories being passed on interpersonally and understand that this interdisciplinary field of inquiry exists largely unfunded and outside of higher education's spheres of power, we also appreciate the value of grassroots activism, the elegance of defining program goals that capitalize on local possibilities, and the importance of knowing and supporting our individual students. Thus, it is in this spirit that we offer our program histories for readers to take from them what they will in hopes that more institutions can find their way to curricular developments that support students interested in LGBTQ inquiry.

Notes

1. Mindful of transformations and contestations, we adopt LGBTQ studies throughout this essay as an operational program title that many will recognize. According to Henry Minton, programs in Europe date to the 1970s and U.S. research centers, such as the Lesbian/Gay Studies Center at Yale, were established in the 1980s (1). Further, many pioneering faculty were queering their courses well before the 1990s.

2. The authors speculate that even more common are internal discouragements and lack of support for the establishment of LGBTQ programs and courses.

3. For a recent account of one such effort, see Cooper (2012), 16–17.

4. While not to deny its significance, we have not included City College of San Francisco in this essay because the department's history has been so thoroughly documented elsewhere; see Collins (1992).

5. Among others, a collection of essays edited by Ronni Sanlo effectively addresses various ways institutions can support LGBTQ student populations; see, *Working with Lesbian, Gay, Bisexual, and Transgender College Students: A Handbook for Faculty and Administrators*.

6. Concerns related to intellectual legitimacy and rigor may provide further impetus. For a recent online discussion evidencing such, see the comments posted to Jaschik (2009, "Defending")

7. This is not to devalue the work of others at Colgate who served the LGBTQ community both outside and inside the classroom prior to 2002. Rather, the Supporters Network represents the first large-scale organization committed to coordinating collective actions.

8. To respect the numerous contributions of people involved over many years in both the Supporters Network and the curricular working group that emerged from it, this case study does not attempt to identify particular individuals.

9. To facilitate their regular rotation, two of the gateway courses belong to and serve the curricula of more traditional disciplines, specifically religion and sociology. The third is located within LGBTQ studies, and the faculty member who typically offers this course holds a joint appointment in the program.

10. LGBTQ alumni were kept informed of the proposal's progress in *Out and About* newsletters being produced at that time through the Supporters Network, and later by LGBTQ Initiatives.

11. Susan Rankin's 2003 report highlights similar curricular discontent that emerged as part of a national survey of LGBT students, faculty, and staff undertaken by the National Gay and Lesbian Task Force (33–34).

12. At the time this essay goes to press, the administration provides no compensation for the program director in terms of a reduction to the university's five-course annual teaching load. Instead, an annual research stipend is awarded to the director.

13. Officially the program name is LGBT Studies. (When we started the program in 2000, we were told that the Q might slow down the approval process.) We have started adding the Q on our unofficial materials and in discussion, and will put through for a name change this academic year when we submit curricular changes.

14. The many other faculty members involved in teaching and developing LGBTQ studies after Dr. Dolores Noll will not be named, but because of her pioneering role in LGBTQ studies and scholarship, we do name her.

15. Ironically, the battle for domestic partner benefits extended after the academic program was developed. Despite having the efforts of the faculty union (AAUP), a larger group of faculty involved in this fight and two separate reports from Human Resources in favor of extending benefits to domestic partners, that victory wasn't achieved until 2008.

16. At that time, most academic programs were either named GLB or LGB studies. Some were emerging with the addition of transgendered or queer. We felt it was essential to include transgendered, and while we preferred queer studies, it was decided to not adapt that name because the dean's office was concerned its addition might raise objections from the university's Board of Trustees or Ohio's Board of Regents. As for the choice between GLBT and LGBT, the faculty contacted other programs and the Center for Lesbian and Gay Studies in New York to see if there were trends or evidence to lend support for one choice or the other: when none was presented, the faculty flipped a coin and LGBT won.

17. In response to the initiatives detailed in this case study, Napa Valley College has improved its score to three stars out of five on the Pride Campus Climate Index.

Works Cited

Bacon, Jen. "Teaching Queer Theory at a Normal School." *Journal of Homosexuality* 52.1–2 (2006): 257–283.

Blumenfeld, Warren J. "LGBTQ Campus Climate: The Good and the Still Very Bad." *Diversity & Democracy: Civic Learning for Shared Futures* 15.1 (2012): 20–21.

Collins, Jack. "Matters of Fact: Establishing a Gay and Lesbian Studies Department." In Henry L. Minton, ed. *Gay and Lesbian Studies*. New York: Haworth Press, 1992, 109–23.

Cooper, Sara E. "Delectable Diversity: Gender and Sexuality Studies in General Education." *Diversity & Democracy: Civic Learning for Shared Futures* 15.1 (2012): 16–17.

Dolan, Jill. "Gay and Lesbian Professors: Out on Campus." *Academe* 84.5 (1998): 40–45.

Jaschik, Scott. "Larry Kramer Questions Gay Studies." Inside Higher Ed, April 28, 2009 (accessed August 20, 2012), Insiderhighered.com.

Jaschik, Scott. "Defending Gay Studies." *Insiderhighered.com.* Inside Higher Ed, July 16, 2009. August 20, 2012 (accessed August 20, 2012), Insiderhighered.com.

Jellison, William and K. G. Valente. "Queer at Colgate: Perceptions of LGBTQ Students." Lecture at Women's Studies Brown Bag Series. Colgate University, Hamilton NY. October 13, 2005.

Minton, Henry L. "The Emergence of Gay and Lesbian Studies." In Henry L. Minton, ed. *Gay and Lesbian Studies.* New York: Haworth Press, 1992, 109–123.

Rankin, Susan R. *Campus Climate for Gay, Lesbian, Bisexual and Transgender People: A National Perspective.* 2003. The National Gay and Lesbian Task Force. *Reports & Research.* (accessed June 12, 2012), http://www.thetaskforce.org/downloads/reports/reports/CampusClimate.pdf.

Sanlo, Ronni L., ed. *Working with Lesbian, Gay, Bisexual, and Transgender College Students: A Handbook for Faculty and Administrators.* Westport, CT: Greenwood, 1998.

"SB 48 Senate Bill—CHAPTERED." *California State Senate.* State of California, 2010. (accessed August 7, 2012), http://www.leginfo.ca.gov/pub/11-12/bill/sen/sb_0001-0050/sb_48_bill_20110714_chaptered.html.

Shepard, Curtis F., Felice Yeskel, and Charles Outcalt, eds. *Lesbian, Gay, Bisexual & Transgender Campus Organizing: A Comprehensive Manual.* 1995. The National Gay and Lesbian Task Force. *Reports & Research.* June 15, 2012 (accessed June 15, 2012), http://www.thetaskforce.org/downloads/reports/reports/Campus OrganizingManual.pdf.

Stewart, Trae. "Vying for an Unsustainable/Inappropriate(d)/Organic Queer Space in Higher Education." *Journal of Curriculum and Pedagogy* 4.2 (2007): 89–95.

Talburt, Susan. "Emergences of Queer Studies in the Academy." *Journal of Curriculum and Pedagogy* 4.2 (2007): 95–99.

Younger, John G. "University Queer Programs." N.p., 1997, (accessed August 7, 2012), http://www.people.ku.edu/~jyounger/lgbtqprogs.html.

Chapter 4

Transgendering the Academy

Transforming the Relationship
Between Theory and Praxis

Pauline Park

Introduction: Situating Myself (the Personal as Political)

I would like to talk about how we can make the T in LGBTQ real. The oft-quoted slogan of the women's movement in the 1960s and 1970s was that "The personal is political," and so I would like to commence by situating myself in the context of my own activism and academic background. After describing my current advocacy work in New York, I will then attempt to articulate a program by which we could advance transgender inclusion in the academy—what I will call "transgendering" the academy.

I was born in Korea, adopted by European American parents, and raised in the Midwest. A German Lutheran upbringing on the south side of Milwaukee is an unlikely background for an Asian American transgender activist working in New York, you might think; but there's nearly half a century between the flight from Seoul on what was then known as "Northwest Orient Airlines" (insert sound of gong here) to Chicago via Tokyo and Anchorage, and the flight from LaGuardia to San Francisco International that brought me to this conference a few days ago.

In between, there have been struggles to come to terms with gender identity and intercountry adoptee identity—I often think I was born to have an identity complex—as well as experiences living in four different Midwestern cities and five different European cities, and working in three different careers in two distinctly different gender presentations. All of which would make for either a crowded and potentially confusing memoir or a novel with a highly implausible plot. A career in public relations in Chicago and a career in academic political science have been followed by my current vocation as an activist—I do not say *career*, because I see activism not as a career but rather a commitment, or a set of commitments. And I would not say that I chose to pursue activism so much as I would say that activism chose me. But if my first career (in public relations) has actually been far more useful to me as an activist than my second, my academic background has helped shape my thinking about activism. And in turn, my experiences doing advocacy work on behalf of a very marginalized community have helped me think about how actual experience with activism can inform academic theory construction just as theoretical work can be used to better inform activism and advocacy.

My Activism

My activism began in 1994, when I joined six others to cofound Gay Asians and Pacific Islanders of Chicago (GAPIC), but activism became a full-time pursuit in early 1997 when I cofounded Iban/Queer Koreans of New York (Iban/QKNY)—which I served as coordinator of from 1997–1999—and Queens Pride House, an LGBT community center in the borough of Queens. The organization with which I am most closely associated is the New York Association for Gender Rights Advocacy (NYAGRA), which I cofounded in 1998. But I also participated in cofounding two political clubs: the Out People of Color Political Action Club (OutPOCPAC) (2001) and the Guillermo Vasquez Independent Democratic Club of Queens (2002).

The accomplishment in which I take the most pride was my role in leading the campaign for the transgender rights law enacted by the New York City Council in 2002. And I have to say that three years of leading a major legislative campaign taught me more about politics than five and one-half years of studying academic political science theory ever did.

But leading the campaign for transgender rights bill (Int. No. 24)— enacted as Local Law 3 of 2002—was only the most prominent public role that I have had the honor of playing as an activist. Following enactment of the transgender rights law, the New York City Commission on Human Rights convened a working group of activists that drafted guidelines for implementation of the statute; ironically enough, my own discrimination case—involving an incident of discrimination that took place in the midst of the process of getting the Human Rights Commission to adopt those guidelines—ended up playing a small but significant role in the process, as well as providing crucial language that helped resolve an impasse we had reached with the commission over the provisions of those implementation guidelines.

NYAGRA is a cofounding member of the coalition seeking enactment of the Gender Expression Non-Discrimination Act (GENDA), the transgender rights bill currently pending in the New York state legislature. But long before the introduction of GENDA, NYAGRA worked with the Empire State Pride Agenda—the statewide LGBT advocacy organization—to cofound the coalition seeking enactment of the Dignity for All Students Act (DASA), which would prohibit discrimination and bias-based harassment in public schools throughout the state of New York. Believe it or not, February 2010 marks the tenth anniversary of the founding of that coalition, and the bill is still pending in the state legislature ten full years after it was first introduced—evidence, if any were needed, that New York does indeed have the most dysfunctional legislature of any of the fifty states.

I also served on the steering committee seeking enactment of the Dignity in All Schools Act, the local DASA bill introduced in the New York City Council in 2002 and enacted by the Council in 2004. Unfortunately, despite the pervasive bullying and bias-based harassment that takes place in New York City schools, the Department of Education—under the direction of the administration of Mayor Michael R. Bloomberg—has refused to implement the DASA statute, substituting instead some weak teacher training efforts that seem to amount to little more than window dressing.

I would like to emphasize safe schools legislation in the context of this discussion because the New York State and City DASA legislation both include comprehensive lists of "protected categories," including race, religion, ethnicity, and disability as well as sexual orientation and gender, defined to include gender identity and gender expression. Safe schools legislation such as New York State and City DASA help move us out of a purely "identitarian" conceptual framework, which can be limiting. Both the New York State and City DASA Coalitions are multiracial and multicommunity, including a broad range of organizations; certainly, LGBT organizations are significantly represented in both coalitions—understandable, since LGBT students and those perceived to be queer are among those most frequently subjected to bullying and bias-based harassment in school.

But while the New York State DASA Coalition is led by the Empire State Pride Agenda, the Dignity in Action Coalition—which is the successor to the New York City DASA Coalition—is led by the New York Civil Liberties Union (NYCLU) and includes a number of prominent API organizations in its leadership, including the Asian American Legal Defense and Education Fund (AALDEF), the Coalition for Asian American Children and Families (CACF), and the Sikh Coalition. In fact, these three API organizations—AALDEF, CACF, and the Sikh Coalition—have emerged as the most prominent and most visible member organizations in the coalition.

It should be obvious—but may not be to everyone—that making higher education more LGBT-inclusive must also mean tackling the problem of bullying and bias-based harassment in elementary and secondary schools, since so many LGBT students drop out of school because of such bullying and never make it to college; that is especially true of transgendered students, I would essay, based on anecdotal evidence (in the absence of any comprehensive study of the problem).

While I may be most closely associated with the work I do on behalf of NYAGRA in the legislative arena, one other important component of my work is training. Over the course of the last decade, I have conducted hundreds of transgender sensitivity training sessions for a wide range of social service providers and community-based organizations, ranging from one-hour workshops to full-day trainings. A small part of my training work has been with academic institutions, focused on issues related to transgender inclusion—including, for example, gender-neutral housing, which has become a major issue on many campuses.

A few years ago, my colleague, Michael Silverman (executive director of the Transgender Legal Defense and Education Fund) and I conducted the first transgender sensitivity training sessions for any major hospital in New York City. And in fact, Michael and I started the Transgender Health Initiative of New York (THINY) with colleagues from TLDEF and the Gender Identity Project of the LGBT Community Center of New York City to enhance access to health care for transgendered and gender-variant people in New York City and the metropolitan area. Last July, NYAGRA published the first directory of transgender-sensitive health care providers in the New York metropolitan area; and while directories of this kind have been posted online for cities such as Los Angeles, Boston, and Minneapolis–St. Paul, the NYAGRA directory may well be the first such directory in the United States ever published in a print edition.

NYAGRA Circles Diagram

Transgender Inclusion: The Circles Diagram

So here is the question that I would like to address today: If our goal is to make higher education fully transgender-inclusive, how would we go about achieving that objective? The first step would have to be to gain a full understanding of just what "transgender" means. Many in this audience will have a very good understanding of transgender identity, but for those for whom this is a relatively new topic, I would like to use a diagram to illustrate the complexity of the community of which I myself am a member. This is the NYAGRA circles diagram http://www.paulinepark.com/index.php/2009/08/ explaining-transgender-the-circles-diagram, which I first began using when we initiated the campaign for Int. No. 24, the transgender rights bill that passed the New York City Council in April 2002; the diagram came out of our first meeting with a Council Member who—though he himself was openly gay—told us that he did not have a clear idea of who or what we meant when we talked about protecting members of the transgender community from discrimination.

As you can see, the diagram (fig. 4.1) represents the community as a series of concentric circles, beginning with transsexuals—those who seek or have obtained sex reassignment surgery (SRS)—often described as being either "preoperative" or "postop," as the case may be. While the mainstream media until recently have tended to focus on those transitioning from male-to-female (MTF), there are, of course, many (possibly just as many) transsexuals who go from female-to-male (FTM). While transsexuals are the segment

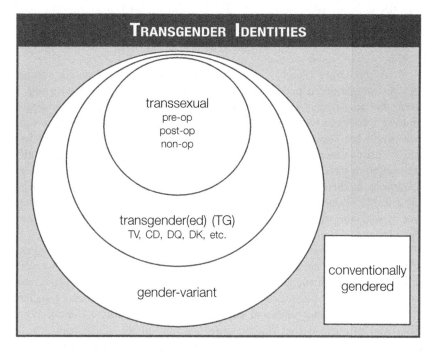

Figure 4.1. The NYAGRA Circles Diagram.

of the transgender community whom many think of first when they think of "transgender," the term transgender is not simply a more politically correct or up-to-date synonym for transsexual. In fact, most transgendered people do not want SRS, and most of those who do (viz., transsexuals) never get it—mainly because of the expense, but for other reasons as well.

Encompassing this first circle is a much larger circle, those I will call "the transgendered," including not only transsexuals but nontranssexual transgendered people as well. The most obvious identity labels in this category of nontranssexual transgendered people are those who identify as—or are identified as—cross-dressers (the old-fashioned term is *transvestite*, though few today use that term to self-identify—except perhaps for Eddie Izzard—and it is now considered overly clinical or even pejorative) as well as drag queens and drag kings—terms best used with reference to performance, whether professional or informal. The "transgendered" in the context of this circles diagram will be used to denote those who present fully in a gender identity not associated with their sex assigned at birth—at least part of the time.

But there are in fact hundreds of different terms that transgendered people use to self-identify, and conversely, many transgendered people do not identify with the term *transgender*. Clearly, the almost bewildering diversity of the transgender community constitutes one of the biggest challenges in attempting to include and serve this population, whether in higher education, health care, or social services.

A still larger category encompassing both transsexual and nontranssexual transgendered people is that which I will label the *gender-variant*, a term that actually has its origins in academic circles but has come into vogue among activists as well. And just who would nontransgendered gender-variant people be? They would include relatively feminine males who nonetheless still identify as men or boys and relatively masculine females who still identify as women or girls. The term *gender-variant* is particularly relevant on college campuses, as there are many who were born male and especially female who disdain the sex/gender binary and terms such as *man* and *woman* that they see as reflecting that binary; many such young people prefer to identify as "gender-queer" and some prefer gender-neutral pronouns.

I contrast these three groups—the transsexual, transgendered, and gender-variant—with another group, the conventionally gendered—those who more or less conform to the gender norms of their time and place, and who (by definition) constitute a majority in every society, as every society constructs norms of gender and imposes those norms on its members. What is crucial to grasp is that this diagram is a map of the gender universe; it does not speak to sexual orientation. As most in this audience will already understand, transgendered people are as diverse in their sexual orientation as nontransgendered people and like them, may be heterosexual or bisexual as well as gay or lesbian. And I also need to emphasize that this diagram is simply my map of the gender universe; there are as many different definitions of transgender as there are transgendered people.

The main point is to avoid the narrowing of discourse around gender identity that is constantly rearticulated and reinforced by the mainstream media—the overreliance on what I call the classic transsexual transition narrative—which focuses almost obsessively on a linear medical transition from male to female through hormone replacement therapy (HRT) toward the end point of sex reassignment surgery; while some do follow that path, most transgendered people do not. Any effort to establish fully transgender inclusive programs and services on a college campus will falter unless it is based on a recognition of the full diversity of transgender identity, and the truth that there are as many ways to be transgendered as there are transgendered people.

Transgendering the Academy: Campus Policies, Curriculum, Student Services, and Faculty and Staff Development

Having situated myself as an activist and ex-academic, and having attempted to describe the diversity of the transgender community, I would now like to set out what I see as four crucial elements in what I call "transgendering the academy." These include: first, establishing campus policies and protocols that explicitly prohibit discrimination based on gender identity and expression; second, advancing transgender entry into faculty positions within academia; third, constructing curricula and building academic programs and departments that advance the study of transgender in the academy; fourth, establishing an institutional infrastructure of services for transgendered students, faculty, and staff; and fifth, constructing theory that is relevant to activism, advocacy, and public policy. I will touch on the first four but devote the bulk of my comments to the last—the task of transforming theory into praxis.

One of the tasks that must be undertaken in order to effect what I am calling the "transgendering" of the academy is the adoption by colleges and universities of policies explicitly prohibiting discrimination based on gender identity and gender expression as well as sexual orientation. I am not currently aware of a comprehensive list of institutions of higher education in the United States or abroad that have adopted such policies, so perhaps the Consortium of Higher Education LGBT Resource Professionals http://www.lgbtcampus.org ("the Consortium") could compile such a list.

There is a curious paradox here: where campuses are situated in jurisdictions that currently include gender identity and expression in nondiscrimination law, explicit policies that do so are somewhat redundant, as such colleges and universities are then under legal mandate to enforce nondiscrimination. But I would argue that campus policies are still useful even in cities, counties, and states with gender identity and expression in human rights law, as they represent an explicit commitment on the part of the college or university to transgender inclusion, and they send a signal to transgendered students, faculty, and staff that their presence and participation in campus life are valued, as well as sending an important signal to those who would discriminate against transgendered members of the campus community.

Of all the items in the project of transgendering the academy, this is, on the face of it, the easiest: simply adding either gender identity and expression to the college or university nondiscrimination policy or—better still—adding a definition of gender that includes identity and expression—requires no elaborate word-smithing or lawyering, merely a commitment on the part of the administration to do so. The difficulty comes when applying such a nondiscrimination policy to specific situations such as sex-segregated facilities, including those where there is the possibility of unavoidable nudity (to use a legal expression). Restrooms, dormitories, and gyms and locker rooms are the most significant "sites of contestation" (to use a term beloved of poststructuralist theorists). Some institutions, such as New York University (NYU), have adopted policies that specifically require the construction of at least one gender-neutral restroom per new building; at the same time that NYU adopted this policy in 2005, the University Senate voted in favor of adopting a policy prohibiting discrimination based on gender identity or expression, consistent with the transgender rights law enacted by the New York City Council in 2002—according to which the university was already under a legal mandate from the City of New York to avoid such discrimination.

Explicit campuswide policies ensuring full access to campus facilities for transgendered students as well as faculty and staff are important but must be drafted in ways that address the potentially thorny issues that arise when it comes to sex-segregated facilities. The rule should be one of reasonable accommodation, backed by an aggressive effort by the administration to ensure full access to such facilities. The prohibition of discrimination based on gender identity and expression must be explicitly included in faculty, staff, and student handbooks along with prohibition of discrimination based on other characteristics such as race, ethnicity, religion, national origin, disability, and so on. Above all, the prohibition of discrimination based on gender identity or expression must be included in legal documents that ensure the right of the student or faculty or staff member to litigate a dispute if necessary; only then can the institution be held accountable, especially in jurisdictions that do not include gender identity or expression in state or local nondiscrimination law.

Single-sex colleges must also address the issue of admissions policies, a particularly problematic issue for women's colleges; but the inclusion of both transmen and transwomen in women's spaces is an issue that will not go away, much as many administrators at women's colleges may wish it to. Clearly, the principle of empowering women through education needs to be subjected to scrutiny, as does the very definition of what constitutes a woman, and what provisions must be made to accommodate and ideally to fully include in the life of the college those female-born individuals who transition to male over the course of their undergraduate careers at women's colleges, as well as those male-born individuals who seek admission to a women's college as women.

Colleges and universities should also mandate transgender sensitivity training for all faculty and staff—and where feasible—for students as well. Where mandatory diversity training already exists for race, ethnicity, religion, and disability as well as sex or gender, that training should include sexual orientation and gender identity and expression as well. In other words, *diversity* needs to be redefined campuswide to include diversity of sexual orientation and gender identity and expression.

Another mechanism for enhancing inclusion would be inclusion in a campuswide census of students, faculty and staff—especially those in leadership positions—that includes self-identification by sexual orientation and gender identity. No doubt such a proposal could meet resistance even at more ostensibly more progressive colleges and universities. But at the very least, surveys of "campus climate" should include questions about climate for LGBTQ students, faculty, and staff.

The second element in the project of transgendering the academy is the inclusion of transgender-relevant courses in the curriculum of institutions of higher education. Inclusion of a course on transgender issues as a requirement for completion of a major or minor in LGBT studies would also represent a significant advance for transgender inclusion in the curriculum. On the curricular front, at least, there has been some progress over the course of the last few decades, as the number of courses offered at colleges and universities in the United States and Canada—and increasingly outside North America—that include a substantial component on transgender issues has grown exponentially, albeit from a small base. Once again, there seems to be no comprehensive list, which would be very useful for LGBT campus professionals as well as for students and faculty. And all too often, even where transgender-inclusive courses are included in a college course catalog, those courses are offered irregularly and by graduate students or adjunct professors who have little institutional influence and limited ability to ensure continuity in course content from semester to semester. But where such courses exist, they are primarily in the humanities and to a lesser extent in the social sciences. In other fields, significant transgender- or even LGBT-specific content in curricula is rare. In schools of medicine, transgender-specific content is sparse, and what little there is focuses almost exclusively on the medical aspects of transsexual transition, even though familiarizing physicians and other health care providers with what might be termed the *psychosocial* aspects of health care provision may be as important in ensuring transgender access to quality health care as "cognate" knowledge of the surgical and endocrinological aspects of gender transition. I would suggest that a minimum of two hours of transgender sensitivity training should be required at every school of medicine that offers an MD.

Inextricably linked with the issue of curriculum development is that of faculty and staff development. Certainly, one of the biggest challenges in advancing a project of transgendering the academy will be that of transgendering the faculty of colleges and universities, few of whom have many openly transgendered members; even fewer transgender-identified faculty members obtain tenure after having been hired while openly transgendered; and still fewer obtain tenure primarily for research focused on transgender issues. And most theorists who focus substantially on transgender issues are in the humanities, with a scattering in the social sciences.

Indeed, one of the most remarkable facts about what might be termed *transgender studies* is that many if not most tenured faculty members who are in the field are not themselves transgender-identified; and those who are for the most part are graduate students and adjunct faculty. What if the faculty of a program or department of women's studies at a college or university was almost entirely male? Or consider for a moment a comparison with ethnic studies: imagine for a moment if a program or department of African American, Asian American, Native American, or Latino studies on a given college campus were mostly or even entirely white; such a situation would be regarded as controversial if not unacceptable by many students, faculty, and administrators alike. And yet, transgender studies—depending on how one defines the field—may be very close to that situation today. There are, of course, significant differences between race and ethnicity, on the one hand, and sexual orientation and gender identity or expression, on the other, and it would be risky indeed to make to glib a comparison between them. And yet, entertaining the analogy for the moment may be useful in pointing out the striking asymmetry in power relations between the majority of those who participate in this nascent field called transgender studies who are students, untenured faculty and independent scholars as well as activists and the minority who as tenured faculty members who constitute the privileged elite of this small society of largely white and upper-middle-class academicians.

Even more problematic is the tendency of transgender studies as a field to mirror the larger academic society's tendency to construct and rigidly enforce orthodoxies of thought as well as hierarchies of power, both within and outside the academy. The clinical literature is dominated by psychiatrists, psychoanalysts, and psychotherapists, with some participation by social workers and other members of the "helping professions," but the transgendered people whose lives are profoundly affected by the determinations of those professionals are excluded from participation in the construction of that literature for lack of the professional credentials required for that participation.

If transgendered people have made little headway in attempting to secure tenure in traditional academic departments, they have made even less progress in schools of medicine where psychiatrists earn their MDs. The American Psychiatric Association (APA) is among professional associations in the "helping professions" that is possibly the least open to participation by the transgendered and the least open to public or LGBT community input of any kind, despite the vast influence over the lives of transsexual, transgendered, and gender-variant children, youth, and adults wielded by the psychiatric profession.

Not unrelated to transgender faculty development is the issue of transgender-inclusive curricular development. Certainly, nontransgendered faculty members can and do participate in the development of transgender-inclusive curriculum; but for the reasons already stated, the asymmetry in institutional power between transgender-identified students and faculty who develop and teach so many transgender-inclusive courses and the tenured faculty who wield decision-making power over them as well as curriculum development poses a serious issue for academic institutions.

Another important issue is the institutional standing of transgender studies and LGBT studies more broadly speaking. First, there is the question of programs versus departments. In most colleges and universities, departments have far greater autonomy than programs and are far better placed to defend faculty lines and budgets against cutbacks than programs; that is no doubt why the faculty members participating in the development of women's studies in the United States have aimed toward the establishment of departments of women's studies wherever possible. So, for example, while offering undergraduate majors as well as minors, the University of Chicago's Center for Gender Studies (http://genderstudies.uchicago.edu/about) has no faculty of its own, only "affiliated" faculty drawn from throughout the university, and therefore no ability to offer tenure-track positions of its own entirely independent of other academic units.

Then, too, there is the question as to whether this field that I am calling "transgender studies" is better thought of as a subset of LGBT studies or of "gender studies," and therefore better housed in a program or department of sexuality studies or one of women's or gender studies. There are, of course, universities that have combined the two: the aforementioned Center for Gender Studies (http://genderstudies.uchicago.edu/about) at the University of Chicago, for example, houses the Lesbian and Gay Studies Project and, according to its mission statement, "consolidates work on gender and sexuality, and in feminist, gay and lesbian, and queer studies."

Then there is the question of institutional infrastructure, especially of student services. Here, the Consortium of Higher Education Lesbian Gay Bisexual Transgender Resource Professionals (http://www.lgbtcampus.org) ("the Consortium") and its members have played a leading role in developing LGBT student services offices at campuses around the United States. There is much to say about services specifically needed by transgendered and gender-variant students, but given that the primary focus of my talk is on public policy and advocacy, I will touch on only a few programmatic elements that I think are important to the development of infrastructure serving undergraduate and graduate students on campus.

Obviously, a fully funded LGBT student services office with at least one or more full-time staff members is the minimum needed to effectively serve transgendered and gender-variant students. Support groups for those coming out and transitioning are also crucial. Support and guidance in navigating the physical infrastructure of a campus are especially important, including access to restrooms and locker rooms in gyms. Housing is also an important issue, and single-sex institutions—especially women's colleges are increasingly confronted with issues of access. Health care is a particularly important and sensitive issue for transgendered students, and the same issues that have come up in the Transgender Health Initiative of New York (http://www.transgender-legal.org/work_show.php?id=8) (THINY) face transgendered students as they attempt to access procedures and care both related to gender transition and not directly gender-related. Offices of LGBT student services can also play a role in assisting transgendered and gender-variant students navigate what might be called the "semiotics of campus life," including negotiating classroom etiquette related to names and pronouns and even posting transgender-affirming signage around campus.

One of the challenges facing offices of LGBT student services is the "siloing" that often results from the construction of offices of multicultural affairs along identitarian lines, such that the office of LGBT students primarily serves white queers, with little engagement with the offices of African American, Latino, or Asian American students, which in turn are inadvertently relieved of the obligation to serve LGBT students of color within their constituencies. Housing the LGBT student services office within the same complex as those serving students of color—such as is done at the University of Connecticut—can help foster collaboration and collaborative programming, as the Rainbow Center at UConn—not coincidentally under the direction of an African American lesbian—regularly engages in. Colleges and universities must work to ensure that LGBT students of color and especially transgendered students of color do not fall between the cracks. "Intersectionality" must not be simply a slogan; it must be a principle on which the work of student service professionals at colleges and universities operate.

Finally, let me mention something of particular interest to me as the alumna of three different academic institutions, and that is the role of alumni in the lives of their alma maters. As anyone working on staff at a college or university will know, alumni wield enormous influence with administrators, above all because of their financial contributions to the institutions they once attended. In that regard, it seems to me that the development of LGBT alumni associations represents one of the most promising recent developments in higher education.

The University of Wisconsin–Madison—which I attended as an undergraduate decades before there were any such LGBT alumni associations or LGBT student services offices of any kind—was the first Big Ten school to confer its official recognition of such an alumni association, the GLBT Alumni Council (http://www.uwalumni.com/home/chaptersandaffiliates/Affiliates/glbtac/glbtac_homepage.aspx) (GLBTAC), established in 1992. I attended the first reunion brunch that summer, hosted by the alumni association known at that time as the Lavender Badgers. By 1999, the association added the *T* to its name and mission. I might add parenthetically that U.S. Representative Tammy Baldwin (JD '89)—the first openly LGBT person elected to Congress—is a Wisconsin alumna and a recipient of a Distinguished Alumni Award from GLBTAC.

I would encourage us as a community to think in terms of LGBT alumni associations that are able to exercise some degree of autonomy from the general alumni associations and the college and university administrators who run them. Such LGBT alumni associations may be positioned to undertake initiatives that would enhance transgender inclusion in the academic institutions with which they are associated. Just to suggest a few such ideas, an LGBT alumni association should consider creating a transgender-specific scholarship fund and perhaps at some point even funding an endowed chair dedicated to transgender-related research.

Activism and the Academy: Turning Theory into Praxis

Let me conclude with the component of this effort that is the most fraught with difficulty. If this project of transgendering the academy is to succeed, the field of what may be termed *transgender studies* must demonstrate its relevance to the community that is the ostensible object of its study. Within the academy, the central justification for that enterprise, which we may term *theory construction* is that it creates new knowledge, illuminating the human condition, or—in social science terms—describing, explaining, and predicting the phenomena which are the objects of its study. What might be called "transgender studies" is in fact a kind of intersection of two overlapping fields—LGBT studies and gender studies (still known as women's studies in many colleges and universities).

There are in fact three distinct literatures concerning transgender identity, none of which communicate with each other. There is, first of all, what might be called the clinical literature of psychiatry, psychotherapy, and social work. Second, there is the literature of gender studies influenced by feminist theory and especially the stream of queer theory that has its origins in the work of poststructuralist theoreticians, above all, that of Michel Foucault ("The History of Sexuality") (http://www.ipce.info/ipceweb/Library/history_of_sexuality.htm) being the *Ursprung* of this literature). And finally, there is a small theoretical literature in the social sciences of a more positivist and empirical nature.

The problem with the clinical literature—especially that developed by psychiatrists—is that it articulates a pathologizing discourse in which all forms of gender variance are viewed as deviant aberration from a heteronormative standard. At the heart of this literature is the diagnosis of gender identity disorder (GID) listed in the fourth *Diagnostic and Statistical Manual of Mental Disorders* (*DSM*), published by the American Psychiatric Association (APA). Even those psychiatrists, psychotherapists, and social workers who are sympathetic to transsexual and transgendered people seeking some sort of gender transition are compelled by the logic of the medicalization of transgender identity to view transsexualism as a condition to be treated through interventions such as psychotherapy, psychiatry, HRT, and SRS. No matter how helpful in practical terms to those seeking to transition in facilitating access to desired medical interventions, the discourse of GID is one that subjects the transgendered individual to treatment for a medicalized condition rather than viewing transgender identity as simply a naturally occurring variant in gender identity and expression.

The deliberations over the revision of the GID diagnosis in the *DSM* are a case in point: the American Psychiatric Association (APA), which publishes the *DSM* is what the British would call a QUANGO—a "quasi-non-governmental organization"—whose determinations as reflected in the DSM have implications for law and public policy. The ability to secure insurance coverage and payment for gender transition-related surgeries and procedures such as HRT and SRS is determined to a considerable extent by the findings of the clinical literature, shaped by a medicalized discourse of transsexualism rooted in a pathologization of transgender identity and gender variance.

A committee appointed by the APA revised of the diagnosis of GID introduced in the fourth edition of the *DSM* (*DSM*-IV) published in 1974, changing it to "gender dysphoria" in the fifth edition, published in 2013; the revision represented a softening of the language, but gender dysphoria, like its predecessor, is still a pathology listed in a directory of mental disorders. And it is important to point out that the committee in charge of revising the diagnosis was led by Dr. Kenneth Zucker, a psychiatrist who advocates "reparative therapy" (http://www.queerty.com/dr-kenneth-zuckers-war-on-transgenders-20090206)—up to and including forced electroshock therapy—for transgendered and gender-variant children and youth. The National Association for Research and Therapy of Homosexuality is a notorious purveyor of homophobic pseudoscience, and NARTH has applauded Zucker for his advocacy of coercive psychotherapy (http://www.narth.com/docs/gid.html) used to enforce rigid heteronormative gender norms on gender-queer children and youth. Among Zucker's confederates in advancing a transgender-phobic agenda within the academy as well as within the public policy arena is J. Michael Bailey (http://ai.eecs.umich.edu/people/conway/TS/LynnsReviewOfBaileysBook.html), a tenured professor of psychology at Northwestern University and the author of *The Man Who Would Be Queen* (http://gaybookreviews.info/review/3437/1013), a book based on shoddy secondhand pseudoscience. Bailey has nonetheless been influential in reinforcing the discourse of pathology in the public mind through interviews on television shows such as *60 Minutes* (http://www.cbsnews.com/stories/2006/03/09/60minutes/main1385230.shtml) (CBS) and through other mainstream media outlets. Even relatively "sympathetic" portrayals of transgender youth such as "Born with the Wrong Body" (http://abcnews.go.com/2020/story?id=3072518&page=1)—a Barbara Walters special on transgendered children that aired on ABC in April 2007—are informed (or perhaps we should say "misinformed") by the pathologizing clinical literature of medicalized transsexualism proffered by Zucker, Bailey, and their ilk.

In a speech I gave at the Trans-Health Conference in Philadelphia in April 2007, I called for the removal of GID from the DSM (http://www.paulinepark.com/index.php/2009/08/transgender-health-reconceptualizing-pathology-as-wellness), contingent on the establishment of mechanisms to ensure continued access to and payment for procedures and surgeries related to gender transition. As I like to say, I do not have a gender identity disorder; it is society that has a gender identity disorder. But I had no access to the *DSM*-V working group chaired by Ken Zucker, and that committee was not open to input from the transgendered people whose lives will be profoundly affected by its decisions. If a transgendered woman with a PhD in political science who is actively involved in the public policy arena is excluded from the deliberations of the APA and the *DSM*-V working group on gender identity, one can imagine how minimal the ability of other members of the transgender community to participate in the discussions that determine the clinical definitions of gender norms both here in the United States and around the world are.

The clinical literature is profoundly compromised by the profound transgender-phobia of the clinicians who dominate that literature and who are largely white, upper-middle-class, conventionally gendered, heterosexual men. But the queer-theoretic literature that is its leading competition in the field of transgender studies, while ostensibly more sympathetic to the transgendered and gender-variant people who are the subjects of its study, is also characterized by limited community participation and problematic discourse.

While the literature of transgender studies influenced by feminist and queer theory is more sympathetic to transgender community members and generally far less pathologizing than the clinical literature of psychiatry, it is nonetheless marred by a similar tendency to objectify and exoticize transgender identities. The dominant figure in this queer-theoretic literature is Judith Butler, and her work is a case in point: accused by some of being abstruse to the point of indecipherability, her work is not based in any lived experience of being transgendered but instead exemplifies an observer's "gaze" that is problematic even if ostensibly more "progressive" and "feminist" than that of the psychiatrists who regard the *DSM* as a kind of clinical Bible. If there is any insight into gender and transgender in Butler's work or that of her followers, it is not of the sort to be useful to either activists or policy makers. Discussion of notions of "performativity" in the context of legislative and policy debates will do little if anything for the transgendered and gender-variant people engaged in life-and-death struggles for survival on the streets of New York, San Francisco, and Los Angeles, not to mention Mexico City, Mumbai, and Marrakesh.

It is one of the most obvious defects of much of the queer-theoretic literature on gender identity and expression that so much of it is inaccessible to so many members of the community that are the subject of the theorist's gaze. Not all, certainly, but much of the literature of transgender studies is written in a style so abstruse if not deliberately obscurantist that it is inaccessible to anyone outside the field, including activists, advocacy organizations and policy makers. None of this is to suggest, of course, that all theoretical literature must be written at a sixth-grade level or in a language that completely excludes all specialized terminology; such a demand would render difficult if not impossible the kind of nuanced and sophisticated discussions of important problems in theory construction that are an appropriate part of academic discourse. And one must resist the anti-intellectualism endemic in American society that is also all too apparent in certain LGBT activist circles.

But any honest academic would have to admit that a goodly portion of scholarly activity is really devoted primarily to the attainment of tenure and promotion; were that set of institutional incentives removed, one suspects that quite a few university presses and even whole journals might go out of publication in short order. One of the problems here is the system of peer review that is central to the adjudication of quality and merit in academic writing and publishing. As we have seen from the scandal that broke in December 2009, with the public dissemination of e-mail messages from scientists at the University of East Anglia regarding global warming and climate change, the system of peer review can be manipulated and undermined by cunning academics such as those caught up in the affair dubbed "Climategate" (see, for example, Jonathan Leake, "The Great Climate Change Science Scandal" [http://www.timesonline.co.uk/tol/news/environment/article6936289.ece] The *Sunday Times of London*, November 29, 2009). If peer review is the gold standard of academic discourse, that gold standard has been tarnished.

Imagine just for the moment if the system entailed the requirement that at least one participant in the peer review of a potential article or book be a member of the community under study and another participant be a member of a relevant policy-making body; would scholars whose writings were under review within such a system be in a position to so blithely ignore the question of "relevance"?

I am not in fact proposing such an innovation; the definitional issues alone would make it difficult to determine qualifications for participation on the part of community members and policy makers; and I am sure that many academics would find such a suggestion to be radical and even outlandish, were it to be made; but such a reaction would simply confirm the suspicion of most nonacademics in the LGBT community that queer theory is removed from the realities and concerns of everyday life for most members of that community.

I am also not suggesting that policy relevance is the primary criterion by which the value of academic research and writing should be evaluated. There is much in the literature of (trans)gender and LGBT studies that is valuable because it contributes to our understanding of transgender identities as well as the relationship between gender variance and sexual orientation. "Three Sexes and Four Sexualities: Redressing the Discourses on Gender and Sexuality in Contemporary Thailand" (http://positions.dukejournals.org/cgi/pdf_extract/2/1/15), an article by Rosalind C. Morris published in the journal *Positions* (2.1 [1994]: 15–43), just to cite one such example, may have no direct relevance to policy—whether in the United States or Thailand—but it is useful in shedding light on the complexities of *transgenderal* identities in premodern and contemporary Thai society. Likewise, Martin Manalansan's book, *Global Divas: Filipino Gay Men in the Diaspora* (http://reconstruction.eserver. org/BReviews/revGlobalDivas.htm) (Durham: Duke University Press, 2003) makes a useful contribution to the literature by examining the complexities of *bakla* identity in the Philippines and the differences with contemporary American society in the way in which transgressive identities are constructed in that culture. Such writings, whether or not they have immediate application to public policy in Europe, North America, or elsewhere, certainly have relevance for activism and advocacy work as well as for HIV/AIDS education and prevent and the provision of health care to transgendered and gender-variant people.

The writing of transgender and queer history is an important component of the project of transgendering the academy, but it is one fraught with peril, conceptual and otherwise. The peril is particularly apparent when activists engage in the writing of that history, as so much of activist discourse is theoretically uninformed and burdened with an overly concretized identitarian politics that lacks conceptual sophistication, to the detriment of the work of the activists and organizations who engage in such discursive practices. Many activists treat LGBT identities as if they are eternal essences with no significant variance across time and place, claiming "famous homosexuals in history," as if Leonardo da Vinci were just another Chelsea Boy or Castro Street Clone.

The transgender variant of this essentializing of identity and identity politics is exemplified by the characterization of Joan of Arc as just one in a long line of *Transgender Warriors* (to cite the title of Leslie Feinberg's 1996 book), as if there were no significant differences in the social construction of (trans)gender identity in France in 1430, or in New York City in 1969 or 2010, for that matter. To describe Joan of Arc as "an inspirational role model—a brilliant transgender peasant teenager leading an army of laborers into battle" (36) who was "burned at the stake by the Inquisition of the Catholic Church because she refused to stop dressing in garb traditionally worn by men" (31) is to use history for contemporary political purposes.

Not only does the *Transgender Warriors* approach to history take an individual historical figure such as Joan of Arc entirely out of historical context—failing to acknowledge that the central reason for her execution by the English was her military leadership of the enemy French forces—that approach produces rather bizarrely ironic discursive practices, constructing a transgender hero out of a woman who in contemporary France is beloved by the far right as the very epitome of French nationalism. But such is the danger of writing transgender history to advance a contemporary political agenda.

In the introduction to *Monsieur d'Eon Is a Woman: A Tale of Political Intrigue and Sexual Masquerade* (http://www.nytimes.com/1995/07/31/ books/books-of-the-times-enigma-of-a-nobleman-pretender-to-femininity. html?pagewanted=1), the biography of the Chevalier d'Eon by Gary Kates, he writes in describing Feinberg's approach to transgender history, ". . . such theorists have little historical sensibility" (preface, p. xiii). Those transgendered individuals who know of d'Eon, "think of d'Eon as an early pioneer who somehow lived centuries ahead of his time. But what makes d'Eon fascinating is that he was no such thing. Neither sick nor ahead of his time, d'Eon's gender bending was lionized in his day and even made emblematic of his generation," Kates writes. An example of historically informed transgender history a profile of the first public transgender figure in Western European history, the Kates biography of d'Eon avoids engaging in the kind of essentializing discourse in which a good deal of transgender history and a great deal of transgender activism engages.

One does not need to endorse the notion that all history is reducible to biography to see that biography is an important component of the project of transgender history. Neither does one need to be transgendered oneself to write transgender biography or history, but the nontransgendered biographer and historian need to be aware of and sensitive to the self-understanding of the subjects that they write about. To call Billy Tipton "the producer of the illusion of masculinity, both onstage and off"—as Diane Wood Middlebrook does in her biography of the twentieth-century jazz artist (*Suits Me: The Double Life of Billy Tipton*, Boston and New York: Houghton Mifflin Company, 1998) comes close to imposing a misunderstanding of a subject who contemporary transgendered people would doubtless wish to call a "transman."

But the danger with autobiography as history is the risk that transgendered authors may project their own individual self-construction on the community as a whole, generalizing from direct personal experience in a universalizing discourse that actually undermines those activists and academic theorists who are attempting to communicate the full diversity and complexity of the universe of gender and transgender identity to a largely uncomprehending society.

Much of what may be termed as *transgender studies*—including that which is written in a queer-theoretic vein—is written from a white, upper-middle-class, U.S.-centric perspective. Transgender studies as a field needs to take into account not only perspectives of transgendered people of color, but the full complexity of intersectionality, examining class, disability, and citizenship and nationality issues, as well as race and ethnicity; and transgender studies must also incorporate the wide world outside the United States in its perspectives and concerns. At the same time, if it is to be valuable, transgender studies must do more than simply preach to the choir. Research and writing that does nothing more than enable the author to strike a pose does nothing to advance our understanding of the complexities of gender identity and expression, much less the marginalized communities that are the ostensible object of the author's screed. Participants in the enterprise of transgender studies must avoid sanctimonious moralizing and instead attempt to engage meaningfully with those inside the academy and out in order to attempt to enlist them as allies.

What poststructuralist theory at its best can do is help deconstruct problematic discursive practices prevalent in public policy discussions, as well as in much of LGBT activism and advocacy work. One of the most problematic such tendencies in transgender activism and LGBT activism more generally is the conjuncture of biological essentialism with liberal rights discourse, as in the formulation, "I was born gay/lesbian/bisexual/ transgendered; my sexual orientation and/or gender identity is an immutable characteristic; therefore, I deserve legal rights." Such a formulation cries out for deconstruction, but attempts to bring academicians informed by poststructuralist theory together with activists advocating on behalf of marginalized communities within a political system characterized by a strongly concretized constituency politics do not always bear fruit. The Center for Lesbian and Gay Studies (CLAGS) at the City University of New York (CUNY) often tries to bring academicians together with activists in order to engage in an exchange of insights and perspectives; but such encounters frequently resemble a dialogue of the deaf, with academics speaking a language indecipherable to activists and activists inevitably frustrating their academic brethren and sistren in the queer theory coven as well.

What I would like to suggest, therefore, is that activists and academic theorists do have something to learn from each other. Transgender and LGBT activists would benefit by subjecting their discursive practices to interrogation and deconstruction of a reflective and productive sort; and academics would profit by examining the relevance of their theory construction by talking with activists and policy makers to—in a postpositivist but nonetheless meaningfully "empirical" sense—"test" their ideas in the "real" world and strive for policy relevance where appropriate. Some direct involvement with activism and advocacy work "on the ground" might also help inform theory construction. Not all theory construction need be "relevant" in a direct way, and not all activism need be conceptually sophisticated. But the gulf between theory and praxis in transgender studies resembles a yawning chasm, a veritable Grand Canyon without the scenic beauty.

And that brings me to the third literature of transgender studies, which is the conventional social scientific sort found in scattered bits and pieces in social science journals as well as in publications of LGBT organizations such as the Policy Institute of the National Gay and Lesbian Task Force or units of academic institutions such as the Williams Institute at the University of California at Los Angeles (UCLA). This is a relatively small literature compared with the clinical literature and the queer theory literature, but some of this empirical literature is genuinely policy relevant, even if it is not always as theoretically groundbreaking as the best of the queer theoretic writing. An example of what I mean is a 2007 Policy Institute report titled, "LGBT Youth: An Epidemic of Homelessness" (http://www.thetaskforce.org/reports_and_research/homeless_youth) by Nicholas Ray, which examines the serious problem of homelessness among queer youth in the United States.

Another example of policy-relevant research is a study on "LGBT Health and Human Services Needs in New York State" (http://www.pride-agenda.org/Portals/0/pdfs/LGBT%20Health%20and%20Human%20Service%20Needs%20in%20New%20York%20State.pdf) a report by Somjen Frazer for the Empire State Pride Agenda Foundation and the New York State LGBT Health and Human Services Network. The report, published in 2009, includes sections on specific populations—the transgender community, people of color, youth, seniors, and LGBT families—as well as on policy areas such as mental health care, substance abuse, housing, social support, and violence. Frazer and her colleagues concluded that "Transgender and gender non-conforming people are more likely to experience barriers to healthcare, homelessness, violence and other negative health outcomes." That conclusion will have come as a surprise to no one in the transgender community, much less to transgender activists and advocacy organizations, but a report that makes such findings available to legislators and other policy makers in New York State government is useful in a way that countless peer-reviewed journal articles in *Social Text* never will be. Indeed, the hoax perpetrated by Alan Sokal would not have been possible had the peer-reviewed articles in *Social Text* not made so easy a target for parody.

The stakes here are far higher than the reputation of an academic journal that few outside of academia will have heard of. Law and public policy have a profound impact on all our lives, but because the transgender community is among the most marginalized in this or any society, it is imperative that the deliberations of public policy makers be informed by research and scholarship that is in turn informed by the lived experiences of transgendered and gender-variant people. And it is equally important that the activists and advocacy organizations pursuing an equality agenda both in the United States and abroad engage the public in a way that does not rely on problematic and even counterproductive notions such as are found at the intersection of biological essentialism and liberal rights discourse.

I would like to see us engage the project of transgendering the academy in earnest, and success of that project can only be premised on a transformation of the relationship between theory and praxis. Only when the academy begins to foster public policy and activism in the United States and abroad that is a informed by feminist consciousness and that takes into account the insights of poststructuralist theory without being overly encumbered by institutional imperatives of publication for tenure and promotion can it make a significant contribution to the pursuit of a progressive vision of social justice and social change. As Mahatma Gandhi would say, we must be the change that we seek to make in the world, and that vision of change is what must guide us as we engage in the project that I have called the transgendering of the academy.

Part II

Case Studies

Chapter 5

Creating Systemic Change Around Lesbian, Gay, Bisexual and Transgender (LGBT) Issues

A Case Analysis and Recommendations

Frank D. Golom

In the fall of 2001, the Princeton Review's annual compendium of the best undergraduate colleges and universities in the United States listed the climate at one of its featured institutions as "pretty homophobic" (Franek 2000). That same year, the campus community at this same institution would read two separate "Letters to the Editor" in the student newspaper detailing frightening accounts of antigay harassment in the college's dormitories. By the spring of 2003, however, the environment that at one time implicitly sanctioned and facilitated such homophobia had changed dramatically. Not only would the college's Board of Trustees honor the work of the lesbian, gay, bisexual, and transgender (LGBT) campus organization, but the student body would also elect several openly gay individuals to key leadership positions for the first time in the university's history. How did an institution that had been publicly acknowledged as homophobic only two years prior come to be one of the leading religiously affiliated colleges and universities in the country regarding sexual orientation diversity and sexual minority concerns? How did the initial publication of two letters in a campus periodical end up as an ongoing institutional change effort of significant consequence for all involved? What are the lessons for other higher education institutions struggling with effecting similar pro-LGBT culture change?

The purpose of this chapter is to: (1) explore an LGBT institutional change effort that occurred at a religiously affiliated university in the eastern United States between 2001 and 2004; (2) consider the key features of that effort that ultimately contributed to its success; and, (3) offer lessons and recommendations from this analysis to other institutions interested in bringing about LGBT-affirming change on campus. Conceptually, the chapter is guided by systems approaches to understanding change and transformation (Burke 2011; Gladwell 2000; Senge 1990). These approaches assume that organizations are best understood as complex, living systems composed of interdependent parts, and that fundamentally altered organizational behavior ultimately requires an altered system. From this perspective, the success of any change effort should be directly related to the extent to which those leading it are able to engage the entire organizational system and its culture in their efforts. The case reviewed throughout the chapter is meant to provide an illustration of this point.

This chapter is written for university administrators and other faculty and student leaders who are responsible for and perhaps struggling with systemic, campuswide challenges related to LGBT inclusion and integration. It is not meant as a theoretical review of the organization change literature, neither is it an exhaustive case study of the institutional change effort at its center. Instead, the chapter is meant to serve as one example of a successful transformational effort and as a possible roadmap for future efforts, using both a basic understanding of the organizational literature on change and transformation as well as evidence from a successful LGBT change case.

Structurally, the chapter begins with brief background information regarding the institution in question and the change effort that occurred. The chapter then continues with additional sections devoted to different systems approaches to organizational change that are rooted in the social science literature, but are also are direct, accessible, and in some cases popularly available (e.g., Gladwell 2000). A choice was made to present the change effort in a way that integrates its actual details with relevant conceptual material rather than offering the reader a chronological summary of the effort. It is my hope that doing so will enable readers to link the conceptual with the practical more directly, and to consider the implications of such connections for LGBT change efforts in their own institutions. The chapter ends with a set of recommendations for initiating, leading, and maintaining LGBT organizational transformation efforts in higher education.

LGBT Institutional Change at an Eastern University

Located in the eastern region of the United States, the institution at the center of this case is a liberal arts college with strong ties to Catholic ideals of education and spiritual and personal development. The college's main campus has an undergraduate population of approximately 3,500 students and includes a small number of graduate and professional programs. The institution has paid significant attention during the previous decade to recruiting racially and ethnically diverse students and faculty and infusing the curriculum with multicultural content and diverse pedagogical approaches, and recent evidence suggests some success in these areas. The percentage of minority students and faculty and the number of diversity-related courses offered on campus have increased significantly in recent years, and a frequently cited aspect of the college's mission has become its emphasis on teaching students to lead in an increasingly diverse and global world.

The LGBT Change Effort

The Institutional Context

Although the LGBT change effort occurred in the context of these strategic diversity initiatives, efforts to promote a more positive LGBT campus climate initially took place in spite of rather than as a result of the institution's overall diversity strategy. That is, sexual orientation was originally excluded from formal and informal discussions of diversity, as issues of race and ethnicity received much of the organization's attention and its resources. There are many possible reasons for the fact that the diversity efforts on campus did not initially acknowledge sexual orientation, but it is likely that the organization's overall culture and its relatedness to Catholic orthodoxy were at least partially responsible. That is, as a religiously affiliated institution, the college's deep and surface structures, including its mission, systems and policies, were not originally designed with LGBT individuals and concerns in mind (e.g., spousal benefits). Additionally, societal attitudes toward homosexuality, particularly in the United States, have traditionally been negative (Herek 2000), and despite substantial improvement in such attitudes during the previous decade, there likely exists a significant lag between individual attitude change and culture change at the organizational level. As a result, the college's conservative, Catholic tradition and the infusion of antigay sociohistorical forces resulted in a climate at the institution that was predominantly LGBT-negative in the fall of 2001.

A variety of data, both anecdotal and quantitative in nature, support this claim. First, as previously noted, two very public instances of antigay harassment and violence occurred in the college's dormitories during the fall of 2001. These instances spurred the larger campus community to address LGBT issues directly and even prompted the campus chaplain, a Catholic priest, to write an editorial condemning homophobia as a sin for the student newspaper. Second, documented reports of antigay harassment were at an all-time high by the conclusion of the 2001–2002 academic year and included three incidents involving homophobic graffiti, one involving homophobic language, one involving antigay harassment, and one alarming incident involving an actual physical altercation. Third, a 1996 campus climate survey conducted by the Office of Multicultural Affairs found that "LGBT individuals were treated worse than any other demographic group on campus," and that the treatment of all minorities and individuals of color remained a significant problem (as reported in an internal campus document). Taken together, these events provided further evidence for what the Princeton Review had already concluded. The general climate on campus with respect to LGBT issues was not only "pretty homophobic," it was also hostile and periodically violent.

The Change Goals

Given the aforementioned realities, the ultimate goal of the change effort was to alter the culture at the university regarding sexual orientation diversity and thereby change the intolerant climate experienced daily by its LGBT students, faculty, and staff. Although such an undertaking was by no means simple or straightforward, the change effort began almost instinctively. The series of severe hate incidents on campus had served not only to alert students and administrators to the serious problem of homophobia at the institution, they had also compelled the administration to action. Reactive and punitive policies were put in place by senior-level administrators, including changes to the way sexual orientation hate incidents were reported, prosecuted, and communicated to the campus community. Each of these changes was publicly revealed to students and faculty through appropriate media, thus sending an immediate message with strong behavioral ramifications that homophobic actions would not be tolerated.

Although these and other policy reviews and modifications were complete by the summer of 2002, the efforts on campus to bring about inclusiveness with respect to LGBT issues were far from complete. Dissatisfied with the administrative response to the hate incidents of the previous academic year, members of the LGBT campus organization began to strategize and consider how they too could influence and in some instances lead the organization change process. Of particular concern to these members were the institutional factors that had permitted such homophobic events to occur in the first place and not just reactive policy responses to antigay attacks. For this reason, the LGBT campus organization began to focus on the larger organizational system as the target of its various interventions. As it turns out, not only is such an approach consistent with the existing literature on organization change and transformation (e.g., Burke 2011; Burke & Litwin 1992; Senge 1990), evidence suggests that it may also be partly responsible for the change effort's eventual success. To understand this point more fully, it may be helpful to consider several key features of successful organization change initiatives, including their applicability to the current case.

Key Features of Successful Change Efforts

A review of the literature on change and transformation in organizations suggests that successful change efforts, particularly those that result in fundamental modifications to the organization's culture, have several features in common (see Burke 2011). Four of these features are reviewed below.

Change Is Systemic

First, and perhaps most importantly, successful change efforts are systemic in nature. That is, change is not fully realized unless the underlying organizational system is fundamentally transformed in some way (Burke 2011). A system is defined as "anything that takes its integrity, form and definition from the ongoing interaction of its elements . . . all of which have a common purpose and behave in common ways" (Senge 1990, 137). To that end, organizational systems have structural, functional and behavioral elements that are inextricably linked to one another and are also impacted by the external environment in which the system resides (Burke 2011). Senge (1990) refers to the first of these elements as the systemic structure, which can be defined as "the basic interrelationships that control behavior and translate perceptions, goals, rules and norms into action" in any organization, including hierarchies, information-flows and general decision making processes (40). The functional element, on the other hand, is seen as the long-term patterns of behavior of a given institution that often result from its structural makeup. In short, the functional element is the organization's personality, or response tendencies, at work. Finally, the behavioral element of any system refers to its specific, individual responses to a given situation, including the particular events that comprise its patterns of behavior, and, more simply, its who-did-what-to-whoms.

According to systems theory, the success of any organization change effort rises and falls on the degree to which it addresses the complex, deep structural levels of any institution over its mere behavioral components. From a systems perspective, singular, event-based attempts at organizational transformation (e.g., isolated diversity trainings), though they are most common, are indeed the least likely to lead to success over the long term. Respondents and change agents commit themselves to reactionary stances, treating only the symptoms of a particular occurrence without ever considering its structural cause (Senge 1990). Efforts at the functional and structural levels, on the other hand, are infinitely more effective at creating sustainable change in organizations because they focus on understanding, maneuvering and assessing the systemic causes of particular patterns of behavior rather than on specific instances of the behavior itself. As a result, a structural approach to organization change can have a significant impact on an institution's culture, correcting deeply embedded and undesirable ways of responding and creating the conditions where certain types of events are no longer likely to occur (Senge 1990).

Change Is Both Revolutionary and Evolutionary

The second feature of successful change efforts is based on conceptualizations regarding the "tempo" of organization change (Weick & Quinn 1999). Weick and Quinn (1999), in their review article on the nature of change, characterize this tempo as either episodic or continuous. Episodic change refers to organizational interventions "that tend to be infrequent, discontinuous and intentional . . . and occurs when organizations are moving away from their equilibrium periods" (365). In other words, episodic or revolutionary change is often the result of some unexpected perturbation in an organization's external environment that punctuates its status quo. Continuous change, on the other hand, refers to interventions "that tend to be ongoing, evolving and cumulative. A common presumption here is that change is not only emergent," but that it is also the cumulative result of continued improvements over time (Weick & Quinn 1999, 375). Although fundamental changes in an organization are unlikely to be reached through evolutionary adjustments alone (Burke 2011), factors related to both episodic change and continuous change should be reflected in any successful organizational transformation.

Change Is Both Transformational and Transactional

A third feature of successful change efforts and one intimately related to the revolutionary-evolutionary distinction is the notion that certain organizational factors can be manipulated to bring about either episodic or continuous change. With respect to the former, those related to episodic change are referred to as the transformational factors and include such aspects of the organization as its external environment, mission and strategy, leadership and culture (Burke & Litwin 1992). Adjustments to these factors result in changes to the organization's underlying or deep structure, impacting the entire organizational system as a whole (Burke 2011). Those related to continuous change, on the other hand, are referred to as the transactional factors. These include the organization's structure, management practices, systems and work unit climate as well as individual level factors related to task and job requirements, motivation and employee needs and values (Burke & Litwin 1992). In contrast to the transformational set, adjustments to these factors are unlikely to alter the deep structure of an organization significantly, only bringing about continuous or evolutionary change as a result. Despite the fact that the transformational factors are considered essential for true, deep structure change to occur (Burke 2011), both transformational and transactional factors should be considered in any change and transformation effort. Each set of factors can be manipulated to bring about the type of change desired, be it revolutionary or evolutionary or some combination of the two. Figure 5.1 depicts various transformational

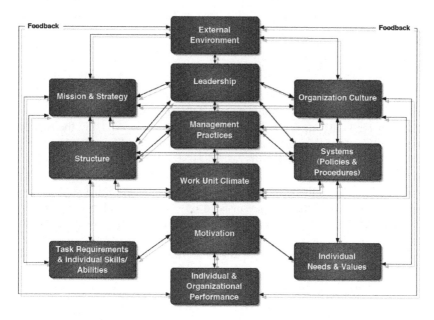

Figure 5.1. Transformational factors include external environment, mission and strategy, leadership, and organizational culture. Transactional organizational factors include structure, management practices, systems, work-unit climate, task requirements and individual skills/abilities, motivation, and individual needs and values. *Source:* W. W. Burke and G. H. Litwin, "A Causal Model of Organizational Performance and Change," *Journal of Management* 18.3 (1992):523–545.

and transactional organizational factors and the interrelationships between and among them (Burke & Litwin 1992).

Change Is Quantifiable

The fourth feature of successful change efforts is the implicit notion that change is and ought to be quantifiable. In any change effort, data should be collected to determine what, if anything, ought to be changed as well as the specific ways in which prospective changes should be implemented and measured. Van de Ven and Poole (1995), for example, describe change as "an empirical observation of difference in form, quality, and state over time in an organizational entity" (512). The present chapter regards change in a similar fashion, and interprets it in the present context to mean an empirical observation of difference in the ways in which LGBT affairs were treated on campus between the years 2001 and 2004. To the extent that a systems framework can be used to quantify these changes, it is not only consistent with Van de Ven and Poole's (1995) emphasis on change as an empirical observation, but also appropriate for viewing the change effort at the center of this paper in quantifiable terms.

Examples from the LGBT Change Effort

As previously mentioned, the LGBT change initiative arose from marked concern regarding the homophobic campus climate and the associated threats it posed for LGBT students. Because that initiative was initially focused on isolated aspects of the college environment (e.g., student life and student code of conduct policies), its ability to create deep structure change in the organization was severely limited. Consistent with the first feature of successful change efforts, members of the LGBT association not only believed that organization change should be systemic, they insisted on it. To that end, these members gradually shifted the college's focus from one that was reactive to one more focused on institutionalizing pro-LGBT efforts. At the organizational level, proposals were drafted calling for the establishment of a resource center for LGBT students as well as an administrative office dedicated to handling LGBT issues. Additionally, the campus association developed a series of normative-reeducative (Chin & Benne 1985) strategic programs aimed at challenging the campus' antigay and hetero-normative culture (e.g., speaking panels, film series, town-hall discussions). In short, the leadership of the campus association seemed to have implicitly recognized what scholars (Burke 2011; Senge 1990) maintain is fundamental: organization change is total system change.

A closer examination of the change effort at the university reveals that the initiative not only became more systemically focused over time, it also included both revolutionary and evolutionary components. To that end, while gradual changes were implemented to make policies, task requirements and job descriptions LGBT friendly, more sweeping interventions aimed at bringing about cultural and attitudinal change also took place. One of the clearest examples of the latter involved the creation of special interest dormitory housing for LGBT and allied students during the 2003–2004 academic year. For this initiative, members of the campus LGBT organization successfully advocated for LGBT students to self-select into housing options that would enable them to live with other LGBT individuals in predesignated locations on campus. Using the safety, psychosocial and developmental needs of sexual minorities to justify such housing, members of the LGBT organization were not only able to bring about its existence, but were also able to convince senior-level administrators, including the university President, to support the initiative publicly.

Taken together, these efforts provide a clear illustration of integrating revolutionary and evolutionary change and also reflect the idea that any successful change effort should address both transformational and transactional organizational factors. For example, the LGBT association's emphasis on altering the college's deep structure dovetailed into an explicit consideration of the institution's various transformational aspects, including its culture, diversity mission and strategy and its leadership. In one particular initiative, a public relations campaign was developed to identify publicly those faculty, staff, and administrators who were receptive to and supportive of LGBT concerns. Another intervention involved successfully advocating for "sexual orientation" to be included in the diversity section of the university's undergraduate educational aims. This latter initiative was particularly transformative in nature, as it affected the institution's overall educational mission and its academic culture in symbolically profound ways; the study of sexual orientation was officially recognized as a legitimate aspect of diversity education at a Catholic university.

In addition to these and other transformational strategies, the change effort also focused on transactional factors to improve LGBT individuals' daily experiences of campus climate. Consistent with the notion that transformational factors relate most closely to culture change while transactional factors are associated with climate (Burke & Litwin 1992), the campus' LGBT leaders developed a series of social and educative programming opportunities aimed at meeting the individual, motivational and developmental needs of sexual minority students. For example, in the period in question, the LGBT organization developed weekly meetings and activities to recruit, retain, and motivate new members, with other campus offices quickly following suit. Peer counseling and support groups were developed for LGBT students struggling with sexual identity issues, and the Office of Multicultural Affairs began to include LGBT-themed content into its recommended diversity readings. Consistent with the features of successful change initiatives, these and other interventions not only became more commonplace as the change effort progressed, they also began to have an impact on several quantifiable outcomes. By the end of the 2004, for example, openly LGBT individuals held a number of leadership positions within and across the college's campus organizations and departments.

Consistent with the proposition that change is quantifiable, other individual and organizational markers of the change effort can be noted as well. With respect to the former, the overall number of out LGBT-identified students increased during the change period, as did membership in the LGBT organization. Some ten or twenty members strong in the fall of 2001, the association had grown nearly tenfold by the spring of 2004, with somewhere between 125 and 150 members on its e-mail distribution list. Additionally, reports from the Office of Student Life documented a dramatic decrease in the number and severity of hate incidents between the 2001 and 2002 and 2003 and 2004 academic years, and the Office of Multicultural Affairs reported an increase in LGBT programming and visibility. With respect to organizational markers of the change effort, the two most noteworthy were the establishment of an LGBT resource center and the previously mentioned creation of special interest housing for LGBT students. In addition, not only were the college's nondiscrimination policy and undergraduate educational aims modified to include "sexual orientation" during this period, but the Princeton Review finally removed its assessment of the campus as "pretty homophobic" as well.

The Tipping Point

Systems approaches to organization change are particularly good at describing the "what" and "why" aspects of change more explicitly than they describe the "when" and the "how." In other words, content is explicitly considered (e.g., transformational and transactional factors; Burke & Litwin 1992), but process with respect to implementation remains unaddressed. The purpose of the next section of this chapter is to better explain how organization change occurs by considering the role of social networks and tipping points (Gladwell 2000) and examining their applicability to the current case.

What Is a Tipping Point?

According to Gladwell (2000), a tipping point refers to the precise moment in a social movement "when everything can change all at once" (9). More specifically stated, it refers to the point at which a small change-effort becomes a widespread epidemic. Through countless case examples and documented research investigations, Gladwell suggests that the tipping of any social epidemic is a function of three specific factors, namely, the types of individuals involved in spreading the change, the nature of the change itself, and the larger context in which the change is occurring (18). As the author (2000) notes, "when an epidemic tips, when it is jolted out of equilibrium, it tips because something has happened, some change has occurred in one (or two or three) of these areas" (18–19). If one considers organization change as a form of social epidemic, understanding these factors should have important ramifications for its planning and implementation.

The law of the few. The first rule of epidemics to which Gladwell refers is the "Law of the Few." Simply stated, the "Law of the Few" maintains that social epidemics are partially a function of the individuals responsible for transmitting some change message. Classified as connectors, mavens or salespeople, these individuals are said to have "particular and rare sets of social gifts" needed to tip any epidemic (Gladwell 2000, 33). Connectors, for example, are responsible for bringing disparate individuals and groups together and are important for both the number and type of people they know with respect to the spreading of a social epidemic. Mavens, on the other hand, are responsible for sharing critical knowledge necessary for an epidemic to take root (Gladwell 2000). As Gladwell writes, they are important to the beginning of any change effort because as information specialists, "mavens know things the rest of us do not" (67). In a similar fashion, salespeople can encourage things the rest of us cannot as well. Responsible for mass persuasion, they are so important to the notion of the tipping point because they often compel others to join social movements and act accordingly. Together with connectors and mavens, salespeople represent those few exceptional individuals capable of starting any epidemic.

The stickiness factor. The "Law of the Few" suggests that "one critical factor in epidemics is the nature of the messenger" (Gladwell 2000, 91). In much the same way, "the Stickiness Factor" suggests that there are aspects of the message itself that are equally as important. One such aspect is the message's "stickiness," or contagiousness. In short, certain messages and epidemics are innately capable of tipping and spreading while others are not. Gladwell discusses a variety of aspects that dictate an epidemic's stickiness, including but not limited to different forms of communication as well as the use of a narrative or story (Burke 2011).

The power of context. Just as the nature of the message is as critical to an epidemic as the nature of the messenger, so too is the context in which the message occurs. Gladwell refers to this notion as the "Power of

Context." Simply stated, this third and final rule of epidemics reflects Lewin's (1951) formula that behavior is a function of the person and his or her environment. Precisely because situational factors often exert as powerful if not more powerful influences on human behavior than dispositional variables, small environmental changes can have a significant impact on the ability of any given social epidemic to tip. Citing anthropological research to suggest that group size is one such factor, Gladwell maintains that "if groups are to serve as incubators for contagious messages, they have to remain below the 150 Tipping Point" (182). When group size grows beyond 150, individuals' capacity to maintain genuine social relationships is overwhelmed (for more information, see Gladwell 2000).

Additional Examples from the LGBT Change Effort

Taken together, the Law of the Few, the Stickiness Factor, and the Power of Context offer a unique perspective with which to analyze the LGBT change effort, particularly with regard to planning and implementation. While the features of successful change efforts were helpful for understanding the content of the change and ultimately why it was so effective, Gladwell's notion of the tipping point addresses how the change happened so quickly and why it occurred when it did. Simply stated, the right individuals with the right message and at the right time came together to promote a change that spread virally across the campus.

Examining each social epidemic rule more closely, the "few" who were responsible for the change initiative illustrate quite well Gladwell's theory of connectors, mavens and salespeople. In particular, the advisers to the LGBT association executed a unique combination of these roles. For example, one faculty member, in part because of his seniority, was capable of connecting and bringing together various individuals at all organizational levels and persuading them to participate in the change process. Another was so knowledgeable with respect to LGBT issues that he offered scholarly justification for the change in a way that no one had been able prior to 2001. Together with a team of campus salespeople, these individuals possessed the extraordinary social gifts needed to communicate the change message and tip the epidemic for the better.

As for the message, one factor that enabled it to stick as well and as long as it did was the fact that the entire LGBT change effort was couched within the college's Catholic values. Almost obsessively, campus leaders consistently linked LGBT inclusion with the institution's stated mission of teaching students to lead in an increasingly diverse and global world. By deliberately using Catholic notions as service, charity, and caring for others, the change message made it clear that transforming the campus climate was not only necessary from a student development or employee engagement perspective, it was also the morally right course of action.

Additionally, the Princeton Review assessment and the public discussion of antigay harassment in the campus newspaper appear to have significantly primed the campus for the change effort that followed. Consistent with Gladwell's notion of the "Power of Context," these very minor events made the college environment ripe for change. Without the very public discussions that would ensue, it seems highly unlikely that the change effort would have ever become as contagious as it did. Further, had the size of the LGBT campus organization not been between 125 and 150 members, its ability to successfully communicate the change message may have been limited (Gladwell 2000). Instead, genuine social relationships between and among LGBT individuals were capable of being achieved, thereby creating a critical mass that could both demand and drive the ensuing change effort.

Recommendations for Effecting Change Around LGBT Issues

A close examination of the change effort in question suggests that other institutions struggling with homophobia and heterosexism consider both the content and process of the change effort in predictable and systematic ways. By integrating the actual details of the case with the conceptual approaches discussed thus far (e.g., systems and social epidemics), this chapter concludes with specific, tangible recommendations for effecting culture change with respect to LGBT issues in higher education.[1]

Recommendation 1: Manipulate the Context by Creating a Strong Sense of Urgency

One of the more tacit pieces of learning from the case and one that is rather consistent with our current understanding of change is the importance of establishing a sense of urgency around the change effort. As Burke (2011) points out, organizations often do not change unless the challenges presented by their current state of affairs become greater than the fear and other restrictive emotions that often follow any proposed change effort. In other words, urgency creates movement and movement, if deliberately captured and catalyzed, can fuel momentum. Urgency, movement, and momentum are also intricately related to Gladwell's ideas related to the power of the larger context in which the change effort occurs. Simply stated, vegetation cannot grow where soil remains untilled and unfertile. Creating a sense of urgency prepares the larger context and organizational environment so that any proposed change effort can take root in the first place.

Creating a sense of urgency may be most easily established by attending to changes in the organization's external environment, its current culture, or its overall leadership and mission. As the case suggests, urgency is a revolutionary, not evolutionary, phenomenon, and thus its production is likely created by attending to or exposing the transformational factors that scholars (Burke & Litwin 1992; Senge 1990) maintain are most closely associated with organization change. Particularly for those higher education institutions that historically have been less than LGBT or diversity-friendly, manipulating the context to support the desired change effort is paramount to all else.

Recommendation 2: Harness and Channel Momentum by Developing a Compelling Vision for the Change Effort that Sticks

If it is not directed toward a particular end state or goal, the energy generated by disequilibrium in a social system is potentially harmful and also increasingly difficult to maintain (Katz & Kahn 1978). Developing a guiding vision for the change effort, however, ensures that the urgency and movement created at the beginning of any change process can help to frame and advance the organization's larger change goals rather than become a counterproductive force. Additionally, a clear vision also serves to remind those involved of the exact purpose of their efforts and acts as a superordinate goal around which disparate parties can organize and toward which they can work. To that end, although urgency is itself a necessary condition of any change effort, it is insufficient for galvanizing and directing individual and organizational stakeholders. In order to be productive, it must be quickly accompanied by a compelling vision that directs movement and momentum toward the larger change objectives.

Developing a compelling vision for change may most easily be established by attending to the overall mission of the organization and integrating the change goals into its larger strategic initiatives. For example, although LGBT issues were initially unaddressed by the college's diversity strategy, the purpose of that strategy was consonant with the overall objectives of the change effort. Said another way, the ensuing vision for LGBT-related change was embedded in a larger and more integrated attempt to increase diversity across various aspects of campus life and in accordance with the university's Catholic values. By utilizing the language of those values and the specific elements of that diversity strategy, the LGBT change effort over time developed a vision or change narrative that Gladwell would likely consider "sticky."

Recommendation 3: Involve the Right People to Communicate and Reinforce the Vision

Once the desired end state of any change initiative is developed, the next step with respect to implementation is to communicate that end to those directly affected by the change effort as well as those whose support and endorsement are critical to its success. With respect to the former, Burke (2011) stresses that an important way to minimize individual resistance to any change effort is to ensure that those affected understand clearly what will not change for them, in addition to what will. As the case illustrates, members of the LGBT community were likely able to push for an increasingly sophisticated series of change initiatives partly because of a tacit knowledge that, although progress could be slowed, given the violence associated with the start of the change effort, it likely would not be reversed. With respect to the latter, the communication of any change effort ought to consider key individuals in the organization whose formal and informal roles assist them in the spreading, supporting, and selling of any given social epidemic or movement (Gladwell 2000).

The easiest way to ensure that the vision is communicated clearly, actively, and engagingly to all parties is to attend to the organization's formal and informal leadership as well as to the individual needs and values of those directly affected by the change effort. As the case suggests, while focusing on both informal and formal leadership increases the likelihood that the organization's connectors, mavens and salespeople will tip the change effort toward the desired end state, focusing on individual needs and values increases the likelihood that those affected remain connected to the change and supportive throughout the change process. This latter point is particularly important, as the creation of a critical mass is needed for any culture change effort to be successful, particularly one as revolutionary as an LGBT change effort on a Catholic campus.

Recommendation 4: Align Day-to-Day Organizational Life with the New Vision (and Stop Behavior that Interferes with that Alignment)

A compelling vision for a change effort is useful insofar as it directs individual attitudes and behavior toward the change goal, but abstract visions in and of themselves are unlikely to produce appreciable changes in the organization's culture given their largely esoteric and distal position relative to individuals' daily workplace experiences. This is particularly true if individual behavior remains dissonant with the new vision, even after the change effort has launched. For this reason, it is important in any change process to intervene at a tangible level so that individual behavior reflects the vision and values the organization wishes to implement.

Aligning everyday organizational behavior with the new vision is likely best achieved by adjusting the organization's management practices and policies as well as the specific task requirements of various jobs and organizational roles. For example, an immediate consequence of the antigay harassment reported during the 2001 to 2002 academic year was a series of procedural changes to the way hate incidents were documented, adjudicated, and reported to the larger campus community, which in effect communicated that bias against LGBT students would not be tolerated by university officials. Additionally, the inclusion of LGBT-related student development responsibilities in various administrators' job descriptions ensured that individuals were for the first time deliberately addressing or encountering sexual orientation issues in their day-to-day work activities. Thus, the new vision was repeatedly and consistently behaviorally reinforced at all organizational levels.

Recommendation 5: Independently Sustain and Institutionalize the Vision

A potential challenge of revolutionary social epidemics is that they are frequently attached to persons, events and narratives that cannot be easily replicated (Gladwell 2000). For example, one of the initial catalysts for the change effort was a series of specific hate incidents experienced by two of the undergraduate students on campus. As a result, the ensuing vision for change was somewhat fueled by specific crisis events and not necessarily by a cross-section of priorities from various campus stakeholder groups. Should such events become less entrenched in both organizational and individual memory, their ability to drive the change effort will likely be attenuated. Institutionalizing various change initiatives such that they cannot be attached to any one person or event is therefore critical to their continued success.

Sustainability and institutionalization can occur by attending to those aspects of organizational life that are not dependent on any one individual, including the organization's structure and systems. To that end, the creation of an LGBT resource center, the inclusion of sexual orientation in the undergraduate curriculum aims and the development of special interest housing for LGBT students all represented attempts at institutionalizing the new vision and embedding it within the college's existing structure, policies and procedures. Each of these efforts was not necessarily sufficient for the continued forward momentum of the change effort, but the structural embeddedness of the new vision did ensure that the consequences of the change were largely permanent in nature.

Recommendation 6: Orchestrate, Reward, and Celebrate Small Successes

Burke (2011) notes that one of the reasons change efforts often fail is that their momentum frequently cannot be sustained over time. A potential mechanism for remedying such tenuous momentum is to plan and execute periodic strategic victories related to the change initiative that are both small in scope and also likely to have significant impact (Sturm, 2006). That is, achieving "small wins" (Weick 1984) can serve to reinforce the goals of the change effort at various levels of the organization while simultaneously motivating those involved to continue working toward the larger strategic objective. Psychologically, such motivation is a critical component of individual and organizational performance and capacity-building (Burke & Litwin 1992).

Increased motivation is most likely achieved by orchestrating strategic victories related to campus climate and individual needs, values, and job requirements. To that end, many of the previously mentioned initiatives included event-based programming that targeted individuals' daily experience of the campus and encouraged the imagination of a more inclusive institutional environment. Such programming was also frequently and consistently acknowledged and celebrated by sexual minority individuals and by the community at large. For example, during the 2002 to 2003 academic year, a series of events were staged to commemorate the eighth year anniversary of the LGBT campus association. Of little significance substantively, the yearlong celebration served as a clear sign of the organization's documented success. It also played an important role in influencing perceptions of the LGBT climate on campus and keeping motivation and institutional progress at the forefront of individuals' organizational experience.

Recommendation 7: Evaluate, Titrate, and Recalibrate the Change Effort

Organizations frequently engage in various people and institutional development initiatives without clearly documenting and demonstrating their actual effectiveness (Saari et al. 1988). To that end, Burke (2011) identifies measurement and evaluation as a key area for further development with respect to the understanding and practice of organization change. As he notes, successful change efforts should be as data-based as possible, both as a mechanism for generating objective information in support of a pending change and also as a means of tracking progress and establishing additional implementation steps. Simply stated, to engage in a planned change effort without evidence of its development or effectiveness is wasteful and potentially harmful to the organization and its members.

A key assumption of most organizational theory and research is that improvement in individual and organizational performance, broadly defined, should be the end goal of most workplace interventions. As a result, although the assessment of any one organizational factor could be used to evaluate and recalibrate a change initiative, it is ultimately the relationship between that factor and individual and organizational functioning that is most indicative of a successful change effort. With respect to the case, such performance data were continuously collected and communicated to those involved in the change effort, including annual reports from the Office of Student Life regarding the frequency and severity of hate incidents on campus as well as such external assessments of the campus climate as the one provided by the Princeton Review. Additionally, data were often considered when determining the next steps of the change process, particularly with respect to whether the organization would be welcoming of or resistant to a pending intervention.

A complete list of all seven recommendations can be found in table 5.1.

Table 5.1. Recommendations for Effecting Institutional Change Around LGBT Issues

Recommendation 1:	Manipulate the context by creating a strong sense of urgency.
Recommendation 2:	Harness and channel momentum by developing a compelling vision for the change effort that sticks.
Recommendation 3:	Involve the right people to communicate and reinforce the vision.
Recommendation 4:	Align day-to-day organizational life with the new vision (and stop behavior that interferes with that alignment).
Recommendation 5:	Independently sustain and institutionalize the vision.
Recommendation 6:	Orchestrate, reward, and celebrate small successes.
Recommendation 7:	Evaluate, titrate, and recalibrate the change effort.

Conclusion

The purpose of this chapter was to describe, analyze and learn from one university's successful attempt at LGBT inclusion and integration on campus. It is my hope that those reading it have gained a broad view of how change occurs in organizational settings, a clear example of the change process as it applies to LGBT issues in higher education and a set of conceptually based action steps that can be used to guide other, similar efforts. To the extent that more rigorous study is needed to understand the nature of LGBT institutional change and integrate it with the existing social science literature, I also hope that the chapter has stimulated future work in this area. Improving the experience of LGBT individuals on campus depends on a deeper understanding of how change and progress can and ultimately should happen.

Note

1. These recommendations are similar to those proposed by Kotter (1998) and Burke (2011).

Works Cited

Burke, W. W. *Organization Change: Theory and Practice*, 3rd ed. Thousand Oaks, CA: Sage Publications, 2011.

Burke, W. W. and Litwin, G. H. (1992). "A Causal Model of Organizational Performance and Change." *Journal of Management* 18.3 (1992): 523–545.

Chin, R. and Benne, K. D. "General Strategies for Effecting Changes in Human Systems." In W. W. Burke, D. G. Lake, and J. W. Payne, eds., *Organization Change: A Comprehensive Reader*. San Francisco: Jossey-Bass, 1985, 89–117.

Franek, R. *Best 331 Colleges*. Princeton, NJ: The Princeton Review, 2000.

Gladwell, M. *The Tipping Point: How Little Things Can Make a Big Difference*. Boston: Little, Brown, 2000.

Herek, G. M. "The Psychology of Sexual Prejudice." *Current Directions in Psychological Science* 9 (2000): 19–22.

Katz, D. and R. L. Kahn, *The Social Psychology of Organizations*, 2nd ed. New York: Wiley, 1978.

Kotter, J. P. "Leading Change: Why Transformation Efforts Fail." *Harvard Business Review on Change*. Boston: Harvard Business School Press, 1998.

Lewin, K. *Field Theory in Social Science*. New York: Harper, 1951.

Saari, L. M., T. R. Johnson, S. D. McLaughlin, and D. M. Zimmerle. "A Survey of Management Training and Education Practices in U.S. Companies." *Personnel Psychology* 41 (1988): 731–743.

Senge, P. M. *The Fifth Discipline: The Art and Practice of the Learning Organization.* New York: Doubleday, 1990.

Senge, P. M., A. Kleiner, C. Roberts, R. Ross, G. Roth, and B. Smith. *The Dance of Change.* New York: Doubleday, 1999.

Sturm, S. "The Architecture of Inclusion: Advancing Workplace Equality in Higher Education." *Harvard Journal of Law and Gender* 29 (2006): 248–333.

Van de Ven, A. H., and M. S. Poole. "Explaining Development and Change in Organizations." *Academy of Management Review* 20 (1995): 510–540.

Weick, K. E. "Small Wins: Redefining the Scale of Social Problems." *American Psychologist* 39 (1984): 40–49.

Weick, K. E. and R. E. Quinn. "Organization Change and Development." *Annual Review of Psychology* 50 (1999): 361–386.

Chapter 6

Network VA

A Case Study of a Statewide Effort to Build LGBTQ Coalitions for Change on College Campuses

Charles H. Ford and Elizabeth P. Cramer

In recent years, Virginia's campuses have come a long way in recognizing the rights and potentials of their LGBTQ (lesbian, gay, bisexual, transgender, and queer) stakeholders, and a catalyst in this unprecedented change has been Network Virginia, a loose, statewide association of the Old Dominion's LGBTQ faculty and staff. Like most reform groups, Network Virginia emerged in 2006 against a stark backdrop of oppression: the hate crimes statute did not include sexual orientation or gender expression; no employment nondiscrimination law covered LGBTQ persons; the Crimes Against Nature law from 1896 was still on the books; and a law was in force prohibiting "civil unions, partnership contracts, or other arrangements between persons of the same sex purporting to bestow the privileges or obligations of marriage" (Equality Virginia 2008, 9). Indeed, a far-reaching marriage amendment to the state's constitution passed by referendum in the fall of 2006, which stated that a valid marriage was between one man and one woman and that similar arrangements between same-sex partners were null and void. Around this same time, too, efforts had been made by Virginia's General Assembly to pass a bill that would have prohibited lesbians and gays from adopting children and a bill that would have discriminated against gay-straight alliances in schools. Partners of LGBT persons who attempted to visit their loved one in hospitals were being blocked from seeing them. Of course, this type of official and legal discrimination came from the same well of poisoned traditions that had maintained slavery and Jim Crow. Virginia had been at the forefront of "massive resistance" to public school desegregation in the 1950s, and it had banned interracial marriage until the U.S. Supreme Court struck down that state law.

Despite this seemingly forbidding landscape, Virginia's college campuses proceeded to go in the opposite direction toward inclusion and respect. By 2005, most public and private colleges and universities had successfully campaigned to include sexual orientation in their institution's nondiscrimination policies, even if none at that time had added gender identity and expression; Safe Zone/Ally programs and LGBTQ student and/or employee organizations were at the largest research universities; and a few of these relatively elite schools had established LGBTQ resource centers. Only a handful of private institutions, of course, featured domestic partner benefits for same and/or opposite sex unmarried partners.

An incident at one of the flagship research universities at the turn of century gave hope for further progress: the case of Karen DePauw and Shelli Fowler, a dual-career academic couple. In 2002, both women had been hired at Virginia Polytechnic Institute and State University (Virginia Tech). After a secret e-mail was sent to conservative members of the Board of Visitors, the Board, in a closed session at its June 2002 meeting, approved all hires on the faculty personnel list except for Shelli Fowler. Following this, collective actions began. A group of faculty created and circulated a petition that was forwarded to the Board of Visitors prior to their November meeting. A group calling itself, Justice for Tech, began a letter-writing campaign. A group of faculty and student activists protested at the November Board of Visitors' meeting. A letter by the American Association of University Professors was sent to the president and to the board condemning the board's actions, and the Chronicle of Higher Education and Virginia newspapers gave coverage to the incident. Eventually, Shelli Fowler was able to obtain a new permanent contract at Virginia Tech (Fowler & Depauw, 2005). Along with discriminatory hiring incidents, there was anecdotal evidence of LGBTQ employees who were leaving Virginia higher education institutions to take positions at colleges and universities in states with more progressive policies and practices.

The time around 2005 and 2006 seemed ripe for harnessing the dissatisfaction and energy of LGBTQ students and employees. While there were many examples of individual campus policies and programs to foster a more welcoming and inclusive campus climate for LGBTQ persons, there was not an ongoing statewide network to address common concerns across most, if not all, of Virginia's college campuses. There had been a few attempts to hold occasional summits, and college students held an annual statewide LGBTQA conference (originally called Virginia Organizations Uniting Together or VA OUT and then called Generation Equality); however, there was not one organization that brought together LGBTQA students, faculty, staff, administrators, and community allies until Network Virginia's emergence in 2006. This article describes and critiques an attempt to bring these stakeholders together for collective political and social activism on Virginia college campuses.

Diversity and LGBTQ-Focused Campus Organizing

There is a growing body of literature on campus organizing around diversity issues in general (for example, American Association of Colleges and Universities 2008; Chesler 2004; Clayton-Pederson et al. 2007; Kezar et al. 2008; Wade-Golden & Matlock 2007), and LGBTQ organizing more specifically (for example, Alvarez & Schneider 2008; Draughn, Elkins, & Roy 2002; Estanek 1998; Finkel et al. 2003; Garber 2002; Meyer 2004; Sausa 2002; Wallick & Townsend 1997). Less common are publications that feature examples of coordinated interinstitutional, regional, or statewide efforts to improve the campus climate for diverse populations. In one example, Clements (1999) describes diversity initiatives at two campuses of a community college system to expose students to differing races, cultures, and religions. Following the diversity initiatives, out of twenty-two items ranked by graduating students in a survey, becoming aware of people different from them in philosophy, culture, religion or way of life was ranked fourth in importance to respondents. In another example, eight higher education institutions in New Jersey were selected to be part of the New Jersey Campus Diversity Initiative (NJCDI) funded by the Bildner Family Foundation in partnership with American Association of Colleges and Universities (AAC&U) and The Philanthropic Initiative. The goals of the project were to decrease prejudice, encourage intergroup understanding, and enact institutional change. As part of the four-year initiative, the institutions received assistance from AAC&U through capacity strengthening meetings, site visits, and the distribution of diversity resources. While the meetings offered opportunities for intercampus exchange of ideas, it appears that the projects enacted by participating institutions were separate rather than a coordinated, collective state effort (American Association of Colleges and Universities 2010).

National Organizing Efforts to Improve
the Campus Climate for LGBT Persons

Several researchers and national organizations have been involved in bringing awareness to campus climate issues for LGBTQ students and employees. One vehicle for this awareness-building is formal assessments of campus climate for LGBTQ students and employees (for example, Gonyea & Moore 2007; Rankin 2003; Rankin et al. 2010; Sherill & Hardesty 1994). The climate assessments over time have shown enduring themes around the concerns and challenges of LGBTQ students, faculty, and staff, even though there has been some improvement in a few areas. Most recently, Campus Pride's 2010 State of Higher Education for LGBT People (Rankin, 2003), delineates several troubling areas, including that LGBTQQ[1] students, faculty, and staff (N = 5,149 from all 50 states) were "much more likely than their counterparts to consider leaving their institution because of experiencing or fearing physical and psychological harassment, discrimination, and violence related to their sexual identity" (Rankin 2010, 2), and most LGBTQQ student respondents reported that they experienced harassment, isolation, and fear while on their campuses. Suggestions for improving the campus climate for LGBTQQ persons in the report included: inclusive policies that welcome LGBTQQ students and employees; commitment to integrate LGBTQQ concerns throughout the institution, including inclusive wording in documents and strong responses to acts of intolerance; integration of LGBTQQ issues in the curriculum and cocurriculum; creation of spaces for student dialogues; comprehensive and LGBTQQ sensitive counseling and health care; and concerted efforts to recruit and retain LGBTQQ students and employees.

Scholars, national LGBTQ political organizations, and academic associations have noticed these reports of the chilly campus climate for LGBT persons and their straight allies, and they have made higher education a focus of their work. In the 1990s, the National Gay and Lesbian Task Force produced a manual to assist organizing efforts on campuses (Shepard, Yeskel, & Outcalt 1995); one of the earlier books on working with LGBT college students was published (Sanlo 1998); and another book on overcoming heterosexism and homophobia was in print, which included chapters focused on academic disciplines (Sears & Williams 1997). Today, several national LGBTQ political groups include campuses as one of their priority issues. The Human Rights Campaign has a youth and campus outreach program, which includes a list of scholarships for LGBT students as well as their own Generation Equality Scholarships awarded annually to LGBT students and allies who have shown an exceptional commitment to promote equality (Human Rights Campaign 2010). The National Gay and Lesbian Task Force still promotes its campus organizing guide and holds an annual Creating Change conference and an Academy for Leadership and Action (National Gay and Lesbian Task Force 2010). The National Black Justice Coalition encourages leadership in Historically Black Colleges and Universities (HBCUs) to create inclusive and safe campuses for LGBT students (National Black Justice Coalition 2010). Finally, the American Association of University Professors' (AAUP) Committee on Sexual Diversity and Gender Identity oversaw the completion of the "Harvesting the Grapevine" project, which featured a scholarly expert, Dr. Lori Messinger then at the University of Kansas (now at University of North Carolina at Wilmington), and her team of interviewers documenting the experiences of faculty and staff members on a variety of campuses who had successfully secured LGBTQ-inclusive nondiscrimination policies or domestic partner benefits. For an overview of the project's making and its conclusions, see Messinger (2009).

These are just a few of the examples of scholars and national political and academic organizations that have been working to improve the campus climate for LGBTQ students and employees. The specific political, social, and cultural contexts in Virginia, along with the growing awareness of campus climate issues for LGBTQ persons nationally, then provide the backdrop for the evolution of the Network Virginia project. The history, purpose, structure, and projects of the initiative will be described in the next section.

Historical Overview of Network Virginia

Network Virginia stemmed from a partially funded grant preproposal. In April 2005, a meeting of statewide LGBT leaders was held at Virginia Commonwealth University, and one of the items on the meeting's agenda was an announcement about the Difficult Dialogues competition put forth by the Ford Foundation. Martin Snyder and Ruth Flower of the national AAUP presented the information about the guidelines and parameters of the solicited preproposals, which were supposed to be about finding reasonable strategies to foster civil debate between different and differing groups on college campuses. Snyder and Flower were quickly joined by Elizabeth Cramer (Social Work) and Janet Winston (English) of Virginia Commonwealth University and Charles H. Ford (History) from Norfolk State University, who, alongside the national AAUP representatives, would contribute to making of the preproposal, which contained an array of ambitious curricular and cocurricular suggestions on how to reflect on and evaluate LGBTQ issues on Virginia's college campuses. The biggest roadblock on our way to success, however, was not a dearth of needs or ideas, but rather it was the Ford Foundation's sensible requirement that institutions commit themselves fully to these Difficult Dialogues by way of a presidential signature on the preproposal's package of documents. The group was unable to get this simple signature from either the head of Virginia Commonwealth University or Norfolk State University because both administrations rightly feared the wrath of legislators and newspapers opposed to gay rights and on the opposite side in the perpetual culture wars.

The story may have ended there, but the people involved thought it was imperative to continue. They asked Snyder of the AAUP to draw on his contacts as a former college president to keep the preproposal alive; Snyder thus went ahead to persuade his friends at the Ford Foundation to consider the group's preproposal without a specified lead agency. This lenience was allowed because it was expected that the group should go out and find a friendly sponsor. Here Snyder convinced Hollins University, a private women's college in Roanoke, Virginia, to become the group's lead institution; Hollins had put forth its own preproposal in the first round that had been turned down, and the faculty members behind that effort, eagerly embraced the chance to work with very different campuses. That summer, the core group, in conjunction with the interested Hollins faculty members—LeeRay Costa (anthropology), Jennifer Boyle (English), and eventually Darla Schumm (religious studies) drafted the full proposal via conference calls and one face-to-face meeting at the Thomas Jefferson Center for Free Expression in Charlottesville. This full proposal featured an array of ambitious projects that ranged from scripting a documentary film on LGBT lives to sponsoring intercampus faculty learning communities on LGBT studies through digitizing important local documents of LGBT history in Virginia held by campus archives, and it was finally submitted in October 2005. Although the full proposal was not accepted entirely by the Ford Foundation, Snyder and the others did learn that they had won $10,000 of the $100,000 for which they had asked.

The intercampus group then decided to use that stipend to launch the Network Virginia: building LGBTQ Coalitions for Change on Campus conference, which was ultimately slated for March 3, 2007 at the University of Virginia's Newcomb Hall in Charlottesville. In preparation for the Conference, the group members clarified the goals of their evolving Network Virginia and tried to set up an interactive website complete with annotated bibliographies and external links. While work on the website always lagged due to personal time crunches and institutional priorities, the following ambitious goals have remained as testimony to the high hopes of the original group members: (1) to build sustainable, professional ties between LGBTQ faculty, staff, and students on Virginia campuses of higher education; (2) to overcome cross-cutting allegiances of race, gender, class, and region that may hinder LGBTQ solidarity within the Old Dominion; (3) to facilitate difficult dialogues among LGBTQ academics and their allies in Virginia about potential strategies and priorities in the ongoing fight for legal equality; and (4) to use and to disseminate anti-oppressive pedagogy as a tool in the making of progressive coalitions in our Commonwealth. Our intended stakeholders seemed to appreciate these goals. This conference, held on a Saturday right before the University of Virginia's spring break, was well attended with eighty-one registrants from all over the state with faculty, staff, students, and community activists represented. The biggest boost in publicizing the conference came from the national AAUP. The July–August 2006 issue of Academe, which focused on the difficult dialogues initiatives, contained an article by Janet Winston, who eloquently explained why she had to get involved with this endeavor in her essay, "Difficult Silences."

At the Charlottesville gathering, the schedule included plenary speakers, Karen DePauw and Shelli Fowler from Virginia Tech University, and morning and afternoon break-out sessions. Each morning break-out session focused discussion on the first three of Network Virginia's four stated goals, while the afternoon sessions came up with practical measures to translate those goals into meaningful steps on their individual campuses. An informal reception rounded out the day's events. People tended to stay all the way through to the end, and discussions continued into the hallways of Newcomb Hall.

After the gathering, the core group had Elizabeth Cramer's graduate assistant, Trenette Clark, to complete an assessment of responses to an evaluative survey distributed at the conference. The survey results found that the conference's program and activities satisfied most attendees, with 93.2 percent appreciating the opportunity to connect with others across Virginia's campuses. In their survey responses, about 45 percent of the attendees also noted a boost of confidence and energy toward their own LGBTQ activism already in progress. The core group went on to analyze and to develop the action steps put forth by the afternoon sessions. Cramer would go on to represent the unique multicampus initiative at the Difficult Dialogues' national meeting at the Ford Foundation headquarters in New York City in September 2007.

Faculty turnover and institutional shifts then led to changes for Network Virginia after its big day of March 3, 2007. Janet Winston had relocated to Humboldt University in California even before the Charlottesville Conference, and the Hollins faculty members no longer wanted the responsibility of sustaining the project after the grant cycle ended. Accordingly, in August 2007, Network Virginia's lead agency changed from Hollins University to the University of Virginia, which led to the website changing sponsors, too. A new Advisory Board was named in January 2008 with core members Elizabeth Cramer and Charles H. Ford included, and that board had its first face-to-face meeting at the Thomas Jefferson Center for Free Expression in Charlottesville in March 2008. Future annual face-to-face gatherings would be held in conjunction with the Generation Equality student conferences in March 2009 and March 2010. Its most significant spinoff was one of the first intercampus faculty learning community in the nation, "Addressing Issues of Diversity and Oppression in the Classroom," which engaged groups of faculty members from Virginia Commonwealth University and Norfolk State

University to grapple with issues of pedagogical inclusion and diversity. For some of the participating faculty members, this was the first time that they had considered how to include LGBT issues and studies into their syllabi (Cramer, Ford, & Arroyo, 2012).

Despite these successes, Network Virginia has ceased to have a formal institutional presence largely because of the lack of formal institutional support. The University of Virginia never fully embraced their role as lead agency, and they gladly handed off the torch to Virginia Commonwealth University. This was fine initially. Indeed, in June 2011 at Virginia Commonwealth, Network Virginia held a successful one-day workshop, "And Justice For All: A Faculty-Staff Symposium on Sexual Orientation and Gender Identity in Policies and Procedures at Virginia's Colleges and Universities." Sue Rankin of Pennsylvania State University's School of Education, a leading expert on campus environments for LGBT peoples and for transgender people in particular, was the plenary speaker, and the conference organizers held concurrent sessions in both the morning and afternoon. Promising local initiatives such as the making of Old Dominion University's Gay Cultural Studies Endowment campaign and Virginia Commonwealth University's recent hiring of a LGBTQ coordinator in the Division for Inclusive Excellence were highlighted. But commitment to a formal structure for the group declined even at Virginia Commonwealth, as local campuses and the national scene began to improve their services and inclusion of LGBT issues and peoples. But even now there is still a need for statewide action, and Network Virginia has made it easier to galvanize the right people. In the fall of 2013, the e-mail list of the last board members—which had representatives from nine campuses and which had five staff members and four faculty members—has proven useful in getting faculty senates to endorse and to replicate the domestic partners resolution passed by the Faculty Assembly of the College of William and Mary.

Analysis of Network Virginia's Strengths and Limitations

Network Virginia has had its share of both successes and failures over its five years of existence. The Charlottesville Conference helped to rekindle enthusiasm among the already committed and allowed diverse campuses to compare notes and to share news of events. More concretely, the coincident panels with Generation Equality in 2009 and 2010 helped to spread practical advice about achieving curricular inclusion of LGBTQ content as well as to have students appreciate the different histories of activism on different campuses in Virginia. Its biggest success was the intercampus learning communities on "Addressing Issues of Diversity and Oppression in the Classroom," sponsored jointly by Virginia Commonwealth University and Norfolk State University. For the

2009–2010 academic year, faculty learning communities on both campuses examined and debated articles and books on pedagogical diversity and inclusion via a wiki and two face-to-face meetings—one in Richmond and one in Norfolk (Cramer, Ford, & Arroyo 2012). The most lasting contribution of Network Virginia, however, was its growing potential as a sounding and bulletin board of information about statewide events, problems, and accomplishments. Even though our webpage seemed to be perpetually under construction, our Facebook page was getting an increasing volume of traffic between its establishment in 2009 and before the advisory board became dormant in 2012.

The biggest obstacle for Network Virginia remained the degree of institutional as opposed to individual commitment. The initial problem of finding a lead agency became permanent; the commitments of Hollins University and the University of Virginia turned out to be temporary and situational. If there is to be a succeeding organization to Network Virginia, then it must insist on memoranda of understanding from participating institutions that specify the expectations and support needed to sustain a intracampus effort . . . This lack of commitment was most reflected in our forlorn web page, which still was never updated by University of Virginia staff These unresolved questions about Network Virginia's home base accelerated the exit of core group members and their successors: by 2011, only Charles H. Ford remained on the Advisory Board out of the original core group. Finally, the detailed mailing list from the Charlottesville Conference became outdated, due to student graduation and faculty migration. Connections with student groups especially had to be constantly renewed and nurtured from scratch, requiring infusions of both energy and time that only a strong institutional rather than individual effort could make.

Network Virginia's uneven development confirms the findings of scholars interested in studying what they have called "interorganizational collaboratives" (Foster-Fishman, Nowell, & Yang 2007; Foster-Fishman et al. 2001). Frequent communications via conference calls and the stalwart commitment of the AAUP via Martin Snyder greatly contributed to the successful buzz around the making of the Charlottesville Conference. Yet other components of collaborative success—"trust in follow-through" and "legitimacy" have been sorely lacking due to the continuing lack of institutional commitment to the endeavor. Momentum and synergy were lost in part because of the perceived lack of permanence or formalized structure of the organization. Thus, systemic or institutional changes directly tied to Network Virginia could not be made, even if the project helped to launch other collaborative projects. In other words, communicating about LGBTQ-related events and happenings have become the most important accomplishment of the group rather than specific policy changes tied to its advocacy. Finally, recent research has questioned whether or not a formalized structure of authority for "interorganizational collaborative" is necessary for mission success (Nowell 2009). Network Virginia's board had always been a committee of equals in which everyone pitched in to do assigned tasks. From the beginning, it did not want to privilege representatives from traditional bastions of white elites: the last thing that Network Virginia wanted to do was to replicate the entrenched inequities inherent in the Old Dominion's institutions. Thus, it was the lack of institutional support rather than the lack of a formalized chain of command that has hampered its effectiveness. (Nowell 2009)

Recommendations for Statewide Collaborations in Other States

From these successes and failures, many lessons have been learned, and a few recommendations can be put forth. The Facebook page, administered by individual board members, was much easier to update and to reach intended audiences than a web page via an institutional host. More fundamentally, sustaining interest in the network must be done, but it is difficult to do so: while conferences are booster shots, no one enjoys the diplomacy and logistical work than goes into implementing the ideas generated by these exchanges of ideas. And, one always runs into the risk of preaching to "the choir" who already have their connections and opportunities laid out for them. Yet, the stunning events of March 2010 with the state Attorney General's retrograde opinion on existing LGBTQ rights on campuses reinforces the need for such a network, despite the stunning gains made at all higher education institutions in the last few years. Cuccinelli's notorious opinion to undermine the nondiscrimination statements of most campuses, while swiftly swatted down, shows the precariousness of these gains and the consequent need for campuses to unite together against any further attempts to turn back the clock. Partnering with other campus advocacy groups such as the AAUP then would be the primary recommendation for similar groups in other states thinking of embarking on the same path. Using conference calls and Facebook pages would be the other recommendation to improve communication between the interested parties. An intercampus faculty learning community is another suggestion for other academic collaboratives. And, finally, gaining real institutional support is absolutely necessary for getting funding and for keeping the network alive long after the core group may have moved on.

Informed by the growing literature on organizing around diversity on college campuses and national efforts to improve campus climate for LGBTQ persons, this case study offers a contextual analysis of the reasons for the formation of a statewide, LGBTQ focused collaborative of higher education institutions in Virginia. Examples of the projects in which the collaboration engaged over a six-year period were offered. A critique of the successes and challenges in our work, informed by the literature on interorganizational collaboratives, was provided. While there is much demonstrated need for coordinated, multi-institutional efforts to combat homophobic cultural and political attacks against LGBTQ persons, the realities of organizing across institutions, securing institutional buy-in, and sustaining leadership in the core group, limit the impact of Network Virginia, and other similar endeavors.

Acknowledgments

A related, briefer essay about Network Virginia was published in the American Association of University Professors' news magazine, Academe, in 2011. The essay can be found at http://www.aaup.org/AAUP/pubsres/academe/2011/SO/Feat/cram.htm.

Note

1. LGBTQQ is defined in the report as Lesbian, Gay, Bisexual, Transgender, Questioning, and Queer

Works Cited

Alvarez, S.D., and J. Schneider, J. "One College Campus's Need for a Safe Zone: A Case Study." *Journal of Gender Studies* 17.1 (2008): 71–74.

American Association of Colleges and Universities. Bildner Family Foundation New Jersey Campus Diversity Initiative, 2010 (accessed September 24, 2010), http://www.aacu.org/bildner/index.cfm.

American Association of Colleges and Universities. *More Reasons for Hope: Diversity Matters in Higher Education,* 2010 (accessed September 24, 2012), http://www.aacu.org/resources/diversity/index.cfm.

Chesler, M. "Confronting the Myths and Dealing with the Realities of Diversity and Multiculturalism on Campus." *Diversity Factor* 12.3 (2004): 5–12.

Clayton-Pederson, A. R., S. Parker, D. G. Smith, J. F. Moreno, and D. H. Teraguch. *Making a Real Difference with Diversity: A Guide to Institutional Change.* Washington, DC: AAC&U Publications, 2007.

Clements, E. "Creating a Campus Climate that Truly Values Diversity." *About Campus,* 4.5 (1999): 23.

Cramer, E. P., C. H. Ford, and A. Arroyo. "An Account of an Inter-Institutional Faculty Learning Community on Addressing Issues of Diversity and Oppression in the Classroom." *Learning Communities Journal* 4 (2012): 5–35.

Draughn, T., B. Elkins, and R. Roy. "Allies in the Struggle: Eradicating Homophobia and Heterosexism on Campus." In *Addressing Homophobia and Heterosexism on College Campuses*, ed. E. P. Cramer. New York: Haworth Press, 2002, 9–20.

Equality Virginia. *Virginia and Its Laws*. Powerpoint presentation, Virginia Commonwealth University, Richmond, VA, 2008.

Estanek, S. M. "Working with Gay and Lesbian Students at Catholic Colleges and Universities: A Student Affairs Perspective." *Catholic Education* 2.2 (1998): 151–158.

Finkel, M. J., R. D. Storaasli, A. Bandele, and V. Schaefer. "Diversity Training in Graduate School: An Exploratory Evaluation of the Safe Zone Project." *Professional Psychology: Research & Practice* 34.5 (2003), 555–561.

Foster-Fishman, P. G., B. Nowell, and W. Yang. "Putting the System Back into Systems Change: A Framework for Understanding and Changing Organizational and Community Systems." *American Journal of Community Psychology* 39.3 (2007): 197–215.

Foster-Fishman, P. G., D. A. Salem, N. A. Allen, and K. Fahrbach. "Facilitating Interorganizational Collaboration: The Contributions of Interorganizational Alliances." *American Journal of Community Psychology* 29.6 (2001), 875–905.

Fowler, S. B., and K. P. Depauw. "Dual-Career Queer Couple Hiring in Southwest Virginia: Or, the Contract that Was Not One." *Journal of Lesbian Studies* 9.4 (2005): 73–88.

Garber, L. "Weaving a Wide Net: The Benefits of Integrating Campus Projects to Combat Homophobia." In *Addressing Homophobia and Heterosexism on College Campuses*, ed. E. P. Cramer. New York: Haworth Press, 2002, 21–28.

Gonyea, R., M. and J. V. Moore. "Gay, Lesbian, Bisexual, and Transgender Students, and Their Engagement in Educationally Purposeful Activities in College." Paper presented at the annual meeting of the Association for the Study of Higher Education, Louisville, KY, November–December, 2007, (accessed March 16, 2014), http://cpr.iub.edu/uploads/GLBT%20and%20Engagement-%20ASHE%202007.pdf.

Human Rights Campaign "*Generation Equality Scholarships*," 2010,(accessed September 25, 2010), http://www.hrc.org/issues/youth_and_campus_activism/12264.htm.

Kezar, A., P. Eckel, M. Contreras-McGavin, and S. J. Quaye. "Creating a Web of Support: An Important Leadership Strategy for Advancing Campus Diversity." *Higher Education* 55.1 (2008): 69–92.

Messinger, L. "Creating LGBTQ-Friendly Campuses." *Academe* (September–October 2009).

Meyer, M. D. " 'We're Too Afraid of These Imaginary Tensions': Student Organizing in Lesbian, Gay, Bisexual and Transgender Campus Communities." *Communication Studies* 55.4 (2004),: 499–514.

National Black Justice Coalition. *About the National Black Justice Coalition*, 2010, (accessed September 25, 2010) http://www.nbjc.org/about/.

National Gay and Lesbian Task Force. *The Issues: Campus*, 2010 (accessed September 25, 2010), http://thetaskforce.org/issues/campus.

Nowell, B. "Profiling Capacity for Coordination and Systems Change: The Relative Contribution of Stakeholder Relationships in Interorganizational Collaboratives." *American Journal of Community Psychology* 44.3-4 (2009): 196-212.

Rankin, S. R. *Campus Climate for Gay, Lesbian, Bisexual and Transgender People: A National Perspective.* Washington, DC: The Policy Institute of the National Gay and Lesbian Task Force, 2003.

Rankin, S. R., G. Weber, W. Blumenfeld, and S. Frazer, S. *2010 State of Higher Education for Lesbian, Gay, Bisexual & Transgender People.* (Executive Summary). Charlotte,NC: Campus Pride, 2010.

Sanlo, R. L. *Working with Lesbian, Gay, Bisexual, and Transgender College Students.* Westport, CT: Greenwood Press, 1998.

Sausa, L. A. "Updating College and University Campus Policies: Meeting the Needs of Trans Students, Staff, and Faculty." In., *Addressing homophobia and heterosexism on college campuses,* ed. E. P. Cramer. New York: Haworth Press, 2002, 43-55.

Sears, J. T., and W. L. Williams, eds. *Overcoming Heterosexism and Homophobia: Strategies That Work.* New York: Columbia University Press, 1997.

Shepard, C. F., F. Yeskel, and C. Outcalt. *Lesbian, Gay, Bisexual & Transgender Campus Organizing: A Comprehensive Manual.* Washington, DC: National Gay and Lesbian Task Force Policy Institute, 1995.

Sherill, J., and C. A. Hardesty. *The Gay, Lesbian, and Bisexual Students' Guide to Colleges, Universities, and Graduate Schools.* New York: New York University Press, 1994.

Wade-Golden, K., and J. Matlock. "Ten Core Ingredients for Fostering Campus Diversity Success." *Diversity Factor* 15.1 (2007): 41-48.

Wallick, M. M., and M. H. Townsend. "Gay and Lesbian Issues in U.S. Medical Schools: Climate and Curriculum." In *Overcoming Heterosexism and Homophobia: Strategies That Work,* ed. J. T. Sears and W. L. Williams, eds. New York: Columbia University Press, 1997, 299-325.

Chapter 7

The One-Year Campus-Climate Turnaround

The University of Rhode Island Strives to Become a Leader in LGBTQ Advocacy[1]

Karen de Bruin

As a small state university located in rural Kingston, just fifteen minutes from Narragansett Beach and three minutes from the closest farm, the University of Rhode Island (URI) is not very used to unsolicited national attention, which is why it came as such a surprise in March 2011, when URI was featured in the headline story of the Chronicle of Higher Education: "For Gay Students, More Room on Campuses."[2] While the headline read positively, the ensuing article, largely dedicated to a history of lesbian, gay, bisexual, transgender, and queer (LGBTQ) life on the URI campus, read, at times, the contrary.[3] "Students in the university's GLBT community are fed up with what they describe as their marginalization," reported Sara Lipka. And, indeed, this "marginalization" had historical precedent. Andrew Winters, the retired director of the LGBTQ Center at URI, explained to the Chronicle that between 1995 and 2000, the Princeton Review ranked URI twice in the top ten most homophobic campuses in the nation. The advent of a LGBTQ Center changed all of that. With one fell swoop, URI left the top ten and joined The Advocate College Guide for LGBT Students one hundred most welcoming institutions in 2006. As if an LGBTQ Center with virtually no operating budget and housed "on the ground floor of an unsought dormitory at the University of Rhode Island, in two conjoined rooms" were enough to counter the homophobic slurs and threats endured by the director and students brave enough to live openly their LGBTQ lifestyle. Bolstered by long-fermented anger, when the new URI president, David M. Dooley, asked a pastor with antigay leanings to speak at his inauguration in the Fall of 2010, the students took matters of discrimination into their own hands: they staged an overwhelmingly successful sit-in at the university library. How did this showdown end? As a model for universities nationwide to follow.

Rapid and sweeping climate-change is possible. However, it requires courage and almost simultaneous commitment from all three constitutive parts of a university: the students, the faculty/staff, and the administration. And each constituency plays a very specific role. Often, as is the case here in Rhode Island, the students are the initial impetus behind the change because they are the most directly affected by a hostile environment. By virtue of their numbers, they can build a critical mass of emotional charge around LGBTQ climate issues. However, due to their relatively short stay at a university, this momentum built by students can very quickly dissipate. Faculty and staff must drive the change because they interface directly with students, they understand the workings of the university, and they represent longevity. Finally, it takes a truly good-faith administration, one willing to reexamine what it means to be committed to each and every one of its students and employees, in order to implement changes. In the case of the University of Rhode Island, as highlighted by the article in the Chronicle of Higher Education, the students ignited the dynamite that had lain dormant for so many years. However, it was a result of the complementary and continuous efforts of the administration and the faculty that the campus climate changed so dramatically over the ensuing twelve months, to the point where in the fall 2011, the new LGBTQ Presidential Commission hosted its first faculty and staff mixer to which Miss Kitty Litter, Rhode Island's legendary drag queen was invited. Needless to say, even a year prior, this event would have been quite simply impossible.

In this article, I will chronicle the exceptional collaborative efforts taken by the students, faculty/staff, and administration of University of Rhode Island to transform the campus *in one year* from apathetic at best with regard to LGBTQ climate to one that strives to be a leader in LGBTQ advocacy nationwide. I will highlight the student demands that set the university into action, the rise of the LGBTQ Presidential Commission and its university plan, and the administration's unequivocal commitment to support climate change. In this article, I will furthermore provide the full LGBTQ report drafted by the Presidential Commission as well as excerpts of the written responses to the report penned by President David Dooley. As such, this article is written with the intention to provide administrators, faculty/staff, and students with tools to emulate the exemplary initiatives and steps taken by the University of Rhode Island community to institutionalize change.

Student Demands and the Rise
of the LGBTQ Subcommittee

Although the library sit-in orchestrated by fed-up LGBTQ students marked a tide-changing moment with regard to attention paid to LGBTQ issues on campus, the subject of hate crimes had been centrally situated on the administration's radar since the "Stop the Hate" silent protest in November 2008. In response to a spate of racial and religious slurs, student activists garnered the attention of the then-president, Robert Carothers. In December 2008, President Carothers formally instated the Equity Council, which has as its mission, "to advocate, promote and sustain diversity and equity throughout the entire university community."[4] However, it wasn't until the second major student protest on campus, namely the library sit-in, that the Equity Council, supported by the new provost and the new president, formally made the decision to create the LGBTQ Subcommittee to the Equity Council. This LGBTQ Subcommittee would pick up on and expand the following demands made by the "bright, courageous [student] leaders," as Provost Donald DeHayes called them, namely:

a. The creation or purchase of a new, freestanding, sufficiently spaced GLBT Center.

b. The publication of resources available to students for the reporting and action to be taken for biased and hate crimes.

c. Mandatory training for RAs on LGBTIQQ issues and how to be sensitive to students who bring up these concerns.

d. Compensation for GLBT center student staff equal to that of the RAs.

e. A substantial increase in the budget for Gay, Lesbian, Bisexual, and Transgender Programs and Services that covers the costs associated with the programs and operations . . .[5]

While the LGBTQ Subcommittee would take on the bulk of the campus-climate analysis, its assessment of issues related to the LGBTQ community and its propositions for solutions could have fallen on deaf ears. However, fall on deaf ears this work did not. Quite the contrary, from the very moment that the students captured the president and the provost's attention with the above-mentioned demands, the administrators shifted LGBTQ concerns to the top of their agenda. Of the sit-in, President David Dooley stated the following:

I want to acknowledge the courage and perseverance of the LGBT students. The students were constructive throughout the week and did a magnificent job in educating the broader campus community about issues of mutual respect, difference, and the true meaning of creating a campus community. Enhancing diversity, equity, and community at URI is one of the premier goals for our institution, and one of the prominent goals of the University's new academic plan.[6]

Provost Donald DeHayes echoed: "With these agreements, the student sit-in ends, and our critically important work to stop hate and bias moves to another level at URI. Both sides have made a commitment to work together. Students will be actively involved, as the University continues to make progress in working toward a campus climate that is safe and free of harassment and discrimination."[7] The vice president of Student Affairs, Tom Dougan, affirmed: "The sit-in has raised our level of awareness of the concerns and sentiment of the students, helping us more clearly understand their frustrations and priorities."[8] And when the Chronicle headline story came to the attention of President Dooley in March 2011, he made a powerful public statement on his presidential blog, claiming:

I suppose it could be argued that such a high-profile presentation of the issues, problems, and progress at the University of Rhode Island is not the most advantageous publicity for the university. I would disagree. Many of you have heard me say that one cannot solve problems while trying to hide them, or by pretending they don't exist. You can only solve a problem by acknowledging that it is real and marshaling the resources needed to resolve it. That is what we are doing at the University of Rhode Island, and we will continue to confront the problems of intolerance and mistreatment of our GLBT students until we succeed in building a community where all of our members are welcomed, affirmed, and supported. As pointed out in the [Chronicle] article, that will take time and will not completely eradicate all incidents of bias or hate. But I think we can succeed in building a community where all our members can say "I fit in; this is a place where I can be myself."

As President Dooley duly noted above, to solve the campus-climate problem, it would take resources. And marshal the resources to meet the students' demands, the president and the provost's offices certainly did. Their first move was to appoint an interim chief diversity officer, a position for which the Equity Council had been lobbying since its inception. They immediately summoned the funds to fulfill the students' demand for a new LGBTQ Center. In the Fall of 2014, the prominent entrance to the URI campus will be the home to this new LGBTQ Center, designed from the ground up to accommodate the needs of the ever-expanding community. In addition, the center has been attributed a new full-time coordinator position with a substantial increase in operating budget. As of spring 2012, Housing and Residential Life, in conjunction with the LGBTQ Center, implemented mandatory (and very successful) resident adviser (RA) and resident academic mentor (RAM) trainings. (An unintended consequence of these mandatory trainings for RAs and RAMs was that student leaders from different halls, on their own initiative, sought out the LGBTQ Center for further informal training.) Finally, to meet all of the student demands, the administration advertised widely, and also through RA and RAM training, the existence of the Bias Response Team to which any and every member of campus is highly encouraged to report acts of bias and crimes of hate.

While the president and provost could have just settled to meet the students' demands, they both chose to go far above and beyond. They immediately enlisted all administrators, ranging from the vice president of Student Affairs and the director of Athletics to the deans of all colleges, in their campuswide effort to build an open and affirming climate for the LGBTQ community. To demonstrate immediately to the students and the faculty/staff their commitment to this community, they actively promoted and participated in highly visible events such as the second Stop the Hate demonstration (under the pouring rain) and the "It Gets Better Project" (which over 1,000 students attended!). They awarded openly gay leader of the pharmaceutical industry and URI alum, Paul Hastings, with the University of Rhode Island's Diversity Award for Lifetime Achievement. And their biggest move was to charge the LGBTQ Subcommittee of the Equity Council with drafting a plan to institutionalize their commitment to support and equitable treatment of all LGBTQ members of the university community. It is this institutionalization of change at the faculty and administrative levels that I will discuss now.

The Institutionalization of Change

In January 2011, a call went out to appeal to faculty and staff interested in serving on the newly conceived LGBTQ Subcommittee to the Equity Council. From the inception of the LGBTQ Subcommittee, Interim Chief Diversity Officer Kathryn Friedman wisely called on members to be the "architects" of a plan to change campus climate, and she emphasized that the execution and the institutionalization of the plan would fall to her office and the Provost's Office. This precision of roles from the outset proved to be invaluable because it relieved the enthusiastic faculty and staff's fear of a disproportional increase in workload. With the knowledge that our role was that of architects, we, faculty and staff leaped into action. The co-Chairs of our LGBTQ Subcommittee were Lynn McKinney, dean of the College of Human Sciences and Services and a self-identified gay man, and Ann Morrissey, special assistant to the provost for Academic Planning, self-identified ally to the LGBTQ community, and expert in the field of leadership and organizational development. Spearheaded by the combined leadership and organizational-development expertise of both these leaders, the LGBTQ subcommittee, composed of twenty-three members (faculty, staff, and student leaders, both LGBTQ and allies) set off to lay the groundwork for its mission.

At the first meeting of the LGBTQ subcommittee, we decided to divide ourselves into three task groups: (1) Equality of Rights and Benefits, (2) Education and Awareness for URI, and (3) Safety and Health. Each task force would meet regularly throughout the spring semester of 2011 to work on findings and recommendations for the interim CDO, which she would then pass on to the president. Each task force had a Chair who recorded the minutes of the meetings and forwarded them on to the subcommittee co-Chairs. During the general meetings of the LGBTQ subcommittee, the task-force Chairs would report on most recent findings and recommendations. At the end of one semester of hard work, each task-force Chair compiled a final list of findings and recommendations that the co-Chairs put together into a report titled, "URI Subcommittee on LGBTIQQ of the URI Equity Council Findings and Recommendations, April 11, 2011."

The final report was organized around three goals: (1) "Realize equity in the benefits and policies related to the URI LGBTIQQ community members"; (2) "Significantly expand the awareness and sensitivity of the university community so that it reflects a LGBTIQQ-friendly community that celebrates and embraces diversity and equity"; and (3) "Ensure that the best possible mechanisms are in place for the safety and health of LGBTIQQ community members." This report was first submitted to interim CDO Kathryn Friedman who then shared it immediately with URI President David Dooley. The LGBTQ subcommittee received a written response from the president who thoughtfully addressed each recommendation, and which began with a sincere thanks to each member of the subcommittee. It is the LGBTQ Subcommittee's report and the president's responses to this report that I will share now.

The first of the three goals and related recommendations in the "Findings and Recommendations" report pertained specifically to union contracts and Human Resource administration.

Goal 1: Realize equity in the benefits and policies related to the URI LGBTIQQ community members.

Findings[9]

1. Language varies widely across union contracts regarding the benefits accorded to LGBTIQQ employees, their domestic partners and children of domestic partners in comparison to language addressing those afforded to spouses and children of spouses.

2. Administration of benefits by HR is somewhat equitable but the communication that benefits may be available to LGB-TIQQ staff is not consistent across various vectors for getting the word out.

Recommendations

1. Letter to President Dooley recommending language changes to unions' contracts to ensure equality of benefits to all URI staff

   Specific areas of language change include:

   a. Nondiscrimination clause to include impermissible basis of discrimination (sexual identity, sexual orientation, gender identity and expression, and HIV status)

   b. Sick, family and bereavement leave—definition of "immediate family" to include domestic partners, their children and family (e.g., partner's parents, grandparents, etc.). Family leave—parental leave, immediate family care or serious illness

   c. Health insurance—domestic partners and their dependent children eligible equally to spouses and children of spouses

   d. Tuition waiver—to include domestic partners and their dependent children

   e. Postretirement health insurance

   In addition—recommend that policy changes regarding benefits are adopted by the University in three areas:

    a. Parental leave: change from maternal and paternal leave to leave for parental reasons (birth, adoption) and provide for equal access to benefits across unions, including paid leave

    b. Postretirement health benefits: include domestic partners on parity with spouses

    c. Taxation of health benefits for domestic partners: university to remunerate employees who opt for health benefits for their domestic partners and/or their children, thus achieving relative economic parity with nontaxation of spouses

2. Communicate widely the benefits that are available to LGBTIQQ staff and their domestic partners

Specifically:

    a. During benefits sign up

    b. During new employee orientation

    c. Establish sessions for existing employees

    d. Link on multiple websites to a comprehensive list of benefits available to LGBTIQQ employees: HR; GLBT Center; associate vice president for community, equity, and diversity; union websites (e.g., ACT/NEA. AAUP, etc.)

In response to this first goal, President Dooley acknowledged the recommendations for "consistent contractual language" and specified that these modifications would have to be made "at the state level and through contract negotiations."[10] In order to facilitate the negotiations with regard to LGBTQ-friendly contract language, President Dooley mobilized the assistant vice-president for Human Resources to work on the committee's behalf.[11] With regard to the taxation issue, President Dooley recognized that this was a "system, legal and collective bargaining issue," and affirmed that he would discuss the recommendation with the board and "report their response." Finally, pertaining to the wide communication of benefits, President Dooley responded that he had already instructed the vice president for Finance and Administration as well as the assistant vice-president for Human Resources to advertise "in a timely manner" benefits available to LGBTIQQ staff and their partners per our recommendation.[12]

The second of the three goals and the related findings focused primarily on education and outreach. Issues deemed particularly problematic included the existing "Welcome Project" (see below), the lack of sufficient funding to the GLBT Center, the lack visibility and support of LGBTQ faculty/staff, and the general feeling of isolation in the LGBTQ community.

Goal 2: Significantly expand the awareness and sensitivity of the university community, so that it reflects a LGBTIQQ-friendly community that celebrates and embraces diversity and equity.

WELCOME PROJECT

Findings

1. Currently, Welcome Project Stickers can be obtained by: attending a Welcome Wednesday or any other Welcome Project event at the GLBT Center; or by arranging a discussion with a Welcome Project or GLBT Center representative. The sticker is an active symbol of support for the LGBTIQQ community, people, families, and friends and by posting this sticker publicly demonstrates one's dedication to the Welcome Project and the LGBTIQQ community.

Recommendations

1. Establish a formalized process for URI faculty and staff to receive a Welcome Project Sticker to ensure that those who receive the sticker are well equipped to assist students. The University of Denver's educational modules can serve as a guide to create sticker trainings taking into consideration URI's culture and needs.

Findings

2. There is much enthusiasm and dedication to increase LGBTIQQ programming, education, and awareness on campus.

Recommendations

2.1. Plans should be developed for more extensive programming and any potential existing funding sources should be tapped as well as grants and other potential funding sources (proposals for funding to divisional heads, grants, and explore possible funding source areas, including URI Foundation, alumni relations, businesses, and grants).

2.2. Create a process for faculty, staff, and students to request funding to attend conferences.

2.3. Ensure that the professional staff at GLBT Center is sufficient to ensure continuing programmatic success.

FACULTY AND STAFF SUPPORT

Findings

3. Presently there are no organized events or groups for LGBTIQQ faculty or staff. Due to this lack of programming there are no structured opportunities for faculty and staff to network, provide support, and share resources. Faculty and staff have expressed interest in opportunities to meet LGBTIQQ faculty and staff in casual and fun environments.

Recommendations

3.1. Organize events for LGBTIQQ faculty and staff to provide a venue to connect with colleagues across the university.

3.2. Develop a network in which faculty and staff can obtain information about events as well as share information with each other.

3.3. Develop and expand opportunities for faculty, staff, and alumni to become involved in LGBTIQQ programming, mentoring, and advocacy work.

COLLABORATION

Findings

4. Currently there are limited opportunities for interaction and sharing between marginalized groups on campus. At present there are a handful of events including: I AM URI Retreat, November URI Community Diversity Project 2010, Diversity Awards Banquet, Diversity Week, Stop the Hate Vigil, and Pangaea Festival. These groups, programs, and events allow the opportunity for people of all races, identities, nationalities, cultures, and creeds, to come together and begin to share a common vision of the world. These opportunities give individuals the chance to know that although there may be differences among them, there are also commonalities and interests that can bring them together.

Recommendations

4.1. Create a more comprehensive Diversity Calendar with greater visibility. Utilize a system where multiple points of access can easily connect all the groups so that individuals can more readily learn about each other and their events. A system that can merge together flyers, newsletters, polls, and so on, and have them available to view online or on a portable device such as a cell phone will allow individuals to take program information with them everywhere they are on campus and encourage them to get involved with what is going on.

4.2. Develop more opportunities for groups to collaborate, support, and learn from each other (i.e., committees, retreats, and trainings).

LGBTIQQ SYMPOSIUM

Findings

5. For seventeen years the university has hosted an annual symposium on gay, lesbian, bisexual, transgender, intersex, queer,

and questioning issues. This symposium covers an array of topics through panels, presentations, and workshops. An opportunity exists to expand the symposium's visibility and amplify its impact on the campus community or to consider how to strengthen the impact of the symposium by reconfiguring it.

Recommendations

5.1. Create a board of faculty, staff, and students to work with the GLBT Center to develop the optimal and most influential series of programs, which may include the symposium and other large- and smaller-scale events. Possible board members could include the Alumni-LGBTIQQ Group and LGBTIQQ Committee Members, collaboration with other student and faculty groups.

5.2. Investigate and articulate plans for funding these events and an effective communication plan for all events to elicit the broadest degree of participation.

5.3. Assess and evaluate the effectiveness of these programs to inform future programming.

EDUCATION

Findings

6. It is unclear how present LGBTIQQ topics/concerns are in the URI curriculum and how prepared faculty are to incorporate LGBTIQ issues.

Recommendations

6.1. Assess what LGBTIQQ topics are being discussed in the classroom and develop processes whereby curriculum can be reviewed for LBTIQQ content.

6.2. Develop a curricular team to work on infusing LGBTIQQ topics where appropriate.

6.3. Develop professional development for faculty about LGBTIQQ issues.

EXTERNAL PARTNERSHIPS

Findings

7. Currently in Rhode Island there are many groups that focus on LGBTIQQ topics.

Recommendations

7. Develop new partnerships with LGBTIQQ groups in Rhode Island that will allow our students to be able to create broader networks.

Expand alliances with other RI Institutions looking for opportunities for programming collaborations and group trainings.

President Dooley had many positive responses to the findings and recommendations related to the second of the three strategic goals. First and foremost, he elevated the LGBTQ Subcommittee to the Equity Council to that of a Presidential Commission that will continue to work toward awareness, sensitivity, and equity pertaining to LGBTQ issues. It will furthermore serve as a consultative board to which the LGBTQ Center will report. To address the problematic Welcome Project, he instructed the chief diversity officer to work with the LGBTQ Center and LGBTQ Presidential Commission to develop educational modules for faculty and staff. He, furthermore, charged her with the identification of sources of funding for more extensive programming, the submission of at least two grant proposals for the 2011–2012 academic year, and the communication of progress to the LGBTQ Presidential Commission. To show support of the LGBTQ Center and its expanded educative purview and in addition to the newly created and funded coordinator position for the LGBTQ Center, President Dooley also considerably increased the center's operating budget. With regard to the findings and recommendations pertaining to faculty and staff support and campus collaboration, President Dooley was quite clear in stating that "creating and expanding community is . . . one of the three missions for the CDO." He thus charged the CDO position to work with the LGBTQ Center and the LGBTQ Subcommittee to "implement social-networking events, communication and opportunities for faculty and staff to participate in LGBTQ programming, mentoring and advocacy work." He furthermore instructed her "to make collaboration, support events and mutual learning between groups one of the Division's priorities for the Academic Year 2011–2012." Pertaining to the recommendation for universitywide education with respect to LGBTQ issues, the president stated that he was already working with the dean of the School of Human Sciences and Services, Lynn McKinney, "to pilot a faculty development program . . . to assist faculty to explore their curriculum and learn about LGBTIQQ issues and knowledge creation," and he stated that he had asked the provost and CDO "to become involved and to assist and support faculty" with this initiative. In addition, he recommended that the newly elevated LGBTQ Presidential Commission work with the LGBT Center "to optimize and improve the effectiveness of the Center, including the Symposium." Finally, with regard to external partnerships, the president stated that he had instructed the CDO to work both with the LGBT center and the LGBTQ Presidential Commission to "expand current external partnerships and develop new opportunities for collaborations."

The last of the three goals, namely, to "Ensure that the best possible mechanisms, protocols, and interventions are in place for the safety and health of the LGBTIQQ community members," entailed evaluating the assessments of climate issues and structures currently available, and suggesting ways to improve existing facilities.

GOAL 3: Ensure that the best possible mechanisms, protocols, and interventions are in place for the safety and health of LGBTIQQ community members.

CAMPUS CLIMATE RELATIVE TO SAFETY AND HEALTH FOR LGBTIQQ MEMBERS

Findings

1. We have not found any current (within the past 2 academic years) URI-conducted assessments of climate issues relative to the safety, health, and well-being of LGBTIQQ community members.

Recommendations

1. Regular assessment of the university's campuses climate is an important and necessary process to understand the safety and well-being of the environment for the LGBTIQQ community.

Specifically:

A. Electronic Snap Surveys or brief ten question surveys (quizzes) to which the URI community may respond should be regularly utilized to determine comfort levels of diverse students on a range of issues.

B. Periodic targeted focus groups should be conducted of different populations of LGBTIQQ (students, alumni, faculty, staff) to help assess the climate relative to their safety and wellness.

C. Any relevant national survey data should be monitored, internally reported, and considered when attempting to understand the university climate for LGBTIQQ community members.

UNISEX, NEUTRAL RESTROOMS THROUGHOUT THE UNIVERSITY

Findings

2. No comprehensive listing or database was available for these types of facilities.

The subcommittee developed a comprehensive resource guide . . . which identifies the campus buildings on the campuses of Kingston and GSO, where such facilities are located. The listing includes the building managers' names, telephone number, and the number of restrooms with the specific locations . . . In all, on the Kingston campus, there are thirty-seven buildings and sixty-seven restrooms on the Kingston campus, which contain gender neutral/unisex facilities. Included in this list is a building with a family restroom and a faculty-only restroom. There are no such facilities at CCE.

Recommendations

2.1 Update and make widely available the resource listing of gender-neutral restrooms and facilities recently established by the subcommittee.

Specifically:

A. This resource listing should be updated on an annual basis and made widely available. It should be posted on several websites (all diversity related websites, human resources, Affirmative Action, general facilities related websites, Student Affairs, and websites for new students among others).

B. The resource guide should be integrated into any new student or orientation materials, perhaps in sections, which reference the value of and resources related to diversity and equity. All of these facilities should have appropriate and clear signage at the site of the facility.

C. All new building construction and renovation projects where bathrooms are part of the project should include gender-neutral bathroom facilities.

D. Locker room layouts (private showers, etc.) and gender-neutral facilities in residence halls should be assessed, monitored, and improved on.

2.2. Consider changing over many of the male and female restrooms that presently exist to gender-neutral by simply changing signage, in most cases.

2.3. All new buildings should install gender-neutral restroom facilities.

2.4. The Roger Williams Wellness Center facility is adding private showers and could be considered a model for inclusion.

2.5. Make it a priority to install gender-neutral restrooms at CCE.

2.6. The assignment of building managers may change. The AAEOD is currently not notified of such changes and should be.

ENSURING SAFETY

Findings

3. A recently implemented student Bias Response Team (BRT) has been implemented to effectively manage a reported issue; develop a plan for resolution; and implement the necessary pieces of an appropriate response to each incident. Once a report is submitted, it is automatically forwarded to key members of the university administration and community.

Recommendations

3.1. Consider the value and feasibility of developing a BRT process for faculty and staff.

3.2. Consider whether it is appropriate and effective to make the community more aware of the various incidents and responses when feasible, in order to expand sensitivity of all community members, awareness about the level of incidents, and the university's work and follow up on these issues. This would need to be balanced with confidentiality and the integrity of the process for filing complaints.

Showing particular concern for the findings related to the safety and health of the LGBTQ community, President Dooley used perhaps the most convincing language yet. In response to the worrisome finding that no current and relevant assessments of LGBTQ climate issues existed, the president confirmed that he had instructed the CDO "to work with the LGBTQ Center and other interested parties to develop electronic snap surveys, periodic targeted focus groups and to monitor national trends and information." He, once again, showed impressive initiative when he stated:

We have begun this work: a team of three URI members have attended a Department of Education conference on the climate and safety for the LGBTIQQ community on university campuses; the University of Rhode Island will soon be a member of the Consortium of Higher Education LGBT Resource Professionals; for the second year, two University of Rhode Island students are attending Summer Pride Leadership Camp; a faculty member is participating in the Camp LGBTIQQ Advisor Boot Camp.

The president continued this show of commitment to all members of the LGBTQ community when he affirmed, in response to the recommendation to make gender-neutral restrooms widely available on campus, that the vice president for Administration and Finance had already begun "an extensive effort to implement recommendations on gender-neutral restrooms on campus." President Dooley furthermore confirmed: "All new buildings and major building renovation projects will include gender-neutral bathrooms. We are also in the process of changing signage on existing single stall restrooms. And we will continue to provide communication, assessment and incorporation of gender-neutral restrooms across the campus." Finally, pertaining to the effectiveness assessment of the Bias Response Team, the president charged the CDO to conduct a study and to report back both to him and the LGBTQ Presidential Commission.

LGBTQ Hip!

In one short year, the University of Rhode Island, inspired by its students, stewarded by its faculty/staff, and buttressed by its administration, certainly come a very long way. In November 2011, the Department of Athletics brought former NFL star and self-identified gay man Esera Tuaolo to speak of "his searing story of terror and hope . . . [from] inside the homophobic world of professional football."[13] However, most emblematic of this amazing progress is both the It Gets Better at URI video produced and filmed by the LBTQ Women's Group and the surprising turnout at the first screening of this video. Thanks to the promotion by the LBTQ Group and the director of Athletics who required all sports teams to attend the screening, over 1,000 people attended this documentary of the incredible mobilization of the URI community to support its LGBTQ members. Students, faculty, and staff, both allies and LGBTQ, shared on camera their moving life stories. Professors, counselors, administrators, and peers declared on film their alliance with the LGBTQ community. And administrators went on visual record to iterate their sincere commitment to making the University of Rhode Island ". . . a community where absolutely everyone is welcomed, affirmed and supported."[14] The final product was so riveting, and the support so amazing, that Rhode Island Public Broadcasting Station asked for the film to be extended to fifty-five minutes so that it could be aired statewide.

In conclusion, I would like to privilege some of the diverse faces of change that voiced clear and unequivocal messages of support during the "It Gets Better at URI" campaign. It is my hope that these messages will serve as inspiration for administrators and faculty/staff that are courageous enough to join the growing chorus of educators committed to each and every student on their university campuses:

Vice President of Student Affairs, Tom Dougan: "I have just always wanted this to be a community where every single person—faculty, students and staff—feels welcome, feels safe, feels secure because once they do that, they can then do their best academic work, they can then be successful here."

Director of Athletics, Thorr Bjorn: "One of the great things about working with an athletic program is the fact that we do believe in teamwork. In order to be successful, you have to be a team . . . We are made up of so many different types of people that I think athletes . . . are great candidates to become support-ers [of the LGBTQ community] and allies . . . We are trying to build an environment of safety, concern and appreciation and love within our department."

Associate Director of Athletics, Gina Sperry: "What we are trying to do here at the University of Rhode Island is we are starting an initiative with our Director of Athletics to start to change the culture in the Department of Athletics . . . We're going to do awareness training with our coaches, with our staff, with our entire department, our student athletes . . ."

Program Assistant of Alumni Relations, Jess Raffaele, on the newly formed LGBTIQ2 alumni group: "A main theme that has been identified is mentoring . . . making sure that when students graduate from URI, they will have resources and fellow alumni out there . . ."

Major of the URI Police Department: "I truly believe that this campus has a lot of resources for all of our students, but they need to know that as a police officer, they can look to us as an ally."

Dean of Human Sciences and Services, Lynn McKinney: "I think it is really important for students to know that there are happy, functioning gay and lesbian people on this campus . . ."

URI Episcopal Chaplain, Jennifer Phillips: "There are so many good helpers available on campus in the counseling center, in the health center, in the religious organizations . . ."

Dean of Arts and Sciences, Winifred Brownell: "If you look in the Academic Plan, if you look at our cornerstone values and at the President's priorities, you will see a consistent message that we want to build an inclusive, diverse community where all are safe and welcome."

President of the University of Rhode Island, David Dooley: "I think an important point for us not to lose sight of is that the issues that the GLBT community faces are not just issues for our students but they are also issues for our faculty and staff, and one of the things that we have to work very hard at ensuring is that they have the freedom to be who they are without any fear whatsoever that their identity will in any way be a negative for them . . ."

Provost and Chief Academic Officer, Donald DeHayes: "If universities aren't going to be the place where we can talk about difficult situations regarding people's sexuality . . . or prejudices that they have experienced then where can you have those conversations? I would like us as a campus to continue to move forward in this area and to find those places, and to make sure that we are, in fact, having those conversations."

While the University of Rhode Island still has much work to do to achieve the status of leader in the field of LGBTQ inclusivity, it took great strides over the course of one year. Faculty, students and staff alike noticed a shift in campus climate. Student Marisa O'Gara confirms:

Yes, I do feel that the campus climate is changing, and I feel that it is doing so in a positive manner. The reason that I think that is that I believe awareness and education highly correlate with positive reform, and events such as the protest and the *It Gets Better* video have offered the student body a unique opportunity to hear a perspective that could otherwise easily fall under the radar . . . I am the first to point out areas for improvement, but I've honestly felt more comfortable and supported on campus recently than I've ever felt before, so I remain optimistic.[15]

Marisa is right to feel optimistic. At the University of Rhode Island, Think Big, We Do.[16]

Notes

1. I would like to thank the Provost's Office at the University of Rhode Island for having sent me to the wonderful *Expanding the Circle* conference in San Francisco in the Spring of 2011. It is thanks to this emblematic show of commitment to LGBTQ issues that the campus climate is evolving in such an exciting and positive manner.

2. Sara Lipka, the *Chronicle of Higher Education,* March 6, 2011.

3. Throughout this article, the reader will notice slippage in the acronym that the URI community has chosen to represent its diverse community of genders and sexualities. This slippage is itself emblematic of the history of the internal debates that have arisen with regard to how to be both entirely inclusive and validating while at the same time remaining pronounceable. These debates are still continuing, but for the moment, the prevailing acronym is LGBTQ (Lesbian, Gay, Bisexual, Transgender/Transsexual/Transitioning, Queer (gender and sexuality)/Questioning). The URI alumni organization is called LGBTIQ2, and the new center has been commonly referred to as the LGBTQ Center, although historically it was called the GLBT Center. This author recognizes the current conversations in scholarship that argue for the reorganizing of the acronym so as to give better visibility to the traditionally underrepresented transgender, transsexual, transitioning, and gender-queer populations of the community.

4. From the Equity Council's website (accessed September 10, 2011): http://www.uri.edu/equity/index.html.

5. As quoted from an e-mail that I received from one of the LGBTQ student leaders, Marisa O'Gara, a French and English dual-degree student, aspiring to a law career in social justice.

6. As quoted from a press release titled "URI officials and LGBTIQQ students reach an agreement on key issues; student sit-in ends," issued by the URI Department of Communications and Marketing on October 1, 2010 (accessed September 10, 2011): http://www.uri.edu/news/releases/index.php?id=5517

7. Linda A. Acciardo, as quoted from a press release titled "URI officials and LGBTIQQ students reach an agreement on key issues; student sit-in ends," issued by the URI Department of Communications and Marketing on October 1, 2010 (accessed September 10, 2011): http://www.uri.edu/news/releases/index.php?id=5517.

8. As quoted from a press release titled "URI officials and LGBTIQQ students reach an agreement on key issues; student sit-in ends," issued by the URI Department

of Communications and Marketing on October 1, 2010: http://www.uri.edu/news/
releases/index.php?id=5517.

9. From the report: "URI Subcommittee on LGBTIQQ of the URI Equity
Council Findings and Recommendations, April 11, 2011," written by the LGBTQ subcommittee to the URI Equity Council. Henceforth, all text in bold and boxed will be
cited from this report.

10. As written by President David Dooley on August 31, 2011, in response to
the LGBTQ subcommittee report titled "URI Subcommittee on LGBTIQQ of the URI
Equity Council Findings and Recommendations, April 11, 2011." All future quotes by
President Dooley, unless otherwise noted, will be from this written response.

11. The LGBTQ Subcommittee has already met with Anne Marie Coleman and
she has given verbal confirmation that she is working to negotiate equitable language
in contracts for all unions.

12. As a side note, when my partner went to Enrollment Services to discuss
tuition for her continuing education, she was surprised and enchanted by the degree
to which the friendly staff identified and explained all her benefits.

13. As quoted from the URI "Events Calendar" (accessed December 20, 2011):
http://events.uri.edu/event/esera_tualo.

14. President David Dooley in the *It Gets Better at URI* video (2011).

15. As quoted from an e-mail that I received from Marisa O'Gara.

16. "Think Big, We Do" is the official URI tag line.

Chapter 8

Queering Harvard Yard

Four Decades of Progress for BGLTQ Equality

Susan B. Marine, Paul J. McLoughlin II, and
Timothy Patrick McCarthy

Introduction

History suggests that institutions with vaunted origins are rarely places where advancing a progressive agenda for human rights is straightforward or smooth. Their very weightiness acts as a kind of inert fulcrum, slackening the momentum of those who aim for greater levels of recognition and agency. Nonetheless, the last forty years of institutional change-making with respect to the advancement of lesbian, gay, bisexual, and trans* rights at Harvard University illustrates the possibilities of patient, sustained forward movement, particularly when such movement is buoyed by shifts in the larger culture. While the path to equity has not been without significant challenges, several factors coalesced to create meaningful change. The voices of many, coupled with the persistent and strategic actions of committed alumni, faculty, staff, and students, have succeeded in "queering Harvard Yard," creating a fertile environment for bisexual, gay, lesbian, trans*, and queer (BGLTQ) visibility and respect at America's oldest institution of higher education. Because Harvard has historically been a bellwether for emerging trends in American higher education since its founding in 1636, the significance of these changes is not to be discounted. As a case study, it portends a complex history of liberal endorsement of equality and a slow but steady evolution of full participation of queer people.

In this essay, we will trace the contours of the movement for queer inclusion at Harvard University over the course of the last four decades. We will name the critical incidents that led to individual and collective action,

*transgender

and define the forces that coalesced to apply pressure (and shift perspective) on a range of issues, including BGLTQ student visibility and status, the advancement of queer, women's, and gender studies, institutional responsibilities to BGLTQ staff and faculty, and the path from marginality to celebration of BGLTQ identities. In tracing this circuitous route, we see in full relief that the effort for inclusion of minoritized genders and sexualities has often been marked by the "one step forward, two steps back" rhythm experienced by many other modern social movements. We recognize, in the struggle, the possibilities that emerge, each one signaling how and why institutions with long histories of heteronormativity may be queered. As active, visible, out members of the faculty and administration working at Harvard from the years between 1998 to the present, we are especially well-positioned to speak with an insider's perspective on what these changes looked like, and ultimately, what they have meant for students, faculty, staff, alumni, and the institution itself.

The history of Harvard's BGLTQ community began with public and vocal shaming, moved through periods of negotiation and adjustment, and has culminated in a gesture toward permanent visibility, as Harvard has now taken its place among only 190 other institutions nationwide in hiring a full-time director to oversee BGLTQ student life. The changes that took place over the last four decades could not have been predicted, but they are nonetheless significant, beckoning a better future for BGLTQ people at Harvard for generations to come.

Harvard in Context: Pre-Stonewall

Harvard has a very queer history when it comes to BGLTQ people. For the most part, Harvard has followed rather than led the great social transformations of the modern era, and this is certainly the case when it comes to the struggle for BGLTQ equality. Like all institutions, whether acknowledged or not, Harvard has had many lesbian, gay, bisexual, and trans* people pass through its gated Yard. Dating back to the mid-1800s, annual reunion class reports, commonly known as the "Red Books," contain no shortage of testimonies—some overt, others not—from which we can glean details about the variety of lived experiences of BGLTQ students and alumni throughout history. From F. O. Matthiessen, the legendary scholar credited with founding "American Studies" in the 1950s, to Bradley S. Epps, Kwame Anthony Appiah, Marjorie Garber, Warren Goldfarb, Diana Eck, Evelynn Hammonds, Mark Jordan, and the late Rev. Peter J. Gomes, Harvard's faculty has boasted a rich array of prominent and prolific queers, many of whom have become increasingly "out," more visible and vocal, in the last generation.

But this is recent history. For most of its more than 375 years, Harvard has been a relatively hostile place for queer folk. Perhaps the most infamous example came in the spring of 1920, when the acting dean of Harvard College, Chester Noyes Greenough, with the full support of Harvard President Abbott Lawrence Lowell, convened a special tribunal to investigate a suspected "network of homosexual activity" among undergraduates (Blount 2005). Inspired by the suicide of undergraduate Cyril Wilcox on May 13, 1920, the five-member clandestine tribunal—known as the "Secret Court"—conducted dozens of interviews and took disciplinary action against eight undergraduates and one graduate student, all of whom were expelled, and an assistant professor, whose relationship with the university was terminated. Though two of these students were ultimately readmitted to the college, many had their lives ruined by this homophobic purge, including dental student Eugene R. Cummings, who, just short of his graduation, committed suicide (Wright 2005). In 2007, Harvard graduate Kevin Jennings, AB '85, endowed an annual thesis prize in BGLTQ studies in memory of Cummings (Jennings, 2007).

The work of Harvard's "Secret Court" was largely lost to history until 2002, when Amit R. Paley, an enterprising reporter for the *Harvard Crimson*, wrote a feature article on the shameful episode (Paley 2002, "Secret Court: Part I") after discovering heretofore undisclosed documents from the hearings in the Harvard archives (the "Secret Court" has also been the subject of a 2005 book by William Wright, a 2008 film by Michael Van Devere, and two plays, one of which—"Unnatural Acts" by Tony Speciale—received a staged reading by the American Repertory Theater in 2012). Paley's revelatory article prompted former Harvard University president Lawrence H. Summers to issue the following response: "These reports of events long ago are extremely disturbing. They are part of a past that we have rightly left behind. I want to express our deep regret for the way this situation was handled, as well as the anguish the students and their families must have experienced eight decades ago. Whatever attitudes may have been prevalent then, persecuting individuals on the basis of sexual orientation is abhorrent and an affront to the values of our university" (Paley, 2002 "Secret Court: Part II"). In 2010, a coalition of activists launched a movement, "Their Day in the Yard," to petition the university to grant posthumous degrees to the students who were expelled by the "Secret Court," a petition Harvard has so far denied (McAuley 2010).

In many respects, Harvard's modern queer history mirrors the larger currents of BGLTQ life and activism in the United States over the last half-century. Before the birth of "gay liberation" in the late 1960s and 1970s, Harvard was an extremely difficult place for gays and lesbians. The "closet"—the compartmentalization or repression of one's sexuality—was a fact of life for most if not all queer folks in this era. For those who were actively homosexual, there were few outlets for social and sexual encounter that did not come with staggering personal, professional, and physical risks. In 2009, Martin Duberman, the pioneering gay historian who received his PhD from Harvard in 1957, reflected on his Harvard experience: "[W]e would sneak off to them [gay bars] in terror of being seen by anybody—a fellow graduate student, a faculty member, an undergraduate who we may have been tutoring. They were terrifying times to be growing up gay in the United States, so much so that I know from my own teaching—and I've taught gay and lesbian studies for many decades now—people simply do not understand, and there's no way that they could or probably even should, because the climate now is so different from what it was back then" (Duberman 2009). From an institutional standpoint, before the rise of the modern "gay liberation" movement, Harvard was an unwelcoming, if not outright hostile, place for gay students, faculty, and staff.

The Contemporary Struggle Begins: Stonewall to 1986

While the Stonewall riots in late June 1969 are often heralded as the beginning of the modern gay rights movement, the effort to gain equality for gay[1] students on college campuses preceded Stonewall. The first known gay student organization—the Student Homophile League—was founded at Columbia University in 1967 by Stephen Donaldson, an openly bisexual man (Highleyman 2007, "First Student"). Because this was the height of the Vietnam era, a sustained movement for gay equality was slow to emerge, as student activists were primarily focused on demonstrating against the war, and what they viewed as the institution's role in supporting it. Harvard's campus was gripped by chaos when a student protest and takeover of University Hall on April 9, 1969, was violently crushed by state police ("Until the April crisis . . ." 1969). This takeover was the culmination of tensions emerging across campuses related to Black Power, feminism, and other civil rights movements. Like the rest of the country, Harvard student activists were working to build broad and meaningful coalitions to advance social justice, of which gay rights was just one of many interests. "Gay Pride," in the form of full and unapologetic openness, was symbolized by the first gay and lesbian march in New York City in June 1970 (Nugent 2007). On the political front, Harvard alumnus Frank Kameny ran for Congress as an openly gay man. The first post-Stonewall national gay rights group—the National Gay Task Force, later the National Gay and Lesbian Task Force—was founded in 1973 (Eaklor 2008). The following year, another alumnus, then-state representative Barney Frank, introduced bills for the protection of gay men and lesbians in the Massachusetts state legislature. ("Conference" 1974). During these transitional and transformative times, the advancement of gay and lesbian rights at Harvard and in the broader political culture were deeply intertwined.

During the 1970s, several small gay and lesbian Harvard alumni groups were established in San Francisco, New York City, Boston, and Washington, DC, connected by Gay Harvard Alumni Newsletter that sought to offer support to fledgling student groups on campus. A student-founded women's center in 1974 included a course on lesbian liberation among its priorities (Bartlett 1975). Using pseudonyms, students began tentatively coming out in the student newspaper (Maclelland 1975), a particularly significant act since the Crimson has long been a feeder publication for the Associated Press. Two student organizations—the Gay Students Association and Gays Organized to Oppose Discrimination—were founded in the late 1970s, providing both safe space and widely attended awareness events for Harvard's out and allied student community (Faludi 1981).

The 1980s saw the beginning of formal efforts to codify gay equality in the school's policies and practices. In 1981, a group of gay, lesbian, and allied faculty and staff wrote a letter to the Faculty Council, asking for inclusion of the phrase "sexual orientation" in the University's nondiscrimination policy, in order to provide formalized protections for faculty, staff, and students in the Faculty of Arts and Sciences (Harvard's largest faculty, and the one, by virtue of its status as the sole granter of the PhD, most frequently associated with the prestige and history of the University) (Baughman 1981). The Faculty Council denied the request, instead opting to go on record decrying discriminatory treatment in admissions, but stopping short of a full commitment to nondiscrimination in all of its services and programs. As an institution that operates by the highly decentralized system of financial management known as "every tub on its own bottom," the Faculty of Arts and Sciences, one of fifty-two discreet "tubs," was a free agent, and was apparently unconvinced of the need for such a policy.

Undaunted, advocates decided to form a collective designed to advance the agenda of gay and lesbian inclusion at the institution. As a concession to the protests over its refusal to include language about sexual orientation in the nondiscrimination policy, the university commissioned the Special Committee to Harvard University on the Status of Gay Men and Lesbians in 1981 to more closely study the issue, and buy time for further consideration of the advocates' demands (Baughman 1981). The issues remained dormant for a few years following this setback, as activists worked behind the scenes to create a more organized effort for advocacy. In 1984, the Harvard Gay and Lesbian Caucus (hereafter, the HGLC)[2] emerged, composed primarily of alumni, faculty, and staff. The group positioned itself both as a mechanism for targeted advocacy on behalf of the community, and a supportive social network for openly gay affiliates of the university. Following two years of intense negotiations, the HGLC and the university's representatives agreed to a reworking of the nondiscrimination policy, to include protection for gay men and lesbians (Harvard Gay and Lesbian Caucus, 2011). While this change was less than perfect, the Caucus viewed the modification as its first big "win" to advance the agenda of full inclusion. While the wording of the policy ostensibly protected those who express same-sex attraction from being subjected to penalties, there was widespread confusion about how, and in what ways, this policy would be observed and enforced in its early years. The university made no specific statements regarding resources for those who felt the policy had been violated; indeed, even today, there remains confusion about the appropriate reporting source should violations occur. Nonetheless, the public statement of support for the gay and lesbian community signaled an important step forward for the goal of full participation and protection in university life.

Though initially a small organization of Harvard and Radcliffe alumni, the HGLC now boasts more than 5,000 members—including current faculty, staff, administrators, and students—and is the largest of the Harvard Alumni Association's Shared Interest Groups, or "SIGs" (Harvard Gay and Lesbian Caucus 2011). Over the years, as the HGLC has grown in both size and influence, it has performed important social and advocacy functions on behalf of Harvard's BGLTQ community. Each year, the Caucus hosts a fall reception, a holiday party, and an annual commencement dinner at Lowell House, whose comasters, Professor Diana Eck and Rev. Dorothy Austin, became the first openly gay or lesbian couple to lead a Harvard House when they were appointed in 1998. The HGLC also oversees dozens of local chapters across the country and publishes regular print and electronic newsletters to keep members informed about Caucus-related news and events. Since 1994, it has also published *The Gay and Lesbian Review/Worldwide*, a bimonthly magazine featuring writing on BGLTQ arts, politics, and culture. In 1987, the Caucus established a charitable foundation, the Open Gate, which has generously supported a range of campus initiatives, including conferences, lectures, academic research, arts programming, public service fellowships, and the like. In terms of advocacy, in addition to being the driving force behind the addition of "sexual orientation" to the University's nondiscrimination policy in 1985, the HGLC has pushed for the extension of benefits to same-sex partners in 1993, the discontinuation of financial support for the Reserve Officers Training Corps (ROTC) in the wake of the "Don't Ask, Don't Tell" policy in 1995, the barring of military recruiters from Harvard's campus, and the addition of "gender identity" to the nondiscrimination policy in 2007 (Harvard Gay and Lesbian Caucus, 2011). As these examples show, the HGLC has played a uniquely powerful role, both in terms of building community and in making Harvard a more equitable and enjoyable place for BGLTQ people.

The climate, then, definitely began to change in the 1980s, even more so in the 1990s, but not without significant controversy from within and without. Students became particularly organized during this time: founded in the mid-1970s, the Gay and Lesbian Students Association (GLSA), later BGLSA, has long been the flagship student group, overseeing the campus resource center for BGLTQ students and sponsoring a broad range of social, cultural, political, and academic initiatives on campus, including HIV/AIDS activism, National Coming Out Day, "Gaypril" events, and the Transgender Day of Remembrance. The history of student activism at Harvard mirrors the larger cultural and political debates in American society—from the ongoing AIDS crisis to the debate over the military policy of "Don't Ask, Don't Tell," antibullying campaigns, and the struggle for marriage equality. The late 1980s and early 1990s was a particularly fierce time for campus political activism. In addition to widespread student concern over the growing AIDS crisis, BGLTQ students had to contend with an increase in campus conservatism during the Reagan-Bush era. At Harvard, the "culture wars" came to a head in the fall of 1991, when a group of right-wing students launched a new campus publication, the *Peninsula*, the first issue of which featured a spate of virulently homophobic articles and an exploding pink triangle on its cover. The magazine's founding editor, Roger Landry, Harvard Class of 1992, justified the publication's existence to the *New York Times*: "The pro-homosexuality movement at Harvard is very strong, and we wanted to reach out to those people who feel same-sex sexual attraction and give them some options" ("Campus Life," December 21, 1991).

The publication ignited a firestorm of controversy, including a pro-gay rally of several hundred people in Harvard Yard, where several prominent members of the Harvard faculty—including the late literary scholar Barbara Johnson and the late Rev. Peter J. Gomes—"came out" as gay publicly for the first time (Galloni 1991). Gomes's announcement caused a particular ruckus, prompting unsuccessful calls for his resignation as Plummer Professor of Christian Morals and Pusey Minister of the Memorial Church. In the wake of this controversy, more BGLTQ students and faculty "came out," and the ranks of the BGLSA began to swell, as more members of the undergraduate community, both queer- and straight-identified, joined to express their public support. In June 1993, the BGLSA garnered national media attention when it organized a highly visible protest of General Colin Powell's Commencement Address, in which he addressed President Bill Clinton's controversial "Don't Ask, Don't Tell" policy (Gammill 1993). During the 1990s the BGLSA changed its name to the Bisexual, Gay, Lesbian, Transgender, and Supporters

Alliance, reflecting a growing awareness of and commitment to the needs of trans* and transsexual students.

Toward a Twenty-First Century Harvard?

What we think of as the contemporary struggle for BGLTQ rights on the American college campus suddenly gained new urgency in 1998, the year that Mathew Shepard was kidnapped, tortured, and murdered while he was a student at the University of Wyoming (Loffreda, 2001). This hate crime garnered national attention and Shepard's eventual death became an important catalyst for the movement to advance queer rights: to many, his death symbolized the countless daily insults and abuses—what some scholars have called "micro-aggressions" (Sue 2010)—as well as more overt assaults experienced by queer youth in primary, secondary, and postsecondary education (Kosciw et al., 2010; Rankin Weber, & Blumenfeld, 2010).

As the world was changing in both harmful and helpful ways for BGLTQ youth on college campuses, their visibility also spiked. Backlash was frequently imminent, and created a sense of urgency about the work that lay ahead. In 1996, the awe-inspiring entirety of the NAMES Project's AIDS quilt was unfolded on the Washington Mall (Burles 2007). Pedro Zamora's struggle with AIDS was visible to the world as he "came out" on Music Television's (MTV's) *Real World* program in 1993, and the nation was riveted when he received a supportive phone call from newly elected President Clinton on his deathbed (Winick 2001). Armed with positive imagery emanating from popular culture—such as Ellen Degeneres's decision to "come out" in 1997 on her nationally televised sitcom, and the Emmy-winning sitcom *Will and Grace* that aired from 1998 to 2006—the conditions created by heightening awareness made it necessary for even the most complacent institutions to become introspective about their practices and policies related to their BGLTQ communities. It was in this mixed environment of progress and peril that the movement to change the experiences of BGLTQ people at Harvard gained serious momentum.

As visibility and tolerance increased in some quarters nationally, BGLTQ life for students at Harvard College followed suit. Benefiting enormously from the strong support of the Harvard Gay and Lesbian Caucus and the Open Gate, Harvard's student groups have flourished. In 2009, the BGLTSA renamed itself again—to Queer Students and Allies (QSA)—marking yet another attempt to broaden the scope of its mandate to include "queer" and "questioning" students, as well as straight-identified and cisgender allies (Kolin, 2009). In addition to the QSA, a broad range of BGLTQ-identified undergraduate groups have emerged, including GirlSpot (for lesbian woman), the Trans Task Force (for trans students and allies), BAGELS (the Jewish BGLTQ student group), and BlackOut and GLOW (for students of color). All of Harvard's graduate schools now also have BGLTQ student groups who work together with undergraduate student leaders under the auspices of the "Mothership," an umbrella group for all BGLTQ student organizations overseen by the HGLC. In recent years, there has been a great deal of coordination among these various constituencies, helping to forge a more integrated and diverse student community across Harvard's various schools. Taken together, they have helped to transform Harvard's culture from one of widespread alienation to broader acceptance for BGLTQ students.

In the last decade, Harvard's BGLTQ community has experienced a period of growing consolidation, integration, and influence. In a sense, the first decade of the twenty-first century was something of a "queer renaissance" at Harvard. Academically, in 2003, Harvard's small women's studies concentration evolved into a more expansive and visible program on women, gender, and sexuality, attracting a number of leading faculty as both permanent and visiting scholars in the next decade, including literary scholars Bradley Epps and Alice Jardine, historians Afsaneh Najmabadi, Michael Bronski, Robin Bernstein, and Susan Stryker, and social scientists Juliet Schor and Kath Weston. In the spring of 2006, author Timothy Patrick McCarthy taught Sex, Lies, and Stereotypes: Queer Culture in the United States from Stonewall to Gay Marriage, Harvard's first-ever LGBTQ history course focusing on politics, culture, and society in the United States. Several WGS courses—including Linda Schlossberg's The Romance: Jane Austen to Chick Lit and Bernstein's Race, Gender, and Performance—have become immensely popular offerings among undergraduates, and are now included in the General Education curriculum. There are now numerous LGBTQ-themed courses offered every year, and a growing call for the creation of a universitywide "sexuality studies" program at Harvard.

The Case for Change: Student Life in the Twenty-First Century

As mentioned, the support for and creation of specific BGLTQ student services on campuses nationwide was slower to arrive to Harvard than other colleges and universities, although the national progress created a healthy pressure on Harvard. Across Harvard College, several small changes were taking place by committed administrators, faculty, students, and alumni/ae that laid an important foundation for the creation of a full-time director of a new Office of BGLTQ Student Life in the spring of 2011 (Massari 2011). One catalyst for progress was a change in the way the college administration began offering more centralized student services for undergraduates instead of treating the twelve upper-class residential Houses as separate "colleges." This change—to provide more centralized services to all students, regardless of House affiliation—was as much a philosophical change as an organizational one. Senior leaders within the college's administration began to provide support for students that were distinct from, yet complementary to, services that students had been receiving in the undergraduate Houses. This push for centralized student services emerged as a result of the implementation of "randomization," the practice of "sorting" students into one of the twelve upper-class Houses through a lottery system. Historically, students had previously chosen their House affiliation; as a result, the undergraduate experience was widely divergent because of self-segregation and House-specific traditions. Instead of each House including a cross-representation of the college population at large—an original goal of the Harvard House system established in the 1930s (Gudrais 2001)—many of the Houses had become homogeneous and distinct. With the new, "randomized" lottery system of housing in place, it was even more important to the senior administration that the experience of undergraduates was not left to chance, and instead operated with consistency and equity across the House system.

One specific change that illustrates this shift by administrators was the appointment of a clinician in University Mental Health Services to work more closely with each of the BGLTQ advisers. These are individuals, primarily graduate students, living in the residential houses who were assigned to promote BGLTQ visibility and awareness, and to serve as support resources for students going through the "coming out" process and other struggles related to sexuality and gender. While each of the BGLTQ advisers (also known as "tutors" within Harvard's system) are individually appointed by each of the twelve faculty House Masters, there was a desire on the part of the college to bring more consistency to the existing decentralized system. While other specialty advisers in the houses—such as those who support survivors of sexual assault and those appointed to promote the improvement of race relations— had formal relationships with liaison offices within the college administration from which they garnered support, training, and resources, BGLTQ advisers were operating with minimal coordination or standards. In addition, they had no formal office or liaison to ensure that they were providing equitable services across the Houses. Students who relied on these advisers for support or advice had begun vociferously complaining about inconsistency and asking the college administration to improve the quality of these tutors and the related programming they offered. The national progress, then, was giving students voice and increasing the expectations they had for the support they received from the college.

Senior leaders within the college's administration also began a concerted effort of examining the undergraduate experience as a whole by working to address widespread student complaints about their experiences outside of the classroom. As a result, several administrators with formal student affairs education and experiences, including authors Marine and McLoughlin, were appointed to support BGLTQ students and connect them with college resources. Closer examination of peer institution data and practices was another indicator that the college administration was moving away from the isolationist view that the Harvard College student experience was too distinct to glean anything helpful from other institutions' practices.

Related to this, a significant catalyst to the examination of undergraduates' experiences both inside and outside of the classroom came when the *Boston Globe* obtained a 2004 internal Harvard memo referencing results of an annual student satisfaction survey conducted by the Consortium on the Financing of Higher Education (COFHE). This memo referenced confidential survey results comparing thirty-one of the most selective and prestigious institutions in the United States, including all eight Ivy League institutions, and put the college on alert that Harvard students' satisfaction with their undergraduate experience ranked near the bottom of the list. The internal memo also stated that the college was taking the satisfaction gap "very seriously," as well as confirmed that a satisfaction gap between Harvard and its closest peers had persisted since 1994 (Bombardieri 2005). That this memo was written at all indicates that administrators in the college had begun to question assumptions and were starting to consider changes in student support practices. This unintended public revelation provided more incentive and a shorter time frame within which to alter the way student life was organized. Moreover, its release provided administrators with a justification to move away from some long-held cultural and administrative practices of focusing solely on the academic experience of undergraduates and provided the rationale for investing more time and energy into the student life of all undergraduates.

The tangible effects of this shift were many between 2000 and 2010, as a critical mass of openly BGLTQ College administrators and faculty emerged, willing to serve as resources to students and to work on behalf of their experience. Routine programming and publications began to include BGLTQ-inclusive language. The College moved away from relying on peer counselors to provide essential health and wellness information to incoming freshmen, and instead created an orientation video in 2004 to highlight resources for students. This widely disseminated video and related guidebook were the new ways that all students were informed about available on- and off-campus resources, including information specifically targeted to BGLTQ students. These materials included names of faculty and staff within the university to whom BGLTQ students and their allies could turn for advice and support. BGLTQ advisers within the Houses also began meeting regularly with the aforementioned centrally appointed coordinator and slowly, as new advisers replaced veteran advisers, the expectation for diverse types of BGLTQ programming became the expectation. Later, the quality and frequency of programs became the focus for these advisers to ensure that BGLTQ students within the houses were having an equitable experience.

As mentioned, progress on the infusion of BGLTQ topics into the curriculum was steady during this time as well, and has picked up significant momentum in the last few years. For example, in 2009, the HGLC and Open Gate again flexed their financial muscle by completing an ambitious $1.5 million fund-raising campaign to endow the F. O. Matthiessen Visiting Professorship in Gender and Sexuality, the first-ever endowed faculty position in gender and sexuality studies in the United States (Henry Abelove was the inaugural Matthiessen Professor in 2012–2013; Gayle Rubin held the post in 2013–2014). In 2009, the Faculty of Arts and Sciences voted to approve a first-ever "BGLTQ Studies" track for students in the Committee on Degrees in Women, Gender, and Sexuality. In addition to this curricular expansion, there has also been a noticeable increase in activity and support coming from Harvard faculty, staff, and administrators. Since its founding in 2005, the BGLTQ Faculty and Staff group has advocated on behalf of more BGLTQ-friendly policies with respect to employee benefits, nondiscrimination, trans* health coverage, and "grossing up" pay in response to federal tax penalties levied on same-sex couples who choose to cover their spouse on their health insurance policy (this policy has now changed as a result of the June 2013 Supreme Court ruling striking down the Defense of Marriage Act). Perhaps nowhere is the culture shift more noticeable than in University Hall, which has undergone a sea change in leadership over the last decade to include many openly BGLTQ administrators and allies, including the appointment of the first lesbian and African American Dean of Harvard College, Evelynn M. Hammonds, as well as two gay-identified associate deans, a lesbian assistant dean, and several other out senior leaders.

Resource allocations in related areas were the inspiration for heightened advocacy among students in the second half of this decade. BGLTQ students and allies saw the success of their peers in securing a women's center and director position in 2006, after more than two decades of repeated pleas to administrators and faculty, as a sign of hope that they could similarly convince administrators of the importance of a BGLTQ center. The creation of the women's center was another illustration of the college's shift away from a long-held administrative philosophy and practice of not providing individual support centers for students. An often-mentioned rationale for not creating centers at the college was that Harvard believed students would best be supported by shared services and support offered within the intimate confines of the twelve undergraduate Houses, and services that did not marginalize or allow for self-segregation. When Princeton created race-specific houses in the 1970s and 1980s, Harvard chose to instead create the Harvard Foundation for Intercultural and Race Relations in 1981, an office meant to support all racial, ethnic, and cultural groups in one effort, and to complement the work of the residential Houses. For the first twenty years of its existence, the Harvard Foundation operated with a staff of one.

The creation of the women's center, then, was a signal that student support would not be provided solely within the upper-class houses and that financial resources would increasingly be channeled to create support that mirrored more traditional student affairs structures. It also created a precedent for "centers" that had been heretofore absent in student life at Harvard. Student activities and campuswide events saw a similar influx of new financial support. Between 2003 and 2006, more than 70,000 square feet of new student spaces were created and staffed, including a student organization center, prayer spaces, a climbing wall, social spaces for freshmen, and an on-campus pub. Campuswide events began with the creation of an events board with an annual operating budget of $200,000, made possible by discretionary funds from the college dean. These new programs and spaces were another sign of increased attention being paid to the cocurricular undergraduate experience by Harvard College's administration, emulating Harvard's peer institutions' success in providing a positive undergraduate experience for their students.

While financial support and the creation of physical spaces matter and certainly signal commitments on the part of institutions, the natural result is for those who are directly affected to question existing practices that appear to run counter to the policy. Two specific inconsistencies have raised questions about the implementation of the nondiscrimination policy in the last few years: the policy's lack of inclusion of those who express a transgressive gender identity, and the ongoing lack of attention paid to differential impact of BGLTQ identity on this community's health insurance access and affordability.

Trans* and other gender nonconforming members of the Harvard community were the first to note the absence of protection for them in the nondiscrimination policy. Erroneously assuming that protecting sexual orientation by default protects those who identify as trans, the university's legal representatives at first resisted the suggestion of expanding the policy to be more directly inclusive of the constructs of gender identity and expression. In 2007, a cross-coalitional advocacy group comprised of the Harvard Trans Task Force, the Harvard Faculty and Staff BGLTQ group, members and board of directors of the HGLC, and students from the then-named Bisexual, Gay, Lesbian and Transgender Supporters Alliance (BGLTSA) came together to craft language—and advance an argument—for the inclusion of those who identify as trans*, including other identities such as transsexual and genderqueer. The group felt it was important to include both gender identity (the way a person identified in terms of male, female, trans, and/or other designation) and gender expression (the varying degrees of masculine or feminine appearance, comportment, and behavior that individuals may choose to express) in the policy.

Through multiple rounds of negotiations, university attorneys declined to include the concept of gender expression, still believing it to be already encapsulated in protection related to one's sex (Pollack 2009). While coalition members viewed this decision to be a compromise of the more fully inclusive goals and parameters of the policy, the decision was accepted as final, and the coalition moved on to applying pressure to the institution in raising awareness of, and enforcing, the policy. The growing national and international visibility and mobilization of trans* activism has been echoed on Harvard's campus. Other desired changes advanced by Harvard's Transgender Task Force in the last five years have included changing the "preferred name" field on the Harvard College application for admission and all subsequent student records, extending insurance coverage for trans* medical care including hormone therapy and various aspects of sex reassignment surgery, and working with the Freshman Dean's Office and the Office of Residential Life to expand options for gender neutral housing (Harvard Trans Task Force 2011). While there have been important advances in raising awareness around trans* issues on campus, equally important challenges remain, namely the expansion of gender-neutral bathrooms, the formal implementation of gender-neutral housing (which was recently vocally endorsed by the faculty of arts and sciences), the broader education of human resource managers and medical professionals across the university, and the ongoing effort to add "gender expression" to Harvard's nondiscrimination policy. As with the broader LGBTQ movement, Harvard still has a long way to go before it can rightly claim to be fully inclusive and accepting of trans* people and concerns.

The Tide Turns: The Working Group on BGLTQ Student Life at Harvard College

The progress made in the last four decades was hard won, but it was clear there was no time to rest: colleges were far from safe heavens for BGLTQ people, as evidenced by the 2010 suicide of a young gay man, Tyler Clementi, who while a freshman at Rutgers University was unknowingly filmed being intimate with another man by his roommate who subsequently put the video footage on YouTube (Nutt 2010). Fourteen years apart, the brutality of Shepard's murder and Clementi's suicide give pause, and cause one to wonder if the significant gains made in society have truly had the desired effect of changing both the world at large, and American higher education, in any appreciable way.

In October of 2010, fueled by concern for the recent uptick in campus- and school-related acts of bullying, harassment, and self-harm (and arguably, a student voice that was more vociferous than the past), a proposal was crafted and advanced to Evelynn Hammonds, Dean of the College, asking for appointment of a commission of faculty, students, and administrators to examine BLGTQ life at Harvard College. This commission's charge would be to consider the question of whether and how the college was doing enough to support the healthy development of BGLT students, and to create a campus climate that was welcoming and inclusive. From our perspective, this request was at least several years in the making and was a result of several factors: the founding of the women's center in 2006, the larger debate about gender-neutral housing and other accommodations for the growing population of trans* students, and the appointment of an out lesbian as the dean of the college.

Hammonds concurred that this was the right moment to examine these questions, and the working group on BGLTQ student life was appointed in October 2010 (Hu & Newcomer 2010). The group was composed of five faculty members, four students representing the range of BGLTQ advocacy and interest groups, and six student life administrators with responsibility for promoting the well-being of all students at the college. Both co-chairs— author Susan Marine, Director of the Women's Center, and Diana Eck, Master of Lowell House and a named professor in the Religion Department—were out lesbians who were well known on campus for making progress on human rights issues with diplomacy and inclusion.

The group convened eleven times during the 2010–2011 academic year, and considered the contours of numerous issues related to BGLTQ student life, including safety, mental and physical health and resources, academic and curricular issues, the support provided by Harvard's residential BGLTQ tutors, and the degree of visibility and support for BGLTQ student organizations, including support and advocacy groups and peer and professional counseling. The group engaged in lively and, at times, contentious debate about the nature of BGLTQ student experiences, and both the structural and incidental features of the Harvard landscape that either bolstered or inhibited BGLTQ visibility and happiness. The final product was hailed by many in the community, including Dean Hammonds herself, who declared that "As a historian I want to say that the working group has made history and will make Harvard a better place for BGLTQ students going forward into the future" (Farjood & Underwood 2011).

The work yielded a number of recommendations, including the formation of a BGLTQ office and a full-time professional director, which were indicative of momentum for a new and increased commitment to establishing a permanent home for BGLTQ students and their interests. Unlike other efforts related to BGLTQ life at Harvard typified by antagonism and resistance, this group engaged in a practice of collaborative transformation (Marine 2011), signaling a new level of partnership and collegiality among students and trustees of the institution's longer-term future.

It was crucial in that moment of high mutual regard for the college's leadership to solidify the commitment by creating a permanent space designated for continued pursuit of the ambitious agenda set forth by the Working Group. The Office of BGLTQ Life was opened March 28, 2012, in the basement of Thayer Hall, strategically proximal to the offices of the Committee on Degrees in Studies of Women, Gender, and Sexuality. The initially appointed director, Lisa Forrest, declined the directorship just as she was about to assume the post, citing "personal and professional reasons" (Nguyen 2011). Emily Miller, a recent graduate of the Harvard Divinity School and graduate student appointee to the Working Group, served as interim director for the next eight months. After a prolonged second search, Van Bailey, former assistant director for Education at the University of California San Diego's LGBT Resource Center, assumed the role of director of the new office (Miraval 2012). Bailey arrived at Harvard just as speculation of a "queer exodus" from Harvard was emerging in the school newspaper (Robbins 2012). Marine, Paul McLoughlin II, and several other well-known out faculty and staff left Harvard that summer. Some involved in this departure were openly critical of the college's efforts, which they felt were too little, too late, and that the campus was a "follower, not a leader" on issues related to queer life and agency (Robbins 2012). But even as the ranks of out leaders that had propelled the Working Group forward were noticeably thinning, Bailey's early work in the community was hailed as unifying, and his visible presence as a trans* person of color was viewed as a significant step forward for those most marginalized in the context of BGLTQ life at Harvard and elsewhere (Kovacs 2013).

BGLTQ Life in Harvard Yard: The Next Phase

As we have demonstrated, much has changed in the last four decades of Harvard's steady if sometimes stalled progress toward full inclusion and participation for BGLTQ people. The forward movement, largely propelled by the coalescence of students and alumni, and scaffolded by faculty and staff advocacy, happened largely through applied and sustained pressure, and shifts in both public and private perception of these issues at Harvard and in the world beyond. Nevertheless, the glacial nature of these shifts in policy and practice leave us to wonder: How do we measure progress?

We can know by the ways that many have stood up to claim space and belonging on campuses across America, from the colleges on the coasts to the campuses in the heartland and everywhere in between. Progress has come in the form of the nearly 200 campus-based BGLTQ centers that now exist, staffed by professionals and funded by the institutions to expand awareness and transform the institutions into welcoming spaces. BGLTQ student organizations host not only support meetings for their members, but large-scale events such as speaker series, panels, demonstrations, and "coming out day" observances, signaling a much greater acceptance of openly identified queer student leadership (Rankin 2005; Sanlo 2000; Sanlo, Rankin, & Schoenberg 2002; Sokol 2003).

Students have demonstrated for the suspension of on-campus military recruiting during the era of "don't ask, don't tell" (French, 2009; New ROTC Unit protested at university, 2008; Steinhauer, 2010), and have lobbied extensively for inclusion of sexual orientation and gender identity and expression in their institutions' nondiscrimination policies (Oguntoyinbo 2009). Recently, one institution (Hoover 2011) announced the inclusion of a question about prospective students' sexual orientation on their applications, signaling a desire for greater diversity on their campuses. Harvard recently announced that it, too, will consider this issue (Villanueva 2011).

At numerous campuses nationwide, students are pushing for gender-neutral housing, asserting its appropriateness for all, but particularly those who live outside of the gender binary (Tilsley 2007). The campus climate, nationally, is inarguably shifting for BGLTQ people, and Harvard is (while not leading that charge) certainly upholding this larger vision of increased access, inclusion, and affirmation for BGLTQ members of its community. Bailey's appointment as the first director of the Office of BGLTQ Student Life (affectionately termed "the Quoffice" by students) at Harvard College brought numerous important changes to Harvard, including centralizing resources for the community; the convening of a Queer Advisory Council made up of faculty, students, and staff; and training a cadre of active student interns. Demonstrating his strong commitment to fostering dialogue, Bailey organized a discussion in the aftermath of professor of history Niall Ferguson's disparaging comments about John Maynard Keynes's economic theories, attributing them in part to the fact that Keynes was gay (Kovacs, 2013). While Bailey's work has made a significant difference to the community, some have cautioned against assuming that an office embedded within the college—even a very effective one—is, or should be, sufficient in ensuring the college's accountability to the needs of BGLTQ students. As voiced by Sandra Korn '14, "I'd like to ask my fellow queer students to think critically about how we can appreciate the Quoffice for the work it does, and ensure that it's not the be-all-end-all of queer organizing on campus" (Korn, 2013). As noted by the Working Group on BGLTQ Student Life, progress is still elusive in several crucial areas, including securing full health care coverage for trans* people, integrating BGLTQ issues more seamlessly into the curriculum beyond the courses offered in the Committee on Degree Studies of Women, Gender, and Sexuality (which is currently working to become a department), and continuing to examine Harvard's support for students suffering from mental and physical impact of homophobia and transphobia experienced in their families as well as on the campus (Marine & Miller 2011). As the new chapter of BGLTQ rights and progress at Harvard begins, it remains to be seen whether Harvard will continue its recent trend of taking responsibility to be a leader on the advancement of BGLTQ rights, or whether it will wait to see what other campuses do before making its next move. As the future unfolds, it also remains to be seen whether higher education institutions collectively will be "queer pioneers," or will fall in line behind other more avowedly progressive social institutions.

The future looked bright indeed when then-Harvard senior (and later Pulitzer Prize–winner) Susan Faludi (1981) affirmed, "Between today and the time the graduating class arrived at Harvard four years ago, a political movement has arisen out of silence, consolidated a large following, dominated campus headlines, and outpaced the other student movements in numbers and staying power. The newborn political presence is the gay rights movement." Nearly thirty-five years later, through small and large wins and by strategically traversing the setbacks documented here, the effort for BGLTQ equality—by all who have thoughtfully commandeered it at Harvard—carries on.

Notes

1. For purposes of historical accuracy, we refer to the "gay rights movement" in the 1960s and 1970s, which became the more inclusive BGLT, and then BGLTQ, rights movement through the end of the twentieth century.

2. In 2013–14, the Harvard Gay and Lesbian Caucus changed its name to the Harvard Gender and Sexuality Caucus, though in this book it is referred to as HGLC.

3. The term *trans** originated from a computer search function allowing one to search for prefix (e.g., *trans-*) with anything else that follows (Killermann 2012). Thus, the use of the asterisk in the term *trans** is used to visually represent the wide array of identities, expressions, and embodiments encapsulated in the trans* community.

Works Cited

Baughman, J. "GSA to Print Discrimination History." *Harvard Crimson* December 8, 1981 (accessed 6 November 2011), http://www.thecrimson.com/article/1981/12/8/gsa-to-print-discrimination-history-pthe/.

Bartlett, A. E. "Women's Center Courses Aim at Goal of Women's Solidarity." *Harvard Crimson* November 19, 1975 (accessed November 17, 2011),http://www.thecrimson.com/article/1975/11/19/womens-center-courses-aim-at-goal/.

Blount, J. M. *Fit to Teach: Same Sex Desire, Gender, and School Work in the Twentieth Century*. Albany, NY: State University of New York Press, 2005.

Bombardieri, M. "Student Life at Harvard Lags Peer Schools, Poll Finds." *Boston Globe* March 29, 2005 (accessed March 16, 2014, http://www.boston.com/news/education/higher/articles/2005/03/29/student_life_at_harvard_lags_peer_schools_poll_finds/.

Burles, K. T., ed. *Great Events from History: Gay, Lesbian, Bisexual and Transgender Events, Volume II (1983–2006)*. Pasadena: Salem Press, 2007.

"Campus Life: Harvard; Magazine Issue on Homosexuality Leads to Rallies." *New York Times* December 22, 1991 (accessed November 27, 2011), http://www.nytimes.com/1991/12/22/nyregion/campus-life-harvard-magazine-issue-on-homosexuality-leads-to-rallies.html.

"Conference." *Harvard Crimson* March 18, 1974 (accessed November 17, 2011), http://www.thecrimson.com/article/1974/3/18/conference-cluding-americans-for-democratic-action/.

Duberman, M. Personal remarks made at HGLC Annual Commencement dinner, 2009 (accessed 27 November 2011), http://hglc.org/extras/duberman_award.pdf.

Eaklor, V. L. *Queer America: A People's GLBT History of the United States*. New York: New Press, 2008.

Faludi, S. "Gay Rights: The Emergence of a Student Movement." *Harvard Crimson* June 4, 1981 (accessed November 28, 2011), http://www.thecrimson.com/article/1981/6/4/gay-rights-the-emergence-of-a/.

Farjood, N., and A. E. Underwood. "College Announces New BGLTQ Resources." *Harvard Crimson* 2011 (accessed November 16, 2011), http://www.thecrimson.com/article/2011/4/29/bgltq-working-students-group/.

French, L. "Ousted ROTC Student Praised: Student's Saga Spurs Protest of 'Don't Ask.'" *Hatchet of George Washington University* February 23, 2009 (Accessed February 3, 2011), http://media.www.gwhatchet.com/media/storage/paper332/news/2009/02/23/News/Ousted.Rotc.Student.Praised-3643205.shtml.

Galloni, A. M. "On Harvard, the Church, and Coming Out." *Harvard Crimson* November 27, 1991 (accessed November 17, 2011), http://www.thecrimson.com/article/1991/11/27/on-harvard-the-church-and-coming/.

Gammill, M. B. "Group to Arrange Anti-Powell Protest." *Harvard Crimson* May 7, 1993 (accessed November 16, 2011), http://www.thecrimson.com/article/1993/5/7/group-to-arrange-anti-powell-protest-pmore/.

Gudrais, E. Housing After Randomization. *Harvard Magazine* November–December, 2001 (accessed November 10, 2011), http://harvardmagazine.com/2001/11/housing-after-randomizat.html

Harvard Gay and Lesbian Caucus Website. "History." (2011) (accessed November 16, 2011), http://hglc.org/about/history.html.

Harvard Trans Task Force Wesbite (2011), (accessed November 16, 2011) http://www.hcs.harvard.edu/queer/ttf/.

Highleyman, L. "August, 1966: Queer Youth Fight Police Harassment at Compton's Cafeteria in San Francisco." In K. T. Burles, ed., *Great Events from History: Gay, Lesbian, Bisexual and Transgender Events, 1848–2006*. Pasadena, CA: Salem Press, 2007, 163–165).

Highleyman, L. "April 19, 1967: First Student Homophile League Is Formed." In K.T. Burles, ed., 172–175). *Great Events from History: Gay, Lesbian, Bisexual and Transgender Events, 1848–2006*. Pasadena, CA: Salem Press, 2007.

Hoover, E. "Elmhurst College Will Ask Applicants About Sexual Orientation." *Chronicle of Higher Education* August 23, 2011, (accessed November 7, 2011), http://chronicle.com/blogs/headcount/elmhurst-college-will-ask-applicants-about-sexual-orientation/28553.

Hu, M. and E. Newcomer. "College Reviews LGBT Support." *Harvard Crimson* October 7, 2010 (accessed November 17, 2011), http://www.thecrimson.com/article/2010/10/7/committee-college-harvard-student/.

Jennings, T. "Lessons from a Witch Hunt." *Gay and Lesbian Review Worldwide* 14.5 (2007, September-October): 6.

Killermann, S. (2012). What Does the Asterisk in "Trans*" Stand For? http://goo.gl/FGT5f4.

Kolin, D. "BGLTSA Votes to Change Name to QSA." *Harvard Crimson* March 1, 2009 (accessed November 17, 2011), http://www.thecrimson.com/article/2009/3/1/bgltsa-votes-to-change-name-to/.

Korn, S. "Institutionalizing Queer." *Harvard Crimson*, September 11, 2013, http://www.thecrimson.com/column/the-red-line/article/2013/9/11/Korn-institutionalizing-queer/#comment-1039333372

Kosciw, J. G., E. A. Greytak, E. M. Diaz, and M. J. Bartkiewicz. *The 2009 National School Climate Survey: The Experiences of Lesbian, Gay, Bisexual and Transgender Youth in Our Nation's Schools*. New York: GLSEN, 2010.

Kovacs, S. "The Community Builder." *Harvard Crimson* May 30, 2013 (accessed March 16, 2004), http://www.thecrimson.com/article/2013/5/30/van-bailey-first-year/?page=1.

Loffreda, B. *Losing Matt Shepard: Life and Politics in the Aftermath of an Anti-Gay Murder*. New York: Columbia University Press, 2001.

Maclelland, C. "Being Gay at Harvard: On Not Being a Sexual Beastie." *Harvard Crimson* November 18, 1975 (accessed November 16, 2011), http://www.thecrimson.com/article/1975/11/18/being-gay-at-harvard-pmy-experiences/.

Marine, S., and E. Miller. *Report of the Working Group on BGLTQ Student Life* April 2011 (accessed November 28, 2011), http://isites.harvard.edu/fs/docs/icb.topic582545.files/BGLTQ%20report%20FINAL%20Forum.pdf.

Massari, P. "A Director of BGLTQ Student Life: New Position will Improve Coordination of College Resources." *Havard Gazette* April 27, 2011 (March 16, 2015), http://news.harvard.edu/gazette/story/2011/04/a-director-of-bgltq-student-life/.

McAuley, J. K. "Degrees for the Dead: 'Their Day in the Yard' Movement Wants Harvard to Award Posthumous Degrees to Expelled Students." *Harvard Crimson* September 28, 2010 (accessed March 16, 2014), http://www.thecrimson.com/article/2010/9/28/harvard-degrees-university-student/.

Miraval, N. R. "Harvard Picks First BGLTQ Director." *Harvard Crimson* July 12, 2012 (accessed March 16, 2014), http://www.thecrimson.com/article/2012/7/3/vanidy-bailey-bgltq-office/.

Nguyen, E. M. "Recently Hire Director of LGBTQ Student Life Turns Down Position." *Harvard Crimson* October 29, 2011 (accessed March 16, 2014), http://www.thecrimson.com/article/2011/10/29/lee-forrest-turns-down-lgbtq-position-harvard/.

Nugent, D. J. "June 28, 1970: First Lesbian and Gay Pride March in the United States." In K. T. Burles, ed. *Great Events from History: Gay, Lesbian, Bisexual and Transgender Events, Volume II (1983–2006)*. Pasadena: Salem Press, 2007, 212.

Nutt, A. E. "Friends Remember Tyler Clementi as Brilliant Musician, Bright Student." *Piscataway Star-Ledger* October 1, 2010 (accessed November 4, 2010), http://www.nj.com/news/index.ssf/2010/10/rutgers_student_tyler_clementi_1.html.

Oguntoyinbo, L. "Non-Discrimination Policies and Support Groups Help Ease Campus Life for Gay and Lesbian Students at HBCUs" July 7, 2009 (accessed January 11, 2011), http://diverseeducation.com/article/12697/.

Paley, A. "The Secret Court of 1920: Part I." *Harvard Crimson* November 21, 2002 (accessed November 27, 2011) http://www.thecrimson.com/article/2002/11/21/the-secret-court-of-1920-at/.

Paley, A. "The Secret Court of 1920 Continued: Part II." *Harvard Crimson* November 21, 2002 (accessed November 27, 2011), http://www.thecrimson.com/article/2002/11/21/the-secret-court-of-1920-part-two/.

Pollack, R. "Policy to Cover Transgender Students." *Harvard Crimson* April 12, 2009 (accessed November 17, 2011), http://www.thecrimson.com/article/2006/4/12/policy-to-cover-transgender-students-harvard/.

Rankin, S. R. "Campus Climates for Sexual Minorities." In R. Sanlo, ed. *Gender Identity and Sexual Orientation: Research, Policy, and Personal Perspectives: New Directions for Student Services*, Number 111: 17–23. http://onlinelibrary.wiley.com/journal/10.1002/(ISSN)1536-0695

Rankin, S. R., G. Weber, W. Blumenfeld, and S. Frazer. *2010 State of Higher Education for Lesbian, Gay, Bisexual and Transgender People*. Charlotte, North Carolina: Campus Pride, 2010.

Report of the Working Group on BGLTQ Student Life (April 2011) (accessed November 28, 2011),http://isites.harvard.edu/fs/docs/icb.topic582545.files/BGLTQ%20report%20FINAL%20Forum.pdf.

Robbins, R. D. "'Queer Exodus' from Harvard Subject of Facebook Discussion." *Harvard Crimson* July 18, 2012 (accessed March 16, 2014), http://www.thecrimson.com/article/2012/7/18/lgbtq-queer-exodus-scholarship/?page=2.

Sanlo, R. L. "The BGLTQ Campus Resource Center Director: The New Profession in Student Affairs." *NASPA Journal* 37.3 (2000): 485–495.

Sanlo, R. L., S. R. Rankin, and R. Schoenberg. *Our Place on Campus: Lesbian, Gay, Bisexual, Transgender Services and Programs in Higher Education.* Westport, CT: Greenwood Press, 2002.

Sokol, D. "Center of Attention." *The Advocate* 892 (June 24, 2003): 127–130.

Steinhauer, J. "House Votes to Repeal 'Don't Ask, Don't Tell.'" *New York Times* December 15, 2010. (accessed January 6, 2011), http://www.nytimes.com/2010/12/16/us/politics/16military.html.

Sue, D. W. *Microaggressions in Everyday Life: Race, Gender and Sexual Orientation.* Hoboken, NJ: Wiley & Sons, 2010.

Tilsley, A. "New Policies Accommodate Transgender Students." *Chronicle of Higher Education* June 27, 2007 (accessed January 3, 2011), http://chronicle.com/article/Colleges-Rewrite-Rules-to/66046/.

"Until the April Crisis . . ." *Harvard Crimson* June 12, 1969 (November 17, 2011), http://www.thecrimson.com/article/1969/6/12/until-the-april-crisis-ported-to/.

Villanueva, I. "Harvard Considering LGBT Option in Admissions Applications." *Advocate* November 17, 2011 (accessed November 27, 2011), http://www.advocate.com/news/daily-news/2011/11/17/ harvard-considering-lgbt-option-applications.

Winick, J. *Pedro and Me: Friendship, Loss, and What I Learned.* New York: Henry Holt & Co., 2000.

Wright, W. *Harvard's Secret Court: The Savage 1920 Purge of Campus Homosexuals.* NY: St. Martin's Press, 2005.

Part III

Changing Student Perceptions

Chapter 9

Student Development

Theory to Practice in LGBT Campus Work

Milton E. Ford, Colette Seguin Beighley, and Ronni Sanlo

This chapter was developed from an all-day workshop presented by Ronni Sanlo and Colette Seguin Beighley at "Expanding the Circle: Creating an Inclusive Environment in Higher Education for LGBTQ Students and Studies"—Summer Institute, 2012. Professionals who attended vetted the student development case studies adding insight based on their experience with lesbian, gay, bisexual, transgender, and queer (LGBTQ) students.

A college student experience is one of developmental navigation with all its predictable ebbs and flows. An LGBT college student experience is all that and more. Ideally, this experience includes defining oneself as a member of a marginalized community, coming to terms with giving up one aspect of dominant-culture privilege—heterosexuality—and establishing a healthy, empowered queer identity.

There are numerous student development theories, several of which help us to better understand the journeys of LGBT students. Our intention is to examine current student development models taught in student affairs curricula and their application to LGBT students.

Since many people who work professionally with LGBT students in college and university settings come to understand LGBT student experience through academic discourse or through a background in activism, they may lack a foundation in student development theory that others have acquired through degrees in Student Affairs. For this reason we wanted to review the major student development theories, including LGBT-specific theories, using the first edition of *Student Development in College: Theory, Research, and Practice* by Evans, Forney, and Guido-DiBrito, and apply them to LGBT student experience.

The importance of understanding these developmental theories is expressed well by Evans, Forney, Guido-DiBrito:

> Knowledge of student development theory enables student affairs professionals to proactively identify and address student needs, design programs, develop policies, and create healthy college environments that encourage positive growth in students. (Evans et al. 5)

We will review the following major student development theories and then examine LGBT student lived experience through each of these frameworks:

- Chickering's Theory of Identity Development

- Josselson's Theory of Identity Development in Women

- Racial and Ethnic Identity Development:

  —The Cross Model of Psychological Nigrescence

  —Helm's White Identity Development Model

  —Phinney's Model of Ethnic Identity Development

- Gay, Lesbian, and Bisexual Identity Development:

  —Cass's Model of Homosexual Identity Formation

  —D'Augelli's Model of LGB Development Process

- Schlossberg's Transition Theory

Chickering's Theory of Identity Development

Chickering is famous for his "seven vectors of development" relating to identity formation. He refers to these as "major highways for journeying toward individuation" with the core developmental issue being the establishment of identity. Chickering's theory addresses development through emotional, interpersonal, ethical, and intellectual lenses (Evans et al. 37–38). Chickering in a 1993 work with Reisser also describes this process as nonlinear and occurring in a progression better described as a spiral or steps (Evans et al. 37–38).

The Seven Vectors

1. DEVELOPING COMPETENCE

    Three processes are at work in this vector to create a sense of competence:

    *   *Intellectual competence*—includes the development of critical thinking as well as the attainment of knowledge

    *   *Physical and manual skills*—includes artistic endeavors, the development of an understanding of personal wellness as well as athletic or recreational competencies

    *   *Interpersonal competence*—includes developing communication skills and leadership abilities including learning to work as a team (Evans et al. 38).

2. MANAGING EMOTIONS:

    In this vector, students learn to identify feelings including the ability to both understand and appropriately express their emotions (Evans et al. 38–39).

3. MOVING THROUGH AUTONOMY TOWARD INTERDEPENDENCE:

    Work in this vector allows students to develop an internal locus of control. This ability allows them the autonomy to be free from the need for constant reassurance and/or approval. Once they develop this level of autonomy, they are able to move toward interdependence—an awareness of our interconnectedness with others (Evans et al. 39).

4. DEVELOPING MATURE INTERPERSONAL RELATIONSHIPS:

    In this vector a sense of self continues to develop and is enhanced and further defined by being in relationship with others. This work includes developing the ability to be in relationship with individuals who have a different lived experience from one's own. Work in this vector also acknowledges the impact that intimate relationships with friends and partners have on the student's sense of self (Evans et al. 39).

5. ESTABLISHING IDENTITY:

    Development that was mastered in previous vectors sets the foundation for the work of establishing identity. As a clearer sense of self has developed, students are able to engage in a more nuanced examination of their complex identities. This further consideration of self may include a revised understanding of the student's sexual orientation and/or gender identity as well as ethnicity. Both a grounded sense of self and an internal locus of control allow students the emotional resources needed to explore nondominant aspects of their identities (Evans et al. 39–40).

6.   DEVELOPING PURPOSE:

This vector is characterized by commitment which is manifest in several areas of students' lives including their abilities to commit to interpersonal agreements, relationships and career paths (Evans et al. 40).

7.   DEVELOPING INTEGRITY:

Like Chickering's other vectors, which he characterizes as spirals or steps, the three aspects Chickering attributes to the development of integrity can be seen as progressing in an overlapping manner.

- *Humanizing values*: In this stage students move from an inflexible, dualistic mode of thinking to a more generous value system that takes into account the needs of others as well as their own needs.

- *Personalizing values*: In this stage students clarify and affirm their foundational values but are also able to understand and honor the values of others.

- *Developing congruence*: In this final stage, students are able to integrate their established values and belief systems with the world around them and, as a result, develop an integrated consciousness and sense of accountability around social issues (Evans et al. 40).

Chickering: Applications to LGBT Student Experience

Two different student responses in the following context: Attendance at a Transgender Day of Remembrance candlelight vigil

Heather is a female-bodied student who has just recently begun to identify as transgender. Heather does not yet have language to describe her lived experience. She is traumatized by the reading of the names of transgender people who have been lost to hate violence and asks, "This is still occurring today?" Heather has not come to understand that violence against the transgender community happens every day. Heather is "Developing Competence" in her new transgender identity.

Linda, a self-identified genderqueer student who uses the pronouns "they" and "them" and is very emotionally fragile, sobs uncontrollably during the candlelight vigil. A counseling center staff member notices their distress and offers to talk at a nearby location. Linda's partner Melissa follows them and remains focused while providing comfort, reassurance, and nurturing to her partner.

Linda appears to be in the "Managing Emotions" stage of development in that they are expressing emotions; but, at this point, rather than controlling their emotions, the emotions seem to be controlling them.

Melissa seems to be "Moving Through Autonomy Toward Interdependence." She is able to focus completely on her partner. She does not need to process her feelings while her partner is in need or be reassured in any way. Melissa is valuing her interdependence with Linda and demonstrating problem-solving ability. This behavior is also suggesting movement toward "Developing Mature Interpersonal Relationships."

Josselson's Theory of Identity Development in Women

To establish context for Josselson's theory, we will look at the 1997 work of Hodgson and Fischer (1979) who examined the differences in development between college men and women. They understood men and women to manifest intimacy and identity development in different ways. Men tend to discover their identities through issues of competence and knowledge. Women's development is defined through relationships with others as well as through deeper levels of intimacy than those experienced by their male counterparts (Evans et al. 65–66).

Josselson found that as women develop their identities, they tend to place value on "the kind of person to be" (Evans et al. 64). This is in contrast to developing an identity based on political, ideological, or religious belief systems and/or vocation. For a woman, interpersonal relationships provide a better sense of her individual identity through the integration of autonomy and connectedness. Women value relationships for the relationship itself; men tend to value relationships in terms of their leading to something beyond the relationship (Evans et al. 65–66).

Josselson's Four Identity Groups

1. FORECLOSURES: PURVEYORS OF THE HERITAGE

After their college experience, women in Foreclosure have not moved from their family's set of ethical values and, as a result, have not experienced individuation. Their identities are anchored in identification with their families. They tend to make confident decisions based on family of origin values but have not questioned that belief system during their college years. These women have not challenged their identities and, therefore, have experienced little identity change (Evans et al. 57–58).

2. IDENTITY ACHIEVEMENTS: PAVERS OF THE WAY

Women in Identity Achievement are able to differentiate from their families of origin. These women have been able to critically evaluate who they are and how that identity was given to them by their families. They are then able to renegotiate that identity to one that is more consistent with who they experience themselves as being. This evaluation and reorganization process leads to a sense of competence that benefits them academically as well. Though Achievers do not demonstrate a higher level of intelligence, they are found in the more demanding academic programs. Achievers are characterized by the balance they are able to maintain in career, relationships, and personal activities. This level of differentiation allows Achievers to successfully manage intimate relationships while maintaining a strong sense of self (Evans et al. 58–60).

3. MORATORIUMS: DAUGHTERS OF THE CRISIS

Women in Moratorium may experience instability as they use their college years as a time of investigating new identities. These women struggle when they realize that there may be more than one way to be right. The outcome of this identity-shaping experience is dependent on their ability to develop a tolerance for ambiguity. As a result of this tailspin, some will continue to struggle until they can move to a higher level of functioning as Identity Achievers; other may regress to an earlier self-identification (Evans et al. 60–61).

4. IDENTITY DIFFUSIONS: LOST AND SOMETIMES FOUND

This identity group is "marked by lack of crisis and commitment" (Evans 61) and encompasses a wide range of women who are characterized by low ego strength. These individuals manifest the most intense anxiety among the identity groups as well as a propensity for withdrawal. This group scores lowest "on all measures of healthy psychological functioning" and may include extreme psychopathology. Women in this identity group lack resources for processing their external experience (Evans et al. 61–62).

Josselson: Application to LGBT Student Experience

Angie comes from a very conservative Christian family. She has been through reparative therapy, which she considers successful. She states knowing she "has changed" and is committed to "not being gay." She demands that the campus LGBT Resource Center carry PFOX (Parents and Friends of Ex-Gays and Gays) materials; and, when the director does not agree, Angie files a harassment complaint against the director with the university.

Angie is demonstrating characteristics of the Foreclosure Identity Group. She is working to negotiate a burgeoning identity that is stigmatized within the context of her family of origin's belief system. Angie is exhibiting focused determination and lack of doubt, reflecting the same traits that characterize her rigid family system. For Angie, family loyalty and inclusion are more important than authenticity and the exploration of emerging possibilities.

Racial and Ethnic Identity Development

In this section, we examine racial and ethnic identity development as it intersects with LGBT identity through the lenses of three theories:

- Cross Model of Psychological Nigrescence
- Helm's White Identity Development Model
- Phinney's Model of Ethnic Identity Development

The Cross Model of Psychological Nigrescence

Cross defines the term Nigrescence as a "resocializing experience" (Evans et al. 73) where identity progresses along a continuum from non-Afrocentrism to Afrocentrism to multiculturalism. Within the psyche of an African American, this process may unfold throughout the individual's life.

The Cross model is a five-stage sequential process:

1. PRE-ENCOUNTER: An individual does not identify in terms of race, but rather desires to be acknowledged as a "human being" (Evans et al. 74). At this point, identity is based on conditions defined in the dominant culture—anti-black/pro-white (Evans et al. 74).

2. ENCOUNTER: Crisis occurs when individuals have a positive or negative encounter that destroys their ability to maintain their previous worldview. This may be one single event or a series of smaller events that cumulatively lead to this crisis. There are two phases to the encounter: first, actually experiencing the event(s); and, second, being profoundly changed by the event. As the individual proceeds through the "Encounter" process, a time of anger toward white people is then replaced by anxiety over "the kind of black person to become" (Evans 75). This angst leads the individual to seek more information and affirmation in pursuit of a black identity (Evans et al. 74–75).

3. IMMERSION-EMERSION: In this process, the former identity is abandoned and the individual commits to a new black identity, withdrawing from encounters with other ethnicities. Cross describes two phases in this journey to self-definition:

   Phase 1: Complete "immersion into blackness" (Evans et al. 75) while experiencing feelings of rage toward white people and white culture. Additionally, the individual experiences guilt for having believed what dominant culture told them about the meaning of being black in our society. Last, the individual develops a sense of pride in their black identity and culture.

   Phase 2: Individual develops an ability to critique black identity which allows them to move away from a dualistic experience (Evans et al. 75).

4. INTERNALIZATION: Individual begins to resolve the conflict between "old identity and new black worldview" (Evans et al. 75). With a sense of security and self-confidence in this

new identity, the individual is able to let go of antiwhite feelings and develop a perspective that is more pluralistic. Black identity is no longer the prominent identity an individual experiences but rather it is one of several ways of experiencing oneself in the world. Black identity becomes internalized, allowing relationships with whites and other ethnicities to be redefined (Evans et al. 75–76).

5. INTERNALIZATION-COMMITMENT: The individual's new identity is manifest in terms of the shared lived experiences of African Americans as well as other marginalized communities; meaningful activities are pursued to address this shared oppression. An individual may or may not continue to be involved in these kinds of activities as their identity is further internalized (Evans et al. 76).

Cross: Application to LGBT Student Experience

The LGBT Resource Center's Pipeline Leadership group was developed to help students build leadership skills; however, since our students do not have their rights, this leadership development is done within the context of activism. During the introductory training, Kiara identifies as African American and is interested in creating a queer newspaper on campus representing voices of all students; Tia identifies as black and angrily states that she is only interested in participating in direct action to improve the campus's racist climate.

There are two ways to interpret Kiara's development: she could be understood in terms of Cross's "Pre-encounter" process if one views Kiara's desire to give voice to all students as a manifestation of not yet having established a black identity. Conversely, Kiara could be seen as experiencing Cross's "Internalization Commitment" process and that her call for representation of all voices is indicative of a desire to include all oppressed communities. However, since she stated that the newspaper would reflect "the voices of all students" and not just marginalized voices, it is likely she would best be defined in Cross's "Pre-encounter" process in that she seems to be identifying all voices as equal without a critique of privilege and power.

Tia appears to display Cross's "Immersion-Emersion: Phase 1" process in that she is presenting with anger and her comments are focused primarily on actions that would benefit African American students. She is clinging to her black identity exclusively and is not yet able to view solidarity with other oppressed groups as central to her own struggle.

Helm's White Identity Development Model

The concept that white identity is anchored in racism has been established in the research (Evans et al. 76). Helm's theory illustrates the journey white individuals take toward a nonracist view of self and an understanding and rejection of racism (Evans et al. 76).

Helm's theory of White Identity Development is based on the idea that individuals move through two phases where there is an intricate relationship between cognitive and emotional processes, as well as accompanying behaviors, throughout development. An individual wrestles with new ways of seeing as well as the feelings associated with these changing worldviews (Evans et al. 76).

Phase 1: Abandonment of Racism

- STATUS 1: CONTACT

  In this first status, individuals become aware of black people through direct experience or indirect knowledge. They may still be unaware of their own privilege or the ways that society advantages whites over blacks. Once they recognize and accept that in the United States the treatment of black people is different from their own experience as a white person, they are able to progress (Evans et al. 77).

- STATUS 2: DISINTEGRATION

  As individuals begin to wrestle with the meaning of whiteness and its accompanying privileges, moral conflict is experienced. During this conflicted time, there may be an attempt to challenge the existence of racism and energy may be expended to try to avoid blaming white people for racism. Additionally, they may attempt to not interact with black people. As these conflicts are resolved and new understandings developed, the individual is able to move to the next status (Evans et al. 78).

- STATUS 3: REINTEGRATION

  During this status, the individuals become fully aware of the reality of white identity. Ideas about the racial superiority of whites are still held, as are stereotypes of blacks. Only when the meaning of whiteness is questioned and an acceptance of the existence of racism is established does movement to the next phase occur (Evans et al. 78).

Phase 2: Defining a Nonracist White Identity

- STATUS 4: PSEUDO-INDEPENDENCE

  During this status, a positive white identity begins to emerge. Individuals start to understand how white people contribute to and benefit from racism. However, responsibility for changing racism is still placed on black people. While individuals at this status tend to associate more with black people than they had previously, black people are still evaluated using white constructions of success (Evans et al. 78–79).

- STATUS 5: IMMERSION-EMERSION

  In this status, the work is both emotional and cognitive as the task is focused on understanding white identity and the power structures that keep racism in place. Stereotypes about whites are replaced with more accurate understandings of white privilege. At this point individuals may seek out other white people who have already taken this journey of understanding. Additionally, greater effort is invested to better grasp the idea of being a member of the dominant group in a white supremacist society. Individuals may read books about this subject or join consciousness-raising groups to aid their understanding of personal, cultural, and institutional racism. The responsibility for creating change shifts from blacks to placing the burden for anti-racism work on whites (Evans et al. 79).

- STATUS 6: AUTONOMY

  This final status is an ongoing process of internalization where individuals continue to renegotiate and manifest their white identity. In this status, ongoing education results in a greater understanding of the intersections of oppression. As a result, a shift occurs to working to fight all the "isms" (Evans et al. 79).

Helm: Application to LGBT Student Experience

At the LGBT Resource Center's "Ongoing LGBT Conference" dealing with racial justice, a white student named Josh suggests that the explanation of structural racism leaves out black people's "bad choices." Josh is demonstrating "Phase 1 Abandonment of Racism, Status 1 Contact." Josh is in the very beginning stage of White Identity Development. He has not yet realized his own privilege or that the experience of black people is different from his own. He applies a white criterion for success onto black people with little awareness of his own personal racism or the impact of institutional racism on communities of color. However, Josh has asserted this opinion in the context of a social justice discussion with a diverse group of people. The feedback he receives provides an opportunity for him to see that the experience of being black in America is completely different from the invisible privilege he has experienced. What Josh does with this feedback will determine whether he moves forward in his White Identity Development or forecloses.

In our Pipeline Leadership group, a white student, Monica, tells Nia she would like her to explain more about black culture and asks her a series of questions about the black experience. Nia tells her to go find out for herself if she is interested. Monica appears to be in Phase 2, "Defining a Non-Racist White Identity," Status 4, "Pseudo-Independence" in that she is pursuing more information about what it means to be black. Though she is asking for more information about black lived experience, she is putting the responsibility for that education onto a black person instead of taking responsibility for doing that work herself. She is also asking Nia to speak on behalf of an entire identity group.

Phinney's Model of Ethnic Identity Development

In Phinney's 1990 model development of an ethnic identity, it is imperative for minority youth to attain healthy self-esteem. There are two major challenges to accomplishing this objective. First, individuals must come to terms with being members of a marginalized community including the stereotypes that accompany that identity. Second, individuals must wrestle with the conflict between the values of dominant culture and those of their identity group, working to the goal of integrating a "bicultural value system" (Evans et al. 80). Phinney's Model views these two challenges as being negotiated through three stages:

- STAGE 1: DIFFUSION-FORECLOSURE

  In this stage, individuals have not yet become aware of the ways they conceptualize and internalize their own ethnicity. This lack of awareness is manifest in indifference toward their ethnic identity (Evans et al. 80).

- STAGE 2: MORATORIUM

  An individual moves into Moratorium as a result of an experience or experiences relating to their ethnicity. At this point, they are no longer able to ignore their ethnic identity. The experience or culmination of experiences causes them to face the ways in which dominant culture diminishes their identity. At this stage, individuals are motivated to learn more about their identity group. Additionally, they attempt to come to terms with their feelings of guilt or embarrassment for their past indifference toward their ethnicity. This stage is often marked by intense emotions (Evans et al. 80).

- STAGE 3: IDENTITY ACHIEVEMENT

  The culmination of Phinney's stages occurs when individuals are successfully able to incorporate a "healthy bicultural identity." At this point, individuals have integrated dominant cultural values as well as those of their ethnic group. This integration leads to both a new sense of confidence as well as the ability to relate more openly to members of other identity groups (Evans et al. 81).

Phinney: Application to LGBT Student Experience

Maria, an out gay senior and second-generation Latina who identifies as "Chicana," is committed to immigration justice, a personal issue for her family of origin. Maria is also passionate about transgender rights, an issue beyond her lived experience. Maria appears to be in Phinney's Stage 3, "Identity Achievement." She exhibits compassion for individuals whose personal histories involve the same struggles her family has experienced. Beyond that, Maria is also able to extend these justice concerns to marginalized communities of which she is not a member.

Emily was adopted from Guatamala and identifies as pansexual and cisgender. She is completing a very successful first year in the engineering program. This year she has taken back her birth name "Lucia," and has been a fierce ally to the transgender community, keeping immense pressure on the university to create an adequate number of gender-neutral bathrooms. In order to bring attention to the crisis facing transgender students, Lucia commits to using only gender-neutral bathrooms. On her blog, she writes about having to plan her day around the scarce location of these bathrooms on campus. The school newspaper picks up this story. By attempting to navigate the oppressive conditions transgender students face, Lucia hopes to better understand how our most vulnerable transgender students might experience our campus. She uses her cisgender privilege to advocate for transgender students.

Lucia is exhibiting Stage 3, "Identity Development." She has become aware and is working to integrate her dominant and subordinate identities. Lucia has reclaimed her Guatamalan ethnicity and is confidently manifesting her complex identity as a young pansexual Latina American woman. This confidence has led to a greater awareness of and compassion for other subordinate identity groups, in this case the transgender community.

Gay, Lesbian, and Bisexual Identity Development

Two theories that already consider LGBT experience in the context of student development are Cass's Model of Homosexual Identity Formation and D'Augelli's Model of Lesbian, Gay, and Bisexual Development.

Cass's Model of Homosexual Identity Formation

Cass's 1979 model works on the assumption that the interaction between individuals and their environments is foundational in the development of a homosexual identity. The Cass model accounts for both cognitive and affective aspects of a person's lesbian and gay identity formation, looking at how individuals perceive themselves as well as their and others' emotional responses to their new identity (Evans et al. 92).

Before Stage 1, individuals view themselves as having a heterosexual identity.

- STAGE 1: IDENTITY CONFUSION

  When individuals first have feelings of attraction to a person of the same sex, those feeling involve "confusion and anxiety." Individuals try to find information to develop a greater understanding of what they are experiencing. This activity can move them forward in their identity development. If they dismiss or retreat from their feelings, the result is Identity Foreclosure (Evans et al. 93).

- STAGE 2: IDENTITY COMPARISON

  This is the stage of first self-acceptance of the possibility that one is gay, lesbian or bisexual. The problem they face is how to deal with the social stigma they will encounter. Individuals may alternatively attempt to maintain a heterosexual identity or seek to alter their homosexual attractions and behavior (Evans et al. 93).

- STAGE 3: IDENTITY TOLERANCE

  In this stage individuals seek to be with other LGB people in order to overcome feeling isolated. When such interaction is established, individuals are on the way to the next stage. If these connections with others are not found, foreclosure can be the outcome (Evans et al. 93).

- STAGE 4: IDENTITY ACCEPTANCE

  Individuals develop positive attitudes toward being lesbian, gay, or bisexual and experience numerous interactions with LGB persons. At this stage, individuals may choose to be out in some circumstances and present themselves as heterosexual in others especially in relation to their families of origin (Evans et al. 94).

- STAGE 5: IDENTITY PRIDE

  Individuals' lives may become centered on LGB matters and they may choose contact with the gay community over contact with heterosexuals when possible. Students at this stage are motivated by pride in anything "gay" and can become irritated by what is "not gay." An individual at this stage may participate in activism on behalf of the LGB community. Negative experience with disclosure can still lead to foreclosure (Evans et al. 94).

- STAGE 6: IDENTITY SYNTHESIS

  Individuals develop a less dualistic view of LGB and heterosexual communities. They relate to others more on their general merit and characteristics rather than their sexuality. They see LGB as one part, rather than the entirety of their identity (Evans et al. 94).

Cass: Application to LGBT Student Experience

As a result of a very cryptic e-mail request, the director of the LGBT Resource Center meets Josh in a neutral location outside the center. Josh is a senior and plays on one of the university's athletic teams. He is experiencing panic about realizing he is gay. He clarifies with the director that he is "not that kind of gay" and that he easily passes as straight. His anxiety is so high that he fears he needs to leave school. Josh is experiencing Stage 2 in Cass's theory, "Identity Comparison," in which there is difficulty dealing with LGB stigma. His rejection of full gay identity is seen in his wanting the director to know that he is "not that kind of gay." As a result of these conflicts, Josh is continuing to present as heterosexual to some groups, while he comes to terms with his new identity.

Sarah is a student worker in the LGBT Resource Center. The center staff knows Sarah has only come out in the past two years but quickly learns she is not out to her parents. Later the staff learns that she has two Facebook accounts: one "out" and one not. Sarah is exemplary of Cass Stage 4, "Identity Acceptance," in that she is comfortable with her lesbian identity but is not out in all circumstances, in this case, at home.

D'Augelli's Model of Lesbian, Gay, and Bisexual Development Process

"Exiting a heterosexual identity entails giving up the privileges and social approval associated with this identity while taking on an identity that is denigrated by mainstream society" (in Evans et al. 95). D'Augelli states that in this process individuals may experience isolation, confusion, panic, anxiety, and denial. This model sees identity development as a lifelong process where individuals continually reassess their place in the world and wrestle with their resulting feelings. This model emphasizes the impact of the individual's agency on this identity journey. Individuals need to carve out a place for positive, healthy development since our heterosexist society provides no healthy narrative in regard to their lives (Evans et al. 95–96).

D'Augelli presents six processes that, he points out, are not stages:

1. EXITING HETEROSEXUAL IDENTITY—Individuals realize they are not attracted to members of the opposite sex and come out as gay, lesbian, or bisexual (Evans et al. 96).

2. DEVELOPING A PERSONAL LGB IDENTITY STATUS—Individuals reconsider what they have assumed to be true about LGB persons. An "identity status" is developed through being in relationship with others who support their new understanding of LGB (Evans et al. 96–97).

3. DEVELOPING AN LGB SOCIAL IDENTITY—Individuals establish relationships with people who are supportive of their sexuality (Evans et al. 97).

4. BECOMING AN LGB OFFSPRING—Individuals establish a revised relationship with their parents by coming out to them (Evans et al. 97).

5. DEVELOPING AN LGB INTIMACY STATUS—Individuals engage in their first significant relationship without the benefits of cultural guidelines. This process can result in feelings of doubt and confusion (Evans et al. 97).

6. ENTERING AN LGB COMMUNITY—Though not all individuals engage in this process due to the inherent risks of discrimination and harassment, individuals commit to social justice activism to some degree (Evans et al. 97).

D'Augelli's theory highlights the importance of safe spaces on campus such as an LGBT Resource Center and LGBT student organizations. As students navigate their identities, LGBT support groups can be vital for those who are in the early stages of exploring their sexuality, gender identity, or both. For students who are more secure in their identities, politically oriented LGBT groups become important venues for expression and continued growth (Evans 104–105). The leadership experience created in this context can facilitate the further development of ego strength.

D'Augelli: Application to LGBT Student Experience

The final week before holiday break in December, the LGBT Resource Center hosts an event for its First-year Queer Alliance—"Homo for the Holidays"— an event title that the students love. The potluck is hosted by our LGBT Faculty and Staff Association as well as our LGBT Ambassadors. Students share what they are anticipating as they look to going back home for the first extended time since coming to campus.

Benjamin shares that he will be coming out as gay to his parents. He will be experiencing the first of D'Augelli's processes, "Exiting a heterosexual identity." Benjamin will also be experiencing the process of "Becoming an LGB offspring."

Christopher shares that he will be coming out to his parents as gender-queer and requesting to be called "Chris." While D'Augelli's theory does not include gender identity development, by extension, Chris demonstrates the second of D'Augelli's processes, "Developing a personal LGB identity status." Again, extrapolating to include gender identity, Chris appears to be experiencing process number four, "Becoming an LGB offspring."

Anna shares that, due to her parents' rejection of her sexuality, she doesn't have a home to go to. She will be going home with Jeff—another First-year Queer Alliance member whose family is very affirming. Anna is experiencing the third of D'Augelli's processes, "Developing an LGB social identity," by finding a new "family" who is supportive of her identity.

Schlossberg's Transition Theory

Schlossberg's 1984 work examines circumstances that often affect the strength of particular transitions adults experience at specifics points in their lives. Schlossberg's theory presents transition as "any event, or non-event, that results in changed relationships, routines, assumptions, and roles" (Evans et al. 111).

Schlossberg defines transitions as falling into three categories:

- *Anticipated*: changes we plan for or at least know are coming

- *Nonanticipated*: transitions that surprise us

- *Nonevents*: events we are counting on that do not happen (Evans et. al 112)

This theory describes the transition process as comprised of three elements:

- APPROACHING CHANGE

  In experiencing transitions, the role of perception is paramount. There is no transition unless it is perceived as such by the individual. Once a transition is so defined, individuals make two types of appraisals:

  1. A judgment of the actual transition in positive/negative/neutral terms

  2. An assessment of his or her means of dealing with the situation (Evans et al. 113)

- TAKING STOCK

  During this process, an individual's ability to cope is based on the ratio of their assets to liabilities. The following, which Schlossberg describes as "The 4 S's," are components impacting an individual's ability to navigate the transition as well as impacting their evaluation of both the transition and themselves (Evans et. al 113).

  1. *Situation*

     The collection of circumstances that bring about a transition. Schlossberg uses the following words and phrases to label these situational aspects of a transition: trigger, timing, control, role change, duration, previous experience with a similar transition, concurrent stress, and assessment (Evans et. al 113).

2. *Self*

   A. "Personal and demographic characteristics," the defining characteristics of the individual including such matters as age, gender, and social status; and

   B. "Psychological resources," the levels of ego strength, attitude and dedication the individual possesses (Evans et al. 113).

3. *Support*

   The relationships an individual has access to, including "intimate relationships, family units, network of friends, and institutions and communities" (Evans et al. 114)

4. *Strategies*

   The means of modifying the circumstances, controlling the meaning to the individual, and managing the immediate and resultant stress from the situation (Evans et al. 114).

- TAKING CHARGE

  Schlossberg et al. in their 1995 work describe transitions as comprised of the following phases:

  "Moving in," "moving through," and "moving out" (in Evans et al. 112).

Schlossberg: Application to LGBT Student Experience

Alex is a transfer student (23) who seems like a lost soul. He stops in the LGBT Resource Center quite a bit but isn't involved in programming or services. Though he received the distinction of being valedictorian in his high school class, Alex has wandered through several unsuccessful stints at various campuses. The year prior to coming out at age sixteen, Alex's maternal grandmother, who was his best friend and incredibly accepting, passed away. After coming out, Alex was rejected by his grandparents, aunts, uncles, and cousins on his father's side, as well as his godparents. Additionally, Alex's father lost his ministerial license as a result of his support for his son. Alex's mom is also very accepting and goes to work for the statewide LGBT advocacy organization. Within the first couple years after coming out, Alex's parents' divorce.

In terms of Schlossberg's "Approaching change" process, one could wonder about the timing of Alex's coming out. The first assessment looks at the event itself, followed by an evaluation of the individual's resources to cope. For Alex, he begins this journey with the devastating loss of his grandmother. It could be that, at this point, it became easier, in terms of emotional resources, to come out as opposed to staying closeted.

"Taking stock," the second of Schlossberg's processes, is also illustrated in Alex's experience, beginning with the first of the "Four S's"—Situation. While it is impossible to fully understand the impact of Alex's loss, it makes sense that he would not view this time after the passing of his grandmother as one where he had the emotional resources to now begin the coming out journey. Instead, it is possible that coming out was a way to manage the lack of resources he was left with following his grandmother's death. This still indicates that Alex, either consciously or unconsciously, conducted a resource assessment of how to best manage his need to come out while in the midst of experiencing profound grief.

Due to the cascading losses that Alex and his family experienced, it seems improbable that Alex was ever able to "move through" or "move out" of these transitions in a way that would feel like mastery. The series of losses he experienced seem to have kept him from ever fully being able to get his feet firmly under him. The complex grief Alex has experienced prevents him from completing Schlossberg's transition processes. This stall is evident in the way Alex continues to present as a lost soul.

Conclusion

Our hope was to provide an overview of some of the major student development theories while intentionally looking through the lens of an LGBT student journey. Our students come to us in complex bodies and are attempting to make meaning of the many identities they ascribe themselves, as well as those ascribed to them by society (Deaux 1993). Until there is a developmental model that can more fully examine multiple identities, our work to best assess our students' journeys continues. We believe it is helpful to find many ways of viewing LGBT students in order to better understand and help them navigate the intricate and beautiful kaleidoscope of identities they embody.

Works Cited

Deaux, K. (1993) "Reconstructing Social Identity." *Personality and Social Psychology Bulletin* 19 (1993): 4–12.

Evans, Nancy J., Deanna S. Forney, and Florence Guido-DiBrito. *Student Development in College: Theory, Research, and Practice.* San Francisco: Jossey-Bass, 1998.

Chapter 10

Queering Service Learning

Promoting Antioppressive Action and Reflection by Undoing Dichotomous Thinking

David M. Donahue and Myles Luber

What if a service learning project was so relevant and meaningful that students went well beyond "going through the motions" of putting in their service hours and writing the perfunctory paper at the end of the semester? What if a service learning project engaged one's mind so deeply that it led not just to new knowledge but to a change in one's thinking and perspective? Isn't this the kind of profound change from service learning that practitioners hope to see?

But what if these changes cause such disequilibrium that it leads to a form of "crisis" that temporarily paralyzes one from action, including action or service expected by the community partner in a service learning project? What if a community partner has expectations from service that do not allow for such a crisis? What if developing balance again takes more time than the weeks from midterms to finals in one semester?

These questions speak to possible dilemmas when service learning is framed as antioppressive work that really matters. They speak to real tensions between the necessary messiness of learning and the bureaucratic tidiness of academic calendars and deadlines for grading. They speak to the tension between balancing support for student learning and meeting the expectations of community partners. Most important, they speak to what students and instructors often construct as a false dichotomy between thinking and learning, on the one hand, and acting and serving, on the other. And they were all real questions for the coauthors, instructor and student, respectively, engaged in a service learning project with on-campus partners to create a queer and trans student center at Mills College.

In this chapter, we present queer theories and perspectives as a way to break down artificial dichotomies and question "natural" assumptions about sexuality and gender, as well as about service learning. We describe what service learning looked like and how it was conceptualized in Schools, Sexuality, and Gender, a course offered at Mills College that bridged the fields of education and queer studies. Author Donahue was the instructor of the course and author Luber was one of the students. We look more deeply at our experiences in one particular service learning project to support the creation of a space on campus for queer students, and use Kumashiro's (2002) "pedagogy of crisis" and conceptions of community and service learning informed by queer theory to analyze the dilemmas resulting from the project for the student and instructor. We conclude with thoughts about how to manage these dilemmas in ways that honor the needs and values of all involved in a service learning relationship—student, instructor, and community partner.

Pedagogy of Crisis

Kumashiro (2002) describes a pedagogy of crisis as an approach to antioppressive education that changes students and society through a process that is personally difficult and that can consequently spark resistance among students. As students learn about the partial nature of their own knowledge (e.g., how some persons, their knowledge, and perspectives are defined as "Other" and excluded from canonical or "commonsense" thinking), they also have to unlearn old assumptions. Such intellectual work is emotionally difficult because it can make visible to students how they have thought and acted in oppressive ways that excluded others and limited their own growth. It can also create in students a state of "crisis" in which, according to Kumashiro (2002), students "are both unstuck (i.e., distanced from the ways they have always thought, no longer so complicit with oppression) and stuck (i.e., intellectually paralyzed and need to work through their emotions and thoughts before moving on with the more academic part of the lesson)" (63).

Because teachers want to provide safe environments (sometimes conflated with "comfortable" environments) for students' learning and because they want to move forward efficiently with their curriculum, many might avoid creating classrooms prompting crisis among students. But as Kumashiro (2002) points out, "education is not something that involves comfortably repeating what we already learned or affirming what we already know. Rather, education involves learning something that disrupts our commonsense view of the world" (63). Such work takes time and a capacity to encounter difference and work through resistance if it is to lead to profound changes in how one thinks and acts in the world. In this article where we examine pedagogical dilemmas about crisis, teaching, and learning, we share our stories as student and instructor and analyze service learning along lines of ethically responsible processes, educative outcomes, and change toward greater social justice. We also bring our understanding of queer theory as applied to service learning, outlined in the next section, to inform our future actions.

Queering Service Learning and Service Learning for Queer Communities

Service learning, when "queered" or framed from the perspective of queer theory, presents possibilities for destabilizing commonsense ideas, and this destabilization can lead to crisis. Further, service learning on behalf of queer communities (e.g., volunteering at an LGBT center), which is not necessarily the same thing as service learning informed by queer theory (e.g., questioning or "troubling" normative assumptions behind an after school tutoring program or soup kitchen), can also raise troubling questions leading to crisis. The service learning described in this article was both framed by queer theory and in some way designed to serve queer communities. This framing contributed to the "crisis" experienced by Luber.

Queering Service Learning

Queer theory questions or "troubles" what is considered "normal" (Butler 1990; Foucault 1979; Sedgwick 1990). It considers the culturally and historically specific ways in which normativity is constructed and given meaning (Derrida 1978; Lyotard 1984). For service learning, this means questioning who is "normal" or "privileged" and therefore serves and who is the "other" or "underprivileged" and consequently needy of service. It also means challenging whether these categories are "natural" (i.e., inherent divisions among people or human constructs subject to rethinking) by asking who decides what is considered privileged and how relationships of power determine who is considered normal and privileged or other and underprivileged.

Queer theory also raises questions about binary thinking, which can be used to challenge the dichotomous terms used to frame service learning. Queering service learning means questioning binary constructions such as "serving"/"being served" and "campus"/"community" (Varlota 1997). Questioning binaries has implications for learning as students are challenged to view contradictions, rather than neat categorizations, as central to understanding. Rather than focusing on fixed and unequal identities or roles such as "one serving" and "one being served" or "learner" and "teacher" that are neither inherent nor required in service learning, queer perspectives encourage us to think about reciprocal relationships in service learning, where borders between providers and recipients of service as well as between learning and teaching are blurred (Hillman 1999). This kind of mutually beneficial relationship is different from sharing power where those serving "give up" some of their power, but clearly identifiable, and unequal, roles remain.

Queer perspectives on service learning can also challenge dichotomies between acting and thinking or in the case of service learning more specifically between serving and learning. Whereas thinking and doing are often seen in opposition, theorists from Dewey (1933) to Schön (1983; 1987) have reminded us of the dynamic relationship between the two. Dewey described how action can cause disequilibrium that leads to reflection and learning. Schön calls this "reflection on action." He also describes an even more immediate connection between thinking and action called "reflection in action," where skilled practitioners are engaged in a back and forth between thinking and action that is almost seamless. Done well, service learning requires students to consider the application of learning and to put thinking into action. Similarly, action, or service, becomes a focus of reflection and is therefore connected to continued thinking and learning or "reflection on action." When students and teachers become skilled practitioners of service learning, they can engage in reflection in action, where thinking and acting are in immediate relationship rather than dichotomous opposed categories.

Service Learning for Queer Communities

Service learning for queer communities also raises questions, including what is meant by "queer communities." Queer theory posits identity as multiple, intersecting, socially constructed, and fluid (Anzaldúa 1987; Kumashiro 2001; Moraga 1996), which necessitates thinking of communities based on identities such as queer identities as equally complex, rather than in totalizing ways that are implied by a term like the queer community, where other aspects of identity are subsumed by one aspect, where sexual orientation is seen as a "natural" category rather than a constructed one for defining community, and where other aspects of identity such as male or white identities can become normative when thinking about or representing "the" queer community. These concerns about essentializing queer communities play a central role in the crisis examined in this case.

Complexity in thinking about community contradicts the binary notion of easily drawing boundaries of inclusion and exclusion and makes difficult the idea of achieving the idealized notions so often associated with community, like that described by the San Francisco Lesbian Gay Bisexual Transgender Community Center (2011), "to connect our diverse community to opportunities, resources and each other to achieve our vision of a stronger, healthier, and more equitable world for LGBT people and our allies." Considering notions of diverse communities under a queer or lesbian, gay, bisexual, and transgender (LGBT) umbrella, Sullivan (2003) writes, "One wonders whether 'our combined community' is in fact the 'paradise' that many have envisaged it to be, or whether it is far from perfect, or perhaps even impossible" (143). Perhaps for this reason, community is used as a metaphor, for example hooks's (2003) "beloved community," or described as a process (Phelan 1994), as much as it is seen as an actual achievement. For Phelan, community is negotiated, much like identity, and in this sense, community is more like building strategic alliances that provisionally shape and are shaped by identities. Secomb (2000) redefines community, focusing less on negotiation and more on what would be seen by many as fractures in a community. She sees community as "an expression of difference and diversity that is made manifest through disagreement and disunity" (134). Such fracturing processes are part of defining identities, queer and otherwise. These ideas about service learning and queer communities inform our thinking about becoming "unstuck" from future crises in service learning.

Service Learning in Schools, Sexuality, and Gender

In fall, 2010, Donahue taught a new course, Schools, Sexuality, and Gender, at Mills College. The course had two complementary aims: to ground students in queer theory and its usefulness for questioning normativity, particularly around gender and sexuality, in education, and to prepare them to be agents of change in making schools places that not only include LGBT and queer people but make the world more just for all. As one colleague commented, the last part of this purpose was no small task. Two essential questions helped organize the course: How do schools shape identities and regulate social norms? How might schools be inclusive places of possibility for all students? By the end of the course, Donahue wanted students to understand that identities are multiple and intersecting; that schools operate as heteronormative, gender-regulating institutions; and that young people, teachers, and school leaders can be agents of change.

All students in the class were required to participate in one of four service learning projects that questioned some aspect of what is considered "normal" or "natural" about schools. One of the projects asked students to develop a lesson plan about Harvey Milk for middle and high school teachers to use as part of the second annual day of commemoration (May 22) in California. The lesson plan was intended to fill in what is a total absence of LGBTQ people from the secondary school history curriculum. Another project involved researching the student handbooks and websites of school districts throughout California to determine whether they were meeting their responsibilities to inform students of their rights under California law (AB 537) to nondiscrimination based on gender, gender identity, gender expression, and sexual orientation. A third project included collecting oral histories of LGBTQ alumnae for an archive in the college library. A final project, which is also the focus of this article, asked students to collaborate with an ad hoc group on campus that was working to create a queer student space (provisionally called QTHQ or Queer/Trans Headquarters) at the college. In the next section, Luber describes how this service learning project led to crisis, and in the subsequent section Donahue describes managing the pedagogical dilemmas of student crisis.

Crisis at the End of the Semester: The Learning Dilemmas of Service Learning (Myles Luber)

I began the semester working with three other students on our service learning project to support the initiative for a queer and trans space on campus. We all shared an investment in supporting queer and trans students and worked on the assumption that creating such a space on campus would be an important way to support these students. The space, which was to be called the "Queer and Trans Headquarters" (QTHQ), had been in the works for at least a year and a half. The request for a space had been met with some resistance and delay by the institution. One student, not in the class, who had been leading the initiative, facilitated meetings between students, faculty, and staff to discuss the initiative and shape the proposal for the space. He also worked with us as an adviser on the service learning project.

The other students and I made a plan to divide the work so that we each would focus on different projects to support the initiative. One student volunteered to contact other schools about their queer and trans spaces to find out what we could learn from them. Another volunteered to create a plan for a lending library in the space, including making a list of books that should be available. However, after a meeting with the student leader of QTHQ, we learned that publicizing the initiative might be more useful and subsequently shifted focus. One student and I took on the task of facilitating focus groups to find out what students' wants, needs, and concerns were about creating a queer and trans space on campus.

After struggling with time management and schedule coordination for weeks, we decided that we could gather information more efficiently through a widely administered survey than we could through focus groups. A survey would allow us to reach more people without having to coordinate schedules for focus groups or having to code hours of qualitative data. We were also under the impression, at the time, that by doing a survey we could bypass the need for approval from the Human Subjects Protocol Committee, saving us time.

We began constructing a survey to send out to students. Our plan was to send the survey to all student organizations on campus that are identity-based (e.g., the Black Women's Collective, but not the Crafters' Collective) in order to get input from a broad base of students. We also planned to post the survey through listservs and social media.

Writing the introduction to the survey was one of our first challenges. We wanted to describe our intentions and describe the space. We first began by describing what we *wanted* the space to be: a space for queer-spectrum and transgender-spectrum people coming from a variety of social locations with a variety of identities. We wanted the QTHQ to be an explicitly social justice–orientated space that would be welcoming to all students. As we wrote this, we tried to create a large, but not exhaustive, list of queer and transgender-spectrum identities. This was an attempt to make participants and future patrons of the space feel that their identities were named explicitly if they identified, for example, as bisexual, but not queer, or gender non-conforming, but not transgender. We were concerned that even the name "*Queer* and *Trans* Headquarters" could be alienating to students from the get-go. We sent an e-mail to students involved with the initiative to try to brainstorm more identity terms for the introduction.

As we did this, I began to question if we could really describe QTHQ in this way. Could we really promise it would be welcoming for all of these people? Were we projecting our hopes into this introduction, at the expense of transparency? Everyone in our service learning group met to address these questions. We concluded the meeting with a much more transparent introductory paragraph; one that acknowledged our hopes for the space, articulated the initiative's current status, and acknowledged the limitations of the working title of QTHQ. We decided to add a question to the survey that would give participants a chance to add their own name suggestions for the space.

In order to get a sense of who did and did not participate in the study, we constructed a demographic question. We struggled to create a question that would make room for participants' many intersecting identities, not privilege any single aspect of identity, and also provide us with concrete demographic information. We chose to ask participants how they self identify, offer a list of categories they could feel free to choose, and provide an empty box in which they could describe themselves. The list of categories included gender, age, race/ethnicity, sexuality, religion/spirituality, ability, class, citizenship status, and national origin. We felt it was important to know the demographics of the participants in order to see if any one group was notably absent. If the results of the survey demonstrated the absence of a particular social group, we intended to seek out their input explicitly.

The middle of the survey focused on questions that would assess the need for a queer and trans space. We hoped that this information would be useful for buttressing the argument at Mills that a queer and trans space is needed and should be funded by the college. We also asked questions attempting to assess the wants, needs, and concerns students may have about the space. We chose to prompt participants, rather than only asking them an open-ended question. For example, when we asked, "Do you have any concerns about the space?" we also provided a list of categories into which their concerns might fall. This required us to think about what our concerns were as students. The list of categories included accessibility, belonging and representation, funding, naming of the space, and the mission statement.

Having finally completed a survey, we made plans to publish and administer it. On the day we planned to send it out, we received an e-mail from Donahue, our professor, informing us that we did, in fact, need Human Subjects approval to go forward with this study. At this point in the semester, we felt it was impractical to put together a Human Subjects Protocol and instead began to focus on what we had learned in the process of putting together the survey and what we had, substantially, to offer the initiative.

One student provided the initiative with publicity, including tabling in the lunch area at student union and tabling at the annual Drag Dance run by the only currently functioning queer group on campus. Another student provided the initiative with information about other institutions' queer and trans spaces. We also produced a survey that is available for use by the initiative, and raised important questions about the nature of the space moving forward.

About halfway through the semester I began to come up against my own ethical dilemma. I became involved with the initiative months earlier after reading a copy of the initial proposal for the space. Although I was, at first, unmoved to participate in the creation of the space, I was driven to action after being troubled by some of the content of the proposal. My involvement was not derived entirely from an investment in creating a queer and trans space on campus, but, rather, from my investment in preventing that space from becoming what I worried would be a white, cisgender, and lesbian space at the expense of queer and transgender students who did not fit into those categories.

After becoming peripherally involved with the project, I questioned the proposal and its stated missions, but failed to question the need for a queer and trans space itself. Having spent much of my teenage years at an LGBT youth center in San Diego, I've learned to value queer and trans youth spaces. However, I've also seen firsthand the pitfalls of queer and trans spaces that fail to be explicitly supportive to queer and trans people of color, people with disabilities, and people whose experiences just generally do not fit dominant gay, lesbian, and transgender narratives.

Having witnessed these sorts of spaces in action, and having only ever seen some of those pitfalls addressed in explicitly queer and trans people of color spaces, I began to question how a queer and trans space on campus could not slip into these same cycles of marginalization. I started to wonder if a queer and trans space was really what queer and trans students needed most on campus. Would the space be used? And, if so, who would use it? For what purposes? Could that energy and money be better spent on different initiatives on campus to support queer and trans students and make our needs visible on an institutional level?

Here I refer back to Kevin Kumashiro's (2002) theory of "crisis" as a stage of learning to explain my process. Having come from direct-action politics into academia, I found myself, as Kumashiro puts it, "paralyzed" from further action at the end of the semester. I was so frozen by my questions and concerns, I found myself grasping for both tools to create, and models for, queer and trans spaces that didn't perpetuate cycles of marginalization. My hesitations became so overwhelming that I felt it was better to take no further action at all than to take an action that might be imperfect. By the end of the semester, I did not feel that I had entirely worked through this "crisis," but have continued to think about how to move forward from this space.

In the short term, the service learning project did not provide our community partner with an immediate result. However, in the long term, this experience was fundamental in shaping my strategies as a student activist. After experiencing and writing about this "crisis," I found myself driven to work through and beyond it. However, this was not a process that could be neatly completed in the course of a single semester. Rather, it is a process I am very much still engaged in.

In my position on campus working as a Social Justice Peer Educator I have used this experience extensively while teaching fellow students, faculty, staff, and administration. While preparing for a discussion about gendered admissions policies at our single-sex institution, my cofacilitator, who was also our partner on the QTHQ project, and I began to imagine the teaching tool I now call the "Three Tiers of Action." I have since extensively expanded the tool and use it regularly as a key framework for workshops on transphobia and cis-sexism.

The framework is intended to move workshop attendees as rapidly as possible from a place of limited knowledge to a place of action. The first tier includes changes we can begin to make *immediately*. This tier is comprised of shifts in interpersonal and day-to-day interactions. The second tier includes changes we can begin to make in the *short term*. This tier presents opportunities to work toward structural and institutional changes. The third tier describes *long-term* questions and changes. This includes cultural and ideological questions and shifts.

The third tier, despite being given the least amount of time in the workshops, is possibly the most important. When presenting this tier I tell workshop attendees that it is important that we recognize that these "big questions" are in the room, and that we continue to think about them. However, what is at stake is the day-to-day survival of trans students on our campus, and endlessly discussing those questions without taking action does little to provide tangible support to trans students. I encourage workshop-goers to recognize that it is possible to move forward as allies and activists without first answering these difficult questions.

The service learning project pushed me to further my work as an activist on campus. And while my experience of "crisis" temporarily "froze" my actions, I was ultimately able to use this experience as a foundation for my own processes of growth as an academic, social justice activist, and individual.

The Unexpected Always Happens: The Pedagogical Dilemmas of Service Learning (David Donahue)

Every year, I renew my long-standing commitment to teach through service learning. I do so because I want students to have authentic opportunities to bridge the dichotomy so often set up between thinking and action. Breaking down such dichotomies, just like implementing a service learning projects is easier said than done, however.

This difficulty is part of what makes service learning vital in a way that pedagogical strategies divorced from action are not. Service learning is messy and I am committed to service learning in part despite and in part because of the "messiness" of service learning. By messy, I mean the predictable result that something unanticipated will happen as well as the ambiguity of taking responsibility for student learning and beneficial community outcomes. It is not hard to imagine why anyone would use service learning despite what seem like immense complications. But I am committed to service learning because of these complications too. The process of any learning that matters is messy and raises dilemmas of competing cultural, moral, and political values. Service learning makes these dilemmas visible and offers them as opportunities for learning that reflect the real world—learning that rarely comes with a single right answer waiting to be discovered. These dilemmas from service learning can also be opportunities to act in ways that respect complexity and messiness. Too often learning in schools is defined only by knowing and is devoid from any imperative to act in any way, let alone antioppressive ways.

Like any other service learning project, the one working with others on campus to create a queer student center had the potential to get messy. I considered the possible complications of students working with a "community partner" also composed of students. I also wondered about the possible complications of students engaged in work on campus that could put them in politically difficult situations with administrators or staff and was aware that faculty implementing such service learning are sometimes accused of indoctrinating rather than teaching (Butin 2006; Robinson "Service"; Robinson "Dare"). Finally, I had difficulty imagining what the final product of service might look like. Whereas other projects were defined from the start by their products—curriculum guides, a data set on policy implementation, oral histories—I knew this project would not result in a queer student center by the end of the semester and needed to define some other interim goal toward which to work. Over the course of the semester, I watched the goals and plans of the group working for QTHQ evolve. Heading into the final weeks of the course, the plan to collect data through focus groups changed into a plan to collect data through a survey and finally, because of the limitations of time, into a plan to create a survey that could be implemented later.

Along the way, I accommodated these evolutions. Only after considering Luber's "crisis" in hindsight and my own nagging questions about whether I responded in the best interest of service for our partner or learning for Luber do I see how this project presented a pedagogical dilemma, which I consider in the remainder of this section.

I describe Luber's crisis as presenting a pedagogical dilemma because it posed questions without any single, correct answer. Unlike problems which have a technical solution, dilemmas, according to Cuban (2001), present "competing prized values," which result in "unattractive choices due to constraints" that require compromise (12). Dilemmas stand in further contrast to problems. Whereas a problem goes away when it is solved, dilemmas can only be managed. Managing a dilemma means being able to act, but the tension creating the dilemma is never eliminated (Cuban 2001; Lampert 1985). Such tensions can be the stuff of crisis.

I initially saw this as a dilemma of balancing responsibilities to students and to community partners. Framed as such it poses a choice between privileging student learning over following through on commitments to the community partner. As an instructor, I unambiguously value students' learning and see it as my primary responsibility. Teachers rarely find anything in competition with their students' learning and, if so, it is hard to imagine what could be as compelling.

Service learning complicates this responsibility, however, because collaboration with community partners makes students and me responsible for following through on commitments that give greater purpose to our activities beyond individual students' learning, as valuable as that is. This additional responsibility leads to many positive outcomes, not the least of which is contributing something valuable to the community. It also contributes to positive outcomes for students as well. I've credited that responsibility with the high quality of work done by students in the past and I draw on it—some might say I manipulate them with it—telling students that service learning projects are never done until the grade is A, because we will not do anything of B quality for a community partner. Because of this responsibility, I usually am clear about expectations and keeping students to those expectations. In the past, I have held students to their responsibility through differences of opinion with community partners and beyond the semester if necessary. If anything, responsibility to others comes as close to a priority as my responsibility to student learning, making this a difficult dilemma.

As I considered my responsibilities to Luber and QTHQ, I wondered about how much direction to apply to the service learning project. I value service learning because it provides opportunities for students and me to think and act in the real world where decisions and timelines are not dictated by fifteen-week semesters and deadlines for entering grades, where we address unanticipated contingencies. I also appreciated that students working in this group thought about what would really be of service and took the initiative to change gears, for example, from outreach about a queer student center to information gathering about students' needs and wants to eventually questioning whether a center was the best way to meet the needs and wants of a diverse group of students. This is exactly the kind of critical and flexible thinking that service learning should encourage in students (Rhoads, 1998).

I also believe in making plans and sticking with them, especially plans that I've helped create and see as producing something of value for students and the community. I worried about not completing the original commitments to our community partner if we changed plans. In the end, the students and I redefined the final product so we were still doing something for a community partner even if it was not what we originally planned. Because the process of creating a queer student center on campus did not have a fixed timeline, letting go of our original plans of collecting data and instead creating only a plan for collecting data felt like "doing something," even if it was a different "something." Managing the dilemma this way meant prioritizing students' learning and giving it the time it needed, but not at the total expense of providing something for QTHQ. Again, I was trying to frame without dichotomizing in a way where clear winners and losers gained or did not gain something from the project. Indeed, I hoped the outcome of managing the dilemma this way was positive for students and QTHQ.

While this project was similar to past ones that have evolved over the course of a semester, it was different because, in contrast to past projects, the changes this time were the result of a student's critical perspective on the service itself. Torn between two valued aspects of service learning—authentic learning that runs according to its own timeline and leads to uncertain results versus following through with a plan that I know can be accomplished in a semester and which I feel confident will yield something valuable to the community and something of educational value to the students, I leaned toward organic change in part because my students believed it would best serve their learning and I trusted their maturity and flexibility in dealing with uncertainty and ambiguity. I saw that Luber's crisis was real and, though not unaware that it created complications for QTHQ and me, saw these complications as secondary to the primacy of student learning. I believed such learning would in the long run also benefit me with more sophisticated understanding of service learning and, I hoped, the community partner with a deeper insight into the multiple meanings of a queer student center on campus. In other words, I was trying to blur the dichotomy between desirable and undesirable results by framing the outcomes as positive for all.

In the moment, I found it easy to answer Luber when he talked to me about his concern with finishing something before the end of the semester, given his state of crisis. I said not to worry, that what was most important was that he take the time to think through what he needed to learn. I wonder if I would have been so quick to prioritize the needs of our partners if, face-to-face with them, they had said they needed to make sure, for example, that a series of reports about LGBTQ student centers were completed. In other words, was I responding to the person in front of me or the primary value of student learning? I suspect that as an educator, I put students and their learning first, no matter what my commitment to the community and service learning. The quickness with which I made this decision reflects that priority. I am aware that students are typically privileged in service learning relationships with the community (Brown 2001; Eby 1998). While I can work for greater reciprocity in those relationships, I cannot imagine doing so at the expense of a student's learning needs.

I have always been attracted to service learning because of the idea that it is about "more than"—more than learning without a meaningful purpose, more than learning disconnected from action, more than learning without benefit to the larger community. Service learning without giving something to the community seems like any other kind of classroom project that might involve a community connection, for example, interviewing community members or collecting information from community institutions.

If service learning is "more than," the baseline of student learning is always present. So requiring any kind of product for the community absent of or as an obstacle to student learning also seems contrary to service learning as well as my own commitment to making sure that students find their service learning experiences educative and not "miseducative." I would worry that requiring students to complete a project about which they had doubts, for example, doubts about the integrity or value of the work, could be miseducative and lead students to think that reflection on ethical or moral questions is not valued or worthwhile.

Concluding Thoughts on Framing Service Learning as Antioppressive

Both of us remained uncertain of our decisions and actions in this case after the semester's end. We questioned whether we let down our community partner and, in various ways, feel the absence of a queer trans space on campus. We began to wonder whether we had done what was most educative as well. As we began to think more deeply, we question framing a dichotomy between students' learning and a tangible contribution to the community. We see that this dichotomy is built on top of another dichotomy, that between thinking and action. As we reconsider this dichotomy, we question the decision to separate and prioritize thinking from acting. As we now consider acting and thinking in more immediate relationship, as we remind ourselves of the value of reflection on and in action, and as we acknowledge the moral imperative to act in nonoppressive ways, we believe in challenging the false dichotomy between acting and thinking, serving and learning. We see service learning projects like this as raising enduring dilemmas between competing values. We do not see those tensions easily resolved. They exist in the third tier of action. We see framing these tensions as dilemmas allows for a way to become "unstuck" from crisis. Rather than avoiding action to privilege reflection on abstract conceptions, however, we believe in the importance of constant reflection on and in action, the kinds of work that can be done in tiers one and two. Most important we believe in action and holding on to such tensions for continued reflection and challenging oppression while nonetheless acting. This is the essence of the third tier.

Embracing contradiction, in other words, holding on to tensions between values while not precluding action, is a necessary part of acting in the world, including acting to be nonoppressive. For service learning practitioners, responsibility to students and community is not mutually exclusive and in opposition but is interrelated and part of enduring dilemmas that cannot be solved and made to go away, but can only be managed and framed in ways that allow for holding on to the tensions and continually acting as well. In supporting—and requiring—students to act and meet responsibilities to a community partner, even if the actions are allowed to evolve, we are also doing what is most educative for students—learning to understand that action is not an option but an imperative and that acting in a world of ambiguity and contradiction means embracing those conditions and continuing to reflect on them in and on action. Framing crises as tensions between conflicting values that can be held while also acting is a more productive way to become "unstuck" from "crisis."

Works Cited

Anzaldúa, G. *Borderlands/La Frontera: The new mestiza.* San Francisco: Aunt Lute, 1987.

Brown, D. *Pulling It Together: A Method for Developing Service-Learning Community Partnerships Based in Critical Pedagogy.* Washington, DC: Corporation for National Service, 2001.

Butin, D. "Disciplining Service Learning: Institutionalization and the Case for Community Studies." *International Journal of Teaching and Learning in Higher Education* 18.1 (2006): 57–64.

Butler, J. *Gender Trouble: Feminism and the Subversion of Identity.* New York: Routledge, 1990.

Cuban, L. *Why Is It So Hard to Get Good Schools?* New York: Teachers College Press, 2003.

Derrida, J. *Writing and Difference.* London: Routledge, 1978.

Dewey, J. (1933). *How We Think.* Boston: D. C. Heath, 1993.

Eby, J. "Why Service-Learning Is Bad," 1998 (accessed July 26, 2011), http://www.messiah.edu/external_programs/agape/servicelearning/articles/wrongsvc.pdf.

Foucault, M. *Discipline and Punish: The Birth of the Prison.* New York: Vintage Books, 1979.

Hillman, T. "Dissolving the Provider-Recipient Split." *Academic Exchange* 3.4 (1999): 123–127. hooks, b. *Teaching Community: A Pedagogy of Hope.* New York: Routledge, 2003.

Kumashiro, K. *Troubling Intersections of Race and Sexuality: Queer Students of Color and Anti-Oppressive Education.* Lanham, MD: Rowman & Littlefield, 2001.

Kumashiro, K. *Troubling Education: Queer Activism and Anti-Oppressive Pedagogy.* New York: RoutledgeFalmer, 2002.

Lampert, M. "How Do Teachers Manage to Teach?: Perspectives on Problems in Practice." *Harvard Educational Review* 55.2 (1985): 178–194.

Lyotard, J. *The Postmodern Condition: A Report on Knowledge.* Manchester, UK: Manchester University Press, 1984.

Moraga, C. "Queer Aztlán: The Re-formation of Chicano Tribe." In D. Morton, ed., *The Material Queer: A LesBiGay Cultural Studies Reader.* Boulder, CO: Westview Press, 1996, 297–304.

Phelan, S. *Getting Specific: Postmodern Lesbian Politics.* Minneapolis: University of Minnesota Press, 1994.

Rhoads, R. "Critical Multiculturalism and Service Learning." In R. Rhoads and J. Howard, eds., *Academic Service Learning: A Pedagogy of Action and Reflection.* San Francisco: Jossey-Bass, 1998, 39–46.

Robinson, T. "Service Learning as Justice Advocacy: Can Political Scientists Do Politics?" *PS: Political Science and Politics* 33.3 (2000): 605–612.

Robinson, T. "Dare the School Build a New Social Order?" *Michigan Journal of Community Service Learning* 7 (2000): 142–157.

San Francisco LGBT Community Center. *History and Mission,* 2011 (accessed July 15, 2011), http://www.sfcenter.org/aboutus.php.

Schön, D. *The Reflective Practitioner: How Professionals Think in Action.* New York: Basic Books, 1983.

Schön, D. *Educating the Reflective Practitioner: Toward a New Design for Teaching and Learning in the Professions.* San Francisco: Jossey-Bass, 1987.

Secomb, L. "Fractured Community." *Hypatia* 15.2 (2000): 133–150.

Sedgwick, E. *The Epistemology of the Closet.* Berkeley: University of California Press, 1990.

Sullivan, N. *A Critical Introduction to Queer Theory.* New York: NYU Press, 2003.

Varlota, L. "A Critique of Service-Learning's Definitions, Continuums, and Paradigms: A Move Towards a Discourse-Praxis Community." *Educational Foundations* 11.3 (1997): 53–85.

Chapter 11

Five Proposals on Homophobia

David William Foster

This essay is divided into two sections. The first examines a series of propositions regarding the nature and practice of homophobia. It is based on the belief that homophobia continues to be a pervasive discursive practice. Yet since many blatant manifestations of yesterday have disappeared, or at least become attenuated, it becomes necessary to think through in greater detail the rhetoric and semiotics of homophobia, toward seeing how it underlies sociocultural practices that may not appear to be directly homophobic.

The second part of the essay turns to certain phenomena in Latin American societies, in the attempt to exemplify with a bit more detail abiding cultural ideologies that can legitimately be identified as homophobic and addressed as such.

Invisible Mutations of Homophobia

One of the considerable ironies of our social life is that, with all the visibility and legalization of certain aspects of queer life, homophobia has increased in many dimensions. Homophobia can be defined as the irrational and frequently violent fear of homosexuals, a fear wielded as much by certain self-identified heterosexuals as by homosexuals in a state of panic brought on by the consequences of their lifetime predicament in the crosshairs of said heterosexuals. Previously, homophobia had fewer social subjects to deal with, due to the "closet" effect imposed by the impunity of homophobia's practice. The effects of homophobia and the fear of falling into the hands of unpunished violence kept the vast majority of those who considered themselves homosexual in the closet, as well as those who contemplated the possibility of either being homosexual or being perceived as such. The definition of a homosexual was relatively meager—certain bodily conduct, including speech and language; a certain way of being in the world; a certain transparency regarding homoerotic desire and an eagerness to act on it. Consequently, the suppression of the signs of homosexuality was considered sufficient to do away with the socio-moral problem it represented.

At its height, psychoanalysis served to increase, enrich, and add depth to these signs of homosexuality, with the ideal goal of demonstrating to one that, despite all his heterosexual self-conscience, his conduct as a macho man, and his prolific fulfillment of heteronormative patriarchy's commandments, he was, in fact, a homosexual. Thus, it was necessary that the psychoanalyst demonstrate this to him, and that he fully come to terms with it in order to embark on the therapeutic project of its elimination. If homophobia dealt mainly with men in a sexist society, it is needless to say that what is being expressed here, with all due rectifications imposed by the differential history of women, was equally applied to women. I could be accused of sexism for speaking insistently about men and not focusing hereinafter on women; but it is precisely because I have a full knowledge of the differential history of women. It solves nothing to write about topics such as homophobia while insinuating that men and women have the same historical experience; the topic cannot even be developed in parallel columns. In simple and straight-forward terms, it's about writing differential histories. One necessarily writes from the historical inscription that is most appropriate to personal experience.

As a responsibility of "refined people" and "liberal and tolerant" com-promise, the open violence of homophobia was usually circumscribed to certain social sectors, sometimes to the sectors of the public officers who provided service to said refined people, who lamented others' brutality but did little to change it, urging their homosexual friends to exercise due discre-tion—that is, to keep their closets firmly locked.

Insofar as there began to be more visibility and legality for homosexuals (there is no unidirectional trajectory, but rather synergetic feedback from one to another), homophobic acts (and even the simple, casual verbal expression of homophobia) began to lose prestige and legality as a global social norm (always understanding that it is a matter of enforced paradigms in determined locales). Yet homophobia does not disappear, but rather assumes different forms: as with sexism and racism, it's the same pig with different lipstick . . .

The Shifting Direct Objects of Homophobia

The first problem for what we could call the business of homophobia—wheth-er in terms of old succinct codes or a wider range of signs—is who counts as "homosexual," or in current terms, "gay," "queer," and so on. In the olden days, it was a "straight" shot to identify "sodomites," because one had evidence (or one fabricated evidence, if necessary) of certain acts according to the watchful agent, who with total impunity hunted for and punished sinners: if an act was committed, a punishment was applied.

In previous times, as well as visual evidence or evidence extracted through inquiry, a process of metonymic chain was practiced: an earring meant an effeminate zeal, which meant an improper desire (heteronormatively speaking), which meant a certain way of being in the world, which meant a certain sexually inappropriate condition, which meant the practice of certain abhorrent acts that became synthesized under the "sodomy" heading, by virtue of which it was possible to refer to the previously enshrined treatment for sodomites.

Today, there has been a multiplication of subjects and a parallel multiplication of signs in play, even though some dimensions of homophobia have been beaten back into retreat (such as submitting the defendant to public derision and adding insult to injury whenever possible). But many new dimensions have opened up. One can cite here, by way of example, the insistence on wielding a series of categories—among fossilized and frozen ones—that are no longer relevant to the range of identities, behaviors, and self-definitions in play: it's what happens when someone calls another person (even with all the respect in the world) "gay," when that person, precisely, is committed to overcoming the categories of identity and all their implied partitions and divisions. One person can say, "I'm a faggot and I love myself," but another person can say, "I am, period. And I love myself." The first one recognizes the process of identity; the second one repudiates it.

Deconstructed Identities

There is no doubt that the deconstruction of identities provides us with a range of sexualities that goes well beyond what is traditionally recognized, to the point that biological masculinity and biological femininity, as inscribed by this binary, remains in our millenary languages, nearly becomes totally denaturalized. If, in Spanish, for example, we have usually said that the gender of *el libro* (book) and *la mesa* (table) are constructed on the basis of a difference in arbitrary grammatical gender, queer theory invites us to contemplate to what point the same can be applied to the binarism on which the grammatical difference between *la mujer* (woman) and *el hombre* (man) rests. If one adheres to the classification proposed by anthropologic researchers on the subject—that we really must talk about five genders—where does that leave the malnourished linguistic categories of Spanish?

Nevertheless, there is no need for homophobia to endorse a similar conceptual perception. In fact, the gap between "street" knowledge of sexuality and queer theory's proposals—neither one founded on privileged, "direct knowledge" of the body—opens a Pandora's box, and homophobes may very well not know where to begin, what with so many potential victims to assail.

This would be a good moment to make note that only recently has the Real Academia Española, in its urgent zeal to keep the language squeaky clean, recognized the existence of homophobia, at least in terms of having an entry in the RAE's *Diccionario*. It isn't unforgiveable to think that the paradigms of sexuality have changed so much that, more than anything else, it is urgent to recognize the existence of homophobia and those who practice it, with its proper adjective: *homophobic*. It isn't that fewer homosexuals were torn to shreds when the semantic nucleus presumably did not exist in the language, but rather that now they are torn to shreds with all the rights and privileges of the language of Cervantes.

Lexicalizing "Queer" in Spanish and Languages Other than English

The recognition of sexual diversity and the queer theory that is sustained within it, that is proposed to analyze it, and that gives us horizons of knowledge with all its philosophical deployment in postmodern society's order of the day, gives rise, almost as if complying with the iron-clad severity of social reaction, to repudiation. On the one hand, it's a matter of conceptual repudiation: queer theory has many ways of being lexically accommodated in Spanish: "twisted theory," "strange theory," "pink theory"—although "queer" is now taking hold in Spain and Latin America. If theory is a conceptual field for analyzing certain phenomena, it goes without saying that it is understood that theory is also committed to defending itself and even promoting itself in a gesture of fervent social activism. Things were quite different when sociology talked about "perverse sexualities," and it was acceptable to speak about homosexuality in the same way that one spoke about drug addiction or alcoholism. But let no one be fooled: queer theory is fundamentally tethered to the premise that its field of study is as natural as Christian theology's assumption of God's existence.

For the homophobia that we could call "tolerant," the sin is no longer in being homosexual, but rather in manifesting one's homosexuality. As they say, "the love that dared not speak its name is now the love that can't shut up." It is seen as a runaway process: first creating visibility, then talking about "those things," and finally promoting queer theory to problematize all the categories, norms, and privileges of heteronormative patriarchy. Where are we going to stop, if being heterosexual ends up being as valid an erotic option as any other?

Queering the Curriculum

Homophobia continues being brutal in a demonstrably violent and fatal way. It is not only in a world deemed less civilized than one's own that homosexuals and those accused of being homosexual are beaten, tortured, and liquidated in a process of identification of which neither proof nor coherence is required and against which there is no possibility of defense or appeal. And that is the case whether it is an officially pursued undertaking or a strictly personal campaign. As with all violent crimes, we have better statistics than before, but there are also more cases, for many of the reasons alleged so far. If in previous times, religions and sects denounced individual acts, now they persecute entire demographics. One significant example: the detainment, torture, and prosecution of all the clients of a gay bar in Cairo. The simple act of being clients of the bar, as another version of the previously mentioned metonymic chain, was understood as proof that those in question were homosexuals, and thus, the dregs of society. (One might believe that this sort of occurrence is an isolated instance of the process of guilt by association. However, the recent death of the Argentine folk singer, Mercedes Sosa, reminded me of what happened at a concert Sosa gave in 1979 in La Plata, the capital of the province of Buenos Aires. Nineteen seventy nine was the height of the military dictatorship's so-called Dirty War against left-wing subversion, and when the police showed up to arrest Sosa and her musicians for subversive acts, they also arrested the entire audience of 200 spectators: the mere act of being at a concert given by Mercedes Sosa was sufficient evidence of the presumed guilt as subversives of those spectators. This example is not impertinent here, as the Argentine military "enhanced" the category of political subversion by subsuming homosexuality within it.)

Insofar as the world of academia is concerned, things are handled with clean gloves (for as much as they conceal "brass knuckles"). The existence of a women's studies program can be admitted; even better if the department has administrative autonomy. Courses on women can be offered, just like courses on African Americans/Afro-Latin Americans, and Chicanos, just as courses can be offered on gay or queer issues. But let's keep them all off in their own stand-alone "programs," with emphasis here on "alone."

Things begin to get complicated when one talks about grounding the entire curriculum in feminism, about studying women and men within the parameters of feminism (or feminisms, as it is now necessary to say, and assuming that we wish to cling to the binary distribution of gender). Likewise, it is quite unheard of when one proposes to study all Latin American culture from the perspectives of racial (and/or ethnic) critical theories. And if being a woman or a Jew weren't enough to disqualify one as a social subject with full exercise of sociocultural rights and privileges, proposing that queer theory ground the curriculum in order to investigate how privileged, obligatory, and patriarchal heterosexism inevitably distorts our understanding of cultural processes is to put oneself once and for all on the path of confrontation. If it isn't a frivolous way of understanding culture, it is at the very least an act of boundary penetration that should be energetically repudiated.

One student—let's be tolerant and say naive, if not ingenuous—asked one of the students working with me in the doctoral program, "Do you have to be gay to work with Foster?" Does anything else need to be said on the subject?

I would like to conclude by turning to an example of what we might call practical queer criticism. I was recently asked to provide the Afterword to a volume of essays intersecting Latin American cultural production and human rights studies. The essays in this volume return at certain important moments of theorizing and analysis to the matter of universal constructs and the messy questions of actual historical realities. At the same time, it is abundantly evident in reviewing these essays that the questions they address are not the consequence of simply tacking onto Latin American historical realities a set of principles formulated elsewhere and that might be justifiably and profitably used in examining certain social matters and cultural interpretations. No longer a linguistic superstructure added as a potentially useful supplement to the Spanish language, the sort of approaches, pioneered in large measure by Hernán Vidal's judicious writings, and exemplified in this volume, involve creating a semantic field from within the language and from within the historical bases of its existence as a linguistic system. One major implication of such an approach is to underscore how one cannot be content to survey a national discourse in terms of how it matches or does not match a predetermined inventory of legal issues, but rather it must be a process of working through the national discourse in terms of what it does address and the complexities of that address. There are many references in these essays (to be published by Vanderbilt University Press) to the patterns of exclusion: who and what social formulations are absent, elided, suppressed, and eliminated in the process of creating semantic realms, horizons of meaning, and ideological exchanges.

I would like to illustrate this by reference to one significant realm of human rights concerns, the issue, within the overarching category of gender, of sexuality. I will refer both to the purported sexism of the Spanish language and to the troubling distortions brought by the so-called gay movement in its Latin American incarnations.

I am not referring to the well-established understanding that Spanish, like most of the world's languages, holds the feminine to be the marked (i.e., the nondefault) category of gender, whether viewed in terms of allegedly natural biological classification or essentially arbitrary grammatical classification. That is, male always prevails over female, with the former being the inclusive common gender, while nouns are grammatically masculine unless they are, with statistical exception, feminine, with new nouns always masculine unless they are derived from already existing feminine nouns. These details are so well established that they are essentially part of even folk knowledge about the Spanish language.

Rather, by the sexism of the Spanish language I refer to the way in which gender marking is virtually an inevitable category of the language and, even more important, how the categorization of gender is inevitably masculine or feminine. This is so to such an extent that one might easily assume (as the speakers of the language must do so unconsciously) that there are only two universal genders, either masculine or feminine. Some playfulness understandably ensues when one's attention is brought to the fact that other languages may have more than two genders grammatically, and that there is a neuter grammatical gender that includes some nouns whose real-world referents are, say, biologically feminine (e.g., German *Das Weib*), but this little serves to enhance any perception on anyone's part that natural gender could be problematical in its rigid binary disjunction between masculine and feminine. A large bibliography now exists on the question of Queer English, which, among other things, is a branch of linguistic inquiry in the language that attempts to understand the consequences of the masculine-feminine binary for the actual universe of meaning the English language refers to, including those affective and poetic attempts to question or go beyond it. We are by now used to the gender-bending work of transsexual speech in which the putative male "speaks in feminine" and vice-versa for the putative female.

But except for the cyber-language utilization of the "at" sign, the arroba, in order to avoid sexist use (e.g., "Querid@s amig@s"), there has been little headway in transcending the binary grip of the Spanish language as far as sexual identity is concerned, and virtually nothing as regards attempting to signal anything like the sort of gender continuum proposed by the 1995 Fourth World Conference on Women in Beijing. And lest one think this to be only a matter of an internationalist feminist or queer agenda, one need only dip into the whole complex issue of gender continuum in native American cultures, from the North Shore to the Straits of Magellan, only one aspect of which is captured by the overworked concept of the berdache. Indeed, part of the historic, colonizing clash between Luso-Hispanic culture and Native American cultures involves the fundamental misunderstanding by the former of the gender continuum of the latter, which it often lumped under the serve-all term of "sodomy," and persecuted accordingly. Or, to put it somewhat differently, the presence of a non-binary-gender continuum among Native American peoples gave the conquerors one more reason to conquer. Thus, when one speaks of "ensuring the rights of indigenous women," it is important to ask exactly what social subjects are we talking about? Does it include, for example, the *muxes* (*muxe* is derived from the premodern pronunciation of the Spanish word *mujer* [woman]) of the Zapotecan cultures of Oaxaca, social subjects who can hardly be simply lumped in with the Western concept of gay transvestites?

One of the effects of neoliberalism in a country like Argentina, recently recovering from neofascist military tyranny and anxious to catch up with the newest forms of modernity that had been suppressed by dictatorship, was to pursue questions of sexual identity. Thus, there is the way in which issues of sexuality would be an inevitable part of redemocratization, since both gender and sexuality were part of the agenda of persecution and elimination of the dominant ideology of military rule. Jews, women, and homosexuals were victims who received "special attention" by the apparatus of oppression and death. These were not disjunctive categories for the torturers, but rather interlocking ones, as viewed by the iteration of anti-Semitic theories on the sexual degeneracy of Jews and the feminization of the homosexual body. In this way, the return to constitutional democracy in Argentina would necessarily address to some extent gender issues, the qualifier "some" here referring, for example, to an enhancement of women's rights, the right to divorce, the recognition of same-sex principles, but not the legalization of abortion.

Of a different order, however, was the sudden visibility of sexuality in, at least, Buenos Aires and other major cities and the imperative to live an openly sexual life. Much of this visibility was directly related to ensuing neoliberalism, because it made possible the purchase of the signs of this dimension of democratic life: clothes, clubs, parades, magazines, and experience-enhancing aids—in short, the lifestyle of sexual liberation. Nowhere was this more evident than in the gay world. If earlier stages of prosperity in Argentina had made possible a visibility for sexual liberation, as in the case of the halcyon late 1950s and '60s, the Argentine equivalent of the mod go-go scene, it did not display much in the way of the homoerotic, remaining even more intransigently heterosexual (most likely as the consequence of the sexual ideology of the Latin American left, which abhorred the homosexual) than its First World sources.

The 1980s, however, brought to the Argentine scene—and, at first, to a lesser extent, other Latin American venues—a veritable eruption of the homoerotic: in a word, of the gay. One cannot but unquestionably applaud the emergence of a new panorama of sexuality in the wake of manifold oppressions of the body, with its attendant social consequences, during the period of dictatorship. However, in the rush to recover the status of *toujours moderne,* there was the wholesale import of a new linguistic superstructure, that of contemporary sexuality and, most notably, that of gay sexuality. Argentine Spanish may now have come pretty much to accept the term *queer* as either a synonym for gay or, more generally, as a term to cover the deconstruction of compulsory heteronormativity, but there has been far less of an easy accommodation in the Spanish of Argentina of gay vocabulary as a whole, or, to judge by the vagaries of Spanish language dictionaries and manuals of good linguistic use, of other nations in which that language predominates. The potential misfits, misunderstandings, and *mépris* were, however, less a matter of the moralistic rejection of what certainly looked alien in the face of what was believed to be the unquestioned legitimacy of the heterosexual matrix, than they were the problem of any suddenly annexed linguistic superstructure: Did they really fit lived human experience?

To be sure, Argentina had always had, as an inevitable component of human sexuality, evidence of what the late nineteenth century came to call homosexuality, and an equally inevitable component of the development of modernity in Buenos Aires (at least) was a record of what came to be called the homosexual lifestyle. We have at our disposal several accounts of this record. But gay culture was something else again, beginning with its visibility and what many perceived to be its aggressive demands for legitimation: there was a certain dimension of the venerable Queer Nation stance to it, and one could hear the old-timers lament that same-sex life was more interesting when it was in the closet and the province of a tight-knit family of persons "in the know." Such romantic attitudes aside, there is no question that whatever had been naturalized in Argentine (and, again, other Latin American) societies as homosexuality, with somewhat of a precise vocabulary and a sublinguistic system those who cared knew how to use (such as the aforementioned "speaking in feminine"), was markedly different from gay sexuality, whose very visibility made even those who didn't care in a way complicitous with its particular speak. This was even more so when it appeared that the "real" way to be gay was to reconstruct in Spanish and its social reality the New York or London or Paris scenes. Such commodifications created a wholly new axis: if to be homosexual meant being willing to play the game, being gay meant being able to pay, and often pay quite a bit, to play the game. As the commodifications of gay sexuality proliferated, so too did the linguistic superstructure required to account for it. Whereas before everyone thought he or she knew what simple *maricón* meant, there was a semantic leap involved in decoding a phrase such as "Soy puto y me quiero," because it involved adjustments in the semantic fields not everyone was willing to accept or able to make (especially since it involved rejecting implicitly the long-held assumption that *putos* were merely male-male prostitutes).

The demise of the neoliberal bubble may have brought an end to the more egregious forms of commodification of so-called alternative sexualities, but it left as linguistic residue that is only now beginning to be fully incorporated into the language, as witnessed by the matter of the word *queer* I mentioned above. What this means for the tenor of the essays in this volume is that, as in the case of other human rights, we are beginning to see a distinct realm of Latin American queer studies in which what is understood by queer—that is, what specifically is involved in terms of the historical realities of a society—is constructed on the basis of the lived human experience of that culture and not merely in terms of canvassing the laws and codes of a society to see if they are in sync with a particular international standard. This research has been perhaps advanced more in the case of the cultures of the Caribbean or in U.S.–Mexican border studies, but there is much to be researched for all Latin American societies.

It is, for example, for this reason that what we in the United States call gay marriage is not really a legal or public policy conundrum in most of Latin America. Marriage is in Latin America, first and foremost, a question of civil unions; some of which those involved may choose to have sanctioned by a religious doctrine. Such civil unions are not in conflict with so-called traditional marriage as U.S. religio-centric society views it to be, where churches have assumed the function of the civil registry. Concomitantly, those civil unions, which are paramount, cannot be construed as somehow second best to in the rituals of the social confirmation of sentimental and sexual bonds, because civil unions are the universal norm of institutional marriage. In short, the semantic domains are conjugated in different ways. This does not mean that churches cannot mount an effective campaign against gay civil unions. It just means that they must do so in terms of juridical practices over which they do not have any recognized control or participation in, as they do in the United States.

While only in very tangential ways do the essays in the Vanderbilt volume have to do with linguistic systems and with that category of human rights related specifically to sexuality, these are areas that will merit investigation as Latin American cultural studies invest in greater measures in the imperative of recognizing the centrality of human rights to the texts that we investigate and the centrality of the humanities to the understanding of human rights. Language is often reputed to be a defining tool of the human species, and linguistic systems are often put forth as the model for the understanding of the universe and experiences in relation to it by humans. Language study, as I have shown it in only a few brief ways in this commentary, will necessarily be central to the contributions of humanities to the principled analysis of human rights. Not to do so, I would argue strenuously, is to engage, precisely, in the sort of sleight-of-hand homophobia to which I allude earlier, grounded as it is on the presumption that things are not that way and to proceed as though that which needs to be proved had already been, irreproachably, proven.

Chapter 12

LGBT Bullying in Schools

Can School Policies Affect Climate?

Erik Green

Bullying and harassment within schools—for both gay and straight students—is not a new topic, and although there is a fair amount of research, there is little consideration of the way school practices (such as antibullying policies) affect school climate. Bullying in schools for lesbian, gay, bisexual, and transgender (LGBT) students (or those perceived as LGBT) has become a national hot-button topic, due to the recent high profile cases of youth suicide blamed on homophobic bullying. This essay examines a slice of the research available regarding LGBT harassment in schools, presents what's been done to connect this topic to educational policies, and proposes a direction and purpose for future research on the subject.

Within three weeks during the fall of 2010, five suicide cases made national news—the deaths of Asher Brown, age thirteen, Billy Lucas, age fifteen, Raymond Chase, age nineteen, Seth Walsh, age thirteen, and Tyler Clementi, age eighteen. Although occurring all over the country, each suicide was attributed to homophobic bullying; on September 9, Lucas hung himself in Greensburg, Indiana ("Billy Lucas"); on September 19, Walsh hung himself in Tehachapi, California (Alexander); on September 22, Clementi jumped off the George Washington Bridge in New York City (Hubbard); on September 23, Brown shot himself in the head in Houston, Texas (O'Hare); on September 29, Raymond Chase hung himself in Providence, Rhode Island ("Gay R.I."). Although these suicides propelled the issue into a national spotlight, bullying based on gender identity and sexual orientation is hardly a new topic—nor one that has gone away as the buzz from these news stories starts to fade. On November 5, 2010, fourteen-year-old Brandon Bitner threw himself in front of tractor trailer in Pennsylvania, just a day after his school held an antibullying assembly that students appeared to joke around about and failed to take seriously (Pursell). Suicide isn't the only concern with bullying either—direct physical assault also occurs, such as the shooting of Lawrence King, age fifteen, on February 12, 2008, in Oxnard, California (Conoley 217).

This "rash" of teen suicides and violence highlights an important problem, begging the question: What is the best solution to not only protect our students from taking their own lives, but to ensure that all students have equal access to a safe learning environment while at school? Among the many viable responses to school bullying, what is the effectiveness of enacting comprehensive antibullying policies and procedures?

Extensive research documents the occurrence of anti-LGBT bullying within schools. Bullying in schools is certainly not a phenomenon unique to LGBT students. In one study, "43% of middle school educators report that student bullying occurs at school daily or weekly. Twenty-two percent of high school and 21% of primary school educators report this same frequency" (Conoley 217). However, "there is a growing body of research evidence to suggest that homophobic bullying is more severe than general bullying [and that] homophobic bullying is not always taken as seriously as other forms of bullying by teachers, even being seen as a 'natural' reaction of young men" (Adams 259). Schools are often the first place harassment occurs for an LGBT student, with one study reporting schools as the most frequent location for someone's first verbal and physical sexual orientation victimization (72% and 56%) (D'Augelli 1469, 1471).

The Gay, Lesbian and Straight Education Network (GLSEN), has attempted to track the concept of "school climate" for LGBT students for the past decade. Through a quantitative analysis of survey responses, the GLSEN National School Climate Survey paints a picture of the experiences of youth (both gay and straight) within our school systems. Indicators of a "negative school climate" include "hearing biased remarks, including homophobic remarks, in school; feelings unsafe in school because of personal characteristics . . . ; missing classes or days of school because of safety reasons; and experiences of harassment and assault in school" (Kosciw xv). In the 2009 survey, the results were telling—88.9 percent of students often or frequently heard the word *gay* used in a negative way; 84.6 percent of LGBT students were verbally harassed because of their sexual orientation, and 63.7 percent because of their gender expression; many students were actually physically assaulted because of their sexual orientation (18.8%) or gender expression (12.5%) (Kosciw xvi). The statistics continued—30 percent of students missed at least one full day of school because they felt unsafe, and LGBT students who were more frequently harassed reported lower grade-point-averages and less desire to pursue postsecondary education (Kosciw xvii). Over the course of the ten years that GLSEN has reported the results of their survey (1999–2009), "there has been a decreasing trend in the frequency of hearing homophobic epithets; however, LGBT students' experiences with more severe forms of bullying and harassment have remained relatively constant" (Kosciw xix).

A variety of studies support the statistics reported by GLSEN, which is considered the touchstone for this type of research. Adams reports that "40% of young gay people in a survey had attempted suicide" (Adams 259) in the UK, and in the United States Biegel observed that "the suicide rate for LGBT students continues to be 3–4 times higher than that of their straight counterparts, and in some parts of the country LGBT runaways may comprise up to 40% of the entire teen homeless population" (Biegel & Kuehl 1). A veritable laundry list of research shows that antigay verbal harassment and epithets are pervasive in many of our secondary schools, that over half of LGB high school students report being verbally harassed in school, and that these students were more likely than other students to be sexually harassed in school (Goodenow, Szalacha, & Westheimer 574). Numerous studies have found "sexual minority youth [are] more likely than heterosexual peers to be threatened or injured with a weapon at school and to skip school because they felt unsafe" (574). The effects can also extend beyond school, as the high levels of harassment among youth either openly gay and lesbian or suspected of being nonheterosexual "frequently resulted in dropping out of school, running away from home, physical violence, drug use, and social isolation" (Barrett, Pollack, & Tilden 167). Early experiences of victimization compiled with a lifetime of harassment were the factors in one study that found "youth who are gender atypical in childhood and who are victimized may have elevated mental health and trauma symptoms, and some may have [posttraumatic stress disorder]" (D'Augelli 1480).

Research on the effects of school policies has been less extensive. Issues of sexual orientation are rarely directly connected to antibullying policies. In the United Kingdom, Adams found that although "sexual orientation is raised in two-thirds of Equal Opportunity documents[,] the theme of 'sexual orientation' is not directly tackled in any of the Anti-Bullying documents received" (Adams 265). Many studies talk about the effect of positive school climate, where "students who were questioning or LGB reported fewer negative psychological outcomes if they were in a school that they perceived to be positive" (Espelage 157–158), or that "[g]ood schools make deliberate attempts to shape school culture in positive directions and to foster health-enhancing behaviors, healthy relationships, and social responsibility in their students" (Goodenow et al. 575). Yet when research has been done on specific attempts to improve school climate, few approaches have been studied specifically for their effects on LGB students (575). Other studies have issues with sample sizes, where studies that focus solely on LGB students have limited ability to compare their results to a control group of nongays on issues like education and occupational achievement (Barrett et al. 166). Time is also a concern; as antibullying policies and the existence of Gay-Straight Alliances have become more prevalent in the past few years, it's unclear if studies done during the 1990s would bear any resemblance to studies conducted now (Goodenow et al. 586).

The GLSEN survey is one of the few research articles which compared the indicators of negative school climate based on whether a school had "No Policy" (or one the students were unaware of), a "Generic Policy" (which did not explicitly state protection based on specific characteristics), or a "Comprehensive Policy" (which may include specific characteristics such as sexual orientation and gender identity, plus elements of guidance to faculty and staff on how to intervene with bullying and harassment) (Kosciw 75). Although the differences weren't always staggering, a clear trend appeared showing differences in the indicators of negative school climate across the types of policies. For biased remarks, having a generic policy revealed no statistical difference from having no policy, whereas remarks dropped as much as 10 percent under a comprehensive policy (75). The likelihood that a student reported an issue rose significantly (11.2% for no policy, 14.1% for generic policy, and 17.8% for comprehensive policy) as did the likelihood that a staff member would have an effective response (28.9% for no policy, 35.7% for generic policy, and 41.2% for comprehensive policy) (Kosciw 77). "Students in schools with comprehensive policies were more likely than students in schools with a generic policy or no policy to report that staff intervened when homophobic remarks (26.6% vs. 15.9% vs. 10.0%) or negative remarks about gender expression (17.3% vs. 13.3% vs. 8.9%) were made" (Kosciw xix). There is also a study that is notable in showing that "antibullying policies had a strong and significant negative association with suicide attempts, even when victimization and perceived support were taken into account" (Goodenow et al. 585), but there have been few replications of research of that caliber.

From reading these studies, a few theories about education and the role of educational policy emerges. First, there is the underlying assumption that all students deserve equal access to quality public education, regardless of their sexual orientation or gender identity. Safety in schools is a driving force behind this—GLSEN posits that "[s]tudents cannot succeed in school when they do not feel safe," and that "[t]he incidence of in-school victimization experienced by LGBT students hinders their academic success and educational aspirations" (Kosciw xvi). The research of Biegel has a goal "to make schools safe and improve the quality of life for everyone within our education system" (Biegel and Kuehl 3). There is also an assumption, posited by the National Mental Health Association, that "[gay and lesbian] distress is a direct result of the hatred and prejudice that surround them, not because of their inherently gay or lesbian identity orientation" (Biegel and Kuehl 4), and that therefore external solutions are necessary to solve the problem of hatred and prejudice within schools.

There is also an assumption that there's a direct relationship between the policies and procedures within a school and the experience of an LGBT youth. The theory holds that "[p]olicies and laws that explicitly address bias-based bullying and harassment can create safer learning environments for all students by reducing the prevalence of bias behaviors and encouraging staff intervention. Comprehensive policies and laws that specifically enumerate personal characteristics, such as sexual orientation, gender identity, and gender expression, among others, are the most effective at combating anti-LGBT bullying and harassment" (Kosciw xix).

However, a question regarding this theoretical assumption arises regarding correlation and causation. Although the initial, limited research proposes that there's a correlation between comprehensive antibullying policies and a decrease in negative social climates, there's relatively little proof of causation. Do we know that policies directly affect climate, or is that climates which are already positive lend themselves toward creating and enacting comprehensive policies? "Administrations that are supportive of LGBT students may be more likely to implement policies and practices that improve school climate" (Kosciw 74)—which leads to a chicken-and-egg question: Which came first, the positive administration or the policy? And which one has greater influence on the school climate? Are there some other factors within the school that lead to both comprehensive policies as well as a decrease in negative social climate? For example, one study found that "[schools] with support groups were more likely than other schools to have a written policy on safety for sexual minority youth" (Goodenow et al. 578). What exactly are the factors that a comprehensive policy would influence? In one online study, "88% of the students said that homophobic remarks were used at least some times [sic] when teachers were present, and many students reported that teachers and staff did not intervene during these incidents" (Espelage and Swearer 157). Would a policy lead to or be a prerequisite for proper teacher training on intervention methods?

Clearly further research needs to be done on the exact correlation between antibullying, LGBT inclusive policies within schools and the effect they have on the experiences of LGBT students. One type of useful study could follow a quasi-experimental model, examining the effects of implementing a new comprehensive antibullying policy in a school (or state), which doesn't have one (or has only a general policy). Quantitative data could reveal if there's a significant shift in the school climate, while qualitative data could track what other policies and procedures change after enactment.

Regardless of the research done on them, more policies need to be developed and implemented specifically enumerating the protection of students based on sexual orientation and gender identity. If we are to believe the assumption that all students, regardless of sexual orientation or gender identity, deserve full equal access to safe schools, as well as the extensive research that has been done regarding the severity and pervasiveness of anti-LGBT harassment and bullying, then this is a critical concern warranting action even if the research thus far isn't conclusive. Correlation has been established between policy and school climate, and although the exact relationship between the two has yet to be fully teased out, the need for educational policies that address harassment and bullying are of paramount importance. Research indicates the potential value of having comprehensive policies, and "steps such as creating, communicating, and enforcing strong anti-bullying policies are within the capacity of even the most conservative schools and communities" (Goodenow et al. 585). Research has shown that for LGBT students, generic policies are not enough to provide a safe learning environment, yet "only 15 states plus the District of Columbia have comprehensive laws that include sexual orientation, gender identity, and/or gender expression" and "only 18.2% of all LGBT students . . . reported that their school had a comprehensive policy that specifically mentioned sexual orientation, gender identity, and/or gender expression" (Kosciw xix). Further research, however, can help support the theory that policy change is required if we expect a change toward positive school climate.

Works Cited

"Billy Lucas, 15, Hangs Himself." *Queerty* September 14, 2010 (accessed September 3, 2013), http://www.queerty.com/billy-lucas-15-hangs-himself-after-classmates-called-him-a-fag-one-too-many-times-20100914/.

"Gay R.I. Student Commits Suicide" *Advocate.com*, October 1, 2010, http://www.advocate.com/News/Daily_News/2010/10/01/Suicide_Takes_Life_of_Gay_RI_Student/.

Adams, N., T. Cox, and L. Dunstan. "I Am the Hate that Dare Not Speak Its Name: Dealing with Homophobia in Secondary Schools." *Educational Psychology in Practice* 20. 3 (2004): 259–269.

Alexander, Bryan. "The Bullying of Seth Walsh," *Time.com*, October 2, 2010, http://www.time.com/time/nation/article/0,8599,2023083,00.html.

Barrett, D. C., L. M. Pollack, and M. L. Tilden. "Teenage Sexual Orientation, Adult Openness, and Status Attainment in Gay Males." *Sociological Perspectives* 45.2 (2002): 163–182.

Biegel, S., and S. J. Kuehl (October 2010). "Safe at School: Addressing the School Environment and LGBT Safety Through Policy and Legislation."

Conoley, J. C. "Sticks and Stones Can Break My Bones and Words Can Really Hurt Me." *School Psychology Review* 37.2 (2008): 217–220 (accessed on March 16, 2014), http://www.nasponline.org/publications/spr/abstract.aspx?ID=1897

D'Augelli, A. R., A. H. Grossman, and M. T. Starks. "Childhood Gender Atypicality, Victimization, and PTSD Among Lesbian, Gay, and Bisexual Youth." *Journal of Interpersonal Violence* 21.11 (2006): 1462–1482 (accessed on March 16, 2014), http://jiv.sagepub.com/content/21/11/1462.refs.

Espelage, D. L., and S. M. Swearer. "Addressing Research Gaps in the Intersection Between Homophobia and Bullying." *School Psychology Review* 37.2 (2008): 155–159.

Goodenow, C., L. Szalacha, and K. Westheimer. "School Support Groups, Other School Factors, and the Safety of Sexual Minority Adolescents." *Psychology in the Schools* 43.5 (2006): 573–589.

Hubbard, Jeremy. "Fifth Gay Teen Suicide in Three Weeks Sparks Debate." *ABC News*, October 3, 2010 (accessed March 16, 2014), http://abcnews.go.com/US/gay-teen-suicide-sparks-debate/story?id=11788128.

Jones, Michael A. "After Students Laugh Off Anti-Bullying Assembly, a 14-Year-Old Commits Suicide." *Change.org*, November 8, 2010 (accessed March 16, 2014), http://gayrights.change.org/blog/view/after_students_laugh_off_anti-bullying_assembly_a_14-year-old_commits_suicide.

Kosciw, J. G., E. A. Greytak, E. M. Diaz, and M. J. Bartkiewicz (2010). *The 2009 National School Climate Survey: The Experiences of Lesbian, Gay, Bisexual and Transgender Youth in Our Nation's Schools.* New York: GLSEN (accessed March 16, 2014), file:///C:/Users/jhawley/Downloads/2009%20National%20School%20Climate%20Survey%20Full%20Report.pdf.

O'Hare, Peggy. "Parents Say Bullies Drove Their Son to Take His Life." *Houston Chronicle* September 29, 2010 (accessed March 16, 2014), http://www.chron.com/disp/story.mpl/metropolitan/7220896.html.

Pursell, Tricia. "Friends: Bullying Led to Tragedy." *Daily Item* November 6, 2010 (accessed March 16, 2014), http://dailyitem.com/0100_news/x603547374/Bullied-student-kills-self.

Chapter 13

Exploring the Boundaries of Self

Using Queer Autobiography to Teach Courses on Identity and Solidarity Across Borders

Juan Velasco

Writing from Life

What happens when we bring our personal narratives to consciousness, share them and analyze them? How can we utilize queer Chicana/o autobiographies to instill a sense of empathy and solidarity in our students? This article aims to include a more salient actualization of justice in teaching through the creation and consumption of autobiographies in the classroom. I explain the use and benefits of personal narratives, methods to encourage students to find their authentic voices and connection with their cultural communities or chosen familias, approaches to improving students' empathy for those culturally different from them, and attempts to expose students to social justice issues and increase the intellectual sophistication with which students approach autobiographical course material.[1]

Despite our fascination with "reality shows" and biographies and autobiographies, only a handful of compelling academic works focuses on the notion of developing justice and solidarity through writing autobiographies in the classroom. And few studies examine the necessary interrelation of justice and the development of identity through the creation and consumption of autobiographies.

Lifewriting offers specific information about the experiential aspects of social justice and identity often neglected in the classroom. By paying attention to the creation and consumption of autobiographies, we understand how the unjust structural realities become internalized in our students, and how their concept of identity affects their sense of self in the world. Chicana/o queer autobiography helps us to understand the complexities of intellectual and experiential knowledge using all the aspects of the person—the creative, the spiritual, and the cultural. The development of a more complex notion of self allows the student to see his or her own links with different communities and allows students to delve deeper into the riches of their own experiential knowledge. Moreover, by looking at how these experiences could be positively transformed through the practice of nonfiction creative writing it becomes possible to grasp the liberatory dimensions of reading and writing, and learn to recognize the mechanisms of violence that define oppressive social systems. More specifically, queer Chicana/o autobiography is also able to create an intellectual framework to discuss the promotion of justice, problematizing the "internal borders" that prevent certain communities from attaining full civil rights, and allows for a kind of teaching that addresses critically cultural "difference" and identity so the consumption of this literature does not become just another shopping choice at a benign multicultural university. Furthermore, in the safe environment of the classroom, students learn how to negotiate the construction of identity and the connections between the process of writing and the process of performing identity in community and the real world.

Excursus: How to Teach: Benefits, Changes, and Growth in Students

Autobiography contributes to our mandate for a critical form of pedagogy that addresses social justice, especially when we face issues of identity and solidarity in the classroom. Perhaps one the most enduring benefits in teaching with this framework in mind has to do with the "point of entry" to the kind of knowledge they reflect.

By combining writing and reading it is possible to learn identity as a celebration of "difference" as opposed to uniformity; there is an emphasis on the "unfolding" of identities as opposed to the "fixed." By writing autobiographies, the students are not only exploring the complexities and multiple possibilities for constructing identity, an empowering pedagogical approach would be able to capture the potential of experiencing texts, which exist in conversation between the local and the global, the experiential and the political, the national and the transnational. Furthermore, through Lifewriting the students can make effective connections between the intellectual and the emotional as well as the historical, the academic, and the experiential knowledge of their own lives.[2]

Recommended Course Goals

This course should include three parts. First, choose the work of contemporary queer writers that can show different models of autobiographical writing.

Inform the students you will read contemporary American forms of autobiography and their conceptualization of identity, history, as well as the new technologies of self-representation (like blogging).

Second, this course should provide students with an introduction to the theory and practice of Lifewriting in the context of writing as re-membering and healing. During the quarter develop their understanding of the principles of Lifewriting techniques and forms, and teach them the craft of writing, and the tools for substantive revision of their dramatic nonfiction pieces.

Third, combine self reflection with writing exercises to trigger the awareness of their early memories, and in general the elements more powerful in their life. Bring a practice of mindful presence to the classroom so students are invited to reflect and see clearly the reality of their experience and the "hunger" for a more authentic "self." In so doing, explore the ways autobiography and self-awareness, if practiced regularly and sincerely, has the effect of increasing one's levels of compassion, and wisdom, while decreasing stress and anxiety.

You can attain these goals through (1) theoretical engagement with autobiography via course readings, presentation, and discussions; (2) actual practice of mindfulness and writing both in and out of class; and (3) critical thinking, via assignments that will ask them to reflect on what they have been learning and experiencing from the reflections explored in the course of the class.

Recommended Assignments

In-class reading should encourage participation and improve their understanding of the basic concepts and theoretical aspects of the autobiographical tradition.

Each student should write a final autobiography as a result of their critical reflection on her or his experience in life. Students should write a twenty-five-page final autobiography using the models discussed in class. The final autobiography should also be an opportunity to learn, through writing, about their "selves," the issues writers face when trying to write about their struggles, and the difficulties of creating a unique voice.

The midterm exam should involve a presentation and a bibliography on a specific problem/text analyzed in class. Students should work in small groups to research and present their findings to the class. Group presentation should consist of an oral presentation to the class on a topic related to one of the books they are reading. Students should work in small groups (your writing *familia*) and submit their questions and discussions to each other for feedback. Everyone is expected to make substantial comments on the other pieces in the group. Request they e-mail or give you the comments they have made on pieces by others' in their writing family. They should receive and learn from everybody's feedback in a space of safety and honesty.

Encourage them to attend a contemplative practice service once a week for a quarter. The writing journal should reflect their regular practice and should include a disciplined reflection on life experiences but it can also be a visual journal where they take notes about the class discussions, their group project, their recording of interesting quotes or ideas that come up during the course readings, and so on. The entries (minimum of two every week) will enhance their ability to reflect on them and on one's own experiences critically, and one's ability to work and learn collaboratively.

Homework Assignments

Use the first two classes to introduce the question: What is an autobiography? These are some possible models to be discussed:

1. Lifewriting as a creative and artistic self-exploration

2. Lifewriting as a contemplative journey and an opportunity for spiritual self-awareness

3. Lifewriting as a tool for intellectual understanding, self-empowerment, and social justice

    • Writing Groups should be like *familias*: They should keep confidentiality. They should commit to safety and collaboration among the writers in order to facilitate re-membering and writing

    • Be sure they understand Lifewriting as an exercise on "being present"—to themselves and to others. The more present they are, the better they will be able to write about it.

In my courses, I have used in the past the work of three gay and lesbian authors who have been very inspiring to me and also address the complex dimensions of culture and identity. I will use Richard Rodriguez's *Hunger of Memory* (1982), Cherrie Moraga's *Loving in the War Years* (1983), and Gloria Anzaldúa's *Borderlands/La Frontera: The New Mestiza* (1987) to address the three main teaching components of the class.

A Hunger for Memories: Richard Rodriguez's Loss of Family and the Need for Belonging

Richard Rodriguez became instantly famous as a writer in 1982 with *Hunger of Memory*. Written as one of the most haunting tales of the gay Mexican-

American experience, the final scene of Rodriguez's book is of profound desolation—a final recognition of a long Christmas evening spent in intense silence, with nothing to say, as he looks blankly at his Mexican father. This ending (in a chapter titled "Mr. Secrets") is revealing of an experience of "difference" that is profoundly alienating and, finally, remote. For Rodriguez, the loss of family is shown through the trace of Spanish sounds slowly fading into the silence of his assimilation and his secrets. This effect is especially important since the "silence and silencing of people begins with the dominating enforcement of linguistic conventions, the resistance to relational dialogues, as well as the disenablement of peoples by outlawing their forms of speech" (Alarcón, 363).

The absence of language and words, and the loss of his culture and family, define his sense of identity. Rodriguez's *Hunger* is revealing of what can go wrong when silencing, and assimilation define "difference" in one's own experience. Richard Rodriguez reactivates the most pessimistic and desolate perspective of self-denial. His text is made of "loss," painful memories lacking meaning or structure, a story that functions as an empty and floating sign, a faint echo of his "voice" sinking slowly into the world of his assimilation.

This text is a warning of the kind of intense pain unable to create an alternative to the void of sexual and cultural assimilation. Thus, his story is translated into an insatiable hunger—the pain of a hungry ghost lost in a world of empty words.

Indeed, *Hunger of Memory* is an autobiography filled with secrets and silences. Secrets permeate every word. Even language, manifested as silence, erases the signs of memory and his connections with a more authentic self. In the chapter titled "The Achievement of Desire," Rodriguez reaffirms as inevitable not only the distancing from his family, but also the loss of any memories of himself, the inevitable price for gaining success through assimilation: "Here is a child who cannot forget that his academic success distances him from a life he loved, even from his own memory of himself" (48).

The erasure of the parents' language and culture extends also to his physical erasure. The relationship between the negation of his body and the negation of his culture and language, finds its symbolic representation in the scene where he applies a razor to his skin to scrape off the last vestiges of his ethnicity: "I was too ashamed of my body. I wanted to forget that I had a body because I had a brown body" (126). Homosexuality, like ethnicity, family, and language, is only present as erasure. The gesture of writing exists only as nostalgia, and the re-creation of this closed, aestheticized writing, turns back against itself as his sexuality, to the very end, remains a secret. But Richard Rodriguez's *Hunger* is also a call for belonging, and for the need to re-create a new family and community. Because his experience is "queer" to Joaquín, the Chicano warrior that appears in the most famous poem of the

Mexican American Civil Rights Movement ("I am Joaquín"), *Hunger* can also be read as the struggle to create a space for queerness within certain sectors of the Chicano Movement since they perceive homosexuality as threatening to cultural nationalism.

Ultimately though, his *Hunger* is manifested in the text as "secrets," as silence, or as a journey toward assimilation. The desire, the hunger to recover what is inevitably lost, becomes the only mark of "difference." Loss is the manifestation of his being, and only the *Hunger* remains.

Identity in this text is a no-man's land, an emptiness that confronts the melancholy of memory lacking meaning and significance—a place where even the body becomes an empty and floating sign. *Hunger of Memory*, then, is one of the most interesting attempts at writing the horror (and the failing) of keeping secrets that cannot be told; it is also an example of choosing to tell the story by branding "loss" of community and family as the ultimate mark of identity working at the center of the narrative. The cultural and sexual anxiety conferred on this autobiography, through this kind of loss, is transcended by other writers we will analyze later. This aspect is important because it becomes the key to understanding the relationship between truth as historic fact and truth as a literary construct. Based on Derrida's assumptions, autobiographical discourse has been described by Paul de Man as a "discourse of self-restoration" (925). But the idea of "self-restoration," as a reaction to erasure or silence, points at the autobiographical text as a space for the reconstruction of loss, or what lesbian writer Gloria Anzaldúa defines as the act of "making faces." From Anzaldúa's point of view, autobiography is not so much the signature of the epitaph (loss), as described by poststructuralists, as it becomes the setting for "making faces." While Paul de Man and others produce an image of speechlessness in their account of autobiography, Anzaldúa's notion of writing is produced as a defiant act of witnessing or *haciendo caras*. Self-restoration is delivered in queer Chicana/o autobiography as the act of "making faces." Anzaldúa argues that "Among Chicanas/Mexicanas, haciendo caras, "making faces," means to put on a face, express feelings by distorting the face (. . .) For me, haciendo caras has the added connotation of making gestos subversivos, political subversive gestures" (1990, xv).

Making Faces is a way to re-create the voices that break away from the demons of silencing and loss while maintaining a guarded space of protection. Furthermore, for Anzaldúa, " 'Making faces' is my metaphor for constructing one's identity" (1990, xvi). Other writers, like Cherríe Moraga, will use the notion of "making *familia* from scratch" to compensate for the lacking (and the loss) of the larger community of support when the voices reveal the secrets. The alternatives offered through Anzaldúa and Moraga's writing will help to transcend the hunger, silence and loss of Rodriguez's life.

Excursus: How to Teach: Exercises that Promote Growth in Students

- Read *Hunger of Memory*. In class discussion and group presentation on Rodriguez's silence and loss as a result of forced assimilation and the keeping of secrets.

- Use Journal Writing to encourage students to write about their sense of loss or pain.

- Possible Exercises in class: Re-create the two most embarrassing moments of their life.

- Writing assignments: Investigate and write your physical, emotional, intellectual reactions to the question for the week: "Who am I?"

- Writing assignments: write a list of twenty joyful moments from your life starting with the line: "I remember/I don't remember"

- Writing assignments: write a list of twenty difficult moments from your life starting with the line: "I remember/I don't remember"

- Techniques to master while writing those exercises: (1) show, don't tell; (2) details, details, details; (3)rising curve of expectation; (4) find your voice.

Cherríe Moraga: Loving in the War Years and Making Familia from Scratch

Cherrie Moraga was born on September 25, 1952, in Whittier, California. With Gloria Anzaldua, she coedited the anthology *This Bridge Called My Back: Writings by Radical Women of Color*, published in 1981. The book won in 1986 the Before Columbus Foundation American Book Award and marked a decisive moment in the development of the feminist movement by disrupting white, middle-class assumptions about women in America. Her lesbian-identified Chicana autobiography, *Loving in the War Years: Lo que nunca pasó por sus labios* ([1983]2000) is a committed reflection on her sexuality and identity, but also the first step to the theme that will become prevalent in her future works. The act of loving who she is as the uniting force of the disparate areas of herself. Moraga's work shows the importance of making a conscious decision to create the space for her identity and the support of the larger community around her: "It's like making familia from scratch / each time all over again . . . / with strangers / if I must. / If I must, I will" (2000, 58).

As part of the same attempts at claiming her multiple identities and the conflating of familia and community, she publishes *Waiting in the Wings: Portrait of a Queer Motherhood* in 1997. Through this book her attempts at reconciliating her lesbian identity, familia, and community, come together full circle: "And how lucky I was to be a lesbian, to have it all—mother, sister, lover—that family of women to see me into motherhood" (54). As an autobiography, the book records the experience of her pregnancy, her son's difficulties to survive, the struggle to reawaken her writing, and the complications of her relationship with Ella. But this is also the story of her new familia: Rafael Angel's birth, Pablo's fatherhood (Moraga's gay Mexican friend and sperm donor), and Moraga's desire to raise her child within a culture free of heteropatriarchal oppressions. In *Waiting in the Wings* she documents the manner in which she conceived (literally, figuratively, and politically) her queer family, and how this aspect of "creating familia from scratch" became the seed for a new consciousness.

This new consciousness is present in the calling to love all the parts of herself and reclaiming a more authentic community. Moraga's *Loving in the War Years*, specially, is a passionate defense of her lesbian and Chicana life as choice while addressing the intersections of political and gender analysis: "Lesbianism as a sexual act can never be construed as reproductive sex. It is not work. It is purely about pleasure and intimacy. How this refutes, spits in the face of, the notion of sex as productive, sex as duty! In stepping outside the confines of the institution of heterosexuality. I was indeed *choosing* sex freely. *The lesbian as institutionalized outcast*" (116). *Loving in the War Years*, the two elements of her title are also addressing the struggle to reclaim the terms by which she could arrive to wholeness. While "loving" is part of the necessary process in order to achieve representation, the "war years" denounces the dismemberment of queers' identity through the aggression of heteropatriarchy. Her autobiography, then, is an exploration of those aggressions perpetuated by culture in the form of dismemberment, while the struggle to re-member, provides the loving, and her sense of wholeness. Her use of the Aztec myth that explains the birth of the moon goddess, Coyolxauhqui, engages directly with the construct. The reality of queer women of color, the need for the healing of dismemberment and the re-membering as an alternative to heteropatriarchal families, is implicit also in the endless struggle between Coyolxauhqui and Huitzilopochtli. As mentioned by Mary Pat Brady, "in turning to Coyolxauhqui, Moraga illustrates at once betrayal, the production and reproduction of patriarchy, and the romanticism that enshrines a disempowered but complicit motherhood" (161).

Regardless of the actions of the god of war, Huitzilopochtli, the myth reminds us how, through careful re-membering, Coyolxauhqui was able to put herself back together as a large disk to become the moon goddess. Describing Coyolxauhqui's mother, Coatlicue, as the victim of rape, the myth engages with the moment the daughter decides to kill her pregnant mother Coatlicue, not only because she wants to stop the birth of a rape, but also because it will give birth to Huitzilopochtli. As Coyolxauhqui is approaching her mother, Huitzilopochtli emerges out of Coatlicue's womb, cutting Coyolxauhqui into pieces and hurling her down the mountainside until she is finally flung out into the night sky, her body littered about like the stars.

Coyolxauhqui, the Aztec moon goddess, becomes herself by acknowledging how her brother, Huitzilopochtli, the war god, "murdered and dismembered her [. . .] and banished [her] into the darkness to become the moon" (2000, 147). Moraga reclaims Coyolxuahqui to represent her experience, but her autobiography reminds us also of the activism and healing necessary to overcome her own dismembering. As she is thrown into the dark sky of heteropatriarchy, her writing must maneuver her way into wholeness through the "unfamiliar" territory of re-membering. Additionally she writes, " 'La Llorona,' 'The Hungry Woman,' 'The Dismemberment of Coyolxauhqui'—these are the stories that have shaped us. We, Chicanas, remember them in spite of ourselves, in spite of our families' and society's efforts to have us forget (. . .) The body remembers" (2000, 147–148).

Through the reclaiming of Coyolxauhqui's myth, Moraga's sense of identity is also an invitation to re-member herself, with all of the pieces of her shattered identity, into a whole. But wholeness is never an arrival point, it is a struggle, a "unified," conscious decision that emanates from her bodily desire, and her loving of the separate parts of her "self." Through her work, Moraga names the sources of oppression as she weaves and conveys together poetry, academic writing and autobiography to create a wholeness that is always spinning and moving, constantly reshaping itself. Coyolxauhqui, then, is represented as a "huge stone disk, which contains the figure of a mutilated warrior-woman (. . .) the circular figure seems to be in motion, her parts rolling around and about, one on top of the other" (2000, iii). Moraga creates the new cartography of her "self," by emphasizing this image: "Maybe I could re-member Coyolxauhqui at least in this writing, this teaching, this praying, this home" (2000, vii).

Just as the moon finds its purpose in shedding light into the darkness, Moraga uses her re-membered writing to shed light into the "hunger" and loss perpetrated by heteropatriarchy, so wrought by racial and sexual oppression, but also to reshape her sense of home and community. Ultimately, her notion of identity is tied up with her rewriting of *familia*: "Familia is *not* by definition the man in a dominant position over women and children. Familia is cross-generational bonding, deep emotional ties between opposite sexes and within our sex (. . .) It is finding familia among friends where blood ties are formed through suffering and celebration shared. The strength of our families never came from domination. It has only endured in spite of it—like our women" (2000, 102–103).

As she struggles for the right of "loving" and the making of *familia*, her autobiography proposes a new form of activism from which the severed parts of herself become a fluid, moving identity, united by the very fact that all her parts are in need to be "re-membered." The strength of her autobiography is precisely this emphasis on writing as a process of re-membering, as a way to reshape community and all the parts of her identity contained within the circle of her powers. Her book serves as a calling to queers to strive for the kind of community and activism that creates a new self, and a genuine sense of wholeness.

Excursus: How to Teach: Exercises that Promote Growth in Students

Read Loving in the War Years. Create safe familia groups and create a process of writing that addresses the need for wholeness and re-membering through different stages of writing.

1. Ask them to develop a list of twenty difficult/joyful moments into a letter to themselves evoking their own suffering/joyful experience in life as part of the "wholeness" of their own spiritual and intellectual journey.

2. Their *familia* group helps the students in the writing of their story. Imagine they are telling the movie of their life to their best friend. What are the best moments? How did it build up? This is a collaborative creation and interpretation of their life.

3. Read their journals; meet with every student during the week to help them envision a project.

4. Work up an outline and treatment for their story.

Gloria Anzaldúa and the Total Self

The intersection of the experiential knowledge of the particular, on the one hand, and the notion of writing as a claiming of a new self, on the other, refuses and transcends an oversimplification of the autobiographical act as "confession." This exploration allows for a type of writing that involves self-understanding and intellectual reflection into what lesbian writer Gloria Anzaldúa defines in her autobiography, *Borderlands/La Frontera: The New Mestiza*, as the "total Self." This is especially important in Anzaldúa's work. The "point of entry" to reclaiming all her experiences emphasizes the notion of total Self as a more complex analysis of experience and identity, one which recognizes the multiplicity of voices as a way of breaking away from the imprisonment of a limited notion of identity. As Anzaldua puts it, "I will no longer be made to feel ashamed of existing. I will have my voice: Indian, Spanish, and white. I will have my serpent's tongue—my woman's voice, my sexual voice, and my poet's voice. I will overcome the tradition of silence" (Borderlands 59). In fact, to the limitations of the traditional "confessional" mode, queer Chicana/o autobiography opposes the articulation of writing as transformation into something than the small I: "Deconstruct, construct. . . . She learns to transform the small 'I' into the total Self" (1987, 82–83).

As the "I" expands into the total Self, a new text emerges—an autobiography that implies personal and communal, experiential and political knowledge. As such, queer Chicana/o autobiographical discourse also allows for a strategic agency. This writing allows one, for example, to emphasize community, but also to replace inherited repressive values within the community with new options. This process involves, then, not only the re-membering and reclaiming of a voice, it also includes a healing vision, a "healing performance" created by the integration of those fragments of identity that have been broken apart by the system. Anzaldúa's notion of the total Self finds resonance within the personal and the political arena. In Critical Legal Studies, Latino/a legal activists have argued for a better court model for deciding cases involving discrimination. Elvia Arriola's article, "Gendered Inequality," points at the reality of discrimination as a daily dismembering of identity. Arriola states that "these paradigms . . . obscure whether or how discrimination occurs, what remedy to use, or why the conflict has arisen" (540). Her holistic irrelevancy model involves understanding identity as part of a "re-membering" of the different categories of experience within a person. Arriola agrees that these categories are very much interconnected parts of one's self, and that the way the court system is handling discrimination cases is flawed. She states that in a courtroom, the "various characteristics of one's identity, such as sexual orientation, gender, and race, are always disconnected (. . .) the various aspects of one's identity may be ranked so that, for example, race may be prioritized over gender (. . .) [and] some characteristics, such as class, do not provide a relevant basis for discrimination claims" (540). Personal characteristics are thus disconnected and ranked, while others are simply ignored. Because the differing parts "may be ranked," certain aspects take priority over others, working to skew the particulars of a court case in unfair ways. Hence, the many areas of experience that make up the whole of a person, "do not provide a relevant basis for discrimination claims" (Arriola 540). What this means is that often times nonfactors in court cases may become factors that make for certain aspects of a person's identity, and an unjust assumption might be made, where "false dichotomies and false power relationships promote limited versions of equality" (Arriola 540). By asserting that the Constitution is color-blind, the "irrelevancy model" disregards certain personal traits as illegitimate classifying criteria to achieve equality, and even though it sees the source of discrimination as coming from a "group-based" generalization, the result legal analysts view the different areas of experience in a person as always being disconnected and in varying degrees of discrimination. As the courts force people into dismembered identities, Anzaldua's total Self and her pursuit of a connected and a holistic subjectivity, empowers queers to take a real step against discrimination. By including this notion in her autobiography, Anzaldúa refuses the logic of the separate "I" to embrace the interconnectedness, crossings, and alliances of the multiple experiences that compose her total Self. Since the early 1980s, Borderlands/La Frontera has been at the forefront of feminist theory since she attempted to put issues of racial and ethnic identity in dialogue with issues of feminism and sexuality. It is her boldness at attempting to confront her multiple identities, and the reclaiming of her own desire for unity that brings a unique strength into her autobiography as a "performance" for social activism.

Her search for connectedness defines the sources of her activism and challenges courts to "recognize that a person's identity is rarely limited to a singular characteristic" (Arriola 540). The notion of the total Self also challenges the courts to recognize that "identity represents the confluence of an infinite number of factors . . . The components of an individual identity constantly shift . . . [So,] no single trait defines [one's] own identity" (Arriola 540).

This writing facilitates a holistic view that allows for a better way to see the compounding of discrimination affecting queers' experience. More specifically, ultimate liberation involves recognizing the many aspects of our identity as all interrelated through the different settings of social oppression.

As her autobiography expands the notion of the individual "I" and rewrites the notion of the "total Self" instead, it is able to create a voice through which we can envision individual self-empowerment and community agency.

Excursus: How to Teach: Benefits, Changes, and Growth in Students

The use of Anzaldua's notion of the total Self allows for an expanding understanding of creation that permits our students to go beyond the effects of loss and trauma. This pedagogy implies imagining this new "self" (a total Self) being able to reenact through a "voice" or performance the sociohistorical implications of institutional and geographic borders along different lines of oppression—gender, sexual identity, religion, citizenship, linguistic codes, class, and racial formation.

The tensions and liberatory potential that lie in the reading, writing, and performing of these stories challenge students to think differently about the effects of systems of power as they relate to privilege: "we are ready to begin to understand difference as a series of relationships of power, involving domination and subordination, and to use our understanding of the power relations to reconceptualize both our interpretation and our teaching of American culture" (Kerber 429).

- A healing performance, or the performing of identity in community and in the real world, can be achieved through readings of their piece. A peer (chosen by them) will reply to their reading and offer his or her feedback. The rest of the class will also offer feedback. This is a collaborative creation and interpretation of their life. Different ways of doing this include:

  1. Discuss effective openings in the context of relationships of power. Reflect and write on "beginnings": Where did you really begin? When do you feel your true self really started? Write "I began . . ." down and let yourself go.

  2. Discuss building a story and creating a climax in the context of liberation: Discover "moments of insight." At what moment you felt you experienced a great insight into the nature of things? Did you experience understanding or having your heart completely opening? In nature? In love? With books? With a dear friend?

  3. Discuss "endings": If you had magic powers, what would bring complete closure to your life? Imagine a scene that resembles being "complete." Write something that brings your life into full circle. Let your imagination take over and be wild. Possible Endings:

     —Endings as a call to action

     —Endings as a parting insight

     —Endings as a look to the future

     —Endings and lessons learned

Final Thoughts on Course Structure

Autobiographies are creative artifacts that provide students with the ability to explore the complexities and multiple possibilities for constructing the self. The search for more complex forms of self allows the student to see his or her own links with different communities by which his or her identity is being shaped, and allows students to delve deeper into the riches of experiential knowledge. Ultimately, we should encourage students to make effective connections between the intellectual and the emotional, as well as between the historical and the experiential knowledge of their own lives. Encourage students to go for a type of writing that involves reflection into what we define as the total Self, which is created by the different links that expand our limited notions of the ego, the oppressed and the repressed. Emphasize these aspects as the process of writing autobiographies takes place in small groups called familia. In these small groups students learn how to negotiate the construction of identity in groups, and learn to see the connections between the process of writing and the process of performing identity in community and the real world.

Be sure that the teaching addresses critically "cultural difference" so the consumption of literature does not become another trip to the mall. Writing autobiography should be a transgression of the boundaries established by dominant culture as we expand the notion of "identity" so we can create individual, communal, and also transnational agency.

The classroom should be a place of relationality and contiguity among students and cultures—a contact zone; it should be a space for a real reenacting of multiple notions of self and an empowering multicultural and multilingual experience. I believe that the sense of self-empowerment provided by Chicana/o queer autobiography is able to address postcolonial trauma, and the intangible and more subtle forms of institutionalized violence and economic injustice against the marginalized in an already globalized, heteropatriarchal world. In this process, reading and writing empower the students to find a dialogical relationship between the communal and the personal, to understand the links between knowledge, history, and power. Through this type of understanding, "difference" becomes not only a means by which we understand the nature of power and domination, but also a tool and a site for the assertion of identity and solidarity.

Notes

1. In this article I use some of the information presented at the Commitment to Justice in Jesuit Higher Education Conference at John Carroll University in

October 16, 2005. In the panel (coorganized with professor Heather Lyons), "Exploring the Boundaries of Self: Using Autobiography to Teach Courses on Identity and Culture," we focused on the use of autobiography in the classroom for the purpose of teaching social justice. I also borrow from some of my previous published articles on Chicana/o autobiography to show its impact on the reading and writing of queer autobiographies. I borrow from my article "*Automitografías*: The Border Paradigm and Chicana/o Autobiography" published in *Biography*; from "*Santitos*: Loss, the Catholic Sleuth and the Transnational Mestiza Consciousness," published in *Mester*; and from my unpublished manuscript "Yo! A Study on Contemporary Chicana/o Autobiography, 1959–2009." While my previous research has been theoretical, I try to show in this article "the practical" benefits of reading and writing autobiography in the context of the queer theory and identity.

2. What is autobiography? According to Fred White, "Lifewriting sometimes goes by other names, such as 'biography,' 'autobiography,' 'personal essays' 'features' or 'creative nonfiction'—but these terms do not convey the purpose of such writing, which is to entertain and edify readers with stories about your experiences, or the experiences of others through your eyes" (6).

Works Cited

Alarcon, Norma. "The Theoretical Subject(s) of *This Bridge Called My Back* and Anglo-American Feminism." *Making Face, Making Soul: Haciendo Caras*. San Francisco: Aunt Lute, 1990, 356–369.

Anzaldúa, Gloria. *Borderlands/La Frontera*. San Francisco: Spinsters/Aunt Lute, 1987.

Anzaldúa, Gloria. "Haciendo caras, una entrada." *Making Face, Making Soul: Haciendo Caras*. San Francisco: Aunt Lute, 1990, xv–xxviii.

Arriola, Elvia R. "Gendered Inequality." *The Latino/a Condition: A Critical Reader*. Richard Delgado and Jean Stefancic, ed. New York: NYU Press, 1998, 539–542.

Brady, Mary Pat. *Extinct Lands, Temporal Geographies: Chicana Literature and the Urgency of Space*. Durham, NC and London: Duke University Press, 2002.

De Man, Paul. "Autobiography as De-Facement." *Modern Language Notes* 94.5 (1979): 919–930.

Kerber, Linda. "Diversity and the Transformation of American Studies." *American Quarterly* 41 (1989): 415–431.

Moraga, Cherrie. *Loving in the War Years: Lo Que Nunca Pasó Por Sus Labios*. Cambridge, MA: South End Press, (1983)2000.

Moraga, Cherrie. *Waiting in the Wings: Portrait of a Queer Motherhood*. Ithaca, NY: Firebrand Books, 1997.

Moraga, Cherrie. *Giving Up the Ghost: Teatro in Two Acts*. Los Angeles: West End Press, 1986.

Rodriguez, Richard. *Hunger of Memory: The Education of Richard Rodriguez*. Boston: David R. Godine, 1982.

White, Fred D. *Lifewriting*. Sanger, CA: Quill Driver Books, 2004.

Part IV

Expanding the Circle

Chapter 14

Show Me Your ID

Jowelle Gomez

There's not much that I can tell trained professionals in the field of psycho-therapy about identity—its formation, use, misuse, concretization, misperceptions, and so on. But I can share with you the journey I've traveled to get to the place where I know what to do when people ask to see my "identification card." And because it is a deeply ingrained habit to think in boxes and packs and groups, it is extremely difficult to even note when we are using those identification boxes and when they're useful or when they're not.

We're in a particularly interesting place right now when we think about identification. The 2008 presidential campaign offers just one of the interesting perspectives on how identification (whether correct or not) shapes our national consciousness and our vision of the world. This is of particular interest to me because of what it says about people in the United States, and our need to keep the ethnicities and genders segregated and the inherent implication in that separation is a hierarchy.

With the entrance of Barak Obama into that race, the politics of running for president in the United States have been played out on multiple fields of identity—both gender and race among them. That play has had the brutality of a heavy-weight boxing championship; the exception being that the punches were often whispered or ignored. But the blood is still flowing from the split lips and gashes. I need only say the name "Hussein," Barak Obama's middle name, and you know how the body slam of identity has been used against him. With the mention of that one name, a middle-class man of color with an exceedingly mild-mannered presentational self is automatically equated with terrorism.

I'll tell some stories that awakened me to the understanding that identity was always going to be a rough sea to navigate—an understanding that Barak Obama's candidacy confirmed. I was raised by my great grandmother (who was part Ioway and part African American) in Boston in the 1960s. I didn't start visiting my mother (Ioway and Wampanoag and African American) in the small Rhode Island (mill) town an hour away until I was thirteen. My mother was light-skinned with the dark, long hair the reflected our Native American roots, and she was married to a French Canadian. Her working-class, mostly white neighbors had never seen her mother, grandmother, or daughter . . . all of us somewhat darker hued than she.

One afternoon a young boy, white, maybe about ten years old, approached me as I sat on my mother's front steps and asked: "What nationality are you?"

I was older and darker so I knew that someone . . . mother, father, or aunt . . . had sent him with the question. I responded insistently: "I'm American," even when he kept repeating the question. We both knew he was not getting the answer they expected back home.

Even at a young age as a person of color I knew what the subtext was, and I had the better vocabulary so I moved through the encounter adroitly leaving him unsatisfied. His use of the word *nationality* did not fool me, so I righteously gave him my nation of origin and reveled gleefully in his confusion. Ultimately, however, I was furious then and now because I knew what he was asking: "Was I white or not?"

I never told my family what had happened; what followed my cleverness was an onslaught of racist phone calls and death threats in the middle of the night. Neighbors burned trash on my mother's postage stamp–sized front yard and routinely harassed her, her husband, and my baby, half-brother. It only relented when Interstate 95 started construction and completely dismantled the neighborhood. This happened in the early 1960s, the civil rights movement was in full bloom in the South, and reports streamed into all of our homes on the national evening news. The news clearly had made the citizens of Pawtucket, Rhode Island feel threatened and unstable.

Traumatized, my mother and her husband lived on their guard for most of their lives, taking extraordinary security precautions even in their new neighborhood. Today, more than forty years later, when I visit Rhode Island to speak at colleges or simply pass through, I feel the same anxiety I felt back then and a small pocket of bitterness I have to consciously swallow down.

Then years later in my early twenties I had another experience that left additional scars. I was teaching in Bronxville, an upper-class, white suburb of New York; it's the kind of town with articles excluding Blacks and Jews; and that has tree-shrouded, winding streets with no signs, because if you don't know where you are you shouldn't be there. I lived in an apartment over a friend's garage (formerly used by the chauffer) and was walking home from teaching my theater class one evening after dark. I was wearing the regulation jeans and T-shirt, topped off by my short natural haircut. Halfway there in the lovely, pine-scented pastoral setting, I was stopped by a police officer who popped out of his patrol car and asked my destination. He was a bit nervous and didn't request my identification, but he made me stand in his headlights while he called for backup.

I knew the tragedies that have grown out of nervous cops faced with unexpected movement so, while I didn't raise my hands in the air, I stood still as a child playing statue. I felt angry, but mostly I felt extremely vulnerable because I could see only his outline in the glare of the car's headlights.

Another patrol car arrived pretty quickly although, to me, it felt like two hours. The second officer peered at me only a moment before saying to his brother officer with the annoyance of someone who needlessly abandoned his personal pursuits back at the police station: "She's a girl!"

As they sent me on my way . . . no apology . . . a shudder of fear swept over me. In his anxiety the police officer wasn't able to see me at all. I was simply a person of color in jeans with short-cropped hair—which translated as man and as danger. His fear and narrow mind prevented him from noticing my not-small breasts in the revealing T-shirt. Once I got home I tried to calm myself with a very big glass of wine. I needed to rid myself of (1) the adrenaline flowing from my fear of being shot, (2) my annoyance that he couldn't tell I was a woman, and (3) fury that *woman* meant *insignificant* to those two men.

I didn't know where to go with those realizations; where does one start with that convoluted level of obliviousness, especially in what are nominally meant to be "peace" officers? I was lucky it was only a blip on the screen of life, not a headline; however, the memory is not a peaceful one.

Those two snapshots reminded me how identity is perceived from the outside and then used to influence your behavior. I didn't know what that young boy's parents had decided about me, except I knew it wasn't an idle inquiry. It was in response to a negative idea of what they perceived my identity to be. Without knowing me, they made choices that changed the shape of my mother's life.

And as much as I like to avoid grouping people together, since that aromatic suburban night, I have never faced a police officer without an initial wariness. Police have to rely on broad ideas and images in order to notice when those who are potential criminals are up to something; however when those ideas make the individual blind it's anxiety provoking. The idea of "profiling" has since become a major issue in the world of policing and civil rights.

When has it been fun having an ID card? Growing up in the 1960s before "community activist" was a suspect phrase, exploring one's identity was an exciting adventure designed to counteract the sort of negativity I met on my mother's doorstep and on that dark suburban street. "Power to the people," "Black is beautiful," "Sisterhood is powerful," are all calls to unity with a group and in that a sense of empowerment.

Identity meant you were identifying with other people, your neighbors and friends in a way that made you all much more effective than when you faced the world as simply an individual. We didn't think of it as separating ourselves from others—that had already been done to us. People of color were segregated from mainstream society into poorer neighborhoods and reservations. Women were relegated to kitchens, the typist pool, and the tight pedestal of the sexual object, But identity allowed us to claim each other in those segregated spaces not as victims but as a group with aspirations.

Of course, that claiming could never be as simplistic as it appeared on the surface or on a banner. Where was the space for me to claim not just the African American part of me but the Native American part and the Cape Verdean part? Where was the room for me to be a sexual being without being an object? Oppression by a dominant culture too often makes singular identity paramount within the oppressed group; then variations or complexities become painful. We see this in every movement, yet it's always a surprise and a disappointment. 'It's not easy to move your arms from fending off body blows to being open and vulnerable.

We see that same impulse to simplicity in the need people had to refer to Barak Obama as the "Black" candidate, when they could just as easily call him the White candidate. In reality he's the biracial candidate (or as some refer to him: the first Pacific Rim president), but that's too complex an identity for a sound bite or for the average Joe Six-Pack or Joe the Plumber to slug down in one gulp.

It's that complexity that led me to the verbal jousting and that sent the young white boy scurrying away from me on my mother's stoop. I knew any direct answer I might try to give to his question about my ethnic identity would feel like a cop-out to me. It would make me feel like I was trying to get out of being just plain Black by bringing in the shades.

If I said I'm Wampanoag and Ioway Indian and Cape Verdean would I be saying, "No, I'm not African American," as if I were ashamed? It felt that way to me. At that young age and in the midst of a Black civil rights movement, navigation of the complexity of identity was often defensive and circuitous.

The seas of identification have gotten no calmer for people of color, for lesbians, or for other queer people. If someone asks for my ID, what part of me do I give them? I pull out my wallet and have my driver's license, library card, insurance card, credit card, bank card, Costco and supermarket cards, the Jewish Community Center membership card, membership cards for the

Museum of Modern Art and Museum of the African Diaspora. What do you know from those ID cards, though?

They are all the same familiar size but each says something different; sometimes they say contradictory things. You do get some picture of me if you sift through: I'm middle class, artsy, and lucky enough to have insurance coverage.

As a card-carrying (virtually speaking) lesbian/feminist I find myself always scanning the horizon for evidence of the misperception of my political identity. And I never have to look far. The first time I saw the cigarette ad in the 1970s with the tag line, "You've come a long way baby," I knew women were in for a rough passage. Men and some women were going to resist passage into twenty-first-century enlightenment with everything they had in them. They meant to keep women from taking themselves seriously—by any means necessary. And as a lesbian, my identity remained completely obscured by my presentation as a femme rather than as a butch lesbian, which puts everyone on notice. Even now I only exist on television prison dramas.

I have hoped that the next generations of feminists and lesbians might have an expanded sense of the layers of human identity, even if they had missed those heady early days of lesbian feminism. I've not seen much evidence that this is the case.

At an event celebrating the lives and friendship of lesbian, feminist poets Audre Lorde and Pat Parker, a number of women of my age (early 60s) were asked to share memories of those women and those times. We reveled in sharing our sexual/social exploits in the 1970s and 1980s. I said out loud that Audre was flirtatious, and many of us spoke of adventures we'd had with lovers.

After the program young women repeatedly commented with surprise that we sounded like we'd had fun back in the day! It was as if plaid flannel and publishing radical magazines inhibited sexual impulses. To the young women in the audience we were simply old women with gray hair, like . . . perhaps . . . their mothers. The concept of the complex lives of lesbian feminists was not in their consciousness. They looked at a woman with gray hair and saw a sexless, conservative, feeble homebody.

Maybe they hadn't heard any of the stories of radical lesbian exploits because they don't appear on almost any syllabus. Or they could only attribute radical acts to the few, well-known lesbians like the two women we were celebrating. They appeared to buy into the same old patriarchal model of the singular hero riding in on a white horse and making change. Despite our insistence that sisterhood is powerful, they could not see us.

This has happened again recently at a community discussion of between members of the transgender and nontransgender community. It was finally a chance to try to get to the root of some of the anxiety and mistrust within our queer community. At one point near the end, we tried to talk about things that came between lesbians and transwomen—not an easy discussion because everyone feels extremely sensitive about how gender and gender training affects our interactions. A transwoman said that lesbians had so much power we should be more welcoming and not so exclusive.

It was like an explosion in the room, suddenly the affinity groups of the 1970s, where women identified with each other and drew power from that identity was threatening to others. Unfortunately we didn't have the time or expertise to "unpack" (as they say) that assertion; but it was clearly an important revelation deserving of more exploration. It made me feel two things at once: How could lesbian feminists begin to stop policing our borders so fiercely and see our connections to others. Some commonalities do exist between transwomen and women and there can be power in that commonality.

At the same time, how could a transwoman see lesbians as having so much power? I don't believe lesbians have an inordinate amount of power in that absolute sense, and certainly not in the dominant culture. But maybe we do have some indefinable strength that comes from growing up as a class that is overtly and covertly suppressed by male culture. We've been developing our cohesiveness and identity longer—that is powerful. However, the transwoman implied that power was effective in a larger context. We did not get to the other side of that discussion: What of the power that accrues to simply being raised with male expectations of privilege that don't go away after the transition? The questions that started to arise in that discussion group explained to me some of the hostilities and misunderstanding within the queer community; and they are not so different from earlier days when gay men and lesbians might as well have been from separate planets.

We couldn't come to an agreement on what power lesbian feminists may or may not have or why we feel so endangered, or why lesbian feminist bonding felt threatening to transwomen and not to transmen. That's something for a psychology student to use as a PhD topic. Ultimately the issue lies within our myopic viewpoint: we were not seeing each other's full identities.

But the point is that the perceptions of me by younger people or transpeople or straight people, as a lesbian feminist, seem so far from what I see as my reality. And I'm sure that my perceptions of them at times have been in conflict with how they identified themselves. How does one alter those perceptions?

All oppressed people in this country have had to dispel the stereotypes that box them in. Those boxes make the people who believe the stereotypes feel more comfortable. So ultimately, what we are doing when we work on recognizing and integrating our identities is going to cause discomfort to someone.

One of the most important revelations for me in the past twenty years was to move away from the conceptualization of identity as absolute. Slaveholders had a very concrete idea of what Black was—subhuman, or three-fourths human, sexual predators, ignorant. In response to the stereotypes, the civil rights movement made Black out to be the exact opposite, that is, saintly repositories of salvation for the modern world. Black people were supposed to have the wisdom of Africa and the solid practicality developed out of urban survival, along with kindliness and shined shoes. The Black Power Movement went a step further and insisted that African Americans were also masters of their own fate, not simply reflections of White culture; we could protect our communities, provided education and food, and not be reliant on the oppressor.

White progressives of the 1960s did something similar with Native Americans. As a reverse projection of their collective guilt about the massacres by their ancestors of entire tribes of people, young hippies turned Native Americans into ecological Joan of Arcs with the answer to all of modern society's ills.

Feminists made a Herculean effort to throw off the mantle of the image of the little woman happy at home with the children clinging to her apron and satisfied with the intellectual stimulation of driving their kids to hockey games and shopping. The result was a superwoman who was supposed to be able to "have it all." One extreme usually begets another. We don't usually counter a solid image with something other than another solid certainty; no "maybe" or "in between" or "sometimes" allowed.

As a writer of vampire fiction, I spend a good bit of my time trying to find those in-between places. Twenty years ago, before *Buffy the Vampire Slayer* and *True Blood* dominated the airwaves, I created an alternate kind of vampire, one struggling to live anonymously within the context of contemporary life. Some are ruthless killers, as in more traditional literary legend; but others exist within a code, a feminist code.

My characters are human but not mortal. They identify as superhuman but not superior to humans. As a writer, I have to interrogate what makes one human and that isn't always the simple thing; just as what makes one person Black and another one White. History shows us that the cover of the book doesn't exactly tell you what's inside, just as my mother's features never aroused suspicion that she was not white until I was seen on her doorstep.

We learn to rely completely on markers and signals and not really look and listen. Then we easily suit our interpretation of those markers to our own needs. The culture around us reinforces these misperceptions, so suddenly your identity becomes "mydentity." No matter what you do, my interpretation of your identity dominates if I have the societal advantage over you.

How long has it been since women first voiced the need for a paradigm shift in gender expectations? The first time was probably a millennium ago, but still popular culture rests on moldy yet comfortable ideas of who women are. There's an amusing country song, "I'm Still a Guy," recorded by Brad Paisley, written by Paisley, John Kelley Lovelace, and Lee Thomas Miller, whose lyrics are:

> When you see a deer, you see Bambi
> And I see antlers up on a wall . . .
> And in a weak moment I might
> Walk your sissie dog, hold your purse at the mall
> But remember, I'm still a guy.

We might dismiss a country song (betraying our identity as urban snobs!), but the lyrics remind us how precarious the male identity is. It has to be protected from any perceptions of femininity. Just as significant, it tells us how important it is for men to keep women in the box they recognize. The Bambi box.

The identity aspect of the issue of "gay marriage" hasn't been discussed at all. Allowing for legal marriage between same gender couples would shift queer people's identity in the most elemental society unity—the family. Although many negatives have been used for queer people, one thing that is a constant in our families is their infantilization of us.

Parents don't know how to look at their own adult queer children as *adults*. Even religious conservatives look at us as wayward children to be saved. But if we can get married it's a corner turned into adulthood. And you can't easily dismiss adults.

We used to laugh at consciousness-raising in lesbian-feminist communities, but that was the seed of real social change because it was a place we went to help us find our identities. We understood that the personal is political, and personal change is the beginning of political change. If we can alter the way we look at ourselves, we can alter the way we look at others.

The only way to make that change is to see identity not as a box but as a door; until we can see identity as a multilayered, many splendored thing we risk not being able to perceive what lies directly in front of us. I can say I'm Wampanoag and once you enter there the next door opens into Cape Verdean and that into being a lesbian and that into my being left-handed and a Bostonian. I've been fortunate to be a feminist and a lesbian and a person of color; these are not identities that allow me to easily ignore the differences within myself and around me. I have learned that each identity is an aspect of myself that makes me more human, more open to the world.

When I teach creative writing I ask those in my workshops to list the identities they have, and then I help them amplify the list to pick up things that get easily lost when one just thinks of him- or herself as a "White person" or "Italian," or "girl." I then ask the workshop participants to spend some time opening all those doors with each other, so we have the full deck of cards . . . identification cards. It may seem cumbersome or superfluous information, but in truth a game is never fun or true if you're not playing with a full deck of cards.

Chapter 15

At the Crossroads

Navigating the Intersection of Spiritual and Sexual Identity Within Lesbian, Gay, Bisexual, Transgender, and Queer (LGBTQ) College Students

Beth Bradley and Brian J. Patchcoski

Introduction

Tricia Seifert (2007) states that educators need to help students develop the ability and willingness to question educational practices and programs that privilege the spiritual identity development of one group over others. Drawing on intentional collaborations between the Center for Ethics and Religious Affairs (CERA) and the Lesbian, Gay, Bisexual, Transgender, and Ally (LGBTA) Student Resource Center at the Pennsylvania State University, this essay aims to provide insight on how to ethically and practically initiate conversations with students on spiritual, religious, sexual, and/or gender identity development. By challenging the conventional notions of affirming and nonaffirming religious groups with the integration of non-Western-based spiritualities, we strive to expand the current practices of practitioner-scholars working to integrate students' spiritual, religious, sexual, and gender identity development through our theoretically based programming experience.

Mutually exclusive assumptions exist about spiritual identity development and the formation of a lesbian, gay, bisexual, transgender, or queer (LGBTQ) identity. Focused on higher education, four out of five college students indicate an interest in spirituality through either active involvement or inquiry within spiritually centered activities (Chickering, Dalton, & Stamm, 2006). Love et al. (2005) indicate that the LGBTQ student population prioritizes their spiritual development; however, this research also suggests a spiritual loss among LGBTQ students as they explore their sexual identities, confirming an assumption of mutual exclusivity between these two identities. Recognizing this loss, LGBTQ students encounter unique and often difficult challenges between spirituality and sexuality, but those challenges remain undefined. Misconceptions between religion and spirituality may provide insight into those challenges, but may not be the only factors influencing student development (Tan, 2005).

The literature in student development acknowledges the complexities and intersections between interpersonal, intrapersonal, and cognitive development. Abes, Jones, and McEwen (2007) state the importance of understanding a fluid intersection of cognitive, psychosocial, and social identity domains of development. Focusing on only one domain does not allow for a holistic understanding of the multiple intersections of identity, especially concerning spirituality and sexuality. Prior research on spirituality and LGBTQ identity formation acknowledges the need to further explore intersectional development and its implications for LGBTQ college students (Love et al., 2005). Previous studies examining LGBTQ identity formation and spirituality qualitatively evaluated students' experiences and provide further evidence for the need to conceptualize nonlinear models of identity development, exploring the multiple dimensions of identity embodied within individual students. Using those experiences as a benchmark, this essay will explore the intersections of spiritual and sexual identity formation among LGBTQ college students and provide examples of theoretically based programs fostering student development.

We begin by exploring former inquiry into spiritual, sexual, and college student identity formation. The literature review will integrate an intersectional exploration of spiritual and sexual identity development. Following the literature review, a detailed explanation of our offices, programs, and collaborations will follow. Last, we will conclude with a synthesis of recommendations based on previous research and our experiences. Through our experiences, we intend to offer a broader and more cohesive practitioner based understanding of spiritual and sexual identity development among LGBTQ college students.

Review of the Literature

Lesbian, gay, bisexual, transgender, and queer college students encounter a significant number of challenges regarding their sexual and spiritual identities (Love et al. 2005). The literature indicates the challenges encountered by LGBTQ individuals and alludes to the misunderstandings of specific religious and spiritual terminology. Existing models of identity development compartmentalize spirituality and sexuality, and restrict an integrated understanding of these two identities. The intersectional exploration of spirituality and sexuality recognizes both differences and similarities within identity construction. Existing literature lacks a concrete model for sexual and spiritual development and highlights the need for scholar-practitioners to promote open dialogue to explore the interplay between spiritual and sexual identity. In this section, we synthesize current research on religion and spirituality, explore models of identity development, describe current inquiry into intersectionality as a theoretical approach in research, and discuss recommendations for scholar-practitioners working with students.

Religion and Spirituality

In order to begin exploration into current literature, it is important to understand that religion and spirituality are two separate entities often used interchangeably. Spirituality pertains to a sense of meaning, purpose, and morality, while religion concerns a specific system of standardized beliefs, practices, and experiences connected to ones' spirituality (Tan 2005). Sexual orientation and spirituality are often seen as mutually exclusive. Love et al. (2005) believe most people perceive this disconnect because they consider religion to be the same as spirituality. Many mainstream religious denominations reject non-heterosexual orientations, which creates a significant dilemma for those who identify as LGBTQ. Misunderstandings of terminology and hostile religious environments characterize some of the factors LGBTQ individuals encounter.

College students develop their spiritual and religious identities through a series of stages. During these stages, students tend to begin a process of separating their identities from their worldviews and "demythologizing" their experiences (Barry& Nelson 2005). The amount of importance an individual places on specific religious and spiritual beliefs reflects a variety of factors such as family ideologies, public involvement in institutional religions, personal importance of their belief system, maternal influence, socioeconomic status, and gender (Pearce & Thornton 2007). Barry and Nelson (2005) describe how emerging adulthood may characterize a time during which college students question familial beliefs, recognize spirituality as more important than religious affiliation, and select aspects of religion which suit them best. When individuals in the process of developing an LGBTQ identity encounter nonaffirming, hostile religious institutions, they may abandon or feel abandoned by their religious communities resulting in a sense of spiritual loss (Lease,

Horne, & Noffsinger-Frazier 2005). Perceiving the changes and challenges college students encounter, institutionalized religious beliefs hold varying levels of importance, especially for those identifying as LGBTQ.

Kiesling et al. (2006) acknowledge spirituality as a persistent sense of self, which confronts ultimate questions about the nature, purpose, and meaning of life, resulting in behaviors that are consonant with the individual's core values. Reflecting on this definition, the spiritual self is individual and oppositional to the institutionalized practice of religion. Love et al. (2005) found spirituality to be a driving force in the work of lesbian, gay, and bisexual students addressing issues of oppression—reflecting evidence that at least a portion of the LGBTQ student population values their spiritual awareness. In general, research indicates spirituality, perceived to share connections with religion, provides significant challenges for LGBTQ students as they develop their sexual identities.

Identity Development

Spirituality and sexuality represent only two aspects of a student's holistic identity. Students often see themselves as a combination of distinct—and sometimes conflicting—dimensions of identity (Abes & Kasch 2007). LGBTQ college students encounter significant challenges in developing their identities. The process of developing an LGBTQ identity is psychological, social, and age-related (Longerbeam et al. 2007). To acknowledge the combination of these factors, it is important to reflect on the multiple dimensions that interact within the formation of an individual's identity. Several models of identity development do not address or include the multitude of identities that many LGBTQ students experience. The majority of LGBTQ identity theories presuppose a narrow conception of what it means to be LGBTQ. These models lack the ability to differentiate the sometimes subtle ways students identify within the confines of LGBTQ labels, which inevitably disregards several other areas of personal development (Renn 2007). It is crucial to not only recognize the multiple layers of identity within an individual but to also identify the salience of those layers and how they can rise and fall over time.

Given the lack of scholarship on LGBTQ identity development, it is imperative to further explore and connect the experiences of LGBTQ students navigating their spirituality and sexuality. LGBTQ students often feel ostracized by the same structures and institutions in which their heterosexual peers develop their spiritual and sexual identities (Love et al. 2005). To better understand the development of LGBTQ individuals and create appropriate resources for them as they navigate a path to wholeness, we must identify ways to acknowledge the disparity that currently exists in the models of sexual and spiritual identity development.

Models of Sexual Identity Development

When conceptualizing the multiple realities of an LGBTQ individual, several models exist pertaining to the development of sexual identity. Bilodeau and Renn (2005) present an overview of literature regarding models of LGBTQ identity development, including stage models, theories specific to LGBTQ people of color, a life span approach, and approaches to transgender identity development. Stage models focus on the resolution of internal conflict related to identification as lesbian or gay, and inform what is commonly termed as the "coming-out" process. Several discrepancies exist within stage models, particularly in addressing complex psychosocial interactions. To address those social interactions, researchers like Bilodeau and Renn provide new perspectives on the experience of multiple and intersecting identities related to race and ethnicity, nationality, and sexuality. New theoretical perspectives reflecting bisexual identity development, Eurocentric notions of culture and its boundaries, and people with disabilities, highlight the social context of nonheterosexual identities across cultures and draw attention to the vast diversity within LGBTQ communities (Bilodeau & Renn 2005).

D'Augelli's life span model of sexual orientation identity development accounts for social contexts and variations in what it means to be lesbian, gay, or bisexual to include a range of personal expressions and comfort (Renn 2007). The D'Augelli model describes six identity processes that operate independently without a specific order. These processes include exiting heterosexuality, developing a personal LGB identity, developing an LGB social identity, becoming an LGB offspring, developing an LGB intimacy status, and entering an LGB community. D'Augelli's framework addresses issues often ignored in other models specific to LGBTQ identity development and creates a corresponding understanding of the processes in bisexual and transgender identity development (Bilodeau & Renn 2005).

Bilodeau and Renn (2005) address terminology and theoretical perspectives that represent innovative thought. The word *transgender* encompasses a variety of meanings inclusive of transsexuals, transvestites, male and female impersonators, drag kings and queens, male-to-female persons, female-to-male persons, cross-dressers, gender benders, gender variant, gender nonconforming, and ambiguously gendered persons. Gender identity reflects an individual's internal sense of self as male, female, or an identity between or outside these categories. Medical and psychiatric literature focuses on a binary construction of gender identity, creating significant issues for those who identity outside of "normality," or broadly defined, biological and gender identity matching as male or female. In terms of new theoretical foundations, feminist, postmodern, and queer theorists suggest dismantling dual-gender systems and promoting greater freedom from rigid social roles. Although these theorists propose new ways of conceptualizing gender, a nonstigmatizing model of transgender identity development has yet to form (Bilodeau & Renn 2005). The models and theories related to sexual orientation and gender identity development differ in perspective and theoretical foundations, but still neglect to acknowledge other aspects of one's holistic identity, such as the influence of spirituality.

Models of Spiritual Identity Development

Contrary to the number of sexual identity development models present within scholarly literature, very few models of spiritual identity formation exist. Helminiak (1996) identified spirituality as a central element of all human experience (Love et al. 2005). He believed spirituality is synonymous with spiritual development because it is the process of growing in authenticity. Love et al. (2005) state how traditional theological understandings of spirituality represent it as a fixed aspect of human experience or a process of development. The process contained three stages: the purgative or movement away from sin; the illuminative, where one grows in virtue; and the unitive, representing union with god. These stages, addressed simultaneously, represented a focus on spirituality and spiritual development rather than personal identity. Helminiak (1987) believed spiritual identity and development involved the whole person and their commitment to wholeness, authenticity, and genuineness. Although literary themes align in defining spirituality as a drive for meaning, authenticity, purpose, wholeness, and self-transcendence, there is little information on how to obtain these measures within one's life. In an attempt to bridge one's various identities, intersectional research provides a way of connecting identities and embracing relationships.

Intersectionality of Spiritual and Sexual Identities

Currently, the complexities between interpersonal, intrapersonal, and cognitive development represent three main areas of scholarly interest within college student identity development (Abes et al. 2007). Social Constructionism considers identity to be socially, historically, politically, and culturally structured. Intersectionality utilizes those structures simultaneously to recognize a multifaceted approach toward identity. Abes et al. (2007) recognize the dynamic construction of identity and the influence of changing contexts on the relative salience of multiple identities. A key tenet of intersectionality is that the process of identifying with more than one social group produces new representations of experience, without minimizing or reducing their original identities (Diamond & Butterworth 2008).

Reflecting on spiritual and sexual identity development, Helminiak (1996) made a strong argument for their interrelationship by indicating how sexuality relates to his tripartite notion of human experience—organism, psyche, and spirit. He believed sexuality is in each aspect of human experience, including spirituality. Love et al. (2005) explored how these intersections between sexuality and spirituality interacted within LGBTQ college students. The collective responses indicated categorizations of identity development and interaction, including reconciliation, nonreconciliation, and undeveloped spiritual identity. Reconciled students embraced being either gay or lesbian and being a religious or spiritually grounded person. These students demonstrated self-efficacy, self-awareness, and self-acceptance. They recognized their spirituality as a source of strength, had a strong sense of spiritual identity, and displayed an interaction between spiritual identity and sexual identity. These students held a relationship with God, god, or a higher power, and several recognized the separation between religion and spirituality. The students with unreconciled identities composed two statuses. One group of students was aware of their nonreconciliation, while the other group was not. The last group of students, those with an undeveloped spiritual identity, appeared to be spiritually undeveloped because of passive or active rejection. The students appeared to lack a purposeful approach to their spiritual development and demonstrated no commitment to the development of their spirituality in any form. Whether active or passive, the students avoided addressing spiritual issues or making commitments relative to their beliefs (Love et al. 2005).

The experiences highlighted by these students provide a small representation of intersectionality. Through their experiences with religion, open and loving environments, having a sexual or intimate relationship, and through thorough self-analysis, these individuals stated how their sexual and spiritual identities interacted to form a relatively cohesive self-identity (Love et al. 2005). Exploring the lived experiences of LGBTQ college students recognizes that they are more complex than most of their daily human interactions reflect, both on and off campus (Clark 2005). Acknowledging these complexities and working with LGBTQ individuals to develop their identities provides a challenge for scholar-practitioners, but development of these identities can be fostered through utilization of current literature and benchmarking with other practitioners.

Collaborative Units

Drawing on intentional collaborations between Penn State's Center for Ethics and Religious Affairs (CERA) and the Lesbian, Gay, Bisexual, Transgender, and Ally (LGBTA) Student Resource Center at The Pennsylvania State University, we seek to provide theoretically based examples of how practitioners can engage students in spiritual, religious, sexual, and/or gender identity development. A basic understanding of each unit and the institution as a whole provides a foundation for understanding our work as practitioner-scholars.

The Center for Ethics and Religious Affairs

A unit of the Division of Student Affairs at the Pennsylvania State University, the Center for Ethics and Religious Affairs (CERA), resides in the Pasquerilla Spiritual Center, which is the largest multifaith facility of its kind in the country. CERA offers a welcoming, safe, inclusive environment for the community to explore a multitude of religious and spiritual traditions in a compassionate, open-minded setting. We aim to promote an environment that stretches beyond tolerance to a genuine appreciation of and respect for religious and spiritual diversity. As a multifaith learning community, CERA is charged with providing programs and a venue for the ethical, religious, spiritual, and character development of the university community. CERA serves nearly fifty recognized religious/spiritual student organizations on campus in addition to its partnerships and outreach initiatives with faculty, staff, and community constituents. Within the confines of a public institution, CERA strives to build active, responsible citizens and raise the consciousness of the community through its spiritual/religious and ethical/social justice resources. With a broad offering of worship opportunities, educational events, and cross-cultural programs that enrich the heart and mind, CERA hosts a culturally diverse multifaith community and celebrates our differences and similarities in a safe, supportive environment.

As a state-related institution, Penn State is unique in offering a venue for spiritual and religious exploration. To that end, CERA has developed partnerships with interfaith organizations to promote interfaith understanding and cooperation through educational and cultural programming and activities.

The expansion of the Spiritual Center in 2003 created more office spaces for student organizations as well as space for a variety of purposes including a Muslim Prayer Room, a space for the Jewish community, as well as a Meditation Chapel, which is the most Christian in orientation of all of the spaces within the Spiritual Center. Nearly fifty student organizations and campus spiritual leaders from a variety of spiritual and religious traditions share space in this facility. Essential to affiliating with CERA is the adherence to a Code of Ethics which encourages trust, mutual respect, the celebration of differences, and promotes religious harmony, as well as the creation of a safe climate where all are welcome.

Traditional Programs

CERA has established partnerships with numerous organizations and constituents including the Interfaith Initiative of Centre County, Interfaith Center of Greater Philadelphia, and various Penn State colleges, units, departments, and student organizations. Each year, CERA recruits and hires one or two undergraduate students to serve in the Fellows Program. These students develop programming and manage events as well as outreach initiatives to help strengthen ties and/or create new partnerships between the CERA, Penn State, and surrounding communities. Some examples of ongoing programming include:

- interfaith initiatives (International Peace Day Program, Interfaith Prayer Breakfast, panels, presentations, Interfaith Conference, Interfaith Action Committee);

- service and service learning projects, including interfaith discussion/reflection;

- ethical Lunchbox Series on a variety of topics such as depression, fair-trade chocolate, human sex trafficking, and so forth;

- speakers—interfaith, ethical, social justice—such as Stephen Prothero, Zainab Al-Suwaij, Reza Aslan, Dr. Phil Jenkins, Arun Ghandi, John Bell, and Christian de la Huerta;

- films such as the *Nefarious Documentary* and *In God's Name*;

- national Hunger and Homelessness Awareness Week programming; and

- exhibits (Clothesline Project, Soka Gakkai International Peace Exhibit);

In addition, the director and assistant director present on various topics related to religion and spirituality, ethics, ethical decision-making, and social justice and service learning initiatives.

The LGBTA Student Resource Center

The Lesbian, Gay, Bisexual, Transgender, and Ally (LGBTA) Student Resource Center is a unit of the Division of Student Affairs at the Pennsylvania State University. The Center offers a safe and supportive environment for exploration of lesbian, gay, bisexual, and transgender people and issues. As a center, we work to assist the community in ensuring the inclusion of LGBTA persons and in eliminating homophobia and heterosexism by providing a comprehensive range of direct service, referral, programming, outreach, and education.

As part of our mission, we provide a variety of programming opportunities for faculty, staff, students, and community members each academic year. During each semester, we provide an LGBTQ mentorship program for LGBTQ undergraduate students. We sponsor events for National Coming Out Day/Week each fall and coordinate and host a Pride Week in the spring of each academic year. The director and assistant director coteach a course for students preparing for involvement within our peer-education program where panels of three to four students go out into the university community to talk about LGBTQA issues and what the university community can do to support and raise awareness of LGBTQ issues. As a center, we also sponsor an internship program for ten to twelve undergraduate/graduate students to work within our office on a variety of outreach endeavors, one of them being our quarterly publication of our an alumni newsletter. Throughout the year, we also sponsor a variety of speakers through our LGBTA Lecture Series, some of which have related to spirituality and religion. Within our physical space, we host a library of resources for the university community and offer ongoing discussion groups in our student lounge, one of which is rooted in spiritually and religion. Finally, as a way of visibly recognizing supportive spaces on campus, our office offers our Support Network, which establishes an identifiable network of persons who can provide support, information, and a safe space to LGBTQ persons at the university.

History of Collaboration

Although the Center for Ethics and Religious Affairs and the LGBTA Student Resource Center have been active on campus for a number of years, these two centers have intentionally begun addressing the needs of LGBTQA students looking to explore their spiritual identities, religious identities, or both since 2008. As a result, there has been increased interest and curiosity among our student population to explore these areas, encouraging us to expand our programming efforts to meet the needs of these students.

Tiers of Collaboration

Over the last four to five years, CERA and the LGBTA Student Resource Center have implemented a variety of programs. These efforts have ranged in levels of student commitment, involvement, and dedication. Through offering programs with varying levels of commitment and participation, we believe we have allowed students to learn about, explore, engage, and advocate on issues of spirituality, religion, sexuality, and/or gender identity. As seen within various models of student identity development, students typically begin to question, explore, engage, and then take ownership of their identities once they have reached a place of comfort and security. It is with a profound respect of student development theory and a strong dedication to our students that we have provided programming with these intentions. Through honoring the "places" where our students have been developmentally, we have provided programs within both of our physical locations, engaged students from both offices through program cosponsorship, increased our visibility and presence within both offices, and highlighted our resources and supportive collaborations for students across campus. Our interventions are described below.

Shared Spaces

Since CERA and the LGBTA Student Resource Center reside in two different physical locations on our campus, it has been crucial to provide programming and events in both spaces thereby allowing students to gain access and become more comfortable entering both of our respective locations. Over the last few years, we have provided a variety of ways for students to engage and learn about these two centers. We have intentionally utilized both spaces for discussion groups, retreats, counseling services, film showings, and programs developed specifically on issues of spiritually, religion, sexuality, and gender identity. Throughout the last few years, we have collaborated to bring discussion groups for student athletes questioning their sexual and gender identity to the Center for Ethics and Religious Affairs' Pasquerilla Spiritual Center. The LGBTA Student Resource Center has utilized the Spiritual Center for the annual fall weekend leadership retreat, allowing students to stay the weekend in the facility and demystify some of the perceptions associated with the space. We have also encouraged our Counseling and Psychological Services (CAPS) unit to utilize spaces in the Spiritual Center when providing their ongoing support group for LGBTQ students.

In terms of a relatively recent initiative, we have now added an ongoing weekly LGBTQA Spirituality and Religion discussion group facilitated by the assistant directors of each center in the student lounge of the LGBTA Student Resource Center. Through our efforts over the last few years, we have intentionally worked to engage students in both locations to expose them to the resources and support provided at each center for the LGBTQ community.

Cosponsorships

The last few years have provided us with significant challenges within our respective communities, but also in designing and implementing programming focused on spirituality, religion, sexuality, and gender. Historically, we have been surrounded by traditionally conservative religious and spiritual groups. We have also encountered beliefs among LGBTQ individuals that spiritually and religion cannot and should not be part of their holistic identities. With these notions in mind, we have worked diligently to expose students, faculty, and staff, to affirming LGBTQ spiritual and religious options.

As stated earlier, the LGBTA Student Resource Center sponsors annual programming for National Coming Out Day/Week and Pride Day/Week each academic year. It has been during these weeks that we have worked to cosponsor programs for students to examine these parts of their identities as well as utilize our spaces. Over the last few years, cosponsorships have ranged in form from bringing national speakers to campus, developing panels with clergy representation from a variety of denominations speaking on LGBTQ issues, cosponsoring a Pride Week Commitment Ceremony, and developing panels with students as the core focus addressing their experiences with religion, spirituality, sexuality, and gender identity. These opportunities have intentionally ranged in student commitment to provide students with the opportunity to engage and participate wherever they are developmentally and personally.

In terms of national speakers, we have hosted a variety of speakers on campus addressing issues of spiritually, religion, sexuality, and gender. Through their discussions, we have examined the intersections of holding a traditionally conservative religious identity and ways to reconcile those experiences with one's sexual and gender identity. Speakers have also addressed issues with sacred texts and their usage against LGBTQ behaviors and attractions. Through these conversations, students have begun to acknowledge and address some of their internal struggles. At the same time, student groups, staff, and community members have been enraged with our cosponsorships. Often, we must defend why these identities are important to explore together. Our partnership has spurred ongoing discussions about how to present these issues in a way that promotes active listening and open minds despite the perspectives or beliefs the students, staff, or community may possess. We continue to strategize creative ways to work with these issues, inclusive of other national speakers offering their services to continue the work we have begun.

The Pride Commitment Ceremony, which was held a few years ago, was a ceremony for LGBT couples sponsored in part by surrounding community organizations as well as CERA and the LGBTA Student Resource Center. Through these cosponsorships, both centers faced community opposition as well as national feedback from organizations *against and for* LGBTQ recognition. The Pride Commitment Ceremony showcased the supportive resources of each Center for students, faculty, staff, and community members—allowing the community as a whole to demystify some of the common stereotypes associated with LGBTQ relationships. As part of this programming endeavor, the Center for Ethics and Religious Affairs compiled a panel titled "The Honeymoon's Over—What's Next?" The panel focused on practical and real-world issues for same-sex couples including human resources topics, like domestic partner benefits and dual-career assistance; healthy relationships and same-sex relationship violence; legal issues like adoption, estate planning, and home ownership; as well as stress and social support.

Additionally, CERA and the LGBTA Student Resource Center has had great success working with panels where faculty, staff, students, and clergy members address issues of spirituality, religion, sexuality, and gender identity. Panels have ranged in topic, composition, and time, but each has brought something new and thought-provoking to our communities. Clergy have addressed issues within sacred texts, their denominations, and world issues associated with the LGBTQ community. Students have discussed how they have or have not reconciled their spirituality and religious identity with their sexuality and gender identity and why. They have spoken in-depth about their personal experiences and discussed how communities of worship have accepted or rejected them for who they are.

A popular and ongoing program has been, "Is Faith Straight? An Ethical Discussion on Spirituality, Religion, and Sexual Orientation." This panel has tailored the LGBTA Student Resource Center's peer education program to include a spiritual and religious component. The program encourages student participants to address religion and spirituality and then hosts a question-and-answer session following their personal stories. The program has grown each year and provides a safe space to address these issues among other students, faculty, staff, and spiritual leaders.

Visibility and Resource Provision

Although we have intentionally utilized both of our spaces for cosponsorship opportunities and created programming to address these issues, we have also worked diligently to ensure that both enters' resources and support for LGBTQ spiritual and religious ideology is present in our respective spaces. In terms of visibility, each center includes brochures and contact information for staff members. We also include events for each center on our semester event calendars and provide weekly updates for students, staff, and faculty in our listserv newsletters. We hope that increased visibility would allow students to access information and address these issues without fear of rejection or further hindrance to their development.

We have also developed and continuously update a list of affirming LGBTQ spiritual and religious communities both on and off our campus. We have surveyed local congregations, campus ministry groups, and student organizations to provide a list of contact information and a statement of inclusion from those organizations who wholeheartedly affirm LGBTQ identities. Although this list has been a tremendous resource for our students, it does not exist without controversy. Remarks have included listing all of the groups who do not accept the LGBTQ community instead of listing the few groups on campus and in the community that do. Why, in their minds, should we pretend or even be hopeful about a plethora of organizations supporting the LGBTQ community? In the geographical area where the university resides, particularly where many rural communities sit outside of the college town and tend to be more conservative as well as mostly Christian in nature, we believe that this list provides students with a resource that keeps them safe when exploring their spirituality and sexuality, despite the small number of organizations who commit to accepting and embracing LGBTQ identities. We hope that in the future as we continue to raise awareness, that the list will highlight more organizations that accept and embrace the LGBTQ community wholeheartedly.

We have also worked diligently to provide an updated list of resources and links on our websites allowing students to learn about and decide what organizations best fit them developmentally. The LGBTA Student Resource Center has also purchased some comprehensive resources from the Human

Rights Campaign addressing issues of spirituality and sexuality, which provide a national outlet for students to recognize that the process to embrace and accept multiple identities is not just a personal or individual struggle, but is an issue many others have sought to overcome in the past.

New and Future Programming

As we previously mentioned, we have tenaciously created, maintained, and designed programming focused on the religious, spiritual, sexual, and gender identity spectrum for several years. Although we believe we need to maintain the tiered programming endeavors we have started, we now acknowledge the need to grow and expand our programming for students who have success- fully navigated their religious and/or spiritual identity relative to their sexual and/or gender identity. During the last year, the LGBTA Student Resource Center has built long-standing cosponsorships with not only the Center for Ethics and Religious Affairs but also the Center for Women Students—offices within Student Affairs that are considered advocacy units. These centers have worked collaboratively to create programming to highlight gender as well as issues surrounding survivors of sexual, emotional, and physical violence. Gen- der is another layer of identity that impacts students already grappling with spiritual, religious, sexual, and gender identity. Therefore, we have brought more visibility to these issues that can deeply affect the well being and safety of our students.

Previous Challenges and Areas of Growth

Throughout the last few years, we have provided several programs to faculty, staff, and students addressing spiritual, religious, sexual, and gender identi- ties, but those provisions have not occurred without opposition. Challenges have ranged from students afraid to disclose their identities due to intense fear of disapproval from religious leaders to religious leaders out rightly rejecting and in some cases, being enraged by our programming efforts. As practitioner-scholars, we have attempted to dispel and erase stereotypes that have existed historically on campus given the geographically conservative area that our campus occupies. Some of these challenges and our approaches to these obstacles that we have taken are discussed below. While we under- stand that our approaches may not be applicable to every campus and every institution, we hope they do provide some guidance for others working with similar issues.

Fear of Disclosure

Although we have experienced a tremendous amount of success surrounding programming on LGBTQ issues and religion and spirituality, we have also encountered students who are still apprehensive of disclosing their sexual and/or gender identity for fear that their communities of practice will disown them or reject them. Often, this can result in alienating them from their core circle of friends, diminishing possible monetary support if employed by their organization, and depriving them of any supportive resources they currently utilize. Restating the conservative overtones of where our institution is located in Central Pennsylvania, it is a reality that a student's entire academic and social life can be uprooted if they engage outside their community of practice. Many of our spiritual and religious groups remain siloed and do not encourage outside group connections or interactions. Some of the clergy or spiritual leaders emphasize that their group is all that the student needs to be successful, so why should they search elsewhere? We have heard from some upper-class students who have attended one or several of our events and have expressed that they regret not having made connections outside of their student organizations earlier in their college careers. They mentioned that they were so caught up in the groups' projects and programs; they did not think to look outside of it and explore other groups, programs, and so forth.

In terms of working with students who have experienced alienation or opposition from their spiritual/religious groups, both centers have agreed to meet one-on-one with them and allow the location to be chosen by the students where they may feel comfortable—acknowledging that they may need to maintain anonymity and distance from their spiritual/religious groups. We have also established other resources for these students providing them with our LGBTQ affirming congregations' materials and assisting them in working through some of the primary obstacles hindering them from connecting their identities. These situations have resulted mostly in one-on-one meetings as well as strong connections with our Counseling and Psychological Services unit.

Stigmas and Stereotypes

Perceptions of CERA and the LGBTA Student Resource Center has affected our programming and challenged us to work harder at eradicating the stigmas and stereotypes associated with both centers. The Pasquerilla Spiritual Center, although a multifaith facility, continues to be seen as "the church" on campus by many while the LGBTA Student Resource Center is seen as "only" for the LGBTQ community. Anyone who walks into the LGBTA Student Resource Center is seen as lesbian, gay, bisexual, or transgender without a second thought about our allies or heterosexual-identified supporters. Students continue to believe that they cannot utilize space within the Spiritual Center on campus because of the hatred that religious traditions have for their sexual identities, gender identities, or both. They believe the individuals within the center, inclusive of faculty, staff, clergy members, and other students, do not accept their identities and would not welcome LGBTQ individuals in such a space. Although students know that some of the programming offered by the LGBTA Student Resource Center has been cosponsored by the Center for Ethics and Religious Affairs, they continue to believe it is the Spiritual Center's way of "pitying" or feeling bad for the LGBTQ community.

In terms of erasing these stereotypes, as we have stated above, we have worked harder to utilize our shared spaces and intentionally collaborate on programming examining these issues. Although these perceptions have not totally been erased, they have been changing as students learn about and engage with members from both centers. Providing visible resources, connecting students, faculty, and staff to affirming groups, and continuously assessing the actions and reactions of students to our programming, we have begun to challenge these stigmas and allowed students to develop their own perceptions rather than take ownership of historical perspectives.

Religious and Spiritual Traditions

Acknowledging the nearly sixty spiritual and religious traditions encompassed within the Center for Ethic and Religious Affairs and on campus, we have struggled with denominational beliefs, religious, and/or spiritual leaders, as well as student willingness to support LGBTQ issues fearing outside perceptions. We have experienced a significant number of issues with spiritual leaders, religious leaders, or both, especially in regard to coordinating panels on affirming LGBTQ groups and cosponsoring programs.

Although we have leaders who are from communities and traditions that embrace and affirm LGBTQ persons, we have had leaders who are still hesitant to work with us especially if they believe, accurately or not, that their churches are divided on the issue and they do not feel comfortable representing their traditions on a particular panel. We have faced leaders who vocally state that it is their job to "love the sinner, yet hate the sin," and other groups who will not respond either way.

As mentioned earlier, both centers cosponsored a Commitment Ceremony on campus. The mayor of the town presided over the four same-sex couples who participated. This ceremony was not a religious event, but show-cased the idea that same-sex couples have a right to be legally recognized and protected. Hundreds of people packed the space and others quietly protested outside. When some of the religious groups, spiritual groups, or both in the facility found out about the Center for Ethic and Religious Affairs sponsor-ship, they complained and spread word to some of the churches in the area who also called in complaints and expressed their outright disapproval. One group approached the director and asked if this means that he could "marry" his best friend or his animals. These groups indicated that if they were going to be affiliated with a religious/spiritual center on campus, it had to adhere to the beliefs/standards that the organization upheld. Being connected to the Spiritual Center, which was supporting the Commitment Ceremony, went against their religious beliefs. The Center for Ethics and Religious Affairs stood strong and reaffirmed their mission to provide ethical, spiritual, and character development of the entire University community, inclusive of the LGBTQ community and to adhere to the University's nondiscrimination policy, which includes the LGBTQ community.

Throughout the last few years, we have forged stronger bonds with some religious leaders, spiritual leaders, or both, while others have encour-aged their members not to attend our events. We have encountered several challenges in building a network of resources for LGBTQ students who want to explore their religious and/or spiritual identities. However, success has by far outweighed the challenges. We continue to work with students on a one-on-one basis and provide tiered programming to encourage students to engage in a place where they are comfortable and safe.

Implications for Scholar-Practitioners

Current research provides some suggestions for scholar-practitioners to help college students develop their spiritual and sexual identities. The research indicates that professionals should provide the means for LGBTQ students to discuss and explore issues of spirituality and sexual identity development. Colleges and universities must address these topics since many students strug-gle with identity issues. Witnessing these struggles, there is a need for broader and more open discussions of sexuality and spirituality on college campuses (Love et al. 2005). Student affairs practitioners are encouraged to support students in ongoing self-work surrounding personal identity (Bilodeau & Renn 2005). Although many institutions do not exclusively explore spirituality relative to sexual identity, researchers state it is the responsibility of student affairs practitioners to advocate for its inclusion. Spirituality should not just exist in small sectors of campus, but rather be incorporated into the lives of students relative to their interest.

Other research recommends professional practice infused within the training of practitioners. Abes et al. (2007) recommend the inclusion of meaning-making capacities and identity perceptions to provide professionals with a deeper awareness of how students understand themselves and the contexts to which they are connected. LePeau (2007) suggests that practitioners explore their own privilege, create ways for students to express themselves, and continuously validate students' beliefs especially pertaining to issues of sexuality and spirituality.

Finally, current research recommends the collaboration and recognition of the influence of faculty in developing a student's intersectional comprehension of sexual and spiritual identity. Research indicates that faculty play a central role in shaping institutional culture and climate and their values lie at the heart of higher education's capacity to change (Lindholm & Astin 2008). Rogers and Love (2007) state how institutions, but specifically faculty, need to increase visibility of spirituality on campuses and intentionally create spaces where spiritual exploration can occur, both in and out of the classroom.

Future Directions

The intersections between spirituality and sexuality warrant further observation and inquiry. Although several research studies extensively examine issues pertaining to sexual and spiritual identity development, there exist multiple areas within current research where further investigations can occur. Research on models of sexual identity development is extensive, but needs to expand to create a model relevant to the experiences of those who identify as transgender. Models pertaining to the life experiences of lesbian, gay, or bisexual individuals should not define the identities of those who identify as transgender.

Through reviewing studies based on spirituality, the research lacks a definitive model of spiritual identity development. Although several explanations exist, such as the attainment of authenticity, there is no set method or theoretical knowledge of how spiritual development occurs. Studies need to examine how spirituality develops within an individual and the resulting effects of that development needs to be articulated.

Intersectionality as a theoretical model provides an analysis of how various identities connect to form an individual's holistic identity. Several concerns exist within current research based on spiritual and sexual identity formation, but only through an intersectional exploration can these identities be fully understood simultaneously. Intersections between spiritual and sexual identity among LGBTQ college students reflects research based on qualitative methods, therefore lacking generalization. These studies lack empirical evidence and may not be representative of the larger college student population.

A model of identity development representing the intersections of spirituality and sexuality requires further exploration and more in-depth discussions of practitioner-derived approaches encouraging college students to share and explore their experiences. Acknowledging this gap, we continue to seek ways to provide and offer students ideas and methods to safely explore and understand their sexual and spiritual identities. Throughout this essay, we have sought to offer a broader and more cohesive understanding of spiritual and sexual identity development and theoretically based programmatic interventions for LGBTQ college students.

Works Cited

Abes, E. S., S. R. Jones, and M. K. McEwen. "Reconceptualizing the Model of Multiple Dimensions of Identity: The Role of Meaning-Making Capacity in the Construction of Multiple Identities." *Journal of College Student Development* 48.1 (2007): 1–22.

Abes, E. S., and D. Kasch. (2007). "Using Queer Theory to Explore Lesbian College Students' Multiple Dimensions of Identity." *Journal of College Student Development* 48.6 (2007): 619–636.

Barry, C. M., and L. J. Nelson. "The Role of Religion in the Transition to Adulthood for Young Emerging Adults." *Journal of Youth and Adolescence* 34.3 (2005): 245–255.

Bilodeau, B. L., and K. A. Renn. "Analysis of LGBT Identity Development Models and Implications for Practice." *New Directions for Student Services* 111 (2005): 25–39.

Chickering, A. W., J. C. Dalton, and L. Stamm. *Encouraging Authenticity and Spirituality in Higher Education*. San Francisco, CA: Jossey-Bass, 2006.

Clark, C. "Diversity Initiatives in Higher Education: Deconstructing 'The Down Low'— People of Color 'Coming Out' and 'Being Out' on Campus: A Conversation with Mark Brimhall-Vargas, Sivagami Subbaraman, and Robert Waters." *Multicultural Education*, 13.1 (2005): 45–59.

Diamond, L. M., and M. Butterworth. "Questioning Gender and Sexual Identity: Dynamic Links Over Time." *Sex Roles* 59 (2008): 365–376.

Helminiak, D. A. *Spiritual Development: An Interdisciplinary Study*. Chicago: Loyola University Press, 1987.

Helminiak, D. A. *The Human Core of Spirituality: Mind as Psyche and Spirit*. Albany: State University of New York Press, 1996.

Kiesling, C., G. T. Sorell, M. J. Montogomery, and R. K. Colwell. (2006). "Identity and Spirituality: A Psychosocial Exploration of the Sense of Spiritual Self." *Developmental Psychology* 42.6 (2006): 1269–1277.

Lease, S. H., S. G. Horne, and N. Noffsinger-Frazier. "Affirming Faith Experiences and Psychological Health for Caucasian Lesbian, Gay, and Bisexual Individuals." *Journal of Counseling Psychology* 52.3 (2005): 378–388.

LePeau, L. "Queerying Religion and Spirituality: Reflections from Difficult Dialogues Exploring Religion, Spirituality, and Homosexuality." *College Student Affairs Journal* 26.2 (2007): 186–192.

Lindholm, J. A., and H. S. Astin. "Spirituality and Pedagogy: Faculty's Spirituality and Use of Student-Centered Approaches to Undergraduate Teaching." *The Review of Higher Education* 31.2 (2008): 185–207.

Longerbeam, S. D., K. K. Inkelas, D. R. Johnson, and Z. S. Lee. "Lesbian, Gay, and Bisexual College Student Experiences: An Exploratory Study." *Journal of College Student Development* 48.2 (2007): 215–230.

Love, P. G., M. Bock, A. Jannarone, P. Richardson. "Identity Interaction: Exploring the Spiritual Experiences of Lesbian and Gay College Students." *Journal of College Student Development* 46.2 (2005): 193–209.

Pearce, L. D., and A. Thornton. "Religious Identity and Family Ideologies in the Transition to Adulthood." *Journal of Marriage and Family* 69.5 (2007): 1227–1243.

Renn, K. A. "LGBT Student Leaders and Queer Activists: Identities of Lesbian, Gay, Bisexual, Transgender, and Queer-Identified College Student Leaders and Activists." *Journal of College Student Development* 48.3 (2007): 311–330.

Rogers, J. L., and P. Love. "Exploring the Role of Spirituality in the Preparation of Student Affairs Professionals: Faculty Constructions." *Journal of College Student Development* 48.1 (2007): 90–104.

Seifert, T. "Understanding Christian Privilege: Managing the Tensions of Spiritual Plurality." *About Campus* 12.2 (2007): 10–17.

Tan, P. P. "The Importance of Spirituality Among Gay and Lesbian Individuals." *Journal of Homosexuality* 49.2 (2005): 135–144.

Chapter 16

New Perspectives on Religion and Spirituality for LGBTQ Students

Scotty McLennan

I hope I can provide an overview of some (but far from all) of the issues and opportunities touching on the intersection of religion and lesbian, gay, bisexual, transgender, questioning (LGBTQ) life that exist on our campuses. My own personal history includes being a minister in the first denomination, I believe, that had an ordained minister come out, back in the 1960s. We then started passing resolutions in 1970 and established an office at our denominational headquarters in 1973, which is now called the Unitarian Universalist Office of Bisexual, Gay, Lesbian, and Transgender Concerns. Starting a couple of years later, I served as a legal services attorney for a decade, ultimately founding and directing the Unitarian Universalist Legal Ministry, which advised some LGBT clients. I am now on the board of the ACLU for Northern California, which worked hard to try to defeat Proposition 8 and is now part of the legal team challenging the proposition's validity. I was the university chaplain at Tufts when the InterVarsity Christian Fellowship was stripped of its status as a student organization for sexual orientation discrimination in refusing a lesbian member a place on the senior leadership team because her beliefs ran counter to the organization's theological teachings on homosexuality; in that case, I worked to get InterVarsity reinstated with an open election procedure. At Stanford, my most recent project in this area has been working with some undergraduate and graduate students, the associate deans for religious life, and religious professionals from Stanford Associated Religions and the Stanford Hospital to establish an LGBT/Religion Leadership Roundtable.

However, I should quickly add that the journey since I entered divinity school forty years ago has not been an always-easy one for me, or, I'm sure, for many others around me. I am, as my university chaplain, William

Sloane Coffin, used to say, a recovering racist, sexist, and homophobe (Glaser and Groves). So my own self-discovery and healing as a white, Anglo-Saxon Protestant straight male is ongoing, and I'll appreciate both your understanding and your criticism of the continuing construction zone of who I am in my sixties.

They used to teach us in divinity school when giving sermons that we should "tell 'em what you're going to say, say it, then tell 'em what you've said." I think that adage may originally have been coined by Dale Carnegie for *all* public speakers. In any case, let me tell you first, now, what I'm going to say. There's a lot of mistrust between many members of the LGBTQ community and many members of the religious community on campuses across the country. This is especially hard on our students who are struggling to develop both their LGBTQ identity and their religious identity. There's actually much support available from university chaplaincies and campus ministries, although that's often not realized. Likewise, there's a lot of effective programming that LGBTQ centers are doing across the country, often unseen, to respond to the religious and spiritual needs of their students. There are genuine problems, though, with religious groups on campus that are not LGBTQ-affirming, but there are also a number of creative strategies and signs of hope available for working with them.

So, let me now say in detail what I'm going to say. The Stanford student with whom I started the LGBT/Religion Leadership Roundtable, Aidan Dunn, keeps reminding me that a critical issue is that many, many students simply don't know that one can be both religious and LGBTQ. It's so often assumed that you can't be religious if you're LGBTQ, and you can't be LGBTQ if you're religious. The fallout from this is a heavy burden, especially given that the national survey results reported this month by the Pew Forum on Religion and Public life establish that three out of four Americans between the ages of eighteen to nineteen are religiously affiliated (Pew Forum). As the Hillel rabbi at Stanford, Mychal Copeland, who has long been out as a lesbian, has explained to me, most of us have spiritual needs, whether we're heterosexual or LGBTQ. Those needs will bubble up to be satisfied even a student has closed the door on religion for him- or herself on the basis that it's homophobic.

Aidan describes some of the dilemmas for students: You can be absolutely terrified to come out, because you're quite sure you'll be rejected by your faith community, and the faith community is a very important part of your life. You don't have the slightest idea how your sexual orientation can possibly be reconciled with your religion's teachings. But even if you begin putting your religion together with your LGBTQ identity, you'll have to go home over vacation and face your family, your church/synagogue/mosque/

temple/shrine, and your community, which usually still will have a negative reaction to your sexual orientation and actions. On the other hand, many queer people and organizations can be very negative about religion, and they can assume that everyone else who is LGBTQ agrees with them. Students of faith then get a clear signal that the LGBTQ community is not a place where they can express this part of themselves. They may be in contexts where everyone in the room assumes it's fine to disparage religion, not even thinking that there might be practicing Catholics or Protestants, Jews or Hindus present. If you do mention your religious commitments, you must not be very aware—somehow you haven't heard the word that all religions hate you. Or you're made to feel a bit eccentric, if not crazy. Or you're treated with condescension or pity.[1]

So, what can be done? One of the most important things, I've been told again and again, is to have the university chaplaincy, office for religious life, or other official umbrella for religious activities on the campus be crystal clear and very public about its support and affirmation for LGBTQ students. A way we've tried to do that at Stanford is to have a prominent, boxed notice, in a contrasting color, inside our Office for Religious Life brochure that describes our university chaplaincy as well as the thirty-five member groups of Stanford Associated Religions. It is called "A Note to Gay, Lesbian, Bi and Transgender Students," and it states, in part, that, "The Office for Religious Life is committed to welcoming students of all genders and sexual identities, all religious and non-religious traditions, and all cultural backgrounds. Please feel free to schedule a visit with a staff clergy or attend one of our regular or special programs." Then it helps that we have an out and outspoken LGBTQ associate dean for religious life, the Rev. Joanne Sanders. There are also a number of well-known professional leaders of our Stanford Associate Religions organizations who are well known to be LGBTQ, like Rabbi Mychal Copeland, but also some Protestant clergy now and in the past. And we have regular programming on spirituality and sexuality that examines the relationship of religion and LGBTQ life.

Similarly, the LGBTQ center on campus needs to be crystal clear and very public about its support and affirmation for LGBTQ students who are religiously or spiritually engaged. Our director at Stanford, who happens not to be religious himself, has described how he's come to assume that virtually everyone entering the center is coming from some religious or spiritual perspective.[2] He's gone out of his way to cosponsor programming with the Office for Religious Life and Stanford Associated Religions groups and to have religious resources that are LGBTQ-friendly, like books, media, and Internet sites, available on the center's website. Over the course of this academic year, the center will have done three screenings on site of films on LGBTQ identity and religion, followed by discussion. *For the Bible Tells Me So* was shown in the fall. It's a documentary portraying how five committed Christian parents, including former House Majority Leader Richard Gebhardt and his wife, and the parents of Episcopal Bishop Gene Robinson, handled the realization that they had a gay child. It brings in other informed voices like Harvard Chaplain Peter Gomes and Bishop Desmond Tutu.[3]

This winter the documentary at the LGBT Community Resource Center was *A Jihad for Love*, followed by a discussion with its gay Muslim film-maker Parvez Sharma. Islam is portrayed with respect from the inside, but we also view conflicts of a number of gay and lesbian Muslims with their clergy, their families, their countries, and even themselves, given that "the majority of Muslims believe that homosexuality is forbidden by the Qur'an and many scholars quote Hadith to directly condemn homosexuality." The believers in the film don't reject their religion, but struggle to reconcile their sexual orientation with the faith they cherish, ultimately pointing to a new kind of relationship with Islam.[4]

In the spring, the documentary at the LGBT Center will *Trembling Before G-d*, portraying gay and lesbian Hasidic and Orthodox Jews who work to reconcile their kind of human love with Biblical injunctions on homosexuality. The world's first openly gay Orthodox rabbi, Steve Greenberg, is featured, along with a variety of Orthodox Jews in a range of relationships to their partners and families.[5]

A third major initiative on university campuses to expand the circle and provide a religiously and spiritually welcoming environment for our LGBTQ students, as well as build respect for religiously committed LGBTQ students, must be widely and boldly publicizing the religious and spiritual groups that are truly affirming. On our campus, that would be the Unitarian Universalists, Quakers, the Episcopal Lutheran Campus Ministry, the United Campus Christian Ministry (a progressive Christian fellowship sponsored by the United Church of Christ, Presbyterian, American Baptist, and United Methodist denominations), Hillel, and AHA! (which stands for Atheists, Humanists, and Agnostics).

I mentioned the history of the Unitarian Universalists earlier. The Palo Alto Quakers' February newsletter, along with soliciting books from older members for the Stanford student group, describes two LGBTQ gatherings upcoming. The student copresident of the Episcopal Lutheran Campus Ministry is also the co-Chair of the campus LGBT/Religion Leadership Round-table. The Presbyterian minister who's the professional leader of the United Campus Christian Ministry also has been active with the Roundtable and written articles in the *Stanford Daily* in support of same-sex marriage and in support of LGBT students as beloved members of the Stanford community.

I've described Rabbi Mychal Copeland's leadership at Hillel. And our atheist group hosted a regional leadership summit recently with a speaker on the LGBT movement and atheism.

But what about the religious groups on campus that aren't LGBTQ affirming? Aidan Dunn, the student with whom I started the LGBT/Religion Leadership Roundtable, has described what he calls a misguided liberal clergy notion that we can or should try to shepherd all religious LGBT students into liberal religious organizations. Many of them are religiously conservative and simply don't want to go there. The director of the Stanford Women's Community Center, who's lesbian, has told me the same thing: "Don't think you can tell a Christian conservative to try liberal Christianity. It won't feel real to them."[6] Evangelical Christians need to hear LGBTQ-welcoming messages from people who believe the way they do, not the way Scotty McLennan does. People who read the Bible within a conservative context as the ultimate authority by which to live their lives, are not going to change their views about homosexuality from someone like me, who claims that the Bible should be read largely metaphorically and allegorically, but not as the literal or inerrant or finally authoritative word of God.

In preparation for this talk, I spoke about this with one of our lead evangelical professional leaders and with two students from one of our largest evangelical groups on campus. They tried to help me see where the cutting edge for LGBTQ-friendliness is these days in evangelical circles and what its limits are. They encouraged me to try to work with it, rather than fighting it or driving it underground on campus. Two important facts, first of all, are that evangelical consciousness is evolving and that evangelical Christianity is not a monolith. There are lots of varieties and shades of evangelicals from very conservative fundamentalists—few of whom are found at Stanford—to so-called Progressive Evangelicals like Jim Wallis who just spoke on campus this week. And younger evangelicals have a very different profile from older ones. For example, the Pew Forum survey found that four out of ten evangelical Christians under thirty say that homosexuality as a way of life should be accepted by society, almost twice as many as those over thirty who would affirm this statement (Pew Forum).

These three campus evangelicals were clear about LGBTQ students being created as much in the image of God as anyone else. They saw nothing sinful about homosexuality per se, but saw sex of any kind before marriage as sinful—heterosexual or LGBTQ. Inconveniently, they also opposed same-gender marriage, insisting that it must be between a man and a woman, but they seemed open to same-gender civil unions with all the rights of marriage. They might also agree that America has a problem in allowing clergy to act both on behalf of the state and on behalf of their religious institution. Would it be better for all if we separated functions as they do in certain European countries, requiring a legally binding ceremony in a state context and a religious ceremony later, if one chooses.

The evangelicals spoke of love as a primary Christian value and of their own love for LGBTQ people just as much as for other fellow evangelicals. Now I know how insulting this can be from an LGBTQ perspective: "We love you as people, but condemn your sexual activity which can never be condoned, as we eventually will for heterosexuals, because we say you can never get married." Yet this seems very different from the official Vatican position for Catholics, which holds that homosexuality as a human condition is itself "objectively disordered,"[7] that all homosexual acts are "acts of grave depravity,"[8] that "all support should be withdrawn from any organizations which seek to undermine the teaching of the Church" or "are ambiguous about it," including use of facilities of Catholic colleges by these groups,[9] and that priests not participate in any gay solidarity events, even including seminars that treat homosexuality in a "positive way."[10]

But then look what's happening at Georgetown University (which may have been reported in yesterday's preconference workshop on creating an inclusive LGBTQ environment at Catholic universities). After two reported antigay attacks on students near campus in the fall of 2007, with a sophomore charged with assaulting a fellow student in one of the cases, the university in 2008 opened an LGBTQ Resource Center with two full-time staff members (Siva Subbaraman, the director, is here at this conference). It provides a place for LGBTQ students to hang out, an LGBTQ prayer group on Monday nights, training sessions and workshops for students and faculty, help for students in finding services on campus, planning of events like Coming Out Week and Lavender Graduation, and lots more. The university president claimed that he would follow church teachings in establishing the center, but he went on to say this: "At a Catholic and Jesuit university, we most certainly can 'advocate' for LGBTQ students. We can and must advocate for respect, inclusion, understanding, safety, mentoring, dignity, growth, and equal opportunity. We can and must advocate for freedom from prejudice, exclusion, discrimination, and homophobia." As one student put it, praising what the opening of the center meant to him, "I have my gay identity and my Catholic identity, and these are two things that are very important to me. But they grew very separately. I needed to live and be as one integrated person" (Johnson 2010) It's also important to note, according to the Pew Forum national survey, that Catholics are one of the most LGBTQ-accepting populations in America. While almost 40 percent of Evangelical Christians under thirty say that "Homosexuality is a way of life that should be accepted by society," that figure rises to 63 percent for the general population of all Americans under thirty, but it goes almost 10 percent higher to 72 percent for Catholics under thirty (and it's at 55%—still a majority—for all Catholics over 30) (Pew Forum 2010).

It should be noted that religious traditions that seem not to be LGBTQ-friendly on campus almost always have alternative groups within them that are. For example, Dignity and New Ways Ministries for Catholics, Affirmation for Mormons, Freedom in Christ for evangelicals, and Al-Fatiha for Muslims. And what is done in pastoral counseling behind closed doors by sensitive Catholic priests, evangelical ministers, Orthodox rabbis, and Muslim imams can be life-enhancing—indeed, lifesaving—for many LGBTQ religious practitioners. I've spoken with both Catholic and Protestant evangelical professionals on campus at Stanford who say that they always try to respond to students where they are and not lead with church doctrine. There's also a lot of moral nuance, they explain, that always needs to be recognized.

There are some very encouraging signs at many secular universities across the country, as I've spoken with colleagues in university chaplaincy. The Rev. Dr. Elizabeth Davenport, dean of Rockefeller Chapel at the University of Chicago, has told me that there's "a general overall acceptance of diversity in relation to sexuality" at her campus. She says that the QueerReligious student group there "has a small but lively following—small only because it's almost passé." She's well accepted herself as a lesbian and the leader of religious life: "It's never been an issue," she says, ever since it came out in the student newspaper during her first couple of weeks as dean in 2008. And her partner is a priest at the nearest Episcopal Church to campus. New to the Midwest, she's been amazed to find Iowa coming out in favor of same-gender marriage, and then Grinnell College in Iowa hiring a gay president who proceeded, during his first speech on campus in the chapel, to introduce his partner—"without whose love and support I would not be here today"—and their two sons.[11]

The Rev. Janet Cooper-Nelson, chaplain of the Brown University on the East Coast, describes how the GLBT community and the Office of the Chaplains and Religious Life are allies—not counterposed or worried about one another. She's found this go be a welcome discovery for a number of new students. She describes their current Queer faith community as "an easily, gently, multi-faith, multi-generational, student and staff community whose laugher is as practiced as its tears." In a videotaped visit by the *Religious and Ethics Newsweekly* to Brown two years ago, an evangelical student leader was asked about his community's response to the "GLBT situation." "He looked tiredly at the camera and then said gently that he didn't think this was the same issue for his generation that it seemed to be for 'older folks.'" Even knowing that the word on campus is that evangelical communities are not safe places for a GLBT student," Rev. Cooper-Nelson told me that she felt chills as this particular student spoke, seeming to be saying, "We're over this, all are welcome, but it will be awhile until the older [religious] authority figures catch up."[12]

One of the most positive experiences many of us at Stanford have had in a long time, ironically, was when the Westboro Baptist Church of Topeka, Kansas, came to campus in January. This is the Rev. Fred Phelps's church, whose web-page address is GodHatesFags.com. They demonstrated outside of Hillel at Stanford, chanting and singing, and holding up anti-LGBTQ signs along with their anti-Semitic signs like "God hates Jews" and "The Jews Killed Jesus." Their homophobic signs included, "Fags are beasts," "Fags doom nations," "Fags can't marry," and "God hates fag enablers." (I take it that last label is intended for people like me.)

What the Stanford community decided to do in response, since we were given a week's warning that they were coming, was to create our own celebration of unity, which turned out to be 1,000 strong, on the Hillel lawn, circled around with our backs to the Westboro church members, singing songs, and reciting a formal pledge together. There were twenty-five cosponsors and partners, including the LGBT Community Resources Center, the Queer/Straight Alliance, and an organization called Jewish Queers, and then evangelical, Catholic and progressive Protestant organizations, the Buddhist Community, the Islamic Society, a new interfaith group called "Faiths Acting in Togetherness and Hope," and the Office for Religious Life. The pledge we recited included these words: "We stand united, from diverse secular cultures and religious traditions. We stand united, gay and straight, bisexual and transgendered . . . We stand united, and with the power of our bodies and our voices, we overcome the ugliness of hate. We stand united, affirming acceptance and inclusiveness. We stand united, affirming respect and diversity. We are Stanford United."

The Presbyterian minister who's the professional leader of the United Campus Christian Ministry, the Rev. Geoff Browning, wrote an op-ed in the next issue of the *Stanford Daily* in the form of an open letter to Mr. Phelps and members of the Westboro Baptist Church. He explained that he'd heard about their prior protests, including at the funerals of homosexuals, "most notably Matthew Shepherd who was beaten to death near Laramie, Wyoming." Then he thanked them for "helping to remind us of the importance of our community and the diversity that we cherish": "You came targeting Stanford Hillel as well as members of the LGBT community. By targeting them, you reminded us that these are beloved members of our community, that our community would not be the same without them. So the students of our community turned your message of hate and doom into a celebration of diversity." In his last paragraph he wrote, "I'm sorry that you couldn't join in with us to experience the power of that moment when we were all there reveling in our shared love and community."

This minister has been an active member of the LGBT/Religion Leadership Roundtable. That's the final sign of hope that I'd like to describe in more detail before ending, so that we have time for some discussion together as a plenary. After Aidan Dunn e-mailed me early last November for support in creating an organization to bridge the religious and LGBT communities on campus, we've been able to gather interested student leaders and religious leaders to meet on a biweekly basis. Our explicit goals are fourfold: (1) to address the needs of LGBT students who have been burned by religion; (2) to build bridges between LGBT and religious communities on campus; (3) to educate students interested in learning about LGBT-affirming views of religion; and (4) to begin discussions around campus about these issues.

We soon formed six committees: One is establishing a blog which will be hosted by a member of the leadership roundtable to provide confidentiality to on-campus participants but allow them to participate fully in an ongoing conversation. A second is creating opportunities for sacred text study, both within and between religious communities. A third is creating panels of students involved in the religious and LGBTQ communities, going into dormitories for discussion programs. A fourth is involved with the ongoing film festival that I've described. A fifth is creating opportunities for discussion—first among religious professionals from diverse religious backgrounds and ultimately among the student leaders of the thirty-five member groups of Stanford Associated Religions. A sixth is doing outreach to athletics, especially given the active involvement of several religious groups that are not known to be LGBTQ-affirming with various Stanford athletic teams. There are LGBTQ athletes and coaches who religiously committed and very much in need of support from the kind of people who are now in the LGBT/Religion Leadership Roundtable.

The college years are a critical time of life for formation of attitudes regarding LGBTQ and religious identities. UCLA's Higher Education Research Institute has conducted a longitudinal study of the evolution of college students' views on spirituality and morality from freshman to junior year, examining 14,500 students attending 136 colleges and universities nationwide. They've found that there's a significant improvement in general attitudes toward the LGBTQ population during the college years. In 2004, 54 percent of freshmen nationwide supported same-sex marriage. That figure rose to 66 percent of the same individuals by their junior year in 2007. When freshmen were asked in 2004 whether they thought it was important to have laws prohibiting homosexual relationships, 68 percent said no, but 79 percent said no as juniors in 2007. These positive attitudes are mirrored for religiously identified students, albeit at different levels (Spirituality in Higher Education 2008). The study also found that although attendance at religious services declines over the college years, attention to spiritual and ethical values show marked increases. For example the percentage of students reporting that they consider developing a meaningful philosophy of life "very important" or "essential" rises from 41 percent to 55 percent between freshman and junior year nationally. "Becoming a more loving person" goes from 67 percent to 83 percent (Spirituality in Higher Education 2008).

So, now let the preacher tell you what I've said! Education is a critically important tool in expanding the circle in two directions—helping all students become more spiritually and ethically aware on the one hand, and helping straight students become more inclusive, welcoming, and affirming of LGBTQ people, on the other hand. Hopefully, education can also help our students see that not all religion is anti-LGBTQ and not all LGBTQ people are antireligious. Education can help our students to find ways to be both LGBTQ and fully a person of faith if they want. But there's lots of hard work that needs to be done on a consistent and continuing basis: like empathetic public dialogue and sensitive counseling one-to-one behind closed doors; careful study of religious texts; close attention paid within the LGBTQ community to its members' spiritual and religious needs; reform of our religious traditions; and greater openness of the LGBTQ community to the positive dimensions of religion. And I haven't even touched on some other important educational activities, like connecting theory and practice in LGBTQ religious studies classes and research.

Thanks again to the conference organizers for including consideration of the relation between LGBTQ concerns and religious perspectives throughout this conference. I believe there's a lot that we can do both within and between our communities to make for much more safe and fulfilling lives for our students.

Notes

1. Aidan Dunn. E-mail to Scotty McLennan on February 21, 2010.

2. Mychal Copeland. Interview with Scotty McLennan on February 21, 2010.

3. Film Synopsis. *For the Bible Tells Me So*, 2007, at http://forthebibletellsmeso.org/film.htm.

4. "About." *A Jihad for Love*, 2007, www.ajihadforlove.com/about.html.

5. "About the Film." *Trembling on the Road*, 2001, www.filmsthatchangetheworld.com/site/about/.

6. Laura Harrison. Interview with Scotty McLennan on February 21, 2010.

7. Vatican. Congregation for the Doctrine of the Faith, "Considerations Regarding Proposals to Give Legal Recognition to Unions Between Homosexual Persons, paragraph 4. June 3, 2003.

8. Vatican. Catechism of the Church, section 2357, February 21, 20.

9. Vatican. Congregation for the Doctrine of the Faith, "Letter to the Bishops of the Catholic Church on the Pastoral Care of Homosexual Persons, paragraph 17, October 1, 1986.

10. Daniel Williams. "New Rules Affirm Pope Benedict's Stance Against Gays," *Washington Post* October 8, 2005.

11. Elizabeth J. L. Davenport. E-mail to Scotty McLennan on February 21, 2010.

12. Janet Cooper-Nelson. E-mail to Scotty McLennan on February 21, 2010.

Works Cited

Glaser, Chris, and Sharon Groves, *For the Bible Tells Me So: Study Guide and Advocacy Training Curriculum*. Washington, DC: Human Rights Campaign, 2008.

Johnson, Jenna. "Georgetown U. Tries to be Catholic and Gay-Friendly." *Washington Post* December 11, 2009 (accessed March 16, 2014), http://www.washington-post.com/wp-dyn/content/article/2009/12/11/AR2009121104654.html.

Pew Forum on Religion and Public Life. "Religion Among the Millennials: Less Religiously Active Than Older Americans, but Fairly Traditional in Other Ways," February 17, 2010 (accessed March 16, 2014) www.pewforum.org/docs/?DocID=510#beliefs.

Spirituality in Higher Education Program, Press Release, Los Angeles: UCLA Higher Education Research Institute, October 13, 2008 (accessed March 16, 2014), http://spirituality.ucla.edu/docs/news/20081013.AssociatedPress.pdf.

Vatican. Congregation for the Doctrine of the Faith. "Considerations Regarding Proposals to Give Legal Recognition to Unions Between Homosexual Persons." June 3, 2003 (accessed June 16, 2014), http://www.vatican.va/roman_curia/congregations/cfaith/documents/rc_con_cfaith_doc_20030731_homosexual-unions_en.html.

Vatican. Catechism of the Catholic Church, section 2357, Latin text © Libreria Editrice Vaticana, Citta del Vaticano, 1993.

Vatican. Congregation for the Doctrine of the Faith. "Letter to the Bishops of the Catholic Church on the Pastoral Care of Homosexual Persons." October 1, 1986 (accessed March 16, 2014), http://www.vatican.va/roman_curia/congregations/cfaith/documents/rc_con_cfaith_doc_19861001_homosexual-persons_en.html

Williams, Daniel. "New Rules Affirm Pope Benedict's Stance Against Gays." *Washington Post* October 8, 2005, http://www.washingtonpost.com/wp-dyn/content/article/2005/10/07/AR2005100701844.html.

Chapter 17

Intersections

A Guide to Working with LGBTQI University Students of Minority Religions or Cultures

Mychal Copeland and D'vorah Rose

Rachel[1] is Jewish and lesbian, of African American and East European decent. She remarks that while each of these identities connects her to a distinct community on campus where she feels a sense of belonging, there is no one place where all of her identities can live simultaneously.

Religion and the struggle for lesbian, gay, bisexual, transgender, questioning, intersex (LGBTQI) self-determination in this country are at odds with each other on our national stage. This political schism conceals the personal struggle for individuals who identify as LGBTQI and religious, including college-age students who are often just beginning to explore their identities. Survey results from a Pew Forum on Religion and Public life study establish that three out of four Americans between the ages of eighteen to twenty-nine are religiously affiliated (Pew Forum). How does this reality affect the LGBTQI community? When campus professionals assume that an LGBTQI or questioning student would never set foot in a religious institution or that he or she would not be trying to reconcile these identities, much of the time, they would be wrong. A longtime director of a university LGBT center remarked that when a student comes to his office to talk about coming out issues, he now assumes that he or she is carrying a religious identity that is playing a significant role in the student's on-campus life as well as at home. This article will explore the multiple identities LGBTQI university students carry when they also affiliate with religious traditions, as well as the intersection of those identities with minority ethnic and cultural backgrounds. We will present tools to help these students navigate the multiple cultural contexts to which they belong, stemming from a pastoral approach to working with students.

Religion is part of the conversation about LGBTQI life on campus for students, and must become so for professionals as well. Students on college campuses publicly or discreetly wear multiple identities: emerging adult, son or daughter, scholar, athlete. They identify as part of one or more ethnicities or cultures as well. Many define themselves loosely or significantly as adherents to a faith or part of a religious community. Students identifying as LGBTQI add one more box to the list, one which may or may not be easily reconciled with the other facets of their identities. These multiple identities are often experienced as being in tension with each other. Each student's situation is unique, but for some, additional layers of identity bring about further challenges. An individual who identifies with an ethnic minority, a religious tradition, and the LGBTQI community can find him- or herself enduring significantly more stress than her or his peers, in that each community represents another distinct group and culture with which to relate (Kundtz & Schlager 2007, 76, 78). Young people navigate, daily, the boundaries between communities, struggling to find ways to bring their whole selves to everything they explore.

So why is the religious or spiritual piece of students' multiple identities so integral to creating safe campuses for them? There are at least three major reasons. Our current political debate about LGBTQI rights is intricately tied to religion, so as LGBTQI people and allies, we need to know how to enter this conversation. Students face these political questions as they balance their identities and come into themselves as adults. We should feel compelled to learn more so we can be present for our students, including learning how religious communities are reading their own and others' texts, how they talk to the queer people in their midst, and how the intersection of religion and politics is playing out on both our campuses and in our country. As Beth Kraig writes, ". . . whether for reasons of personal spiritual belief or pragmatic political policy, LGBT people and their heterosexual allies need to understand the language and nature of faith organizations. LGBT people need to engage in, rather than spurn, opportunities to situate their identities and human rights within the larger frameworks of religion and theology in the United States" (Kraig 1998 384).

The second reason that we cannot excise religion from the conversation has more to do with the health of LGBTQI students themselves. If LGBTQI students decide as they are coming into their identities that religion belongs to someone else, namely religionists who define gay people out of their texts and communities, then these young people have nowhere to turn for meaningful religious or spiritual support. These negative definitions of who they are may leave them feeling vulnerable and without spiritual or community grounding at a time when they need them most. Those who define religion as antigay have then successfully robbed these youth of a spiritual and nurturing home community. Raising this topic on campus helps address the needs of LGBTQI students who are redefining themselves spiritually.[2] Addressing the need for religious and spiritual community will support their healing, growth, and possibly even help heal past centuries of pain and exclusion.

The third reason is that the more we ignore the intersection of religious and queer identity, the more lives we lose to suicide. As campus professionals, it is imperative that we sit beside students in their struggle and show them compassion as they attempt to integrate the many facets of their lives. Contemporary religious leaders and institutions, including or perhaps especially those with a campus presence, must find ways to creatively address and embrace *individuals* who are LGBTQI, even if their institutions' theologies condemn the behavior. How many more teens and college students will commit suicide before this becomes evident? We can let students know that we are with them on their journey to find room—theologically, spiritually, and communally—within their religious traditions. We can all be part of this sea change, but we can only enter the conversation if we understand that positive religious or spiritual identity is a key factor in creating the welcoming, safe campuses for which we all strive.

There is both hope and frustration for those of us striving to find ways to help LGBTQI students live and integrate all of their seemingly disparate identities. On the one hand, suicide rates for LGBTQI youth are higher than for their peers. Among lesbian, gay, and bisexual youth, the risk of attempting suicide is 20 percent greater in unsupportive environments compared to supportive environments (Hatzenbuehler 2011). Furthermore, lesbian, gay, and bisexual youth who come from families that reject them are more than eight times as likely to have attempted suicide than lesbian, gay, and bisexual peers who reported no or low levels of family rejection (Ryan & Huebner 2009). Many families' tendencies toward nonacceptance stem from religious or cultural biases against homosexuality, so the threat of familial abandonment may be exacerbated for those from traditional religious and cultural backgrounds.[3] Young people are also beginning the coming out process at younger ages, so more students arrive on campus as freshmen who have already been dealing with personal, familial, and religious struggles for years, often within unsafe environments. Depending on the acceptance level at a student's particular university, there may also be a threat from classmates, some of whom may be hostile to LGBTQI people on religious grounds.[4] Furthermore, students attending institutions based in nonaccepting religious frameworks may experience additional barriers.

On the other hand, our students are growing up in an era in which many religious communities are carving their own path to meaningful engagement with the LGBTQI people in their midst. Even some of the communities that seem most unfriendly toward LGBTQI folk are working sincerely to at least *accommodate* LGBTQI members—a tremendous shift, considering the leaders of these religions have traditionally declaimed homosexuality as one of the worst sins. Many campus professionals came of age in an era in which to come out as LGBTQI equated closing the door to religion, spirituality, and often the family that was bound up in those religious communities. But that is not necessarily the case anymore. There is more space than ever before for LGBTQI people within religious institutions. From queer churches and synagogues to the rise of out clergy and the hundreds of LGBTQI religious groups and welcoming institutions, it *is* getting better.

Students explore their emerging multiple identities in many different ways. As a result of increased openness within some religious institutions, many college students are remaining within their religious traditions or adopting new ones that are more queer-friendly than their traditions of origin. The latter may entail a great deal of loss in that one religious or cultural milieu cannot be simply and painlessly substituted for another. Others remain within nonaccommodating traditions, trying their best to either remain closeted in that realm, living with the inconsistencies, or suffering harassment from clergy, fellow laypeople, or both. Many are, indeed, able to sustain being private about their personal lives in the context of a nonaccepting religious institution. Of course, others walk out the door of their house of worship as soon as they come out. While this self-preserving solution is absolutely understandable (and often lauded by members of the LGBTQI community), there is loss in this decision. We all have spiritual needs, whether we are heterosexual or LGBTQI. Those needs will arise and demand attention, even if the student has closed the door on religion for him- or herself. Students may find themselves struggling to find a spiritual home and a way to fill the emptiness that has been left by a culture, a tradition, or a theology that once contributed to a sense of meaning and purpose in the world. With or without the strictures of a religious institution, the pain of believing that a God who was once present is now hostile and punishing will leave deep wounds. If family is deeply intertwined with that religious tradition, the loss is excruciating and complex. Parents, themselves, struggle to reconcile personal pain with advice they seek from their trusted religious leaders.

As campus professionals, understanding the campus climate and confronting our own assumptions can help us better serve the students who struggle to reconcile being queer, religious, and/or a member of a cultural minority. It is pertinent to note that the psychological literature concerning the coming-out process has paid little attention to the effect young people's cultural background may have on how they choose to integrate their identities.[5] Yet a student emerges from a complex network and family system, and culture and religion are important pieces of that constellation (Szapocznik & Kurtines 1993). A student's background affects the way she or he defines who constitutes "family," and introduces cultural and familial values surrounding sexuality, childbearing, gender roles, and being in relationship. We may assume that "being out" equates everyone in one's life knowing about a sexual identity, while some students may define it as disclosing to certain people or being out in only certain arenas. For example, a student's decision to be "out" in all environments except for a religious one may actually be healthy and appropriate for her or his process. Students may preference a racial, ethnic, or religious identity far above a sexual one and may make personally consistent decisions based on that hierarchy of identities (Smith 1997, 288).

In order to help guide interactions with religiously or spiritually engaged students, we have developed the following questions for university staff, instructors, and other campus leaders to ask themselves and their colleagues. These questions can help cultivate self-awareness of personal religious or spiritual background:

1. Within what religious or spiritual tradition did you grow up, if any?

2. Did you find anything meaningful within that tradition, as a youth or young adult? For example: Did it help establish a sense of community, connection to something transcendent/ bigger than oneself, a sense of connectedness to others? Did it provide useful guidelines for establishing life priorities?

3. If you did not grow up with a particular religious or spiritual framework, do you recall how religion was spoken about in your home? What were familial attitudes toward people who were religious?

4. Is your tradition of origin still meaningful to you? If so, what parts of it are meaningful? Why?

5. If you moved away from this tradition, why did you do so? And at what age did you make this move?

6. Have you found a way to meaningfully reconcile your critiques or discomfort with this tradition? If so, how did you do this? At what age? Who or what helped support you in this process?

7. Even though you may now be highly critical of this tradition, do you retain any positive feelings or meaning from this background?

8. If you currently are not engaged in any formal religious or spiritual activity, how do you cultivate that which provides

meaning in your life? Do you find this by being with loved
ones? Through music, art, poetry, dance? By being in nature?
By engaging in physical activity, or through science, math,
philosophical quest, or social action?

9. Reflecting on questions 1–8, are you able to recognize why an
LGBTQI student might find positive meaning by participating
in a religious tradition or spiritual practice community, even
though there might be legitimate critiques of that tradition?

10. Reflecting on questions 1–9, how might you be able to offer
sincere and meaningful support and guidance to your religiously or spiritually active LGBTQI students?

It may be helpful when answering these questions to acknowledge that
each of us carries a certain amount of religious "baggage"—positive, negative,
or neutral. Just as our own identity formation was affected by our families
of origin, our education, our ethnicities, our opportunities or lack thereof,
we have also been influenced by subtle or explicit attitudes about religion
growing up or in our adult years. Religion is part of our "story," as it is for
our students. Whether we embrace, reject, or feel ambivalent toward religion
or spirituality, the more we are able to confront our own presuppositions
the better equipped we will be in working with our students. Applying these
questions to the story of a college student, we see how challenging our own
assumptions can lead to deeper understanding.

Rosa is a Latina student who comes out on campus, and is then
outed to her parents without her knowledge. They seek counsel
with their Catholic priest, and he tries to perform exorcisms on
Rosa, urging her "evil spirit" to flee. The priest advises Rosa's parents to force her to attend a program to "rehabilitate" her. After
a few years, her parents still do not return her phone calls. Rosa
continues to attend church every Sunday on campus and wears
a cross around her neck. She is also very active in the LGBTQI
community on campus, running a queer Latino group. While she
always exhibits a positive outlook, she speaks of the pain of being
severed from her family, the uncomfortable periodic interactions,
and the judgments she hears from other members of her family
who are in contact with her. She also experiences hostility from
the LGBTQI community for being part of an institution that they
feel is oppressive to queers.

Here are some questions we might consider in working with Rosa:

- Who is the Catholic priest on campus? What are his views on sexual identity? On pastoral counseling with queer students? If he cannot be a resource, are there other Catholic staffers? If not, are there other Christian leaders who can be of help to Rosa, acknowledging that they do not exactly represent her community?

- Are there other students who can be resources for her, either from the Latino or Catholic communities?

- Is it necessary for Rosa to be "out" in all of the communities in which she lives and thrives?

- Is the LGBTQI community on campus educated about religious/LGBTQI issues? If not, who on campus might be able to speak to the community to ensure that students like Rosa are not ostracized by their gay friends because they are religious?

- How is Rosa reconciling her own faith/spirituality with the rejection of her parents' church? How does she view her relationship with God? What about her current involvement with the church is bringing her fulfillment?

By applying the self-awareness questions suggested above, it is possible that for a secular or even antireligious university staff member working with a student like Rosa, he or she may come to have a greater understanding of and appreciation for the student's religious and spiritual needs.

As we sit with students who are balancing multiple identities, the more we can come to understand our own background and perspectives, the better we will be able to serve the students and to sympathize if conflicts arise for them. However, we do not only interact with students in the realm of one-on-one counseling. Many campus professionals work with LGBTQI students in student affairs and other areas of event planning and campus education. While individual campuses will work to identify their particular issues and to creatively find the best solutions for their communities, there are some common pitfalls that can be easily avoided. LGBTQI students with multiple identities or from minority religions face ongoing ignorance at best, and outright prejudice and stereotyping at worst, by their classmates, instructors, coaches, and the immediate communities surrounding and supporting universities. Sometimes, even with the best intentions, students with multiple identities are placed in highly uncomfortable circumstances with their peers or adults on campus. The following questions can serve as a guide to those of us working closely with LGBTQI students with multiple identities:

1. When planning an event, for whom is the program intended?

2. What barriers might exist to attending this event for students with multiple identities? What might be the impact of the event's particular location on campus?

3. What could be done to remove or at least lessen these barriers?

4. What are the needs and experiences of students from multiply persecuted groups?

5. What are the needs and perceptions of students who are recent immigrants?

6. What types of overt teaching can be offered on campus to expose students, staff, and instructors to the existence of multiple identities?

7. What type of support can be offered on campus for students with multiple identities?

8. What type of assumptions are promulgated on campus about LGBTQI students? Do people assume that:

   • they are only politically liberal?

   • they support abortion?

   • they are not religious?

   • if they *are* religious, there is obviously a conflict with their sexual identity?

   • they are liberal in their religious practice?

   • they are politically active?

   • if given the legal opportunity, they would choose to marry?

We will approach another student story with these questions in mind.

Ahmet, a student from a Muslim background, has just come out to himself but is still largely in the closet. He had formerly been the president of the Islamic group on campus. As he slowly confides in friends on campus outside of his Muslim community, many remark that his coming out must mean the end of his involvement with that religious group. Their assumptions frustrate him since he sincerely wants to continue practicing Islam and is struggling to stay connected. At one point on campus, an LGBTQI group screens a movie about gay Muslims, Jihad for Love, but he cannot see it because he knows that to merely attend would result in being shunned by his local Muslim community.

- What tools does Ahmet need to be able to talk to his non-Muslim friends about where he stands with his intersecting identities?

- Is there a way to screen the film in a venue that would make it possible for him to attend?

- Are there other students, groups, or clergy on campus who can be of support to him?

- Are there national or international organizations within the Muslim community that serve as a resource for him?

By applying these questions, university staff may be more successful at creating safe and effective environments and opportunities for students' learning and development. However, the few student stories told here cannot be understood as representative of the vast number of college students grappling with intersecting identities. Each student narrative is unique, and each individual's coming-out process is just that—a lifelong process without a clear beginning or endpoint. For LGBTQI students who identify with a religious, minority ethnic, or cultural heritage, they could be just beginning the search for their authentic, spiritual selves. While the self-reflection and programming questions listed in this essay are, hopefully, a meaningful start to better understanding the needs of religiously affiliated students, each campus will discover how these questions and issues need to be answered within its own particular environment. Regardless of our campuses' orientation or our own personal histories, as campus professionals, we have the unique privilege of standing alongside our students on their journeys toward wholeness.

Notes

1. All student names have been changed.

2. On the need for faith discussions on the college campus see Laura C. Engelken.

3. Althea Smith. See p. 286 for a detailed discussion about the complexity of religion, coming out, and abandonment in minority cultures. See also E. Dube, R. Savin-Williams, and L. Diamond, pp. 143 and 206.

4. Robert Rhoads addresses intolerance and bullying in *Coming Out in College: The Struggle for a Queer Identity*. Westport: Bergin & Garvey, 1994. Indicative of hostility toward GLB students, one subject comments that "Gay, lesbian and bisexual

lifestyles are immoral and should not be accepted as an ok lifestyle. I don't want my children to grow up thinking because everyone's doing it, it is all right. The Bible calls it sin!" (16).

5. Althea Smith (282). Furthermore, Smith argues in this article that "Many assumptions about coming out have been developed through research involving pre-dominantly White or White-identified lesbians, gay men, and bisexuals, for whom individualism, independent identity, and separation from family of origin are impor-tant parts of growing up" (281).

Works Cited

Dube, E., R. Savin-Williams, and L. Diamond. "Intimacy Development, Gender, and Ethnicity Among Sexual-Minority Youths." In Anthony D'Augelli and Charlotte Patterson, eds., *Lesbian, Gay, and Bisexual Identities and Youth: Psychological Perspectives*. New York: Oxford University Press, 2001.

Hatzenbuehler, Mark. "The Social Environment and Suicide Attempts in Lesbian, Gay, and Bisexual Youth." *Pediatrics* April 18 2011 (accessed March 16, 2014), http://pediatrics.aappublications.org/content/early/2011/04/18/peds.2010-3020. abstract.

Kraig, Beth. "Exploring Sexual Orientation Issues at College and Universities with Religious Affiliations." In Ronni L. Sanlo's *Working with Lesbian, Gay, Bisexual, and Transgender College Students: A Handbook for Faculty and Administrators*. Westport, CT: Greenwood Press, 1998.

Kundtz, David, and Bernard Schlager. *Ministry Among God's Queer Folk*. Cleveland: Pilgrim Press, 2007.

Pew Forum on Religion and Public Life. "Religion Among the Millennials: Less Religiously Active Than Older Americans, but Fairly Traditional in Other Ways." February 17, 2010 (accessed 2013), www.pewforum.org/docs/?DocID= 510#beliefs.

Rhoads, Robert. *Coming Out in College: The Struggle for a Queer Identity*. Westport, CT: Bergin & Garvey, 1994.

Ryan, C., D. Huebner, et al. "Family Rejection as a Predictor of Negative Health Outcomes in White and Latino Lesbian, Gay, and Bisexual Young Adults." *Pediatrics* 123.1 (2009): 346–352 (accessed March 16, 2014), http://pediatrics. aappublications.org/content/123/1/346.full.pdf+html.

Trevor Project (accessed 2013), http://www.thetrevorproject.org/suicide-resources/ suicidal-signs.

Smith, Althea. "Cultural Diversity and the Coming-Out Process: Implications for Clinical Practice." In Beverly Greene, ed. *Ethnic and Cultural Diversity Among Lesbians and Gay Men, Psychological Perspectives on Lesbian and Gay Issues*, vol. 3. Thousand Oaks, CA: Sage Publications.

Szapocznik, J., and W. M. Kurtines. "Family Psychology and Cultural Diversity: Opportunities for Theory, Research, and Application." *American Psychologist* 48 (1993): 400–407.

Chapter 18

Culturally Appropriate Information Support Services for Lesbian, Gay, Bisexual, and Transgender (LGBT) South Asians[1]

Representing Multiple Shades of Identity Based on Sexual Orientation and Ethnicity

Bharat Mehra, Eric Haley, and Dylan Lane

Introduction

Lesbian, gay, bisexual, and transgender (LGBT) people belonging to ethnic minority groups have "special needs" different from their white counterparts as a result of double jeopardy experienced while facing racism in white homosexual communities and homophobia in their ethno-cultural environments (Dube & Savin-Williams 1999; Tremble, Schneider, & Appathurai 1989). Their feelings of self-worth, practicing safe-sex, and achieving professional and personal success are impeded (Savin-Williams 2001) as a result of perceived disownership in their ethnic communities owing to their sexual orientations (Gibson 1989; Gupta 1989; O'Donnell et al. 2002). Additionally, internalized racism and everyday marginalizing experiences in a white dominant context also present key challenges to self-fulfillment and social well-being for LGBT ethnic minorities (Minwalla et al., 2005).

Similar to other ethno-racial minority homosexuals (Gil-Gomez 2000), LGBT South Asians trying to construct their LGBT identities and express cultural revisions that acknowledge their homosexual experiences encounter a lack of acceptance and support from their ethnic peers (Fernandez 2006; Blakey, Pearce, & Chesters 2006). This lack of support and acknowledgment of LGBT South Asians in their ethnic communities is related to the social construction of what is considered normative in a contemporary South Asian cultural milieu. The South Asian cultural norms are historically represented in extended familial ties, monogamous heterosexual ideals, arranged marriage prospects, inequities in gender roles and behavior, and patriarchal traditions unique to South Asian circumstances and practices. Such defining characteristics dictate the expected cultural standards that have got transmitted across generations "embedded and embodied in citizenship and nationalism, circulated through capitalism, and mobilized in the discourses of postcoloniality" in modern South Asian society (Desai 2002, 66). The process has disallowed for any transgressions that present alternative cultural narratives and perceived deviances from the idealized norm (Rastogi 2005). LGBT South Asians over the ages internalized, interrogated, and challenged such cultural hegemony, while attempting to resist its disempowering hierarchies and stereotypes that were established by the postcolonial nation state and based on biased intersections of racial, ethnic, and gender classifications (Sarker 2002).

There is also the experienced reality that LGBT South Asians face in their interactions with dominant white LGBT communities in the diaspora, similar to the experiences of LGBT individuals from other communities of color, of prejudice and exclusion, indifference and invisibility (Summer 1995), and exoticized objectification that considers them alien and marginalizes them as "outsiders" on society's margins (Dang & Hu 2005). What is unique to LGBT South Asians (compared to other communities of color) is a situated nature of their experiences and a resulting deep impacts of their perceived and real marginalization, that are internalized as ongoing conceptualization, construction, and enactment (Appadurai 1996) within a dynamic South Asian identity formation process (Hall 1997), while simultaneously immersed in a continuous sense of "being and becoming" (Heidegger 1991, 136). This formation of sexual subjectivities in a neocolonial South Asian cultural environment is a consequence of liberalization and its consumerist production activities in market economies, as well as of dominant hegemonic desires in Indian nationalism to reify rigidly articulated conservative sexualized, racialized, religious, classed, and gendered forms of social regulation and normalization in the postcolonial world (Bhaskaran 2004). In a globalized and electronically networked information society, the significance of physical location is highly reduced and LGBT South Asians encounter and experience the complex interplay of cultural heterosexism and racialized behaviors irrespective of their geographic settings. This is owing to globalizing forces such as: a pervading homogenization of cultures and expansion of global markets (O'Hara & Biesecker 2003), media manipulation of aesthetic sensibilities and semiotics (Pieterse 2003), and the high intensity of worldwide electronic communication and information exchanges (Uimonen 2003).

An LGBT South Asian located anywhere in the world, thus, encounters a wide range of emotional, cultural, symbolic, and physical resistance within and outside her or his ethnic environment. The process of consciously and/or unconsciously resisting these resistances and recognizing the "outsider" status of their LGBT thoughts, feelings, and experiences is what ultimately renders the LGBT South Asian isolated and confused while negotiating her or his sexual orientation and gender identity (Kukke & Shah 1999/2000). Additionally, LGBT South Asians face a cloak of invisibility that becomes difficult to breach owing to the following typical behavior experienced in their ethnic communities:

- ridicule and cultural signals of deviance and disorder (Hom 1994);

- deliberate ignorance (Sullivan 2001);

- apathy about engaging in communication in matters of sexuality (Laurent 2005);

- unavailable language discourse to effectively communicate on LGBT concerns (Erni 2003); and

- sheer avoidance, lack of support, and inaccurate information (Narrain & Bhan 2005).

Recognition of minimal cultural support and information resources available for LGBT South Asians to meet their needs has not led to a significant increase in provision of appropriate materials or research on the concerns and experiences of this disenfranchised population (Ratti 1993). This is because LGBT South Asians are still considered peripheral to the South Asian diaspora and cultural sensibilities, and they are treated as outside the realm of mainstream narratives in South Asian colonialism and nationalism as well as those espousing liberal feminism and queer theory and politics (Gopinath 2005). Moreover, what LGBT resources do exist are considered culturally inappropriate for LGBT South Asians since they only cater to the needs of white LGBT people and do not acknowledge or address issues associated with the South Asian cultural experience (Leong 1995). For example, design of social support services for LGBT people often leave out cultural-specific attention to topics such as gender and sexuality constructions, oppression and minority politics, and identity and language, to name a few, that are significant to LGBT South Asians in their coming out process (Kwong-Lai Poon 2006). This pilot study identifies specific needs of LGBT South Asians that are reflective of their multiple shades of identities based on sexual orientation and ethnicity. Findings address missing gaps by providing guidelines for the design of culturally appropriate information support services for LGBT South Asians in academic communities to meet their specific needs and expectations.

Research Methods

This paper addresses the following research questions:

- What are the specific needs of LGBT South Asians?

- What should a culturally appropriate information support service for LGBT South Asians in academic communities include in order to support their dual struggles of acceptance within South Asian ethnic communities and white LGBT populations?

The archives of khush electronic mailing list (http://groups.yahoo.com/group/khush-list/), the oldest cogender electronic mailing list for LGBT South Asians provided by Yahoo!, were used as a dataset to identify the components of a culturally appropriate information support service for LGBT South Asians in academic environments. The purpose of the khush electronic mailing list, according to its administrators, is to discuss South Asian LGBT culture/experiences/issues and form a social support network for its users. The uses of the khush electronic mailing list as an information resource for LGBT South Asians to meet their specific needs were identified during summer 2009. The study was based on a content analysis of 693 electronic messages posted during a six-month January to June period by ninety-four registered members, averaging 7.37 messages per user and 115.5 messages per month. Two researchers independently created a draft coding scheme based on grounded theory principles, content analysis, and application of open, axial, and selective categorization (Glaser & Strauss 1967; Hunter et al. 2005) to fifty-four randomly selected electronic messages posted to the khush electronic mailing list. The two-draft coding schemes were merged and modified in-process based on mutual agreement and detailed discussion with a coder who was hired to apply the merged coding scheme to the dataset of electronic messages. Each electronic message was coded to identify the following: electronic message content topic and focus related to LGBT and/or South Asian concerns, impact of electronic message content (positive, negative, or neutral), and region of electronic message focus (India, USA, other, not applicable). The process helped document the purposes of use of khush electronic mailing list as an information resource for LGBT South Asians to meet their specific needs. Patterns of user demographic information were manually generated and confirmed via the use of the advanced search engine provided by Yahoo! The study has implications for providing culturally appropriate information support services to effectively meet the specific needs of LGBT South Asians in academic environments.

Who Are LGBT South Asians?

The following are salient characteristics of the LGBT South Asian population based on resulting interpretations from extrapolation of the demographic data gathered during the content analysis of the electronic messages posted on the *khush* mailing list:

- LGBT South Asians are located in almost every geographic part of the world, from urban to rural environments, from regions in the South Asian subcontinent to the Americas, Europe, Australasia, and Africa. This dispersed spread of LGBT South Asians around the globe is connected to the high degree of migrations, adventurous spirit, and a love for travel found in the South Asian community (Van der Veer 1995). The physical location of *khush* users during January to July 2006 reveals this geographic diversity, with twenty-one users in the United States (e.g., Atlanta, New York City, Silver Spring), six users in India (e.g., Chennai, Bangalore, Jaipur), one user who declared her or his location as USA/India, one user each from Australia (Melbourne) and United Arab Emirates (Dubai), and sixty-four users who left their location undeclared.

- The pervasive use of networked information and communication technologies (e.g., Internet) around the globe has resulted in greater information flows, communication exchanges, and awareness about LGBT issues within and outside the LGBT South Asian population (Kole 2007). This is reflected in the content analysis of the *khush* messages during the period of study, which shows that there were 227 messages about LGBT and/or South Asian issues in India, 124 messages about LGBT and/or South Asian issues in the United States, and 94 messages about LGBT and/or South Asian issues in various other parts of the world.

- In spite of the world becoming "flat" owing to globalization (Friedman 2005) and the increased awareness of progressive civil rights efforts for LGBT people in different parts of the world (Cruz-Malavé & Manalansan IV 2002), there is still much fear of cultural ostracization and prejudice against LGBT people in South Asian communities, even though this is slowly changing. Positive and progressive news coverage and information from Westernized nations is providing some impetus to

LGBT South Asians to venture out of their closets and challenge heterosexist sexuality/gender-related constructions and conceptualizations in their local communities.

- Applying the popular (though controversial) 10 percent estimate of homosexuality in the general population (Kinsey, Pomeroy, & Martin 1948) to the approximate 1.3 billion people in South Asia and the 24 million in the South Asian diaspora (Rangaswamy 2005) provides significantly large numbers of LGBT South Asians around the world. Without getting into the controversy of specific numbers we can safely say there is much variation in LGBT South Asians in terms of their conceptualizations, language of identities, and behaviors associated with sexuality and sexual orientations that do not always follow Westernized constructs related to alternative sexualities (Sherry 2005). For example, research findings identify significant numbers of South Asian men who have sex with men regardless of whether they self-identify as LGBT (Pradeep 2002).

- LGBT South Asians fall in the range of all possible age groups, incomes, occupation backgrounds, and marital status (Khan 2001). Since the closing decades of the twentieth-century LGBT South Asians in their twenties and thirties have been more proactive in seeking fulfillment of their needs and desires, though in recent years we are finding younger LGBT South Asians becoming more forthcoming in using the Internet to express their LGBT identities (Bolding et al. 2007). Age of *khush* users during the period of study ranged from 13 to19 years (one user), 20 to 29 years (10 users), 30 to 39 years (16 users), 40 to 49 years (three users), to 50 to 59 years (one user). Sixty-three users did not declare their age. Examples of *khush* users' self-identified occupations included professionals/students from disciplines such as information technology, event planning, journalism, research, management, cultural geography, accounting and administration, graphic design/filmmaking, entrepreneurship, computers, activism, and enterprise facilitation.

- Recent research shows more male LGBT South Asians active online since females have other avenues (e.g., offline informal social networks) to express their LGBT identities (Yip 2004). This was true also of *khush* users during the period of study for there were only fourteen self-identified female users, fifty-one male users, and twenty-nine users did not declare their sex.

Needs of LGBT South Asians

LGBT South Asians have multiple intersecting needs resulting from their LGBT sexual orientations and South Asian ethnicities. These needs are created as a result of the individual's immersion in an encompassing social and cultural environment that presents a real and/or imagined reality, situating and contextualizing a sense of marginalization for the individual. Needs relating to their LGBT sexual orientations and South Asian ethnicities intersect to create unique thoughts, feelings, and actions experienced by LGBT South Asians that makes their contexts different from those experienced by other LGBT people and those encountered by other ethnic minorities.

The paper does not distinguish between the specific needs/expectations of LGBT South Asians relating to their sexual orientation and those needs/expectations relating to their ethnicity in order to refrain from minimizing the nature of their experiences. The rationale is based on an understanding of the integrated nature of experienced situations where facets of lived experience cannot be separated and distinguished (or wholly explained using the existing constructs of language) based on one factor or another (Merleau-Ponty 1968). This also relates to the complexities associated with experiences reflecting intersections between issues of sexual orientation, ethnicity, or both. Use of the phrase *needs/expectations* expresses these considerations in recognizing that the specific needs of LGBT South Asians resulting from the intersections of their sexual orientation and ethnicity create a context of desired expectations from the external social and cultural environment as well as within the individual LGBT South Asian. When the social and cultural environment and/or the individual are lacking in these expectations various barriers and challenges get established for LGBT South Asians to overcome.

Table 18.1 presents a summary of the needs/expectations of LGBT South Asians resulting from their sexual orientation and ethnicity. Needs/expectations of LGBT South Asians with regard to the external social and cultural environment relates to their lives and experiences as the marginalized "other," where either their alternative sexual orientation is regarded as "deviant" from the idealized cultural norm and/or their ethnicity becomes a symbol of difference that marks them as "different" from the dominant majority (De Beauvoir 1980; Said 1979). Needs/expectations of LGBT South Asians emerge in the enactment of social and cultural expectations, values, behavior,

Table 18.1. Need-Expectations of LGBT South Asians Related to Their Sexual Orientation, Ethnicity, or Both

NEEDS/EXPECTATIONS FROM THE SOCIAL AND CULTURAL ENVIRONMENT	
South Asian Ethnic Communities	**LGBT White Communities**
Lack of acceptance of alternative sexualities	Minimum acknowledgment of cultural diversity in values and behavior
Prejudice and discrimination by heterosexuals (e.g., ridicule and use of demeaning language and behavior)	Indifference and invisibility
Heterosexist assumptions	Exclusion from LGBT cultural activities
Lack of legal protection	Exoticized objectification or xenophobia
Ignorance about LGBT-related information	Misinformed/stereotyping racist labels
Physical abuse and harassment	Negative focus on differences in physical appearances and ageism
	Racist aesthetic standards based on cultural models of "whiteness"
	Rigid Western conceptualizations and constructions of sexuality

NEEDS/EXPECTATIONS WITHIN THE INDIVIDUAL

Internalized homophobia/heterosexism based on South Asian cultural values and expectations (e.g., expectations of gender characteristics and behavior)

Internalized racism and white aesthetic standards

Misperceptions of social isolation from other LGBT people of color

Lack of knowledge of etiquette, norms, and behavior in LGBT social interactions

Lack of awareness of culturally sensitive information support services

Mental health issues (e.g., depression and questioning self-worth)

and practices in specific situations that create marginalizing circumstances for them to experience.

Based on the *khush* data collected during this research, the needs/expectations of LGBT South Asians in their interactions with the external South Asian social and cultural environment emerge from a perpetuation of rigid culturally defined gender roles and expectations that are patriarchal, chauvinistic, and heterosexist in their assumptions. It leads a denial of their existence and physical, emotional, and mental abuse of LGBT South Asians that creates an environment of fear that becomes difficult to resist or challenge. Lack of legal and political will to support their equal rights and protection, fairness of representation, and social justice and tolerance worsen the situations LGBT South Asians encounter. Challenges in LGBT white communities for LGBT South Asians are related to a cloak of invisibility and lack of respect for cultural diversity that is based on stereotyping, racist assumptions, misinformation, and narrow and petty constructions of human behavior, appearance, and etiquette. It leads to a treatment of LGBT South Asians as "outsiders," and creates needs/expectations at the individual level concerning social isolation and psychological loneliness that are often worsened as a result of lack of representation in media channels and avenues of communication and information support services. Internalizations of the various intersecting "phobias" LGBT South Asians experience in South Asian ethnic and LGBT white communities result in self-loathing and self-damaging behaviors and feelings that only accurate information, critical reflection, sensitive support, and socially accepting environments are able to nurture toward self-awareness and growth.

Framework of Information Support Services for LGBT South Asians

Progressive changes in the heterosexist and racialized environments around the world can be initiated via provision of culturally appropriate information support services that help LGBT South Asians overcome barriers and challenges faced in the external social and cultural environment as well as internalized within the individual. These changes can help meet the needs of LGBT South Asians resulting from the intersection of their sexual orientations and ethnicities. They can alleviate some of the difficulties LGBT South Asians face in their process of self-fulfillment and social acceptance. Additionally, part of the mission and activities of administrators of information support services for LGBT South Asians in academic environments should go beyond providing services and facilities only for LGBT South Asians. Their work should also include focusing on the larger communities in which LGBT South Asians (and other disenfranchised populations) are embedded to address ignorance, create awareness and tolerance, and provide supportive climates via policy formulation, programming of events and activities, planning of dialogue workshops, among other strategies (Mehra & Braquet 2006; 2007).

Table 18.2 summarizes topics of concern related to sexual orientation and/or ethnicity for LGBT South Asians as reflected in their electronic messages posted to the khush electronic mailing list during the study period. An analysis of the posted messages provides a good indication of what culturally appropriate information support services for LGBT South Asians in academic environments should look like. The following are five essential components of such an information support service:

- Multimedia news channel

- Information resource

- Communication and discussion avenue

- Social support and counseling center

- Community referral to local events and activities

News sharing formed the most important use of khush electronic mailing list during the six-month period with a total of 312 electronic messages that contained content on topics of activism, entertainment, health, legal issues, politics, religion, and research. Study of LGBT-related news content on these different topics provides an awareness of their interrelated nature of impact serving multiple purposes. For example, the following is an excerpt from an online scientific report based on a televised program on the topic of sexuality that was shared in an electronic message posted by a khush user during the period of study. The electronic message was coded for multiple categories of news on research, entertainment news, and information resource sharing, since it contains the information source of the article and was televised as entertainment and research-based news.

Subject: CBS television segment: The Science of Sexual Orientation

Some interesting viewpoints and study findings put forth. This is from last Sunday's 60 Minutes News Magazine Program

http://www.cbsnews.com/stories/2006/03/09/60minutes/main 1385230.shtml

Table 18.2. Topics of Concern Related to Sexual Orientation and, Ethnicity, or both for LGBT South Asians

TOPIC	NUMBER	E-MAIL CONTENT FOCUS		
	Total	LGBT	South Asian	LGBT + South Asian
NEWS (N)	**312**	**248**	**202**	**138 (44.23%)**
N-Entertainment	137	97	90	50
N-Activism	71	67	52	48
N-Legal	57	50	37	30
N-Politics	28	20	13	5
N-Health	10	6	7	3
N-Research	8	7	2	1
N-Religion	1	1	1	1
ONLINE INFORMATION RESOURCES (O)	**290**	**181**	**147**	**38 (13.10%)**
COMMUNICATION/ DISCUSSION	**226**	**167**	**106**	**47 (20.80%)**
O-Entertainment	128	90	38	0
O-Politics	47	31	34	14
O-Activism	26	25	22	21
O-Health	10	8	6	4
O-Research	6	4	2	0
O-Religion	5	5	0	0
O-Legal	4	4	4	4
COMMUNITY REFERRAL	**152**	**127**	**128**	**103 (67.76%)**
CIVILITY	**8**	**NA**	**NA**	**NA**
OTHER (includes 12 e-mails that contained non-LGBT and non–South Asian content)	**18**	**5**	**1**	**0**
TOTAL	*1,006*	*728*	*584*	*326*

The Science of Sexual Orientation, March 12

(CBS) There are few issues as hotly contested—and as poorly understood—as the question of what makes a person gay or straight. It's not only a political, social, and religious question but also a scientific question, one that might someday have an actual, provable answer. The handful of scientists who work in this underfunded and politically charged field will tell you: That answer is a long way off. But as Lesley Stahl reports, their efforts are already yielding tantalizing clues. One focus of their research is twins . . .

[The report was inserted in the message.]

The taxonomic subclassification of news-related information needs of LGBT South Asians to include activism, entertainment, health, legal issues, politics, religion, and research helps identify the different topics to represent in a multimedia component in an information support service for LGBT South Asians in academic environments. Such an effort can address the needs of LGBT South Asians by helping them overcome social isolation, keeping them well-informed on current LGBT concerns from around the world, and providing access to measures to ensure healthy and safe practices, to name a few.

Within the category of news, the most popular news subjects for *khush* users were entertainment (137 electronic messages) and activism (71 electronic messages). For example, the following is an excerpt from an electronic message that was coded for activism news item from USA that had a positive impact on LGBT concerns:

Subject: International News axn5678

Filed from New Orleans: Push to report antigay abuses to U.S. State Dept.

Activists in London and San Francisco are urging people around the world to report antigay abuses to the U.S. State Department. They hope to increase the number of such incidents that are included in the department's country-by-country human-rights report, which the agency must produce and send to Congress each year. Submissions must be received at the State Department before the end of . . . "[This] will help improve the U.S. State

Department's monitoring of such abuses and expand a data base that can be used by human rights campaigners pressing for an end to homophobia," said longtime independent activist Michael Petrelis . . .

[The news item was inserted in the message.]

Such a news item serves to meet the needs of LGBT South Asians in providing information about effective strategies being adopted from around the world to address LGBT prejudice and discrimination. It can develop awareness of possible political and legal recourse available to LGBT South Asians, irrespective of their geographic locations that they and others can replicate to tackle institutional, communitywide, and individual actions of homophobia in their local environments.

The fact that *khush* users posted the largest number of electronic messages in the category of news related to LGBT, South Asian, and both LGBT and South Asian concerns has an important lesson for the design of information support services for LGBT South Asians in academic communities. The need to gather current news and information from around the world about LGBT and South Asian concerns seems to be a high priority need for LGBT South Asians. Additionally, the high percentage of the news electronic message content focus on both LGBT and South Asian concerns (44.23%) indicates the importance of news reflecting both LGBT and South Asian issues for LGBT South Asians and a lack of availability of offline information resources to meet this specific need. Providing LGBT-relevant news on these topics in electronic, print, and other media formats from the South Asian geographic region and from around the world to the entire campus population and surrounding communities will expand knowledge about global efforts regarding LGBT issues in local situations, address ignorance and develop empathy toward this disenfranchised population, and provide concrete strategies for LGBT South Asians and others to participate in to make their campuses and communities better places to live and learn.

The high number of electronic messages posted by LGBT South Asians sharing online information resources with each other (total = 290) and the large number of electronic messages with LGBT and South Asian content indicates a demand and availability to meet this information need online. A culturally sensitive information support service for LGBT South Asians in academic environments must provide access to such online resources that are accurate, authentic, easy to navigate and use, simply organized and well structured, and provide bias-free information in multiple levels of readability and information literacy. The low percentage of messages that shared information resources with references to both LGBT and South Asian concerns (13.10%) indicates an urgent need to identify such resources owing to the lack of online availability of sources that provide information based on intersection of LGBT and South Asian issues.

Figure 18.1 summarizes the kinds of online information resources that were shared via the *khush* electronic mailing list during the period of study. Online news articles (120 electronic messages) and electronic information about specific organizations associated with LGBT and/or South Asian concerns (49 electronic messages) headed the list of online information resources shared during the period of study. Other categories of online information resources shared through *khush* electronic mailing list included: attached files and images (27 electronic messages), personal websites (23 electronic messages), listserv information (21 electronic messages), electronic description of books/films (19 electronic messages), videos (17 electronic messages),

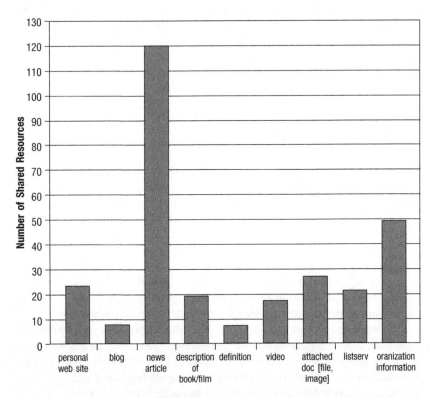

Figure 18.1. Types of online information resources shared on the *khush* electronic mailing list during the six-month period from January to June 2009.

blogs (7 electronic messages), and online definitions of specific terms (e.g., homosexuality) (7 electronic messages). Such information provides a good description of what online information to provide access to in the design of a culturally appropriate information support service for LGBT South Asians in academic environments.

Communication and discussion generating electronic messages formed the third important use of *khush* electronic mailing list during January through June 2006, with a total of 226 electronic messages that contained content on topics of activism, entertainment, health, legal issues, politics, religion, and research. These electronic messages provided a rich avenue for communication exchanges and generated engaged online discussion that highlights the need for such online and offline spaces in the design of culturally revenant information support services for LGBT South Asians in academic communities. These spaces will also generate positive impacts as centers providing social support and formal and informal counseling for LGBT South Asians. For example, the following is an excerpt from an electronic message that was coded for opinion on activism and information resource sharing that had a positive impact on LGBT concerns:

Subject: Re: [Khush] Censorship on the khush list

In re: to what I think was the original aspect of this discussion . . . discriminating against fem gays (please correct me if I am wrong) but I ran across this on someone's gaydar profile, thought it was rather a good idea . . . here is part of the content of the site (http://www.sexualracismsux.com/).

This web page is aimed at confronting racist behavior and speech in gay men, particularly those of us who use online personal services like gaydar. If you're after more general material about racism check the links page. What we're saying in summary is, sexual behavior is no more justified a place for racial prejudice than any other area of life. We should stop making racist statements in essentially public forums like personal ad sites. If our sexual preferences have had an ethnic or racial bias, we should challenge ourselves to confront those limits and, if we can, exceed them. We believe these things because we think that narrow-mindedness, hurtful speech and exclusionism have no place in the gay community . . .

[The website content was inserted in the message.]

Exchanges in the online world (such as those on the khush electronic mailing list) can also provide access to negative information related to LGBT and/or South Asian concerns. It is important for LGBT South Asians to be aware of negative information (in addition to positive information), since it helps them gain recognition of the reality of the opposition and lack of support LGBT South Asians face around the world. It also provides knowledge of the strategies available for them to address these opposing forces. For example, the following is an excerpt from an electronic message that was coded for opinion sharing on religion and research in the United States, since it presents negative opinions about religious interpretations based on homosexuality research in religious canon and cites an American context:

> Subject: Re: it's only natural . . .
>
> Thanks again for a good article. Regarding the revelation you have as to his attitude . . . actually (and i am not well trained in religion—so someone may want to correct me) but the basis of the sodom and gomorra story is about inhospitality . . . men want to have another man who is not interested. they are condemned for their inhospitality not the fact that they want to have sex with another man. An interesting article on this guy . . . let's hope he does not get stoned by the rabid religious right. A friend of mine recently told me about some evangelicals who are attending the funerals of US servicemen killed in Iraq and taunting their families that they died as God's punishment for homosexuals in the United States and gay rights here.
>
> Talk about perverse . . .

The high number of communication messages with LGBT, South Asian, and both LGBT and South Asian content on topics related to activism, entertainment, health, legal issues, politics, religion, and research reflects a need of LGBT South Asians for a social space (online and/or offline) to discuss these topics and the applications of these topics to their everyday lives. This seems especially true for the topics of entertainment, politics, and activism that formed the top three most popular topics under the category of communication. The relatively high number of community referral electronic messages posted on notices and announcements to local events (152 electronic messages), and the extraordinarily high percentage of such messages containing content related to both LGBT and South Asian concerns (67.76%) reflects the importance of this information to meet the needs of LGBT South Asians.

For example, the following is an excerpt from an electronic message that was coded for community referral event announcement and news activism in Turkey with a positive impact on LGBT concerns:

Subject: International Anti-Homophobia Meeting in Ankara, Turkey

Dear List,

International Anti-Homophobia Meeting in Ankara, Turkey

As Kaos GL, we are organizing an International Anti-Homophobia Week in Ankara/Turkey from May 17th till May 21th. We hope that both gay and lesbian as well as heterosexual individuals will join the activities during this week, and you are invited. If you can't attend the meeting personally, we would appreciate if you could share with us your information, experiences, ideas and suggestions. With best regards,

Kaos GL Kaos Gay-Lesbian Cultural Researches and Solidarity Association Ankara / Turkey

[The conference meeting program and details were inserted in the message.]

Information Support Services for LGBT South Asians in Higher Education

What does this study on the online behavior of LGBT South Asians and a content analysis of electronic messages posted on an electronic mailing list for LGBT South Asians tell us about their real-life experiences and specific needs? What should a culturally appropriate information service to effectively meet the specific needs of LGBT South Asians look like in the American academy? Based on findings reported in this chapter, we conclude with a brief discussion on possible answers to these questions and draw implications for improving the design of information support systems for LGBT South Asians in academic environments.

Researchers have documented the close connections between online behavior and offline experiences of Internet users from its early phases of use (Castells 1999; Jones 1999) to its current stages of development (Silver & Massanari 2006). A contemporary need has been identified for critical research in cyberculture studies to support progressive social changes in the day-to-day lives of disenfranchised and underserved populations (Mehra 2006; Mehra, Albright, & Rioux 2006). This pilot study responds to the necessity of the hour and provides an example of application of Internet research to make recommendations to improve the everyday information experiences of marginalized lay users. It extends prior research on the use of the Internet by sexual minorities (Mehra, Merkel, & Bishop 2004) via contextualizing Internet use practices to empowerment of LGBT South Asians and providing suggestions for improving their information realities to accomplish changes that are meaningful to them (Mehra & Braquet 2006).

An analysis of online data reported in this chapter has special significance for design of culturally appropriate information support services to meet the specific needs of LGBT South Asians in academic environments. Several *khush* users from around the world were immersed in academic surroundings, and often their electronic messages, as well as those of others, made explicit and implicit references to their colleges, universities, and a lack of suitable resources and information services to support a positive learning experience for LGBT South Asians in those settings. One significant aspect revealed in such electronic messages is related to how people in academic settings were viewed as not being disconnected from the larger community and other stakeholders such as government agencies, nonprofit organizations, corporations, institutions, informal social networks, and individual activists, among others. Several electronic messages made references to a need for an expanded role of the academy in building partnerships and collaborative efforts with these other community stakeholders to address intersections of discrimination based on multiple variables (e.g., based on sexual orientation and ethnicity for LGBT South Asians), as well as specifically target issues particular various forms of discrimination (e.g., homophobia, sexism, racism, etc.).

As noted in the literature review of this paper, an LGBT South Asian encounters uniquely harsh experiences as compared to her or his ethnic peers or other LGBT people owing to double marginalization based on sexual orientation and ethnicity (Mao 2002). The present study on the online behavior of LGBT South Asians using *khush* electronic mailing list shows how the information resource is being used to counter, to a limited extent, the real-life issues faced by LGBT South Asians. For example, sharing of positive news, information resource sharing, and communicating opinions to generate online discussions among LGBT South Asians via *khush* electronic mailing list encourages dialogue about LGBT matters, provides a language discourse for understanding issues, removes the cloak of invisibility by allowing LGBT

South Asians to connect with others like themselves, and ultimately may creative a sense of belonging and empowerment. It seems that greater knowledge and distribution of information about discussion groups like *khush* electronic mailing list would be of benefit to LGBT South Asians and others who are facing lack of social and community acceptance owing to their sexual orientation and/or ethnicity. Archiving the information shared on such electronic resources and making that information findable via a directory and search navigation feature would be significant in the design of information services to specifically meet the needs of LGBT South Asians.

Lessons learned in this study about the role of *khush* electronic mailing list in meeting the specific needs of LGBT South Asians can be applied in the design of culturally appropriate information support services in academic environments to make them more effective and meaningful to LGBT South Asians. For example, any information support system (offline and/or online) for LGBT South Asians in the academy must provide adequate opportunities for sharing news, information resources, communication and discussions avenues, and announcements on local events, amongst other functionalities. Information support services so designed must also provide resources that address the specific needs of LGBT South Asians related to activism, entertainment, health, legal, politics, religion, and research. These should include information that relates to both LGBT and South Asian concerns in the same resource.

Identifying a framework for the design of culturally appropriate information support services for LGBT South Asians in academic communities that is inclusive of these categories of information is the first step in the right direction. Implementing such information support services to meet the unique needs of LGBT South Asians is the next step to ensure future support and sustenance to the population that will help them address their needs/experiences resulting from their sexual orientation and/or ethnicity. Making improvements in the design of existing information support services to meet the specific needs of marginalized users in academic environments (e.g., LGBT South Asians) will lead to positive changes in their lives and contribute in furthering the role of social equity and social justice in the enactment of democracy, liberty, and freedom from discrimination and prejudices for all people.

Notes

1. The term *South Asian* is used in this chapter to refer to people who are inhabitants of, or are descended from the inhabitants of the following countries: Bangladesh, Bhutan, India, the Maldives, Nepal, Pakistan, and Sri Lanka.

Works Cited

Appadurai, A. *Modernity at Large: Cultural Dimensions of Globalization.* Minneapolis, MN: University of Minnesota Press, 1996.

Bhaskaran, S. *Made in India: Decolonizations, Queer Sexualities, Trans/National Projects.* Hampshire, UK: Palgrave Macmillan, 2004.

Blakey, H., J. Pearce, and G. Chesters. *Minorities Within Minorities: Beneath the Surface of South Asian Participation.* York, UK: Joseph Rowntree Foundation, Bradford University, 2006 (accessed on May 25, 2009), http://www.jrf.org.uk/bookshop/eBooks/1972-involving-south-asian-communities.pdf.

Bolding, G., M. Davis, G. Hart, L. Sherr, and J. Elford. "Where Young MSM Meet Their First Sexual Partner: The Role of the Internet." *AIDS and Behavior* 11.4 (2007): 522–526.

Braquet, D., and B. Mehra. "Contextualizing Internet Use Practices of the Cyber-Queer: Empowering Information Realities in Everyday Life." *Proceedings of the 69th Annual Meeting of the American Society for Information Science & Technology 2006: Information Realities: Shaping the Digital Future For All* 43. Austin, TX, November 3–8, 2006.

Castells, M. (1999). "The Information City Is a Dual City: Can It Be Reversed?" In D. A. Schon, B. Sanyal, & W. J. Mitchell, eds. *High Technology and Low-Income Communities: Prospects for the Positive Use of Advanced Information Technology.* Cambridge, MA: MIT Press 1999, 25–41.

Cruz-Malavé, A., and M. F. Manalansan IV, M. F. *Queer Globalizations: Citizenship and the Afterlife of Colonialism.* New York: NYU Press, 2002.

Dang, A. and M. Hu. *Asian Pacific American Lesbian, Gay, Bisexual and Transgender People: A Community Portrait. A Report from New York's Queer Asian Pacific Legacy Conference, 2004.* New York: National Gay and Lesbian Task Force Policy Institute, 2005 (accessed on June 24, 2014), http://www.thetaskforce.org/downloads/reports/reports/APACommunityPortrait.pdf.

De Beauvoir, S. *The Second Sex.* New York: Alfred A. Knopf (Vintage Books Edition), 1980.

Desai, J. "Homo on the Range: Mobile and Global Sexualities." *Social Text* 73.20.4: 65–89.

Dube, E. M., R. Savin-Williams. "Sexual Identity Development Among Ethnic Sexual-Minority Male Youths." *Developmental Psychology* 35.6 (1999): 1389–1398.

Erni, J. N. "Run Queer Asia Run." *Journal of Homosexuality* 45.2–4 (2003): 381–384.

Fernandez, S. "More than Just an Arts Festival: Communities, Resistance, and the Story of Desh Pardesh." *Canadian Journal of Communication* 31.1 (2006) (accessed on May 25, 2009), http://www.cjc online.ca/viewarticle.php?id=1764&layout=html.

Friedman, T. L. *The World Is Flat: A Brief History of the Twenty-First Century.* New York: Farrar, Straus, and Giroux, 2005.

Gibson, P. "Gay and Lesbian Youth Suicide." In M. R. Feinlieb, ed. *Report of the Secretary's Task Force on Youth Suicide* 3. Washington, DC: Department of Health and Human Services, 1989, 109–142.

Gil-Gomez, E. *Performing La Mestiza: Textual Representatives of Lesbians of Color and the Negotiation of Identities* (Literary Criticism and Cultural Theory: The Interaction of Text and Society). New York: Routledge, 2000.

Gopinath, G. *Impossible Desires: Queer Diasporas and South Asian Public Cultures.* Durham, NC: Duke University Press, 2005.

Hall, S. *Representation: Cultural Representations and Signifying Practices.* London: Sage, 1997.

Heidegger, M. *Nietzsche: Volumes One and Two.* San Francisco, CA: Harper, 1991.

Hom, A. Y. "Stories from the Homefront: Perspectives of Asian American Parents with Lesbian and Gay Sons." *Amerasia Journal* 20.1 (1994): 19–32. Print.

Hunter, K., S. Hari, C. Egbu, and J. Kelly. "Grounded Theory and Application Through Two Examples From Research Studies on Knowledge and Value Management." *Electronic Journal of Business Research Methods* 3.1 (2005): 57–68.

Jones, S. Preface. In S. Jones, ed., *Doing Internet Research: Critical Issues and Methods for Examining the Net.* Thousand Oaks, CA: Sage, 1999, ix–xiv.

Khan, S. "Culture, Sexualities, and Identities: Men Who Have Sex with Men in India." *Journal of Homosexuality* 40.3/4 (2001): 99–115.

Kinsey, A. C., W. B. Pomeroy, and C. E. Martin. *Sexual Behavior in the Human Male.* Philadelphia, PA: W. B. Saunders, 1948.

khush-list-owner@yahoogroups.com. *Khush List: For South Asian Queer Topics* (n.d) (accessed June 24, 2014), https://groups.yahoo.com/neo/groups/khush-list/info.

Kole, S. K. "Globalizing Queer? AIDS, Homophobia and the Politics of Sexual Identity in India." *Global Health* 3 (2007) (accessed on June 25, 2014), http://www.pubmedcentral.nih.gov/articlerender.fcgi?artid=2018684.

Kukke, S., and S. Shah. "Reflections on Queer South Asian Progressive Activism in the U.S." *Amerasia Journal* 25.3 (1999/2000): 128–137.

Kwong-Lai Poon, M. "The Discourse of Oppression in Contemporary Gay Asian Diasporal Literature: Liberation of Limitation?" *Sexuality & Culture* 10.3 (2006): 29–58.

Laurent, E. "Sexuality and Human Rights: An Asian Perspective." *Journal of Homosexuality* 48.3/4 (2005): 163–225.

Leong, R. *Asian American Sexualities: Dimensions of the Gay and Lesbian Experience.* London, UK: Routledge, 1995.

Mao, L. "Ethnic and Gay Identification: Gay Asian Men Dealing with the Divide." *Culture, Health, & Sexuality* 4.4 (2002): 419–430.

Mehra, B., and D. Braquet, D. "Process of Information Seeking During 'Queer' Youth Coming-Out Experiences." In M. K. Chelton and C. Cool, eds., *Youth Information Seeking Behaviors: Contexts, Theories, Models and Issues.* Toronto: Scarecrow Press, 2007, 93–131.

Mehra, B., and D. Braquet, D. "A 'Queer' Manifesto of Interventions for Libraries to 'Come Out' of the Closet! A Study of 'Queer' Youth Experiences During the Coming Out Process." *Library and Information Science Research Electronic Journal* 16.1 (March 2006) (accessed on June 25, 2014), http://libres.curtin.edu.au/libres16n1/.

Mehra, B. "An Action Research (AR) Manifesto for Cyberculture Power to 'Marginalized' Cultures of Difference." In D. Silver, and A. Massanari, eds. *Critical Cyber-Culture Studies*. NYU Press, 2006, 205–215.

Mehra, B., K. S. Albright, and K. Rioux. "A Practical Framework for Social Justice Research in the Information Professions." *Proceedings of the 69th Annual Meeting of the American Society for Information Science & Technology 2006: Information Realities: Shaping the Digital Future for All* 43. Austin, TX, November 3–8, 2006.

Merleau-Ponty, M. *The Visible and the Invisible*. Evanston, IL: Northwestern University Press, 1968.

Minwalla O., B. R. Rosser, J. Feldman J., and C. Varga. "Identity Experience Among Progressive Gay Muslims in North America: A Qualitative Study within Al-Fatiha." *Culture, Health & Sexuality* 7.2 (2005): 113–128.

Narrain, A., Gautam Bhan, Gautam, eds. *Because I Have a Voice: Queer Politics in India*. New Delhi, India: Yoda Press, 2005.

O'Donnell, L., G. Agronick, A. S. Doval, R. Duran, Athi Myint-U, and S. Stueve. "Ethnic and Gay Community Attachments and Sexual Risk Behaviors Among Urban Latino Young Men Who Have Sex with Men," *AIDS Education and Prevention* 14.6 (2002): 457–471.

O'Hara, S., and A. Biesecker. "Globalization: Homogenization or Newfound Diversity?" *Review of Social Economy*, 61.3 (2003): 281–294.

Pieterse, J. N. *Globalization and Culture*. Lanham, MD: Rowman & Littlefield Publishers, 2003.

Pradeep, K. "Interventions Among Men Who Have Sex with Men." In P. Samiran, A. Chatterjee, and A. Abdul-Qader, eds. *Living with the AIDS Virus: The Epidemic and the Response in India*. New Delhi: Sage Publications, 2002, 112–129.

Rangaswamy, P. "South Asian Diapsora." In B. V. Lal, P. Reeves, and R. Rai, eds. *The Encyclopedia of the Indian Diaspora: Immigrant and Refugee Cultures Around the World*. Honolulu, HI: University of Hawaii Press, 2007.

Rastogi, P. "From South Asia to South Africa: Locating Other Post-Colonial Diasporas." *Modern Fiction Studies* 51.3 (2005), 536–560.

Ratti, R. *A Lotus of Another Color*. San Francisco, CA: Alyson Books, 1993.

Said, E. W. *Orientalism*. New York: Vintage Books, 1979.

Sarker, S. *Trans-Status Subjects: Gender in the Globalization of South and Southeast Asia*. Duke University Press, 2002.

Savin-Williams, R. C. *Mom, Dad. I'm Gay: How Families Negotiate Coming Out*. American Psychological Association Press, 2001.

Sherry, J. *Social Work Practice and Men Who Have Sex with Men*. New Delhi: Sage Publications, 2005.

Silver, D., and A. Massanari, A., eds. *Critical Cyber-Culture Studies*. New York: NYU Press, 2006.

Sullivan, G. "Variations on a Common Theme? Gay and Lesbian Identity and Community in Asia." *Journal of Homosexuality*, 40.3/4 (2001): 253–269.

Summers, C. J. *Gay and Lesbian Literary Heritage: A Reader's Companion to the Writers and Their Works from Antiquity to the Present*. London: Routledge, 1995.

Tremble, B., M. Schneider, M., and C. Appathurai. "Growing Up Gay or Lesbian in a Multicultural Context." In G. Herdt, ed. *Gay and Lesbian Youth.* Binghamtom, NY: Harrington Park Press, 253–267.

Uimonen, P. "Networks of Global Interaction." *Cambridge Review of International Affairs* 16.2 (2003): 273–286.

Van der Veer, P. *Nation and Migration: The Politics of Space in the South Asian Diaspora* (South Asia Seminar Series). Philadelphia, PA: University of Pennsylvania Press, 1995.

Yip, A. K. T. "Negotiating Space with Family and Kin in Identity Construction: The Narratives of British Non-heterosexual Muslims." *Sociological Review* 52.3 (2004): 336–349.

Contributors

Joshua G. Adair is an assistant professor of English at Murray State University, where he coordinates the Gender and Diversity Studies program and serves as associate adviser for Alliance, the university's LGBT student group. His recent publications include "'Christopher Wasn't Satisfied with Either Ending'": Connecting Christopher Isherwood's *The World in the Evening* to E. M. Forster's *Maurice*" (*Papers on Language and Literature* 48.3, 2012), "House Museum or Walk-In Closet? The (Non)Representation of Gay Men in the House Museums They Called Home," which appeared in *Gender and Sexuality in Museums: A Reader* (Amy Levin, ed., Routledge, 2010) and "One must be ruthless in the cause of Beauty": Beverley Nichols's and John Fowler's Queer Domesticity in 1950s England" (*Visual Culture and Gender* 5, 2010).

Colette Seguin Beighley became director of the Grand Valley State University LGBT Resource Center in 2010 after holding the assistant director position for two years. Prior to her work at GVSU, Seguin Beighley was director of communications for Triangle Foundation—Michigan's antiviolence and advocacy organization serving the LGBT communities. Seguin Beighley holds an MS in Counseling and Mental Health and is licensed as a marriage and family therapist in both California and Michigan. She has served as co-Chair of the Great Lakes region of the National Consortium of Higher Education LGBT Resource Professionals. Currently, she serves on the Advisory Board for "Expanding the Circle: LGBTQ Studies and Services in Higher Education." In 2008, Seguin Beighley received the West Michigan Pride ACE Advocacy Award for her work on behalf of the LGBT community. In 2012, the GVSU Women's Commission presented her with the Maxine Swanson Award for leadership in support of the rights of women at Grand Valley State University.

Beth Bradley, MEd is currently the assistant director of the Center for Ethics and Religious Affairs (CERA) at the Pennsylvania State University. While working at the largest multifaith center in the country, the Pasquerilla Spiritual Center, Bradley has provided the means for conversations on issues of ethics, justice, and religious/spiritual identity, especially as it relates to the welcoming of all groups and identities. Beth is also a trained speaker for the Faculty/Staff Speakers Bureau Program and collaborates with the LGBTA Student Resource Center and the Center for Women Students, among others, to develop and implement programming.

Donna Braquet is associate professor and Life Sciences Librarian at the University of Tennessee Libraries in Knoxville, where she serves as a subject librarian to the Department of Ecology and Evolutionary Biology; Department of Biochemistry, Cellular, and Molecular Biology; and Department of Microbiology. Her research focuses on diversity issues in academic libraries, library services, and collections for underrepresented populations, and information behaviors during disasters.

Mychal Copeland is the Bay Area Director of InterfaithFamily. Over the past thirteen years, she served as rabbi and senior Jewish educator with two Hillels, UCLA and more recently, Stanford University. Copeland is the founder of a national *Rosh Hodesh* (new moon) project for teens, *It's a Girl Thing*, that celebrates the monthly lunar cycle and strengthens teen girls' self-esteem and spirituality with over 100 groups around the country. She writes a monthly Torah column for the *J: Jewish News Weekly of Northern California*. Her biweekly blog about interfaith family life can be found at InterfaithFamily.com.

Elizabeth P. Cramer, PhD, LCSW, ACSW, is a professor in the School of Social Work at Virginia Commonwealth University. Her primary practice and scholarship areas are lesbian and gay issues, domestic violence, and group work. Cramer has published on educational strategies to reduce the homophobia of social work students and she edited the book, *Addressing Homophobia and Heterosexism on College Campuses*. She cofacilitated an intercampus Faculty Learning Community on addressing issues of diversity and oppression in the classroom. Cramer serves on the editorial board of the *Journal of Gay and Lesbian Social Services*.

Karen de Bruin is head of the French Section and associate professor of French at the University of Rhode Island. She has been appointed to the LGBTQ President's Commission, where she is currently working to improve policies, education, and awareness with regard to gender and sexuality.

David M. Donahue, PhD, is professor of education and associate provost, Mills College, Oakland, California. He has worked with teacher credential students preparing to teach art, English, and history in secondary schools, and with graduate students investigating teaching and learning with a focus on equity in urban contexts. His research interests include teacher learning, generally, and learning from the arts and service-learning, specifically. Most recently, he is coeditor of the book *Artful Teaching: Integrating the Arts for Understanding Across the Curriculum*, published in 2010 by Teachers College Press. He is also coeditor of *Democratic Dilemmas of Teaching Service Learning: Curricular Strategies for Success*, published by Stylus in 2011. In 2008, he was selected by Campus Compact as one of ten Engaged Scholars for New Perspectives in Higher Education.

Calle M. Fielden is a graduate of the Social Work Graduate program at the University of Tennessee and is currently working as a therapist in Indianapolis, Indiana.

Charles H. Ford, PhD, is a professor of history at Norfolk State University (NSU). He also serves as the director of the Quality Enhancement Plan (QEP) at NSU and as Chair of its History Department. In the 1990s, his primary research areas were in eighteenth-century Britain and the Atlantic world, and he published *Hannah More: A Critical Biography* in 1996. In this century, Ford has pursued and published—along with his colleagues, Cassandra Newby-Alexander of NSU and Jeffrey Littlejohn, once of NSU and now at Sam Houston State University in Huntsville, Texas—a number of projects explicitly dealing with the desegregation of public schools in Norfolk, Virginia. Most significantly, Ford and Littlejohn's *Elusive Equality: Desegregation and Resegregation in Norfolk's Public Schools* was published by the University of Virginia Press in 2012.

Milton E. Ford was professor of Liberal Studies at Grand Valley State University, and author of *Playing It Straight: Gay Men and Heterosexual Marriage*. He died during the production of this book.

David William Foster (PhD, University of Washington) Regents' professor of Spanish and women and gender studies at Arizona State University. He served as Chair of the Department of Languages and Literatures from 1997 to 2001. In Spring 2009, he served as the Ednagene and Jordan Davidson Eminent Scholar in the Humanities at Florida International University. His research interests focus on urban culture in Latin America, with emphasis on issues of gender construction and sexual identity, as well as Jewish culture. He has written extensively on Argentine narrative and theater, and he has held Fulbright teaching appointments in Argentina, Brazil, and Uruguay. He has also served as an Inter-American Development Bank Professor in Chile.

Frank D. Golom is an assistant professor of psychology at Loyola University Maryland, where he specializes in organizational psychology and the application of psychological principles to workplace and organizational settings. His expertise is in the area of change leadership, team effectiveness, and workforce diversity. Previously, Golom served as associate director of Executive Education Programs at Teachers College, Columbia University, where he led key functions for the university's executive education offerings in organization development, consultation, and executive coaching, including the design and launch of an executive-level master's degree program in leading and managing change. Golom has authored several articles related to sociodemographic diversity in organizations and continues to conduct research in this area. He also maintains a small consultation and executive coaching practice. Previous clients include Fordham University, the Hetrick-Martin Institute, and Tiffany and Co.

Jewelle Gomez is a novelist and playwright. Her Black, lesbian vampire novel, *The Gilda Stories*, has been in print continuously for twenty years, and her theatrical adaptation of the novel toured thirteen U.S. cities. Her play about James Baldwin had its world premiere in San Francisco in 2011. Her new play about Alberta Hunter will premier in 2015.

Erik Green Erik Green is a PhD student in the Education Department at the University of California–Santa Cruz. His research explores how gay men become socialized into gay communities through Discourse.

Eric Haley is a professor in the School of Advertising and Public Relations at the University of Tennessee.

John C. Hawley (editor) is professor of English at Santa Clara University, and editor of the three-volume *LGBTQ America Today* (ABC-Clio).

Dylan Lane is Communications Specialist and K-12 MindSET Coordinator for the Tau Beta Pi Association in Knoxville, Tennessee.

Myles Luber majored in Critical Social Theories of Race, Gender, and Sexuality at Mills College in Oakland, CA. As a student there, he advocated for the rights of queer and transgender students and applicants. He now works on making change outside of academia and engaging critically with the boundaries and limitations of the university. Currently he is authoring a zine and recording music that explores and expands the concept of "gender dysphoria" and illuminates the experience of transitioning as a nonbinary transgender person. He works as a child-care provider and as a receptionist for a local acupuncture clinic. He can be found online at feverdreamsforpansies.ban-camp.com.

Susan B. Marine is assistant professor and program director in the Higher Education graduate program at Merrimack College. She writes about issues of feminist agency and queer inclusion in American postsecondary education, and recently authored the ASHE monograph *Stonewall's Legacy: Bisexual, Gay, Lesbian and Transgender Students in Higher Education.*

Timothy Patrick McCarthy, PhD, is lecturer on history and literature and on public policy at Harvard University, where he directs the Sexuality, Gender, and Human Rights Program at the Carr Center for Human Rights Policy at the Harvard Kennedy School. A historian of politics and social movements, his most recent book is *Stonewall's Children: Living Queer History in an Age of Liberation, Loss, and Love* (New Press, 2014). A respected leader in the LGBTQ community, McCarthy was a founding member of Barack Obama's National LGBT Leadership Council, has given expert testimony to the Pentagon Comprehensive Working Group on the repeal of "Don't Ask, Don't Tell," serves on the advisory board of the Harvey Milk Foundation, and is currently vice president of the Harvard Gender and Sexuality Caucus.

Scotty McLennan is the dean for Religious Life at Stanford. His duties include providing spiritual, moral, and ethical leadership for the university, teaching, and encouraging a wide spectrum of religious traditions on campus. He is an ordained Unitarian Universalist minister and an attorney. He teaches ethics in several faculties, including Urban Studies and the Graduate School of Business. He is the author of *Jesus Was a Liberal: Reclaiming Christianity for All* (Palgrave Macmillan, 2009) and *Finding Your Religion: When the Faith You Grew Up with Has Lost Its Meaning* (HarperSanFrancisco, 1999).

Paul J. McLoughlin II (PhD, Boston College; MEd the University of Vermont; BA, Miami University, Ohio), former associate dean of Harvard College and senior adviser to the dean of Harvard College, has worked to create inclusive student communities throughout his higher education administrative career. He is a Paul P. Filder grant recipient for his original research on socioeconomic class and its role in student success, titled "The Transition Experiences of High-Achieving, Low-Income Undergraduates in an Elite College Environment" (University of South Carolina, 2012). He is currently serving as Lafayette College's dean of students.

Bharat Mehra is associate professor in the School of Information Sciences at the University of Tennessee. His research explores diversity and intercultural issues in library and information science to achieve social justice and social equity to meet the needs of minority and underserved populations. The efforts have involved working with international groups, sexual minorities, racial/ethnic minorities, and rural librarians, among others, to achieve action-oriented socially relevant outcomes that further communitywide progressive changes on behalf of people on society's margins.

Molly Merryman is co-coordinator of LGBT Studies at Kent State University, and the author of *Clipped Wings: The Rise and Fall of the Women Airforce Service Pilots (WASPS) of World War II*, New York: NYU Press (1997).

Pauline Park, PhD is Chair of the New York Association for Gender Rights Advocacy (NYAGRA), which she cofounded in 1998, and president of the board of directors as well as acting executive director of Queens Pride House, which she cofounded in 1997. She led the campaign for passage of the transgender rights law enacted by the New York City Council in 2002. Park has written widely on LGBT issues and has conducted transgender sensitivity training sessions for a wide range of organizations.

Brian J. Patchcoski, MEd is the founding director of the Office of LGBTQ Services at Dickinson College. He joined Dickinson from Penn State, where he served as the assistant director of the LGBTA Student Resource Center. As assistant director, Patchcoski held primary responsibility for gender- and sexuality-related programming offered to the university community while also teaching in the Sexuality and Gender Studies minor. While at Penn State, he participated in several national research projects examining student identity development and campus climate, and has served as the Mid-Atlantic Representative for the Consortium of Higher Education LGBT Resource Professionals. Patchcoski has worked extensively providing trainings and discussions exploring issues of sexuality and gender identity and has presented at several national conferences. He currently serves as the Chair of the Pennsylvania College Personnel Associations LGBTQ Committee.

D'vorah Rose, MA, RN, BCC, consults with and advises healthcare institutions and universities throughout the United States and internationally on religious and cultural diversity, the needs and experiences of LGBTQI patients and students, multifaith health-care chaplaincy, bioethics, and end of life care. Rose is currently the senior manager of Customer Experience for a large national hospice. Prior to this, she was the Spiritual Care Coordinator and

Palliative Care Consultant for Washington Hospital Healthcare System, serving one of the country's most religiously and culturally diverse communities. She began her health-care chaplaincy career at Stanford University Medical Center while also holding the position of adjunct lecturer in Spirituality and Health at Dominican University of California–San Rafael. Rose is an ordained rabbi, registered nurse, and board certified multifaith health-care chaplain.

Ronni Sanlo is a retired UCLA professor and LGBT Center director. She is a well-known author, speaker, and workshop presenter at colleges, universities, organizations, and businesses around the country. She is currently the facilitator of writing retreats for LGBT people. She may be contacted at ronnisanlo@gmail.com.

K. G. Valente is professor of mathematics and Lesbian, Gay, Bisexual, Transgender, and Queer (LGBTQ) Studies (Joint Appointment) at Colgate University, where he also serves as director of the Division of University (Interdisciplinary) Studies.

Juan Velasco is an associate professor in the Department of English, where he teaches courses in nonfiction creative writing and Chicana/o Literature. His first novel, *Enamorado*, was published in Spain in 2000. He wrote the foreword for *Under the Fifth Sun: Latino Literature from California* in 2002. In his book, *Moving Borders: Tradition, Modernity and the Search for "Mexicanness" in Contemporary Chicano Literature (2003)*, Velasco examines cultural and literary traditions from both south and north of the Mexican–U.S. border. With photographer David Pace he created the poetry DVD, *Call Me When I Am Gone* in 2008. He published *Massacre of the Dreamers/La masacre de los soñadores* in Spain in 2011. *Automitografia: A Study on Contemporary Chicana/o Autobiography* is Velasco's scholarly work in progress. It examines contemporary Chicana/o autobiography from 1959 to 2009.

Index

Made in the USA
Monee, IL
24 September 2021

78677650R00215